'This book is an indispensable cornucopia of fresh Everest perspectives across a range of disciplines, edited by three of the best Everest academics around.'

Ed Douglas, author of *Himalaya: A Human History*

'A huge milestone in scholarly research on Chomolungma/Mount Everest.'

Jon Mathieu, author of *The Alps: An Environmental History*

'Jomolangma, Sagarmatha or Everest… however you might know the mountain, this is the book we all needed. It reflects the plurality of the world we live in, written from the vantage point of "Everest".'

Pasang Yangjee Sherpa, Assistant Professor of Lifeways in Indigenous Asia, University of British Columbia

'Finally, the history of the world's highest mountain as the flashpoint of colonial ambition, dreams of national glory and mountaineering heroism gets the serious treatment and critique it deserves, with essays on expedition history, gender issues, climate change and more. Want to know more about Everest? Read this collection.'

Julie Rak, author of *False Summit: Gender in Mountaineering Nonfiction*

'Everything you always wanted to know about climbing Mount Everest – that you won't find in the standard accounts.'

Maurice Isserman, co-author of *Fallen Giants: Himalayan Mountaineering from the Age of Empire to the Age of Extremes*

'*Other Everests* is a wide-ranging and absorbing set of essays that decisively reframes the received history of the world's highest mountain.'

Stewart Weaver, author of *Exploration: A Very Short Introduction*

Other Everests

Manchester University Press

Other Everests

One mountain, many worlds

Edited by Paul Gilchrist,
Peter H. Hansen, and Jonathan Westaway

MANCHESTER UNIVERSITY PRESS

Published by Manchester University Press
Oxford Road, Manchester, M13 9PL

www.manchesteruniversitypress.co.uk

British Library Cataloguing-in-Publication Data
A catalogue record for this book is available from the British Library

ISBN 978 1 5261 7916 6 paperback

First published 2024

The publisher has no responsibility for the persistence or accuracy of URLs for any external or third-party internet websites referred to in this book, and does not guarantee that any content on such websites is, or will remain, accurate or appropriate.

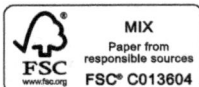

MIX
Paper from
responsible sources
FSC
www.fsc.org   FSC® C013604

Typeset
by Cheshire Typesetting Ltd, Cuddington, Cheshire
Printed in Great Britain
by CPI Books (UK) Ltd, Croydon, CR0 4YY

Contents

Contents

Figures

List of figures

Contributors

Ankit Babu Adhikari is an author, musician, and researcher from Nepal. He has a master's in sustainable development from Kathmandu University and is actively involved in storytelling through research, narratives, and musical endeavours. As a journalist, Ankit has worked for major national dailies the *Kathmandu Post* and *Himalayan Times*, and his work has appeared in the *Asian Geographic* and *Washington Post*. In 2014, Ankit switched from mainstream journalism to a career in musical storytelling. He has performed theatrical plays and has several single releases in his name. For his musical prowess, he was profiled as 'Nepal's Singing Storyteller' by the *Diplomat* and *DW*, and as 'Master of His Own Style' by *Republica*. In 2020, Ankit partnered with Pradeep Bashyal to author *Sherpa: Stories of Life and Death from the Forgotten Guardians of Everest* (Octopus, 2022), a narrative nonfiction chronicling Sherpas' struggles, sacrifices, successes, and tragedies over five decades. The book was shortlisted for the 2023 Boardman Tasker Award for Mountain Literature and has been published in Italian and Czech. He currently works at the UN World Food Programme.

Pradeep Bashyal is a journalist and author from Nepal. He has a master's in international relations and diplomacy from Tribhuvan University, with a dissertation on China's Belt and Road programme (BRI), for which he researched at the Institute of South Asian Studies, Sichuan University, Chengdu. For over a decade, he has worked with different media outlets in Nepal and abroad. His works have appeared in the *Washington Post*, *Diplomat*, *BuzzFeed News*, *Pittsburgh Post-Gazette*, *Asian Geographic*, *Nepal Magazine*, and *Kathmandu Post*, among others. He has reported from different corners of Nepal including the Everest Base Camp. Pradeep has a keen interest and expertise in long-form storytelling. He is also a radio presenter and has interviewed top mountaineering personalities and political figures of Nepal. In partnership with Ankit Babu Adhikari, he authored *Sherpa: Stories of Life and Death from the Forgotten Guardians of Everest* (Octopus, 2022), an oral history of Sherpas' evolution in the mountaineering industry surrounding Everest. *Sherpa* was shortlisted for the 2023 Boardman Tasker Award for Mountain Literature and has been published in Italian and Czech. He currently works at the BBC World Service.

Ian Bellows is an interdisciplinary social scientist whose research examines tourism and rural livelihoods in mountain communities in Nepal, with a special focus on vulnerability and adaptation to changing social-ecological conditions in the Himalayan region. As an undergraduate researcher, he studied the political economy of the Himalayan mountaineering industry and how rumours of Maoist involvement influenced public discourse surrounding the 2014 Mount Everest disaster. Ian's scholarly work draws on his professional experience in mountain tourism and recreation, including as an outdoor educator, park ranger, and mountaineering expedition leader. He earned his MA in Asian Studies from Cornell University and his BA in Geography and International Studies from the University of Washington. He also completed a summer programme in the Anthropology of Travel, Tourism and Pilgrimage at SOAS University of London.

Tim Chamberlain, FRGS, is a PhD candidate at Birkbeck College, University of London. He is currently researching and writing a thesis upon Western explorers in East Tibet during the first half of the twentieth century. He gained a BSc in Anthropology from the University of East London in 1997 and an MA (with distinction) in World History from Birkbeck in 2014. He has previously published articles on three generations of writers from a Western family who were resident in China from the late nineteenth to the early twentieth century and on British diplomatic diaries during the Boxer siege of Peking in 1900 in the *Journal of the Royal Asiatic Society China* (2013 and 2017). He also writes a popular blog on history, museums, and travel writing called *Waymarks*.

Felix Driver is Professor of Human Geography at Royal Holloway, University of London. He specialises in collections-based research and public engagement on the history of geography, exploration, and empire, and has undertaken many projects in partnership with museums, botanic gardens, and visual artists. As Chair of the Royal Geographical Society's Collections Advisory Group, he has taken a particular interest in the development of new policies and practices around its collections, including its extensive Everest expedition archives. He is Chair of Royal Holloway's Centre for the GeoHumanities and is currently co-investigator of an AHRC-funded project on the Oral History of the Environmental Movement in the UK.

Ruth Gamble is a Senior Lecturer in the Department of Archaeology and History at La Trobe University and is currently an Australian Research Council DECRA Fellow. Her first two books, *Reincarnation in Tibetan Buddhism: The Third Karmapa and the Invention of a Tradition* (Oxford University Press, 2018) and *Rangjung Dorje, Master of Mahamudra* (Shambhala, 2020), trace the links between Tibet's reincarnation lineages and its sacred geography. She co-wrote her forthcoming book, *Rivers of the Asian Highlands: From Deep-Time to the Climate Crisis* (Routledge, 2024), with earth scientists and other humanities scholars and is working on an environmental and cultural history of the Yarlung Tsangpo River.

Paul Gilchrist, PhD, is a Principal Lecturer in Human Geography in the School of Applied Sciences, University of Brighton, UK and is a Fellow of the Royal Geographical Society–Institute of British Geographers and the Higher Education Academy. He has teaching and research interests in the geographies of leisure. His research focuses on how people encounter outdoor environments for leisure, sport, and tourism and the regulatory practices that emerge to establish claims to access, belonging, and ownership. He is a founding co-editor of the Taylor & Francis book series Advances in Leisure Studies. He is currently co-investigator on the AHRC Research Network *Other Everests: Commemoration, Memory and Meaning and the British Everest Expedition Centenaries, 2021–2024*.

Jenny Hall is a Senior Lecturer at York St John University, UK. She is a cultural geographer who specialises in the geographies of tourism, leisure, sport, and heritage. Jenny's work is interdisciplinary and draws from across the social sciences. Issues of social and ecological justice are central to her work, and she has focused on the intersectional experiences of inequality in adventure. Working with public agencies, her research has influenced policy in mountaineering organisations in the United Kingdom. Jenny is currently working with Mountain Rescue England and Wales to understand women's experiences of being in mountain rescue, with an aim of creating a practical toolkit to enable rescue teams to improve equality, diversity, and inclusion. As an expert in governance and policy in tourism concerning urban heritage, spatial justice, and regenerative tourism, she is currently working with National Parks on research-ing climate crisis and conservation through public engagement programmes. She is a Fellow of Royal Geographical Society, a mountaineer, and a member of her local mountain rescue team.

Peter H. Hansen is Professor of History and Director of International and Global Studies at Worcester Polytechnic Institute, USA. He is the author of *The Summits of Modern Man: Mountaineering after the Enlightenment* as well as articles on yaks, colonialism, documentary films, mountaineering, and modernity. He has been a visiting fellow at Durham, Harvard, Cambridge, and Australian National University and Fulbright Scholar in France. He has reached a wider audience in television series and public programmes. He is writing a book on Mount Everest.

Agnieszka Irena Kaczmarek, PhD, is an Assistant Professor in the Department of Modern Languages at the University of Applied Sciences in Nysa, Poland. Her current interests concern twentieth- and twenty-first-century Polish and American literature, with a focus on nature and moun-tain travel writing. In 2013, she published her doctoral dissertation entitled 'Little Sister Death', which constitutes the analysis of William Faulkner's *The Sound and the Fury* while bearing in mind the philosophies of death as presented by Max Scheler, Martin Heidegger, and Emmanuel Levinas. She has also published articles on Charles Dickens, Mark Twain, Harold Pinter, Thomas Merton, Edward Abbey, Eva Hoffman, Wanda Rutkiewicz, Arlene Blum, Bill Bryson, and Cormac McCarthy. Since 2018, she has been coordinator for the International Book Club, a reading promotion project. She has also received a Fulbright Senior Award (2020–21) to conduct research at California State University, Bakersfield.

Peter Mikša, PhD, is head of the Centre for Public History at the Institute of Science of the Faculty of Arts, University of Ljubljana, Slovenia, and Associate Professor of Contemporary Slovenian History at the Department of History. His research is devoted to the themes of border studies in Slovenia; nationalism in southeast Europe, primarily in the Slovenian mountainous region/the Alps; the position of Slovenes in different states; the dissolution of Yugoslavia and attitudes towards Yugoslavism; Slovenia's democratisation and independence; the history of mountain tourism; the history of sport. Since 2016, he has been professional assistant of the Gornjesavski Museum of Jesenice, the Slovenian

Alpine Museum unit, managing the field of mountaineering, alpinism, and mountain cultural and material heritage. He was founder and editor-in-chief of www.friko.si, the most important alpine and sport-climbing web portal in Slovenia. He is an alpinist and instructor for alpinism, rock climbing, and sport climbing. He is leader of the Research Group of the Alpine Association of Slovenia, which encourages students and researchers to study mountaineering, alpinism, and related activities.

Felix de Montety is a human geographer at the Université Grenoble Alpes, France. His work is situated at the crossroads between mountain geography, archival methods, and linguistics. He received a PhD at the University of Nottingham in 2019, with a thesis on 'Mapping Other and Self: Language, Space and Identity in the Modern European Geographical Imagination of Central Asia'. His current interests focus on place-naming processes, cartography, and language geography in the Alps, Turkey, and Central Asia.

Young Hoon Oh, PhD, is Lecturer in the Department of Archaeology and Anthropology at the Jeonbuk National University, South Korea. He has been researching the histories and cultures of mountaineering in Nepal, where he began his ethnographic research about Sherpas, since 2012, and in Korea, where he was born, raised, and climbed. His first monograph, *Climbing Sherpas in the Himalayas: An Ethnography of Sherpa Ethnicity* (Asia Culture Center), published in 2021 in Korean, examines ethnographically the rise of a new generation of Sherpas in the industry. Dr Oh is also an experienced mountaineer, and during his doctoral research joined nine Himalayan expeditions, including three on Mount Everest. As an anthropologist, he uniquely applies his own climbing experiences to the consideration of how insiders see the worlds of climbing and mountaineering, especially in non-Western contexts. Since the COVID-19 pandemic, he has been focusing on Korean mountaineering, investigating how the country's past, dotted with colonialism, war, and authoritarianism, intersects with ever-intensifying biopolitics and neoliberalism on mountains, rocks, and ice in Korea and beyond.

Sarah Pickman is an independent historian and freelance writer, editor, and curator, whose research examines the intersections of exploration and science, material culture, and extreme environments in the nineteenth and early twentieth centuries. She holds a PhD in History from Yale University, with a specialisation in History of Science and Medicine, and an MA in Decorative Arts,

Design History, and Material Culture from the Bard Graduate Center. Her writing has appeared in scholarly volumes and journals as well as popular venues such as *Alpinist* and *Material Intelligence* magazines. Dr Pickman also serves as an editor for the journal *Endeavour* and the *History of Anthropology Review*, and has curated exhibitions in a number of venues including the Yale School of Medicine and the Bartow-Pell Mansion Museum. www.sarahmpickman.com

Jonathan Pitches is Professor of Theatre and Performance and Head of the School of Performance and Cultural Industries at the University of Leeds, UK. He is an influential scholar, author, and editor of theatre training, digital pedagogy, and eco-criticism and the founding co-editor of the Routledge journal *Theatre, Dance and Performance Training*. He has published several books including *Vsevolod Meyerhold* (2003/18), *Science and the Stanislavsky Tradition of Acting* (2006/9), *Russians in Britain* (2012), and *Stanislavsky in the World* (with Dr Stefan Aquilina, 2017). He is sole editor of *Great Stage Directors Vol 3: Komisarjevsky, Copeau, Guthrie* (2018) and author of *Performing Mountains* (Palgrave, 2020), supported by the Arts and Humanities Research Council. In 2023, he co-edited (again with Aquilina) the *Routledge Companion to Vsevolod Meyerhold* comprising twenty-seven essays by scholars and practitioners from all over the world. Most recently he has been working on mapping the relationship between Scottish literature and its extensive mountain landscapes for the *Routledge Companion to Scottish Literature*.

Yvonne Reddick is an award-winning author, documentary scriptwriter, and environmental humanities scholar. Her book *Burning Season* (2023) won the Laurel Prize for Best First UK collection of Ecopoetry, was shortlisted for the Saltire Scottish Poetry Book of the Year Award, and was named a BBC Radio 4 Poetry Extra Book of the Month. She is the recipient of an AHRC Leadership Fellowship and grants from the Arts Council England, Leverhulme Trust, and Engineering and Physical Sciences Research Council. Her scholarly books include *Ted Hughes: Environmentalist and Ecopoet* (2017) and *Anthropocene Poetry* (2024). With the filmmaker and biologist Aleksander Domanski, she made the environmental documentary *Searching for Snow Hares*, shortlisted for the British Mountaineering Council's Women in Adventure awards. Yvonne's research has revealed Nobel Laureate Seamus Heaney's determination to save a peatland that inspired his poetry, and how poet Ted Hughes lobbied politicians about water pollution. Her current work for trade publishers includes *Fire on Winter Hill*, about mountains and climate change, with the support of a

Northern Writers' Award for nonfiction; and *Hope Brink*, about women in the outdoors, forthcoming from Broken Sleep Books in 2025.

Anna Saroldi is Lecturer in Italian at the University of Oxford and obtained a DPhil in English Literature from Oxford. Anna's research focuses on translation and collaborative practices across English, Italian, and French in the twentieth and twenty-first centuries. Anna has published on self-translation, heteroglossia, and retranslation from an archival and genetic perspective. Anna is a committee member of the *Oxford Comparative Criticism and Translation* (OCCT) Research Centre and General Editor of the *OCCT Review*. Anna's most recent project looks at the translation and transmission of mountaineering literature in Europe in the twentieth century, from the perspective of feminist translation studies. On the topic, Anna published the article 'Translation and Mountaineering, a First Case-Study: Nea Morin and Janet Adam Smith between Collaborative Translation and cordée féminine' (2023).

Jayeeta (Jo) Sharma is an Associate Professor of the Culinaria Research Centre, the School of the Environment, a Graduate Faculty Member of the Departments of History and the Study of Religion, and a Faculty Affiliate at the School of Cities, the Asian institute, and the SDG Academy at the University of Toronto, Canada. She is a Fellow of the Royal Geographical Society and a Life Member of the Association of Indian Labour Historians. As an applied scholar of food, environment, and justice, Jo directs the Feeding City lab and co-directs the Sustainable Food and Farming Futures Cluster of Scholarly Prominence. As a publicly engaged scholar of the environmental humanities, she is deeply committed to global academic and community-engaged collaborations towards north–south knowledge sharing and dissemination and connecting those to broader sustainable development goals.

Jolynna Sinanan, PhD, is a Lecturer in Digital Anthropology in the Department of Social Anthropology and the Granada Centre for Visual Anthropology at the University of Manchester. She has conducted extensive fieldwork in Trinidad, Nepal, Australia, and Cambodia and has published widely on digital and data practices, digital visual communication, intergenerational mobilities, work and gender. Her books include *Social Media in Trinidad* (UCL Press, 2017), *Visualising Facebook* with Daniel Miller (UCL Press, 2017), and *Digital Media Practices in Households* with Larissa Hjorth et al. (Amsterdam University Press, 2021). Jolynna's current research is developing a long-term ethnography of the Everest economy.

Jonathan Westaway, PhD, is a Senior Research Fellow in History in the Institute for Area and Migration Studies, School of Psychology and Humanities, University of Central Lancashire, UK and is a Fellow of the Royal Geographical Society–Institute of British Geographers (RGS-IBG), the Royal Anthropological Institute, and the Royal Asiatic Society. He is a cultural and environmental historian. His research focuses on imperial cultures of exploration in both polar and mountain environments. His recent research has examined British imperial governance, knowledge practices, and leisure cultures in Highland Asia and Central Asia c.1850–1947 and their representation in travel writing, photography, and film. In 2021–22 he was a Royal Geographical Society–Wiley Digital Archive Fellow working on a project entitled *Encountering the Indigenous Body in the Himalayan Borderlands: Gurkhas, Sherpas, and the Embodied Construction of Martial and Mountain Races in British India, 1890–1947*. He was Project Lead on the AHRC Research Network (AH/W004917/1) *Other Everests: Commemoration, Memory and Meaning and the British Everest Expedition Centenaries, 2021–2024*. He is currently Project Lead on the follow-on AHRC Impact and Engagement award (AH/Z506035/1) linked to the Other Everests project, working with project partners the RGS-IBG, the National Trust, the Kendal Mountain Festival, Archive Nepal, and The Confluence Collective (India).

Matija Zorn, PhD, is the head of the Research Centre of Slovenian Academy of Sciences and Arts (ZRC SAZU) Anton Melik Geographical Institute, Ljubljana, Slovenia, and was head of the institute's Department of Physical Geography. He also holds a position of an associate professor at University of Primorska, Koper, Slovenia. His research mainly focuses on physical geography, and especially on geomorphology, climate geography, and geography of natural hazards. In addition, he also studies land degradation, environmental history, and historical geography. His extensive bibliography includes nine scientific books. He is currently Chair of the Commission on Land Degradation and Desertification of the International Geographical Union, member of the executive committee of the Association of Slovenian Geographers, editor-in-chief of *Geografski vestnik/Geographical Bulletin*, chief editor for physical geography of the SCIE and *Acta geographica Slovenica*, and member of the editorial boards of several international scientific journals.

Acknowledgements

Other Everests: one mountain, many worlds would not have been possible without the generous support of the Arts and Humanities Research Council (UK) networking grant (AH/W004917/1), *Other Everests: Commemoration, Memory and Meaning and the British Everest Expedition Centenaries, 2021–2024*, on which Jonathan Westaway was project lead and Paul Gilchrist co-investigator. AHRC funding enabled the Other Everests network to host a symposium at the Royal Geographical Society–Institute of British Geographers in London in June 2022 attended by scholars from around the world, including many of the contributors to this volume. Many thanks to Prof. Katy Shaw at the AHRC for her support and encouragement. The AHRC also has generously supported public engagement activities during 2024–25 through follow-on funding for impact and engagement grant (AH/Z506035/1). Initial AHRC funding also supported publication in print and open access editions. We also gratefully acknowledge the support of Manchester University Press in making this possible, especially our editor, Kim Walker.

A key objective of the Other Everests network has been to mobilise the knowledge embedded within archives, which is only possible with the close collaboration of many professional societies, archives, archivists, curators, and librarians. The active support and collaboration of the Royal Geographical Society–Institute of British Geographers (RGS-IBG) has been critical, and we would like to thank Joe Smith, Alasdair Macleod, Catherine Souch, Sarah Evans, and Eugene Rae. This book has made extensive use of photographic images from the RGS-IBG archives, and we thank Jamie Owen and Joy Wheeler for help in securing images for the book and associated public exhibition. Jonathan Westaway also benefited from an RGS–Wiley Digital Archive Research Fellowship in 2021–22 that contributed to the formulation of themes and objectives on this project.

Acknowledgements

Another goal has been to engage diverse publics and audiences with Other Everests and we are very grateful for the partnership of the National Trust (NT) and the Kendal Mountain Festival. For having the vision to make possible the Other Everests exhibition at Wray Castle, Windermere, during summer and autumn 2024, we particularly thank at the NT Mike Innerdale, Jez Westgarth, and Harvey Wilkinson. At NT we also gratefully thank Laura White, Caroline Haine, Amy McGowan, and Laura Ruxton. At the Kendal Mountain Festival, we would like to thank the directors, particularly Paul Scully, for programming Other Everests events. Thanks also to our friends Archive Nepal, The Confluence Collective (Kalimpong, India), and Nyema Droma, artist (Lhasa, Tibet, China).

For their collaborations with Other Everests, we also would like to express our thanks to friends at the Alpine Club (AC), Mount Everest Foundation (MEF), and the Mountain Heritage Trust (MHT): John Porter, former AC president and honorary secretary of the MEF, who has long championed the cause of high-altitude workers in the Himalaya; Ed Douglas, editor of the *Alpine Journal*; Emma Macdonald and Glynn Hughes at the AC library and archives; and David Johnston-Smith at the MHT collections. Our thanks also to colleagues at other institutions: Meghan Backhouse and Alex Blakeborough at Liverpool Museums; Prof. Clare Harris at the Pitt Rivers Museum, University of Oxford; and Prof. Graham Dawson at the Centre for Memory, Narrative and Histories, University of Brighton. Thanks to Kristina Dy-Liacco at the C.V. Starr East Asian Library, Columbia University, and the Tharchin Estate, for reproduction of an image from *Melong* (*Mirror*). Prof. Felix Driver is not only a contributor to this volume but has been an unwavering supporter of Other Everests and generously shared his considerable expertise. As a pioneering scholar, academic colleague, and friend, we owe him a debt of gratitude.

For additional funding and support of Other Everests, at the University of Central Lancashire we would like to thank the Centre for Migration, Diaspora and Exile (MIDEX), the Institute for Area and Migration Studies (AMIS), Prof. StJohn Crean, Dr Alexis Holden, Prof. Alan Rice, and Prof. Erik Knudsen. We also thank the professional services staff in the Research and Enterprise Service at the University of Lancashire who have helped develop, manage, and generally keep the project on track: Vaida Kazlauskaite, Diane Brewer, Kate Hutchinson, and Stephen Parr. Very special thanks are due to Dr John Law, Research Bid Development Officer at the University of Central Lancashire, who nurtured the Other Everests project from its inception. The project and this book would not have been possible without him.

Acknowledgements

Our warmest, heartfelt thanks to our colleagues around the world that contributed chapters to *Other Everests*, who are listed elsewhere, for sharing their scholarship, wisdom, and creativity in exploring the contours and shaping these stories of other Everests. We are also very grateful to members of the network who contributed in other ways or at other stages of this project: Amrita Dhar, Jan Faull, Shae Frydenlund, Abbie Garrington, Dawn Hollis, Nokmedemla Lemtur, Carmen Nasr, Mridu Rai, Nathan Smith, Himani Upadhyaya, Paula Williams, and Jase Wilson. We look forward to more stories of the many worlds that 'fit' on this mountain.

Paul would like to thank his wife Sophie and children Fabian and Aubrey for their love, understanding, and forbearance throughout the project and the completion of the book. Peter would like to thank Allison, Will, Katie, and Anne, and the memory of Hogie, for their love. Jonathan would like to thank his wife Julia for her love and support during the development of this book and his children Jago and Thea for their critical engagement with their dad's mountain obsession.

Introduction: one mountain, many worlds

Peter H. Hansen, Paul Gilchrist, and Jonathan Westaway

Footprints break the surface of the snow, heading towards the summit of Mount Everest. Who made them? For the past century, many people looking at such footprints have imagined a singular heroic figure, certainly male, probably Western, or perhaps a pair of climbers sharing a rope, such as George Mallory and Andrew (Sandy) Irvine in 1924 or Edmund Hillary and Tenzing Norgay in 1953. The footsteps in the cover photograph of this book lead upwards on the snows of the 'Hillary Step', the imposing obstacle below the summit on the Nepali side of Everest, named after one of the pair who together made the first ascent of the world's highest mountain.

In June 1924, Mallory and Irvine left similar footprints on the northern, Tibetan slopes of Everest that were visible to observers watching through telescopes below. After they disappeared near the summit, Mallory and Irvine were celebrated for embodying the spirit of man. Yet their deaths were not the first on the mountain. Two years before, in 1922, seven porters were killed in an avalanche on the slopes of the North Col. The porters' names were later added to a memorial for Mallory and Irvine at Everest Base Camp in Tibet, but their contributions remained largely hidden in the Everest expedition archives, overshadowed by the stories of heroic white men.

Since the 1950s, 'other Everests' has implied a mountaineering metaphor to elevate the significance of other endeavours. 'There are other Annapurnas in the lives of men', Maurice Herzog famously concluded in *Annapurna*, his account of the first ascent of an 8,000-metre peak in 1950. Echoing Herzog, the leader of the successful 1953 British expedition, Sir John Hunt, thought the ascent of Everest was justified by the 'seeking of their "Everests" by others'. Hunt concluded 'the spirit of man' could overcome any obstacle and the ascent should inspire enterprising explorers, mountaineers, and adventurers in climbing and other pursuits.[1]

1

Since then, climbers have often followed the footsteps of Sherpas, the ethnic group in Nepal that became the leading porters and guides on Mount Everest.[2] In the 2020s, fresh footprints in the snows of the Hillary Step were being made by Sherpas, both men and women, and the climbers following their footprints are as likely to be from India and China as from Europe or North America. By the first quarter of the twenty-first century, 'other Everests' highlights the contributions and perspectives of diverse communities on and beyond the mountain.

Other Everests is the culmination of a UK-funded research network initially concerned with the commemoration of the centenaries of the early British Mount Everest expeditions.[3] The network examined multiple ethical, social, and political challenges raised by Mount Everest, with attention being given to the meaning of historical commemoration, the agency of Indigenous labour, and the evolution of contemporary mountaineering cultures. The earliest British expeditions were linked to a geostrategic 'forward policy', including the military invasion of Tibet, which aimed to realign Tibet away from Republican China towards British India.[4] After the First World War, the assault on Everest became a gesture of imperial redemption, an effort to restore British morale and reassert the vitality of an imperial masculinity considered critical to ruling a multiethnic empire.[5] The 'epic of Everest' became a metaphor for the expedition organisers and filmmakers who saw Mallory and Irvine embodying the 'spirit of modern man'.[6] This language persisted into the 1970s, when the global counterculture transformed relations with Sherpas, Junko Tabei became the first of many women to climb Mount Everest, and a new breed of climbers entered the scene who began to replace imperial masculinities with corporate masculinities drawn from transnational business boardrooms.[7] With the advent of commercial guiding services and the discovery of Mallory's body in the 1990s, older imperial narratives were exhumed and resurrected along with artefacts from the body. Mountaineering narratives still celebrate heroic men conquering mountains in ways that perpetuate racial and gender stereotypes and continue to inform quasi-colonial practices in contemporary Himalayan mountaineering.

Postcolonial scholars examining such stereotypes and practices highlight the role of 'Othering', whereby 'individuals and groups are treated and marked as different and inferior from the dominant social group'.[8] Since the 1920s, Everest expeditions have relied on vast pyramids of Indigenous labour, an embodied infrastructure that was seldom acknowledged, except when identifying Gurkhas or Sherpas as embodying a 'martial race' or 'mountain' people.

While traditional Everest narratives often adopt such colonial perspectives, the 'Other Everests' research network attempted to invert and subvert this rhetoric and reintroduce a plurality of perspectives – a world of multiple or alternative Everests.[9]

Other Everests attempts to clear a space to engage the many worlds that share the same mountain, the multiple ways of being-in-the-world, 'a world where many worlds fit'.[10] This introductory chapter highlights some of these 'worlds' and overlapping themes in Everest's many names, nations, genders, tourists, climates, and stories. Throughout this volume, the international and interdisciplinary array of contributors reactivate old and new archives, engage with multimedia and live performances, and participate in historical or ethnographic fieldwork. They shed light on the different ways of being in relationship with the mountain and how these are navigated by climbers and high-altitude workers alike, from ritual ceremonies to the mountain's immovable goddess through to contemporary digital practices, as global adventure tourists and guides curate their Everest experiences. The authors in the volume contribute to a plurality of new histories and perspectives. Everest can be viewed as a 'fallen giant' or the height of global prestige; a tourist's quest for adventure or a commodified package in a global adventure tourism industry.[11] Avalanches and natural disasters in the 2010s caused deaths that highlighted risks from a changing climate, but as many of our contributors make clear, these vulnerabilities co-emerged with inequalities in high-altitude labouring practice over the last century. The other Everests presented in this volume have shaped the present but do not determine the future approaches to the world's highest mountain.

Many names

Mount Everest – Chomolungma – Sagarmatha represent perhaps the most prominent example of many worlds shared by one mountain. Surveyors in British India announced in 1856 that a snowy mountain visible from the plains of India was 'probably the highest in the world, without any local name that we can discover'. After Andrew Waugh invoked his privilege as Surveyor General to name the peak after his predecessor, 'Mount Everest' was challenged by British and German naturalists in the Himalayas who advocated the place names Deodunga or Gaurishankar. Yet, as Ruth Gamble and Felix de Montety demonstrate in their chapters, Waugh as well as his British and German critics were mistaken. The mountain was known locally by yet another Tibetan name, Chomolungma.

The mountain was Chomolungma / Chomolangma in honour of the goddess Miyo Langsangma, 'the immovable, good woman of the willows', in Gamble's fresh and vibrant translation.[12] The immovable goddess was one of the five sisters of long life, Tseringma Chenga, deities who resided in mountain abodes after being subdued by Padmasambhava and Milarepa, a process recorded in Buddhist narratives and embedded in Tibetan landscapes. By the 1890s, European antiquaries retold these stories in garbled versions or in mistranslations that expressed prejudice or misunderstanding. A British medical officer, L.A. Waddell, identified Tseringma Chenga with Mount Everest after hearing stories from natives of Khumbu and studying ritual objects and texts that he purchased in Sikkim or looted from Tibet.[13] Emil Schlagintweit, a German scholar of Buddhism, read the Milarepa biographies collected by his elder brothers in India and Nepal and argued that any learned monk would identify the Mount Everest range with Tseringma Chenga. Schlagintweit proposed Gaurishankar-Everest as more melodious and memorable than cumbersome Tibetan names: 'it is always advisable to use Indian names instead of Tibetan names, which have to be ranked with Polish names due to the difficulties in pronunciation and spelling'.[14]

In the early eighteenth century, Chomolangma had appeared on maps of Tibet made by senior Buddhist monks trained in survey techniques at the imperial court in Beijing during the reign of the Kangxi emperor.[15] After the lamas' surveys, the Kangxi Atlas included *Jomolangma alin* in Manchu and Mandarin on maps before 1720 that were subsequently copied in Europe with the name transliterated as *Tchoumou lancma Mont* in French and *Mount Chumu Lankma* in English. The 1741 English edition of J.-B. Du Halde's description of China included this name and explained that its maps of the Mongol empire retained the names given by the lamas 'as being much more to be depended on, than those which travellers set down'.[16]

In 1921, British mountaineers returned from the mountain reporting that 'Everest is known and called by the Tibetans Chomo-lungma, Goddess Mother of the Country.'[17] Sven Hedin noted the resemblance between Chomo-lungma and Tchoumou-lancma on the French maps, and teased that Chomolungma was a 'French not British discovery' and 'the discovery was made by the emperor's lama topographers, and discoveries by natives naturally do not count'.[18] Climbers' testimonies and Hedin's comments were met with indignation by British surveyors. Sidney Burrard, a former Surveyor General, responded to Hedin with outrage, arguing that Mount Everest was on the border 'between the Aryan and Mongolian races' and 'the European mind is different from the

Tibetan'.[19] As Felix de Montety points out in his chapter, the British preference for exonymy – non-local place names used by outsiders – was deeply entangled with imperial and racial politics of mountain names in the nineteenth and twentieth centuries.

The most important figure in the continuing sacralisation of Chomolungma in the early twentieth century was Zatul Rinpoche (Dzatrul Ngawang Tenzin Rinpoche), the Head Lama at the Rongbuk (Dza Rongpu) monastery.[20] Zatul Rinpoche founded the monastery around 1902 on a site where nuns had practised for centuries, and he blessed visiting climbers and porters during many Everest expeditions in the 1920s and 1930s. In his chapter, Felix Driver convincingly shows that the exchange of gifts at the monastery that John Noel filmed in 1922 took place not at the beginning of the expedition but *after* an avalanche on Mount Everest that killed seven porters. The White Tara icon that Zatul Rinpoche gave to the expedition leader, General C.G. Bruce, represented not boldness, as Bruce thought, but a deity of compassion and healing. After these encounters, Zatul Rinpoche wrote an autobiography in the 1920s expressing concern that the sahib's 'back-the-front' views threatened the sacredness of the mountain.[21]

The many worlds that fit the mountain in the 1930s were obscured, but not erased, by the politics of empire. In 1931, the *Statesman* newspaper in Calcutta published extracts from Zatul Rinpoche's spiritual autobiography about the climbers' visits to the monastery. Zatul Rinpoche reported that he asked General Bruce early in the expedition where they were going. Bruce indicated Everest and replied: 'This mountain is the highest in the world. If we can ascend it and reach the summit, the British Government will give us big pay and a great title.' After seven porters died in the avalanche, Zatul Rinpoche performed a service of blessing for the dead 'with great zeal thinking in my mind how these souls had suffered so great and untold difficulties and all for the sake of nothing'.[22] The 1931 translator of these extracts, Johan Van Manen, a Dutch orientalist and secretary of the Asiatic Society of Bengal, also sent a translation of the Tibetan name to Sidney Burrard, the former Surveyor General, but advised him not to trust it: 'The ritualistic Tibetan who reads mystical names in books cannot identify them with geographical features', and geographers could be misled 'by information from ignorant porters'. In his guidebook to Himalayan geography, Burrard asked whether a sentence from Zatul Rinpoche that identified the location of 'Jomo-Langma' was evidence of a Tibetan name for Mount Everest. Not at all, he claimed in 1933, summing up decades of opposition to Tibetan names: 'The best service which explorers will be able to do in future is to teach the Tibetans to adopt the name Mount Everest.'[23]

Zatul Rinpoche was also a spiritual teacher, and he wrote a pilgrim's guide-book to Rongbuk in 1932 to show visitors how to perceive this sacred place: 'Rongbuk is renowned as a supreme, sacred spot that brings liberation by hear-ing about, seeing, remembering, or touching it'.[24] He gave copies of his guide-book to visiting British climbers in 1936, and they published extracts a year later. The pilgrim's guide left climber and schoolmaster E.G.H. Kempson in no doubt that 'the best-known local name for Mount Everest is Chomo-langma'.[25] Gegen Dorje Tharchin also considered the proper local name of Mount Everest in 1933 in the pages of *Melong* (*Mirror*), the first Tibetan-language newspaper. In her chapter, Ruth Gamble notes that Tharchin considered the possibility of Tonting Gyelmo (*Gangs mthon mthing rgyal mo*), a name conventionally associated with Gaurishankar, before hearing from a Sherpa trade official in Calcutta and consulting Zatul Rinpoche's collected works which indicated that the British were climbing a different mountain, the abode of 'Miyo Langsangma or Chomolungma'.[26]

Visits to the Rongbuk monastery and sacred areas near Chomolungma inspired multiple stories of sacred valleys and 'ways of seeing' Tibet and Mount Everest.[27] In his chapter, Tim Chamberlain locates *Lost Horizon*'s utopian visions of 'Shangri-La' – in James Hilton's 1933 novel and Frank Capra's 1937 film – in a much wider field of films, articles, and travelogues of Tibet. Driver, Chamberlain, and Jayetta Sharma all highlight the dependence of travellers and climbers on local people and animals whose labour, mobility, and agency is visible in texts, films, and photographic images. The large quantities of com-fortable gear, supplies, and imported food described by Sarah Pickman in her chapter served to insulate the climbers from the local milieu even as they relied on cooks and 'coolies' in their expeditions. This tourist infrastructure had been in place for decades as 'globe trotters' such as Mark Twain visited Darjeeling hoping to see Mount Everest. In the 1890s, Twain turned away from the mountain and was entranced by the bazaar, 'watching the swarthy strange tribes flock by from their far homes in the Himalayas'.[28] Sharma's chapter uses photographs of this marketplace to bring into focus the long-established networks of Sherpas and Sherpanis working within Himalayan labour regimes that facilitated the entry of famous Sherpas such as Tenzing Norgay and Ang Tharkay into the worlds of tourism and Mount Everest.[29] The reinterpretation of artefacts, writings, films, photographs, and gear from the early Everest expe-ditions by the contributors to this volume powerfully demonstrate the potential to reactivate histories of Indigenous agency and local knowledge in expedition-ary, monastic, cinematic, and photographic archives.

More frequent use of 'Chomoluṅgma' on maps and by international media in the 1930s led a Nepali historian to the 'discovery' or invention of the name Sagarmatha. By 1938, Baburam Acharya, an education administrator, felt aggrieved that the world's highest mountain had no Nepali name and pro-posed 'Sagarmatha' in a literary journal, with an etymology he translated as 'brow/head reaching up to the sky'. Years later, a Nepali linguist interviewed Acharya and was disappointed to learn that his third-hand sources were col-leagues in the education department and dismayed at Acharya's questionable view that 'sweet-sounding' Indo-Aryan names had long ago replaced 'harsh sounding' Tibeto-Burman names in Nepal.[30] The name Sagarmatha was little used until the 1950s – after the first ascent of Everest, Chinese invasion of Tibet, and controversies over the border between states in these mountains. Contested sovereignty over the mountain led to disputes over names, and Chinese officials viewed 'Everest' as a British imposition. China and Nepal resolved their border dispute by placing the boundary line along the summit ridge in a 1961 treaty.[31] Since then, Sagarmatha and Qomolangma (in vary-ing transliterations) have become firmly established as official names alongside Mount Everest.

Many nations

Ascents of Mount Everest were considered matters of national impor-tance during imperial, postcolonial, and Cold War eras throughout most of the twentieth century. Access to Everest was transformed by the independence of India in 1947, communist revolution in China and the invasion of Tibet, and by the opening of Nepal to visitors in 1950. A series of Everest ascents by British, Swiss, Chinese, American, and Indian expeditions in the 1950s and 1960s deepened and expanded the heroic, masculine norms associated with earlier imperial models from the 1920s. After the Second World War and the British withdrawal from India, attitudes towards Sherpa high-altitude workers slowly began to change. In the late 1940s and early 1950s, Sherpas increasingly asserted their agency, assumed more responsibility, and demanded more egali-tarian relationships in mountaineering expeditions.[32] In 1952, the Swiss Everest expedition made Tenzing Norgay a full member of the climbing team, a team led by professional alpine guides. Raymond Lambert, a professional guide from Geneva, praised Tenzing's physical and moral strength but was confused by

7

their relationship: 'Quite simply, I must say that I, the guide, have the confused impression, for once, of being the "client".' On Everest's highest slopes, Lambert recalled feeling like a deep-sea diver walking against an underwater current and reflected again on their relationship: 'this curious feeling comes over me: am I the client? Is Tenzing the guide? Or the opposite. I don't know, but the impression is new.'[33]

The next year, Tenzing Norgay and Edmund Hillary reached the summit of Everest together on 29 May 1953 in a British expedition led by Col. John Hunt. News of the ascent was published in London on the day of Queen Elizabeth II's coronation, and the climbers were hailed as national heroes in Britain, Nepal, India, and New Zealand.[34] The climbers were frequently asked 'who was first' on the summit. Jonathan Pitches' chapter examines the theatrical staging of their partnership in plays about Everest. In Matt Kambic's *The Sherpa and the Beekeeper*, the play starts with the controversy over who stood on the summit first. Tenzing and Hillary engage in Socratic dialogues that hew closely to the historical record and amplify their voices. Pitches notes that Kambic and other playwrights create performances that crystallise multiple historical disputes over Everest for theatrical audiences – ownership of a sacred mountain, contested nationalities of the climbers, divisions between Sherpas and climbers, and contrasts between once untrammelled snows and slopes now littered with debris and human remains.

By the 1970s, flag-waving national expeditions with significant commercial or government sponsorships continued to be prominent, especially for women climbers, something often overlooked in mountaineering histories that emphasise the countercultural and hypermasculine individualism of elite Euro-American men. In 1975, for example, large expeditions from Britain, Japan, and China reached the summit of Everest with sponsorship from Barclays Bank, Japanese media companies, and the Chinese Communist Party. In her chapter, Jenny Hall highlights the importance of women-centred networks of national and transnational scope in leading to successful ascents of Everest by women. As leader of an all-women Japanese team, Junko Tabei became first woman to climb Everest on 16 May 1975, followed eleven days later by Pan Duo from China. On the summit, Tabei posed with Japanese and Nepali flags, and the Chinese team later flew its flag from a tripod. Wanda Rutkiewicz led an all-women Polish expedition that topped two Gasherbrum summits in 1975, which led to an invitation to climb Everest. Agnieszka Irena Kaczmarek's chapter describes Rutkiewicz's driving ambition and challenging experience on a German–French Everest expedition in 1978, when she became the first Polish mountaineer and third woman to climb Mount Everest.

At the time, Rutkiewicz was criticised for demonstrating the same hypermasculine qualities for which male climbers received kudos. After Doug Scott and Dougal Haston became the 'first Britons' to climb Everest via the Southwest Face on 24 September 1975, Scott told reporters they had no flag because they climbed only for themselves: 'Reaching a summit was purely for you. It's the most selfish thing you can do.'[35] In 1978, Reinhold Messner made the first ascent of Everest without bottled oxygen alongside Peter Habeler, demonstrating a similar bravado. Messner paid a large fee to join the 1978 Austrian Everest expedition. Messner rejected the nationalism of his fellow German speakers in the South Tyrol, a formerly Austrian region that had been part of Italy since the First World War: his handkerchief was his flag, Messner announced, and he climbed for himself, not for any nation.[36]

Nationalism remained prominent in some places that came 'late' to Himalayan mountaineering. In their chapter, Peter Mikša and Matija Zorn describe the 1979 Yugoslav ascent of Everest via the West Ridge Direct as the culmination of Yugoslav Alpinist Himalayan Expeditions since the 1960s and the harbinger of Slovenian alpinism's continuing prominence and success. The flag of Yugoslavia that Nejc Zaplotnik tied to Everest's summit tripod represented multiple nationalisms in one banner. Since the early twentieth century, alpinism had been a symbol of Slovene national identity whether in multiethnic empires, monarchies, or states. The 1979 Yugoslav expedition was organised by the Alpine Association of Slovenia, funded by a range of Yugoslav companies (whose names were given to climbing camps), and the summit team and most of the climbers were Slovenes. A second climbing team to reach the summit included a Slovene, a Croatian, and Ang Phu, the sirdar or leader of the climbing Sherpas. Ang Phu slipped on the descent and fell to his death because he was unable to arrest his slide, having dropped his ice axe.[37] The importance of such snow and ice skills, like being able to self-arrest with an ice axe, had been evident to the Slovenian alpinist Aleš Kunaver, who turned down the leadership of the 1979 Everest expedition to start the first climbing school for Nepalis in Manang.

Unlike mountaineering schools established by India in 1954 or through foreign philanthropy in Nepal in 2003,[38] the Manang Mountaineering School was a hybrid endeavour that combined Kunaver's sense of mission, solidarity funds from Yugoslavia, and the nationalist ambitions of the Nepal Mountaineering Association (NMA), founded in 1973. The NMA took over the Manang school in 1980 with Slovene alpinists and doctors volunteering as instructors for several decades.[39] The alpine associations of two small mountain states whose national identities were tied to their climbing prowess collaborated to create this mountaineering school in a geopolitical context that encouraged international co-operation and integrated development of mountain areas.[40]

Many genders

The mountaineering achievements of women, especially Asian women, are often dismissed or downplayed in popular writing and mountaineering histories of Everest. Julie Rak's ground-breaking *False Summit* and Jenny Hall's work in this volume and elsewhere suggest adventure and mountaineering are often visualised and materialised through masculinised bodies that symbolise heroism, bravery, strength, speed, and risk-taking.[41] Yet as Sharma and Hall demonstrate in their chapters, Sherpa women were on the earliest Everest expeditions in the 1920s and joined climbing teams on other mountains in the 1950s. Hall focuses on the empowered women who have navigated gender inequalities and multiple axes of social difference on Everest since the 1970s. The women-centred approaches of Junko Tabei, Wanda Rutkiewicz, or Arlene Blum elicited misogynist criticism from some men but inspired other women to follow in their footsteps. Many climbers summited Everest in all-women teams from India led by Bachendri Pal in 1984 and from South Korea led by Ji Hyeon-ok in 1993, including Ji's ascent without supplemental oxygen. The deaths of women climbers often led to criticism, whether after the deaths of Alison Chadwick-Onyszkiewicz and Vera Watson on Annapurna in 1978, Wanda Rutkiewicz on Kangchenjunga in 1992, or Alison Hargreaves on K2 in 1995. Pasang Lhamu Sherpa became the first Nepali woman to summit Everest in 1993 and her ascent and death during the descent was a landmark event in Nepal. While Pasang Lhamu was celebrated as a national hero in Nepal and commemorated with national honours like those Tenzing Norgay had received in 1953, her achievement was derided by many Western arbiters of mountaineering status.

Ascents of Everest by women from the global North – such as Rutkiewicz, Lydia Bradey, Rebecca Stephens, or Alison Hargreaves – received much more attention than Asian women in Western media. The all-women expedition to Annapurna led by Arlene Blum used this attention to their advantage, raising USD 80,000 to pay for the ascent by selling T-shirts with the slogan, 'A woman's place is on top'.[42] In mixed-gender expeditions, women were and are expected to conform to a climber's version of hypermasculinity, which Kaczmarek defines in her chapter as involving the glorification of risk, physical hardships, strength, machismo, and displays of dominance. The hostility, tension, and masculine selfishness that Rutkiewicz experienced from male teammates on Everest made it difficult for her to collaborate with Marianne Walter, who climbed with her husband on the same expedition. For Kaczmarek, Wanda Rutkiewicz's behaviours on the expedition embodied combinations of femininity and masculinity consistent with a hybrid identity, exemplifying many genders, not just one.

During the first decades of the twenty-first century, women climbers from the global South still rarely receive the recognition or rewards enjoyed by their counterparts in the global North, though signs of change are emerging in the 2020s. Lhakpa Sherpa first climbed Everest in 2000 and completed her tenth ascent in 2022. Lhakpa challenges gendered stereotypes of Nepali women as a ten-time summiteer, divorced single mother, abuse survivor, and worker at low-status jobs in the US. After her tenth ascent, Lhakpa has started a guiding business, received some sponsorship, and is the subject of a Netflix documentary, *Mountain Queen*.[43] A younger generation of Nepali women climbers also harness social media and online marketing, including Shailee Basnet, who organised all-women ascents and climbing projects that seek to empower women and girls. On Instagram, Dawa Yangzum Sherpa, the first Nepali (and Asian) woman to be certified as an international mountain guide, as well as the Pakistani mountaineer Naila Kiani, have garnered thousands of followers.[44] These media practices have the potential, write Jenny Hall and Martin Hall, to 'decolonise the outdoors, by foregrounding the visibility of people excluded from the narrative in tandem with realigning the histories of mountains themselves'.[45]

Women writers, editors, and translators have been at the forefront of recentring marginalised figures on Everest in response to histories that exoticised or feminised women and men in mountaineering. Walt Unsworth's well-regarded *Everest* (1981 and later editions) viewed ascents by women as stunts and called on climbers to approach the mountain with a more sporting ethos, 'less rape and more seduction'.[46] Audrey Salkeld's research in the archives of the British Everest expeditions laid the foundation for Unsworth's *Everest*, and she became a leading Everest historian in her own right. Anna Saroldi's chapter focuses on the contributions of Salkeld and Julie Summers in rewriting the history of Mallory and Irvine and asks why we do not 'see' and value women writing histories of mountaineering when they are there in plain sight. Salkeld's work as a mountaineering researcher, journalist, and translator led to invitations to coauthor *The Mystery of Mallory and Irvine* and to serve as 'expedition historian' for a search party in 1986. After Mallory's body was rediscovered in 1999, Salkeld wrote several histories of Everest and encouraged Julie Summers, Irvine's great-niece, to write her great-uncle's biography using family papers found in an attic trunk. Unsworth, Salkeld, and others had previously documented Lytton Strachey's adoration of Mallory's male beauty as well as Mallory's romances and nude portraits in the Bloomsbury circle that led to speculation that Mallory chose Irvine as the result of an infatuation.[47] Even non-titillating accounts of Mallory and Irvine's partnership portrayed Irvine as a passive and feminised figure, an object to be chosen, without agency of his own.[48]

Letters in the family archives enabled Summers to document Sandy Irvine's love affair with his best friend's stepmother, who was near his own age, at the time of the Everest expedition. Summers' rediscovery of Irvine's hypermasculinity made it possible to see him as an embodied person with desires of his own. Summers observed that Irvine looked at Mallory as a role model and actively sought to convince decision-makers including Mallory to put him in a summit team. Saroldi notes that highlighting Irvine's agency was a critical move for women historians to gain credibility within the mountaineering community, and she recommends multivocal approaches to include the multiple voices and standpoints of Sherpas, women, and non-Western climbers.

Many tourists

After Dick Bass climbed Mount Everest in 1985 to complete ascents of the 'seven summits' – the highest peaks on seven continents – professional mountain guides actively extended their services for clients from peaks like Mount Rainier and Mont Blanc to the highest mountain in the world. On Everest, a 'race among mountain guides to put a paying client on the summit and bring them down safely' culminated with ascents of Everest by clients of two guiding companies in 1992.[49] Everest guiding services expanded rapidly in the 1990s with operators touting adventure packages catering for different tourist desires, from Base Camp to the summit.[50] Everest Base Camp has comforts of home that rely on extended supply chains and networks of labour bearing a strong resonance to the early Everest expeditions discussed by Sarah Pickman and Jayeeta Sharma. The Base Camp facilities that irked Jon Krakauer in 1996 seem rustic in comparison with the luxurious amenities available in the 2020s to 'A-listers' paying the highest fees, described in their chapter by Pradeep Bashyal and Ankit Babu Adhikari. Providing pleasurable Himalayan experiences for large numbers of client-members is one of the central purposes of the mega-expeditions on Everest that Young Hoon Oh calls 'expedition conglomerate'. Ian Bellows also highlights the proliferation and professionalisation of Nepali expedition operators and asks whether the increased role of Nepali firms has altered structural inequities in the Everest industry.

Everest ascents were transformed in the twenty-first century. In his chapter, Ian Bellows characterises a series of events in the 2010s – from the 'Everest brawl' of 2013, the Icefall avalanche in 2014, and the earthquake in 2015 to the COVID-19 pandemic in 2020–21 – as constituting a critical juncture in Everest's history. The conflicts and cancellations of these years suggest continuities with a century-long struggle for control, recognition, and better working conditions on Everest. High-quality training programmes at mountaineering schools improved climbing skills, deepened cultural and language proficiencies, and broadened opportunities for employment on mountaineering expeditions for Nepalis. Many Nepalis have received international certification as guides and now lead ascents of peaks around the world as well as in Nepal. The commercial guiding companies from North America, Europe, and New Zealand that dominated the Everest industry from the 1990s to 2010s are being displaced by Nepali-owned expedition operators in the 2020s.

Young Hoon Oh's chapter offers an insider's perspective on the industrial practices of Everest expedition conglomerates. The organisation of work and rates of pay for the role of climbing Sherpa (once simply called 'Sherpa') are shaped by neoliberalism, neocolonialism, ethnic politics, and weak regulation of mega-expeditions in Nepal. Colonial legacies include 'equipment fees' and rates of pay that incentivise carrying multiple loads between camps, practices established by British expeditions in the 1920s that have continued for a century. Summiting Everest provides the biggest bump in pay, yet reaching the summit depends mostly on a client's fitness rather than the climbing Sherpa's ability. Clients and loads to carry are assigned through patronage networks based on ethnicity, belonging, and social ties to the team guide (formerly sirdar, another colonial legacy role), who in turn retains or embezzles a portion of their pay as compensation for this patronage. Oh estimates that a climbing Sherpa who reaches the summit earns on average about USD 4,000 for three months on Everest and Bashyal and Adhikari estimate an average of USD 5,000 from guiding for a year – in comparison to an average per capita income of a little more than USD 1,000 in Nepal. A small number of Nepali guiding services pay their best-known and often internationally certified Nepali guides much higher rates that match the earnings of international guides.

A diverse group of commercial outfitters offer expedition packages for different consumers. With Everest ascents priced from less than USD 30,000, with special discounts, to more than USD 200,000, customers at the eye-watering top end of this range enjoy an array of perks – appetising gourmet meals provided by expedition chefs, advanced weather forecasts, almost unlimited access to supplemental oxygen, and remote support teams acting as mission control. At the lowest price points, clients have little support and must look after themselves. Some express concern that such arrangements have lessened social ties on the mountain, though similar complaints have been made since the 1990s. Margret Grebowicz viewed the 2019 climbing season as 'a profound breakdown of how most people imagine the social fabric, as climbers ignored or left behind climbers who were struggling, in an every-person-for-themselves focus on summiting'.[51]

The Nepali-owned guiding services that became prominent after the conflicts and natural disasters of the 2010s also emerged out of personal networks over a longer period. Bashyal and Adhikari note that Konjo Chumbi became the main provider of local support for international Everest expeditions in the 1950s and 1960s, and his son, Ang Tshering, founded Asian Trekking in the 1980s. Asian Trekking became the leading Nepali-owned mountaineering company competing with the largest international guiding firms on Everest in the 1990s. Moreover, several of Ang Tshering's protégés have founded their own firms including Seven Summits Treks and Tag Nepal, among others. In the 2010s, Sherpas have leadership roles in climbing agencies as well as the lucrative but less dangerous trekking industry. Many porters – who were formerly ethnic Sherpas – are increasingly from Tamang and Rai ethnic groups from nearby valleys or districts or other parts of Nepal. As the number of Everest permits and ascents has reached record levels, a deadly 'numbers game' has ensued. Everest permits raise millions of dollars in foreign currency for the government of Nepal, which provides a financial incentive not to limit the number of permits despite increasing risks of death or injury due to overcrowding on the mountain.

Visiting climbers and tourists as well as Indigenous guides and porters share mobile media and the digital infrastructure on Everest that reaches well beyond the region. In her chapter, Jolynna Sinanan notes the mediatisation of Everest throughout its history as a mountaineering destination and draws our attention to the emergence of new mobile livelihoods in the twenty-first century. Legacy climbing media in books, magazines, and films – whose content is often problematically dominated by visual and textual records of male achievement – compete with social media platforms that appear to have a

14

democratising effect. Instagram, for example, enables climbers as well as porters to curate visual records and 'mini-memoirs' that communicate instantaneously with followers. These platforms enhance the professional credentials of local guides and porters. The 'selfie' and other digital practices on Everest or other Himalayan landmarks have become essential to future employment for porters. Sinanan shows that controlled curatorship of images elides potentially troublesome critical perspectives of the high-altitude mountain tourism industry, which find their voice in other quarters.

Photographs of climbers stuck in long lines on Everest have made an impression around the world. Young Hoon Oh was stuck in one of these lines on the Lhotse Face in a photograph that went viral in 2012. Yet the photograph could not convey, Oh notes, the miscommunication, political squabbling, and institutional failures that caused this dangerous traffic jam. Another widely shared photograph from 2019, showing a 'conga line' of hundreds of climbers queuing on the summit ridge, was taken by Nepali-born mountaineer Nirmal Purja. Hundreds reached the summit on that day and the photograph was circulated as evidence of the mountain's surging appeal, under-regulation, and limited carrying capacity.[52] Rival guiding companies accused Purja of depicting the queue as an everyday event rather than an exceptional occurrence due to a narrow window of fine weather.[53] Purja went on to complete ascents of the fourteen highest peaks in record time, recorded in a Netflix film, and launched companies selling guiding services and merchandise. Viral photographs and widely screened documentary films of the conflicts in the 2010s, though, have raised awareness of crowded conditions and prompted questions about sustainability.

Nonetheless, as Sinanan and other contributors suggest, visual images tend to focus attention on certain kinds of technical 'solutions' – such as increasing fees, collecting garbage, posting liaison officers, or requiring prior experience – and divert attention away from broader structural contexts, such as the precarity of Nepali livelihoods highlighted by Oh or the polarised and politicised society of Nepal underscored by Bashyal and Adhikari. Questions remain about the economic and environmental sustainability of the whole Everest industry and the future viability of climbing Everest in a period of rapidly accelerating climate change.

Many climates

The 2010s witnessed climate instability on Everest and growing concern about threats posed by rising temperatures to the mountain's cryosphere and surrounding communities.[54] Himalayan temperatures are rising faster than global averages, which causes glaciers to retreat and ice that took millennia to accumulate disappears in decades. Visitors to the mountain are struck by the dissonance between the vision of Everest fashioned by the early explorers as an unspoiled snow-capped summit to a present-day reality of thinning ice and exposed rock. Yvonne Reddick draws a contrast between the Everest as first glimpsed by Mallory in 1921, 'a prodigious white fang excrescent from the jaw of the world', and her view of Everest a century later whilst on a trek to Base Camp, where she finds a sombre and stolid peak, 'stark and dark and bare'. We are, as she says, 'balanced on the brink of a tipping point'.

Mountain residents make similar observations. Villagers in Khumbu and surrounding districts, for example, discuss winters getting shorter and warmer and the surrounding mountains getting darker.[55] Yet climate change narratives often focus on techno-managerial solutions to problems such as risks of glacial lake outburst floods. The contribution of local knowledges and personal experiences in climate change assessment and the legitimacy of more participatory and locally rooted management regimes are too often sidelined.[56] Other contexts such as the sacredness of the area, land practices, and restrictions on living within national parks also deserve attention.[57] Yet the affective dimensions of relations with mountains and glaciers across the Himalayas can still be heard. Consider Dolma, an elderly Ladakhi woman, who blames people who have become careless and unmindful rather than 'climate change' for disappearing snows: 'To care for the glacier, you have to see the glacier, you have to know the glacier, like you know a friend.'[58] Indigenous ways of understanding sentient and agentic landscapes offer other ways of understanding the landscapes and cryosphere of the Greater Himalaya region, other worlds focused on the critical interdependencies between human and nonhuman worlds.[59]

Voices concerned about climate justice have raised questions about the institutional power of Western science in monitoring Himalayan climate change. Advances in forecasting speak to important continuities on Everest in the labour of scientific mapping and monitoring that attempt to make the mountain knowable.[60] Climate assessments predict further warming in the Himalaya which may lead to more unpredictable weather, shifting monsoon patterns, shorter climbing windows, and narrower margins for climbers in the 'death zone'. A scientific study on Everest's South Col in 2022 found ice that had taken 2,000 years to accumulate disappeared in 25 years.[61] Commentators imagine future Everests transformed by instability of the regional cryosphere and threats to Himalayan 'water towers', the vast reservoirs of ice that maintain the flow of rivers in South Asia. Receding snowpack and retreating glaciers also confront people with more macabre consequences of climate change. Would-be Everest summiteers must also contend with a ghoulish 'mortuary landscape' as they encounter the dead, given up by the mountain's thinning ice.[62]

The Khumbu Pasang Lhamu Rural Municipality – the local authority that oversees rules and regulations for Base Camp – periodically offers proposals to stem flows of waste into their communities. Bashyal and Adhikari note that abandoned tents high on the mountain are only the most visible examples of consumer and human waste on the mountain. In frozen conditions, some materials, including human waste, will never decompose until warming temperatures result in reemergence from the ice. Waste removal has been limited mostly to lower camps. More stringent regulations have been issued though waste streams exceed existing capacity to deal with them. Young Hoon Oh draws attention to the 'rationalised absurdity' evident in clean-up campaigns which pay more to bring trash down than to carry loads up the mountain. Oh suggests that the 'media fantasy' of Everest as a sewer of human debris also frames clean-up campaigns as acts of willpower and heroism, so much so that clean-ups can become semi-colonial interventions. Perversely, bounties to bring back garbage expose high-altitude workers to additional objective risks in the Khumbu Icefall. These risks are not borne to the same degree by mountaineering clients who may acknowledge principles of 'leave no trace' but also take more than photographs and leave piles of equipment and large carbon footprints.

Many stories

Thirty-five years after climbing Mount Everest without bottled oxygen with Peter Habeler in 1978, Reinhold Messner argued that Everest in the 2010s had 'nothing to do with classic alpinism. People don't climb Hillary's Everest or my Everest. They climb another mountain, even if it is geologically the same.'[63] For Messner, Everest represented many mountains and one lost world, a world of 'classic alpinism' that began at Base Camp where tourism ended. Yet even the mountain of 'Hillary' (note the singular) or 'my Everest' (note the possessive) was never an unpeopled and uniform space outside of time and history. To imagine the mountain as a vacancy and the solitary male climber as an explorer (not a tourist) are enduring fantasies that authorised the naming of Everest in the 1850s and animated visions of 'classic alpinism' even longer.[64] For more than a century, Everest climbers have relied on existing infrastructures – networks of people and nonhuman animals, gear and material culture – which were created to provide logistical support for militaries or creature comforts for 'globe-trotting' tourists including mountaineers. It does not diminish the accomplishments of Hillary and Tenzing, Messner and Habeler, or later climbers, to point out that elite climbers remain dependent on the Everest industry even when they climb elsewhere in the Himalayas. As Young Hoon Oh observes, the predominant framing of an Everest ascent as 'man versus mountain' casts into shadow anything that happens before setting foot on the mountain (and much after that point as well), obscuring the contributions of others, and clouding the view of many worlds and other Everests.

Theatrical performances try to bring these Everests out of the shadows.[65] Jonathan Pitches' chapter on the staging of multi-sensorial plays about Everest in the 2010s and 2020s finds that Everest-as-conquest and man-versus-mountain narratives have fractured and are being replaced by a layered complexity. The partnership of Hillary and Tenzing and pairings of solipsistic tourist-climbers and business-savvy Nepali guides are staged not as documentaries but as dialogues of historical context and the theatrical imagination. *On Everest* by Lone Twin, the performance duo, mocks mountaineering masculinity in a play that can end either on the summit or by not making it to the top at all.

Exhibitions also provide opportunities to spotlight other Everests through curatorial or artistic works. Felix Driver's chapter describes the visceral impact of exhibits with enlarged, life-sized images of Indigenous intermediaries – such as a youthful Tenzing Norgay or victims of the 1922 Everest avalanche – for the 'hidden histories' of exploration at the Royal Geographical Society. Exhibition design, images, and documents combine to name the Everest 'coolies' of 1922 and tell new stories that restore something like dignity and agency to these porters. The collaboration of artists and scholars is also evident in 'Scaling the Heights', an exhibition of archival materials, artefacts, and 'action man' figures which are staged in poses to reenact British ascents in the Himalayas.[66] The action-man figures toured the UK staging 'ascents' in libraries, archives, and climbing or leisure centres. The Everest centenary in 2024 occasioned a wide range of collaborations – including this book and related exhibitions – bringing together artists, scholars, climbers, mountain festivals, and heritage institutions to reinterpret and tell new Everest stories.[67]

Creative works in poetry, mixed genres, or narratives with multiple viewpoints also highlight Everest's many worlds. 'Chomolongma' is a 'bridge between worlds', writes anthropologist Sienna Craig in sonnets on Himalayan sacred geography.[68] Faye Latham's erasure poetry blots out a text by F.S. Smythe to reveal a poem telling a story from the perspective of an avalanche victim trapped under the snow. White correction fluid represents the avalanche but also how the 'history of mountaineering tends to be written about, erasing landscapes by transforming them into moral testing grounds for the human soul'.[69] Or consider 'Three Springs', Jemima Diki Sherpa's moving response to the deaths of family or friends in three spring seasons including the 2014 Icefall avalanche. Deaths created 'gaps, like missing teeth' in the lines of women and men in the village, gaps slowly filled by adolescents who moved 'closer to the fire to fill the spaces of the ones that are missing'.[70] Helen Mort's poems about women mountaineers engage in dialogue with Victorian women climbers, Alison Hargreaves, and Lene Gammelgaard, as well as Jemima Diki Sherpa. In the poem 'How much can you carry?', a porter shoulders oxygen tanks, hopes, and dreams, and asks 'when do I stop?' In one of the Everest poems, Mort writes from the point of view of oxygen itself, held in a bottle and breathed through a mask.[71]

Other Everests provides multiple perspectives on the many worlds of this mountain. Footprints in the snow might tell many different stories. Clearly, people following the footsteps of Mallory and Irvine on Everest in the 2020s do not have the same experience as their predecessors a century ago. Just as clearly, many people on Everest at any time in its history do not have the same experience as their own contemporaries. How should these stories be told? As Pasang Yangjee Sherpa has remarked, 'The story should be about the existence of multiple stories and about bringing them to light …. It should involve shifting our focus from one-way-of-being to recognizing the multiple-ways-of-being.'[72] The contributors to this book offer steps in this direction by reinterpreting existing archives as well as breaking new ground. The many worlds of *Other Everests* begin with Chomolungma.

Notes

1 Maurice Herzog, *Annapurna* (New York: Dutton, 1953), p. 311; John Hunt, *The Ascent of Everest* (London: Hodder & Stoughton, 1953), pp. 231–2.

2 Pasang Yangjee Sherpa, 'Ethnographies of the Sherpas in the high Himalaya: themes, trajectories, and beyond', in Jelle J.P. Wouters and Michael T. Heneise (eds), *Routledge Handbook of Highland Asia* (London: Routledge, 2022), pp. 182–94, https://doi.org/10.4324/9780429345746-16

3 'Other Everests: commemoration, memory and meaning and the British Everest Expedition centenaries, 2021–2024', funded by the UK Arts and Humanities Research Council; www.othereverests.com

4 Alex McKay, *Tibet and the British Raj: The Frontier Cadre 1904–1947* (Dharamsala: Library of Tibetan Works and Archives, 2009).

5 Wade Davis, *Into the Silence: The Great War, Mallory, and the Conquest of Everest* (London: Bodley Head, 2011).

6 John Noel, *Through Tibet to Everest* (London: Arnold, 1928), pp. 147, 284; John Noel (dir.), *Epic of Everest* (UK: BFI, 2013 [orig. 1924]); Francis Younghusband, *The Epic of Everest* (London: Longmans, 1926).

7 Sherry Ortner, *Life and Death on Mt. Everest: Sherpas and Himalayan Mountaineering* (Princeton, NJ: Princeton University Press, 1999).

8 Gabrielle Griffin, *A Dictionary of Gender Studies* (Oxford: Oxford University Press, 2017), e283, www.oxfordreference.com/view/10.1093/acref/9780191834837.001.0001/acref-9780191834837-e-283

9 Homi K. Bhabha, 'The other question', *Screen*, 24:6 (November–December 1983), 18–36, https://doi.org/10.1093/screen/24.6.18

10 Arturo Ecobar, *Designs for the Pluriverse: Radical Interdependence, Autonomy, and the Making of Worlds* (Durham, NC: Duke University Press, 2017), p. xvi; Marisol de la Cadena and Mario Blaser (eds), *A World of Many Worlds* (Durham, NC: Duke University Press, 2018), p. 1; Kikee Doma Bhutia, '"A world where many worlds fit": understanding cosmopolitics through narratives of possession and spirit invocation among the Lhopos (Bhutia) in Sikkim', *Narrative Culture*, 8:2 (2021), 263–80, https://doi.org/10.13110/narrcult.8.2.0263; Ruth Gamble, 'Surviving Pemakö's pluriverse: Kunga Tsomo, the goddess, and the LAC', *Critical Asian Studies*, 54:3 (2022), 398–421, https://doi.org/10.1080/14672715.2022.2069140

11 Maurice Isserman and Stewart Weaver, *Fallen Giants: A History of Himalayan Mountaineering from the Age of Empire to the Age of Extremes* (New Haven, CT: Yale University Press, 2008); Mark Liechty, *Far Out: Countercultural Seekers and the Tourist Encounter in Nepal* (Chicago, IL: University of Chicago Press, 2017).

12 Chomolungma, Chomolangma, Jomolangma are transliterations of the Tibetan *jo mo glang ma*, and spelling varies among sources. See Chapter 1 for further discussion.

13 L.A. Waddell, *Among the Himalayas* (London: Constable, 1899), pp. 345–59; L.A. Waddell, 'The environs and native names of Mount Everest', *Geographical Journal*, 12:6 (1898), 564–9, https://doi.org/10.2307/1774275

14 Emil Schlagintweit, 'Der Name des höchsten Berges der Erde', *Petermanns Mitteilungen*, 47 (1901), 40–3.

15 Mario Cams, *Companions in Geography: East-West Collaboration in the Mapping of Qing China (c.1685–1735)* (Leiden: Brill, 2017).

16 J.-B. Du Halde and Emanuel Bowen, *A Description of the Empire of China and Chinese-Tartary, Together with the Kingdoms of Korea, and Tibet*, vol. 2 (London: Edward Cave, 1741), p. 388, map between pp. 384 and 385. J.-B. d'Anville's 'carte générale du Thibet ou Bout-tan…' (1733) was included in several atlases in the 1730s.

17 C. K. Howard-Bury, 'The Mount Everest Expedition', *Geographical Journal*, 59:2 (1922), 81–99, https://doi.org/10.2307/1781386

18 Sven Anders Hedin, *Mount Everest och andra Asiatiska problem* (Stockholm: Bonner, 1922), pp. 77–8.

19 Sidney Burrard, *Mount Everest and Its Tibetan Names* (Dehra Dun: Survey of India, 1931), p. 16.

20 Sherry Ortner, *High Religion: A Cultural and Political History of Sherpa Buddhism* (Princeton, NJ: Princeton University Press, 1989).

21 Ruth Gamble, 'The mountain's many faces: how geologists mistook Chomolungma for Everest', in Alison Bashford, Emily M. Kern, and Adam Bobbette (eds), *New Earth Histories: Geo-Cosmologies and the Making of the Modern World* (Chicago, IL: University of Chicago Press, 2023), p. 53. See also Chapter 1 by Gamble in this volume.

22 'Lama of the Rongbuk Monastery', *Statesman* (Calcutta), 1 January 1931. Van Manen provided his translation to E.O. Shebbeare in the 1930s, which was printed by W.H. Murrary, *The Story of Everest* (London: Dent, [rev. Nov.] 1953), pp. 208–9. For a longer version, see Alexander W. Macdonald, 'The lama and the general', *Kailash: A Journal of Himalayan Studies*, 1:3 (1973), 225–33. Bruce recorded his reply as they were on a pilgrimage. C.G. Bruce, *Assault on Mount Everest, 1922* (London: Edward Arnold, 1923), p. 46.

23 S.G. Burrard, H.H. Hayden, and A.M. Heron, *A Sketch of the Geography and Geology of the Himalaya Mountains and Tibet*, 2nd ed. (Delhi: Manager of Publications, 1933), p. 25.

24 Translation in Jamyang Wangmo, *The Lawudo Lama: Stories of Reincarnation from the Mount Everest Region* (Boston, MA: Wisdom, 2005), p. 15.

25 E.G.H. Kempson, 'The local name of Mount Everest', in Hugh Ruttledge, *Everest, The Unfinished Adventure* (London: Hodder & Stoughton, 1937), p. 288; translation by F.W. Thomas.

26 See Gamble in this volume, and Bhuchung K. Tsering, 'Mi ti gu ti cha pu long na', *Tibet Bulletin*, 8:4 (October–November 1985), 20. For *Melong*, see Columbia University and archive.org; for the writings of Ngawang Tenzin Norbu (1867–1940), see Buddhist Digital Resource Center.

27 Edwin Bernbaum, *Sacred Mountains of the World*, 2nd ed. (Cambridge: Cambridge University Press, 2022); Veronica della Dora, *Mountain: Nature and Culture* (London: Reaktion, 2016); Jon Mathieu, *Mount Sacred* (Winwick: Whitehorse Press, 2023).

28 Mark Twain, *More Tramps Abroad* (London: Chatto & Windus, 1897), pp. 369–70.

29 See also Nandini Purandare and Deepa Balsavar, *Headstrap: Legends and Lore from the Climbing Sherpas of Darjeeling* (Seattle, WA: Mountaineers, 2024); Bernadette McDonald, *Alpine Rising: Sherpas, Baltis, and the Triumph of Local Climbers in the Greater Ranges* (Seattle, WA: Mountaineers, 2014).

30 Kamal P. Malla, 'Sagara-māthā: the linguistic conquest of Mount Everest', *Nepalese Linguistics*, 15 (1998), 19–28, himalaya.socanth.cam.ac.uk/collections/journals/nepling/pdf/Nep_Ling_15.pdf

31 Baburam Acharya, *China Tibet and Nepal* (Kathmandu: China Study Center, 2018), pp. 166–72.

32 Ortner, *Life and Death on Mt. Everest*, pp. 151–3.

33 Raymond Lambert, 'Altitude 8600', in *A l'assaut des 'quatre mille': dix récits de haute montagne*, 2nd ed. (Geneva: Editions Jeheber, 1953), pp. 215, 225–6.

34 Peter H. Hansen, 'Coronation Everest: the Empire and Commonwealth in the "second Elizabethan age"', in Stuart Ward (ed.), *British Culture and the End of Empire* (Manchester: Manchester University Press, 2001), pp. 57–72, https://doi.org/10.7765/9781526119629.00009

35 *Sunday Times* (19 October 1975); Peter H. Hansen, 'Scott, Douglas Keith (Doug) (1941–2020)', in *Oxford Dictionary of National Biography* (Oxford: Oxford University Press, online edition, 2024), https://doi.org/10.1093/odnb/9780198614128.013.90000381698

36 Isserman and Weaver, *Fallen Giants*, p. 435.

37 Bernadette McDonald, *Alpine Warriors* (Victoria, BC: Rocky Mountain Books, 2015), pp. 131–6.

38 Himalayan Mountaineering Institute (HMI), founded by India in 1954, and the Khumbu Climbing Center, founded by the Alex Lowe Charitable Foundation in 2003. For HMI, see Purandare and Balsavar, *Headstrap*.

39 Manang Mountaineering School, https://web.archive.org/web/20231004165636/ https://www.nepalmountaineering.org/manang-mountaineering-school

40 Bernard Debarbieux and Gilles Rudaz, *The Mountain: A Political History from the Enlightenment to the Present* (Chicago, IL: University of Chicago Press, 2015).

41 Julie Rak, *False Summit: Gender in Mountaineering Nonfiction* (Montreal/Kingston: McGill-Queen's University Press, 2021); Jenny Hall, Emma Boocock, and Zoë Avner (eds), *Gender, Politics and Change in Mountaineering: Moving Mountains* (Cham: Palgrave Macmillan, 2023).

42 Arlene Blum, *Annapurna, a Woman's Place* (San Francisco, CA: Sierra Club Books, 1998 [orig. 1980]); Katie Ives, 'An oral history of the first U.S. ascent of Annapurna (Oh yeah, and it happened to be the first female ascent, too)', *Outside Magazine* (May 2017), https://web.archive.org/web/20220524224820/https://www.outsideonline.com/out door-adventure/climbing/annapurna-women/

43 Lucy Walker (dir.), *Mountain Queen: The Summits of Lhakpa Sherpa* (USA: Netflix, 2024); Anna Fleming, 'Herstory 6: Lhakpa Sherpa's long dream of Everest', *UK Climbing* (31 May 2023), https://web.archive.org/web/20231002160212/https://www.ukclimb ing.com/articles/features/herstory_6_lhakpa_sherpas_long_dream_of_everest-15196; *Cloudscape Climbing*, https://web.archive.org/web/20240424025826/https://cloudsca peclimbing.com/

44 Dawa Yangzum Sherpa, www.instagram.com/dawayangzum/; Naila Kiani, www.ins tagram.com/naila._.kiani/

45 Jenny Hall and Martin Hall, 'Politics of representation in mountaineering: conclusion', in Martin Hall and Jenny Hall (eds), *The Mountain and the Politics of Representation* (Liverpool: Liverpool University Press, 2023), p. 292.

46 Walt Unsworth, *Everest* (London: Grafton, 1991), p. 196.

47 Paul Deslandes, *The Culture of Male Beauty in Britain: From the First Photographs to David Beckham* (Chicago, IL: University of Chicago Press, 2021).

48 The discovery of Irvine's remains on Everest in 2024 also may prompt reassessment of his role. See Grayson Schaffer, 'Exclusive: Remains of Andrew "Sandy" Irvine believed to have been found on Everest', *National Geographic* (11 October 2024), https://www. nationalgeographic.com/adventure/article/sandy-irvine-body-found-everest

49 Will Cockrell, *Everest, Inc.: The Renegades and Rogues who Built an Industry at the Top of the World* (New York: Gallery, 2024), p. 74.

50 Paul Beedie and Simon Hudson, 'Emergence of mountain-based adventure tourism', *Annals of Tourism Research*, 30:3 (2003), 625–43, https://doi.org/10.1016/S0160-7383(03) 00043-4

51 Margret Grebowicz, *Mountains and Desire: Climbing vs. the End of the World* (London: Repeater Books, 2021), p. 49.

52 Tim Mutrie, 'The Everest climber whose traffic jam went viral', *New York Times* (18 September 2019), https://web.archive.org/web/20211203202921/https://www. nytimes.com/2019/09/18/sports/the-everest-climber-whose-traffic-jam-photo-went-vi ral.html

53 Nimsdai Purja, *Beyond Possible: One Soldier, Fourteen Peaks – My Life in the Death Zone* (London: Hodder & Stoughton, 2022), pp. 195–7. See also, 'Most days, it's not so crowded on Mt Everest', *Nepali Times* (28 May 2019), https://web.archive.org/web/20230315101306/ https://nepalitimes.com/here-now/most-days-it-s-not-so-crowded-on-mt-everest

54 Dani Inkpen, 'Ever higher: the mountain cryosphere', in Klaus Dodds and Sverker Sörlin (eds), *Ice Humanities: Living, Working, and Thinking in a Melting World* (Manchester: Manchester University Press, 2022), pp. 72–88; Dani Inkpen, *Capturing Glaciers: A History of Repeat Photography and Global Warming* (Seattle, WA: University of Washington Press, 2024).

55 Pasang Yangjee Sherpa and Ornella Puschiasis, 'A reflexive approach to climate change engagement with Sherpas from Khumbu and Pharak in northeastern Nepal (Mount Everest Region)', in Susan A. Crate and Mark Nuttall (eds), *Anthropology and Climate Change*, 3rd ed. (London: Routledge, 2023), pp. 224–41, https://doi.org/10.4324/97810032 42499

56 Ritodhi Chakraborty and Pasang Yangjee Sherpa, 'From climate adaptation to climate justice: critical reflections on the IPCC and Himalayan climate knowledges', *Climatic Change*, 167:49 (2021), https://doi.org/10.1007/s10584-021-03158-1; Georgina Drew and Mabel Denzin Gergan, 'Imagining Himalayan glacial futures: knowledge rifts, disciplinary debates and icy vitalities at the Third Pole', *Social Anthropology/Anthropologie Sociale*, 32:1 (2024), 80–95, https://doi.org/10.3167/saas.2024.320107

57 David L. Haberman (ed.), *Understanding Climate Change through Religious Lifeworlds* (Bloomington, IN: Indiana University Press, 2021); Dan Smyer Yü and Erik de Maaker (eds), *Environmental Humanities in the Himalayas: Symbiotic Indigeneity, Commoning, Sustainability* (London: Routledge, 2021).

58 Karine Gagné, *Caring for Glaciers: Land, Animals, and Humanity in the Himalayas* (Seattle, WA: University of Washington Press, 2019), p. 140.

59 See Whitney Barlow Robles, 'On nonhuman agency', *Journal of Interdisciplinary History*, 54:3 (Winter 2024), 305–21, https://doi.org/10.1162/jinh_a_02000

60 Lachlan Fleetwood, *Science on the Roof of the World: Empire and the Remaking of the Himalaya* (Cambridge: Cambridge University Press, 2022); Thomas Simpson, 'Imperial slippages: encountering and knowing ice in and beyond colonial India', in Dodds and Sörlin (eds), *Ice Humanities*, pp. 205–27.

61 Mariusz Potocki et al., 'Mt. Everest's highest glacier is a sentinel for accelerating ice loss', *npj Climate and Atmospheric Science*, 5:7 (2022), https://doi.org/10.1038/s41612-022-00230-0

62 Doug Scott, Ian Wall, and Jonathan Westaway, 'The Everest Mess', *Alpine Journal*, 123 (2019), 129–37.

63 Stefan Nestler, 'Messner: "First ascent a magic moment of mountaineering"', *DW* (29 May 2013), https://web.archive.org/web/20220813030534/https://www.dw.com/en/messner-first-ascent-a-magic-moment-of-mountaineering/a-16844185

64 Peter H. Hansen, *The Summits of Modern Man: Mountaineering after the Enlightenment* (Cambridge, MA: Harvard University Press, 2013); Caroline Schaumann, *Peak Pursuits: The Emergence of Mountaineering in the Nineteenth Century* (New Haven, CT: Yale University Press, 2020); Dawn Hollis and Jason König (eds), *Mountain Dialogues from Antiquity to Modernity* (London: Bloomsbury, 2021); Dawn L. Hollis, *Mountains before Mountaineering: The Call of the Peaks before the Modern Age* (Cheltenham: History Press, 2024).

65 Jonathan Pitches, *Performing Mountains* (London: Palgrave Macmillan, 2020).

66 Stephen Livingstone and Abbie Garrington, *Scaling the Heights – Miniature Mountaineering* (Durham: Oriental Museum, 2018). Scaling the Heights, www.instagram.com/scalingtheheights

67 See Acknowledgements in this volume for the 'Other Everest' network, and related work, *Everest 24: New Views on the 1924 Mount Everest Expedition* (London: Riverside Press, 2024).

68 Sienna Craig, 'A sacred geography: sonnets of the Himalaya and Tibet', *Anthropology and Humanism*, 35:2 (2010), 240–7, https://doi.org/10.1111/j.1548-1409.2010.01071.x

69 Faye Rhiannon Latham, *British Mountaineers* ([Yorkshire]: Little Peak Press, 2022); quotation from *LittlePeak.co.uk*: https://web.archive.org/web/20220131124725/https://www.littlepeak.co.uk/news/news10/

70 Jemima Diki Sherpa, 'Three springs', *Whathasgood* (23 April 2014), https://web.archive.org/web/20190602072640/https://whathasgood.com/2014/04/23/three-springs/; *Financial Times* (2 May 2014), and multiple literary anthologies.

71 Helen Mort, *No Map Could Show Them* (London: Chatto & Windus, 2016), pp. 58–63.

72 Quoted in Katie Ives, 'Sharp end: between the lines', *Alpinist*, 51 (Autumn 2015), 11–12, https://web.archive.org/web/20240217210337/https://alpinist.com/departments/sharp-end/

The immovable goddess: the long life of Miyo Lang Sangma

Ruth Gamble

After determining that one of the central Himalayan peaks was the world's highest in the early 1850s, Andrew Waugh, the head of the Great Trigonometric Survey of India, was responsible for naming it. He asked around and decided it had no one local designation and named it after his predecessor and mentor, George Everest. The name Mount Everest has stuck ever since.

Waugh was mistaken. The people who lived at the mountain's base, Tibetans in Dingri and Shelkar to the mountain's north and the Sherpas in Solu Khumbu to the mountain's south, had known the mountain as Chomolungma for centuries, perhaps longer. It was named for the lifelong goddess who occupied its peak, a goddess whose full name is Miyo Langsangma, 'the immovable, good woman of the willows'. Waugh's decision to name the mountain after a British man obscured the goddess's central role in the mountain's story. Although Tibetans and Sherpas have continued to revere her, the mountain's international history has misrepresented or ignored her. Waugh's mistake lives on, but we can bring the goddess out of the surveyor's colonial shadows by telling and retelling her story.

When Buddhist religious teachers and texts introduce their audiences to a deity, they often begin with a physical description. As Himalayan gods can be multi-headed, multi-armed, multi-coloured, hold precious objects in their hands, and ride a variety of animals, their descriptions start with the enumeration of the deities' appendages, their facial expression, their colour, the things they hold, and the animals they ride. All these heads, hands, colours, possessions, and animals tell us something about the deity to whom we are being introduced.

Getting to know Miyo Langsangma means learning what she looks like and what this look means. She has one head and two hands, a peaceful expression, golden yellow skin, and rides a tiger. In some images, she holds a bowl of rice in her left hand and a mongoose that spits jewels in her right hand. In others, she holds a tray of riches with her left hand and a banner with the other. Her singular head, two hands, and peaceful expression tell us she is approachable. Her golden colour associates her with the south, the earth element, autumn, harvests, material increase, and giving, which is also why she holds trays of riches, a jewel-spitting mongoose, or rice. The banner she sometimes holds marks her as a worldly deity, a bodhisattva rather than a fully awakened Buddha. The banner's presence in some images and absence in others suggests there is some debate about her status. Those who draw her without it are claiming she is awakened. The goddess is, furthermore, usually drawn as part of a group with her five sisters, the Tseringma Chenga, who are all long-life deities (see Figure 1.1).

This description gives us a sense of the goddess and her connection to a broader sacred geography that stretches across the Himalaya and back through multiple Buddhist lineages and community histories. If we follow these lineages and histories back through time, we discover the origins of the goddess's names and what they tell us about her. We also learn she has a thousand-year story, much of which was preserved in the biographies of two famous Buddhist yogis, Guru Rinpoche and Milarepa. Rituals and stories accreted to her and her sisters as highland settlements pushed into the valleys below their mountains. This process of settlement and sacralisation continued into the early twentieth century, when a young Tibetan reincarnate guru named Dzatrul Ngawang Tenzin Rinpoche (1867–1940) established a monastery at Dza Rongpu (Rongbuk) below the mountain's north face. While in retreat there in the 1930s, Dzatrul Rinpoche wrote the *Guide to Dza Rongpu's Sacred Sites*,[1] which describes the goddess's abode in detail.

Like Waugh's surveying, the longer sacralisation recorded in Dzatrul Rinpoche's *Guide* has also had an enduring legacy. It described an alternative vision of the mountain that long preceded the surveyors or mountaineers. Tibetans and Sherpas maintain its legacy by insisting on the goddess's continuing presence despite pressure from nationalist projects to reimagine the mountain as a Chinese and Nepali national space and the climbing industry's commodification of it.

Into the etymological willows

Much of the goddess's story is encoded in the connected local names by which she and the mountain are known. These names are from the Tibetic languages

Figure 1.1 The Tseringma Chenga (Five Sisters of Long Life). This nineteenth-century image depicts the central deity of Tseringma, associated with Gaurisankar, and her sisters including Miyolangsangma, associated with Chomolungma (Everest), the yellow goddess in the top right corner. Courtesy of the Rubin Museum of Art, gift of Shelley & Donald Rubin Foundation, F1996.10.2 (HAR 433).

spoken around the mountain: the Tó and Tsang languages spoken north of the mountain, and Sherpa, spoken to its south.[2] In these languages, the most common contemporary names for the mountain and the goddess are Chomolungma – also transliterated as Jomolangma – and Miyo Langsangma.[3] These are two versions of the same name with many of the same components. Miyo Langsangma has three parts. *Miyo* is a Tibetan neologism invented to reflect the Sanskrit term *acala*, which means 'immovable'. *Lang* has several meanings. It most likely means 'willows', but it could also mean 'ox' or even 'elephant', which is called a 'great ox', *langchen* in most Tibetic languages. The syllable *ma* indicates the thing being described is female. *Sang* means excellent or wholesome. These syllables most likely mean 'immovable, good woman of the willows'.

Chomolangma contains the same *lang* and *ma* syllables. They are preceded by the word *chomo*, also transliterated as *jomo*. Chomo/Jomo is an honorific title meaning 'noble lady', used to address royalty, religious adepts, mountain deities, and those beings, like Chomolungma, who are considered royal, religious, and divine. The name Chomolungma, therefore, most probably means 'noble lady of the willows'. The mountain is sometimes also called Jomo Kangkar or Gangkar, which means 'noble lady of the white snow', 'goddess of the white snow', or, at a stretch, 'goddess of the glaciers'. This term is more of a descriptor than a name and describes all female snow mountain deities.

The title Chomo/Jomo connects the goddess and the mountain to other sacred female peaks. One of Gaurishankar's (7,181 metres) Tibetan names is Jomo Tseringma, named for Miyo Langsangma's divine older sister. Jomolhari (7,326 metres) sits on the Chinese–Bhutanese border, and there is a mountain in central Tibet named Jomo Khanag. Cho Oyu (or Chowo Yu, 'turquoise lady'; 8,188 metres) contains a version of the same title. It is also worth noting that the mountain goddesses are not the region's only famous Chomo/Jomo. The central Himalaya were also home to a group of human female adepts titled 'Jomo' who lived in Dingri, just north of Chomolangma and Cho Oyu, in the eleventh century.[4]

For much of the goddess's history, the two versions of her name, Chomolungma and Miyo Langsangma, were used interchangeably to describe her and her mountain. When Dzatrul Rinpoche wrote the *Guide to Dza Rongpu's Sacred Sites* in the 1930s, for example, he listed 'the well-known Chomolungma' among the region's 'beautiful snow-mountain deities'.[5] The goddess and the mountain are still both called 'Chomolungma' in contemporary Tibetan sources.

Over the last few decades, however, Buddhist teachers living south of the mountain have become more specific in their use of these versions of her names, referring to the mountain as Chomolungma and the goddess as Miyo Langsangma. They seem to have done this for pedagogical reasons. In the Buddhist worldview, it is important to distinguish the goddess from the mountain. The mountain is one of the goddess's *né* (abodes), but her existence stretches beyond it in time and space. As Buddhism holds that all matter arises in dependence on the mind, she may infuse the mountain with her presence or manifest a physical mountain, but that mountain is not her. She can travel away from it and will outlive it. Giving the mountain and the goddess two different names clarifies this separation.

In Tibetan written sources, the meaning of the goddess's name is relatively straightforward, but as there are many homonyms in Tibetan, some who have heard rather than read her name have understood it differently. The early twentieth-century British emissary to Tibet, Charles Bell (1870–1945), who arranged the passports for the first British expedition to the mountain in 1921, heard the mountain's name as 'Lho (southern) Cha-ma-lung'. *Chama* can mean 'female birds', and he read *lang* as *lung*, which means 'valley' or 'land' in Tibetan. Combining the meaning of these words, he chose to translate the mountain's name as 'the southern district where birds are kept'.[6] Everyone I asked while visiting Khumbu in January 2023 also associated the mountain's name with a bird, but this time a chicken. The mountain's name, they assured me, meant 'standing chicken's comb' because their view of the mountain from Khumbu looked like a raised chicken's comb. Etymologies of the goddess's name grew more creative as they crossed cultures. For example, her name is often translated as 'goddess mother of the world'. While it may be understandable to gloss Chomo as 'goddess mother', her name can only mean 'of the world' by following Bell's misreading of *lang* as *lung* and ignoring his reference to birds.

The other name that has stuck to her remarkably well is, of course, 'Everest'.[7] Unlike other colonial names, which are slowly falling out of use, 'Mount Everest' remains the mountain's most common international title, and even locals, who view the mountain as the goddess's abode, refer to it as 'Everest' when they speak to foreigners. There are multiple reasons for this. The mountain and the goddess have always been known by multiple epithets, and in this cultural context, Everest can be added to the mountain's list of names without displacing the others. The name 'Everest' also performs a significant socio-cultural function for the local, minoritised communities that live around the mountain. 'Everest' connects them directly to the international community, allowing them to bypass the Nepali and Chinese nationalist stories of the mountains. They are known as the people of the mountain, and the mountain is connected directly to them.

These communities rarely use, by contrast, the names their national governments insist on calling the mountain. According to official Chinese history, Chinese geographers first mapped, named, and, therefore, 'discovered' the mountain during the Qing Empire's reign. The current government's claim that this map is 'Chinese' ignores the fact that the Qing Empire, and therefore their mapping project, was Manchu, and Tibetan monks conducted the surveys that produced the maps. But they are correct in stating that the Qing court produced Manchu and Chinese language maps of Tibet with the goddess's name on them as early as 1720.[8] Since 1720, various Chinese governments have written the mountain's name in at least six transliterations but seem to have settled on two transliterations by the second half of the twentieth century: Zhumulangma Feng (珠穆朗玛峰) in Chinese characters or Qomolangma in the official Pinyin transcription of Tibetan. Many Tibetans view these spellings and the pronunciation they suggest as symbols of China's disputed sovereignty over Tibet and refuse to use them.

The Nepali government calls the mountain Sagarmāthā, a Sanskrit name. The origin and etymology of this name are unclear. Some argue that *māthā* means 'forehead' or 'head', and *sagara* means 'sky', so the name means something like 'head in the sky'. The Nepali nationalist historian and school administrator Baburam Acharya (1888–1971) was the first to publish this name for the mountain in an essay entitled 'Sagarmāthā or Jhyāmolongmā' in the Nepali-language monthly *Shāradā* in 1939.[9] At the time, this publication got him in trouble with the Nepali government, which threatened to deport him for insulting the British by proposing a Nepali name for Everest. He later claimed he had heard the name Sagarmāthā from locals living near the mountain. Given the rarity of Nepali speakers in the region at that time, and the even lower rates of Sanskrit literacy, this seems strange, and his claim that this was an old name for the mountain is unlikely. Despite the name's history, the Nepali government accepted Sagarmāthā as the official Nepali name after Nepal–China boundary talks in the early 1960s and now insists it is the mountain's national name.[10]

In the god's realm

The local histories of the goddess, found in Tibetan texts, images, and rituals, are centuries older than their Nepali, British, or Chinese counterparts.

Texts written over almost a millennium describe or invoke the goddess. She is part of a larger community of supernatural beings that, according to Asian Highland lore, are the Highlands' original inhabitants. These supernatural beings are roughly divided into three categories, depending on where they live: (1) *lha* (territorial deities) live in mountains and heavens; (2) *sinpo, tsen, and nojin* (demons) live in intermediate spaces; and (3) *sadak* (earth lords) and amphibious, snake-like *lu* live underground and underwater. The most common term to describe these beings is *lha-lu*, meaning 'from the gods in the heavens to the *lu* underground'. *Lha-lu* control the elements – earth, water, fire, air, and ether – and create disasters when insulted. As it is hard for ordinary beings to know when, how, and why they have offended *lha-lu*, they rely on people with great spiritual power, either yogis or royalty, to intervene with the *lha-lu*.

The *lha-lu*'s abodes are called *né*, and the mountain abodes of *lha* (territorial deities) are particularly revered. These mountain deities were often associated with clans, and clan leaders were sometimes said to have descended from them. The importance of individual mountains changed over time as clans' power rose and fell and settlement patterns changed. Early human settlements were concentrated in central Tibet's river valleys, and they venerated deities like Yarlha Shampo, whose mountain sits at the head of the Yarlung Valley in central Tibet. He is said to be the ancestor of the Tibetan Empire's rulers (sixth to ninth centuries CE). Over time, however, other mountain deities, such as Nangthen Thanglha on the plains north of Lhasa and Amnye Machen in the Plateau's northeast, rose in prominence.

The central Himalaya's mountains were visible to larger settlements to their north across the Pelmo Thang Plain for millennia, but they tended to see them from afar and describe them as a collective. At some point before the tenth century CE, these mountains became associated with two groups of goddesses that both belonged to a class of *lha* known as Zhingkong Sungma (Earth Guardians). The Tenma Chunyi (Twelve Stabilising Deities) congregated on Pelmotang Plain, and the Tseringma Chenga (Five Sisters of Long Life) lived among the mountain's peaks. Both groups of goddesses were fierce. The Tseringma Chenga were known to eat the flesh of those who entered their realm.

The life stories of the adepts who converted the goddesses to Buddhism preserve knowledge of their fierce pre-Buddhist lives. As Hildegard Diemberger notes, the *lha-lu* did not make 'specific ontological claims' – like those of a universalistic creator god – and could, therefore, be incorporated into the Buddhist world.[11] The adepts' tales are set in the sixth to tenth centuries but were written down from the eleventh century onwards. One of their central themes is the protagonists' calming and conversion of the *lha-lu*.

As the *lha-lu* became Buddhist, so did their abodes, and the Buddhicisation of the *lha*'s mountain abodes was a significant marker of Buddhism's success in the Highlands. Some mountain *lha* were reimagined as fully awakened Buddhas, and their *né* rose in importance.[12] Others were still considered worldly gods, and their influence remained local. The status of others was open for debate; one person's *lha* was another's Buddha. Chomolangma and her sisters, the Five Long-Life Goddesses, belong to this last category; their status was and is an object of debate. Different authors described them as one or the other. The two most well-known versions of this story were their guest roles in episodes of Vajrayana Buddhism's two most famous life stories, those of the beloved yogis Guru Rinpoche and Milarepa.

Two Buddhist gurus and Five Long-Life Goddesses

Guru Rinpoche, also known as Padmasambhava, is one of the most influential figures in Tibetan and Himalayan history and one of its most historically elusive. Extant eighth-century sources say that an Indian specialist in tantra named Padmasambhava visited the Tibetan Emperor's court to teach Buddhism.[13] He may also have offered advice on rearranging Tibet's irrigation systems.[14] However, the version of his life story better known in the mountains is the one retold in the eleventh and twelfth centuries by a series of *terton* (treasure revealers). The *terton* claimed to be reincarnations of his eighth-century disciples and to have access to revealed *ter* (treasure texts) that Guru Rinpoche had hidden away centuries earlier for them to find. In these texts, Guru Rinpoche is reimagined as the second Buddha who brings the *dharma* to Tibet, converts its people, and calms its *lha-lu*.

The 'calming' or 'subduing' process – *dulwa* in Tibetan – is a complicated cultural phenomenon that manifests differently across the Highlands and through the centuries. In Guru Rinpoche's stories, he engages in supernatural competition with the deities, outperforms them, and then extracts from them a vow to practise Buddhism and aid Buddhists. In later stories, other yogis and *tantrikas* remind the *lha-lu* of this vow and then re-negotiate, asking them to forgive offences or bring boons.

Guru Rinpoche's story became rooted in the sacred landscapes of the Highlands. The many caves, lakes, and mountaintops where he meditated or tamed *lha-lu* are local and trans-local pilgrimage sites. All Vajrayana Buddhists revere him, but he is mainly associated with the Nyingma (Old Ones) lineage, which is very influential in the central Himalaya.

Milarepa (1040/52–1123/35)[15] continued Guru Rinpoche's work negotiating with the *lha-lu*, converting non-Buddhists, and encouraging those who had converted to practise. He started life as a black magician, causing many deaths, before seeking redemption through a life of solitary meditation in the mountains. He mastered the yogic technique of inner fire and became renowned as a *repa* (cotton-clad one) who could withstand the fierce, high-altitude winters in caves. He was also celebrated for his songs, through which he communicated his realisations. Milarepa spent much of his life in the central Himalaya, and his most sacred sites are just west of Chomolungma, in the Rongshar, Labchi, and Nyalam Valleys. Like Guru Rinpoche, Milarepa is revered by all lineages of Vajrayana Buddhism but, unlike his predecessor, he is mainly associated with the Kagyu (oral transmission) lineage.

Although Guru Rinpoche's story is understood to be older, the geo-biographies of these two adepts developed around the same time and over-lapped and enhanced each other. Their stories also contained, maintained, and promoted the narratives of central Himalayan goddesses. One of the most significant episodes in Guru Rinpoche's story was his calming of the Twelve Tenma (stabilising deities) on the Pelmotang Plain, eighty-six kilometres north of Chomolungma.[16] The oral traditions Dzatrul Ngawang Tenzin Rinpoche relied on to write the *Guide to Dza Rongpu* in the early twentieth century also claimed that Guru Rinpoche visited the Dza Rongpu Valley, where he tamed a flesh-eating demoness. Guru Rinpoche's visit prepared the Dza Rongpu Valley for human habitation, and after he had blessed it with his presence, it was considered a good site for meditation.[17]

Milarepa's geo-biography misses Dza Rongpu Valley but includes the most detailed descriptions of Miyo Langsangma and her sisters, who were his partners in sexual yoga. Sexual yoga, it should be emphasised, is not sex but the transmutation of sexual energy to bring about insight into reality. As it brings direct insight into the nature of reality to all who engage in it, the story of Milarepa's awakening can also be read as the story of the five sisters' awakening, but not everyone reads it this way. Some writers and painters describe and paint them as Buddhas; others as non-awakened deities. Their colours, positioning, and attributes align them with the Five Great Self-Arising Buddhas: Vairocana, Amoghasiddhi, Amitābha, Ratnasambhava, and Akṣobhya. Miyo Langsangma's eldest sister, Jomo Tseringma, is white like Vairocana, sits at the centre of her sisters, and represents wisdom.

Miyo Langsangma is yellow like Ratnasambhava, sits to the south, and represents giving. But unlike these Buddhas, the sisters are not seated and ride animals like other non-realised protector deities. Their role as non-awakened protector deities is clear when they are depicted with banners. When they are not, their status is ambiguous.

All five sisters are said to abide on Gaurishankar, which the Tibetan texts describe as a 'five-peak' mountain. The texts sometimes name the mountain Jomo Tseringma for the Tseringma Chenga's oldest sister and sometimes call it Tonting Gyelmo (azure queen).[18] None of the goddesses spend all their time on this mountain. They maintain *né* (abodes) in Bhutan's Paro Valley, among other sites, and several of them are associated with other central Himalayan peaks. A number of ritual texts prepared between the fourteenth and seventeenth centuries describe the second sister, Chomolungma/Miyo Langsangma, maintaining a *né* on another peak near her sister.[19] Miyo Langsangma's *né* existed, therefore, within this cultural geographic web. It was not the region's most important sacred site, but it was not unimportant either.

From the fifteenth century onwards, the central Himalaya's sacred geography also came to include a series of *beyul* (hidden lands) south of the watershed, hidden by Guru Rinpoche so that his followers could access them during times of strife. This strife came in abundance during the sixteenth and seventeenth centuries as various Mongol and Manchu armies aligned with Tibet's religious lineages competed for power across the Highlands. At the end of this period, the fifth Dalai Lama, Ngawang Lozang Gyatso (1617–82), and his Gelug lineage had established the Ganden Podrang government in Lhasa, and the Kagyu and Nyingma lineages had been pushed to the periphery. The primarily Nyingma Sherpa made their way from eastern Tibet to the *beyul* south of Chomolangma in the Khumbu region. They continued to be called Sherpa, 'easterners', even after living in the Khumbu for hundreds of years.

Chomolungma was not prominent in Khumbu's sacred geography; all but its 'chicken comb' was hidden behind closer mountains. Another closer mountain, Khumbila (or Khumbu Yul-Lha, 'Khumbu's territorial god'), became the *beyul*'s most important mountain deity. But the Sherpa maintained close associations with Nyingma and Kagyu Buddhist yogis who lived north of Chomolungma and circulated stories of the goddess. After the Gelug's ascendancy, the Nyingma and Kagyu lineages became more closely linked, along with the stories of their most famous adepts, Guru Rinpoche and Milarepa. Guru Rinpoche's taming of a flesh-eating demoness in the Dza Rongpu Valley was intertwined with Milarepa's story, particularly his interactions with the

Tseringma Chenga, who had been flesh-eating demonesses before their conversion to Buddhism. Proponents of each lineage respected each other's sacred sites but tended to promote those associated with their own lineages. Thus, the Dza Rongpu Valley, home to Nyingma practitioners, was more closely associated with Guru Rinpoche than Chomolungma.

New mountain views, new mountain names

Along with these Tibetan texts, another unexpected place where the goddess's name appears is on the previously mentioned maps produced by the Qing imperial court in the early eighteenth century. The Qing court composed these maps after expelling the Dzungar Mongols from Tibetan territory and establishing a *choyon* (priest-patron) or protector relationship with the Dalai Lamas in the early 1700s. As Tibet was not a Chinese province and was difficult to reach, the map makers sent Tibetan monks trained in cartography to survey it. The monks' surveys led to the most comprehensive series of maps of Tibet hitherto produced, and the transliterated names of the goddess and her sister, Jomo Tseringma, appear on several maps at the edge of Tibetan territory in the central Himalaya. The maps were reproduced in French later in the same century by cartographer Jean-Baptiste Bourguignon d'Anville in his *Nouvel atlas de la Chine, de la Tartarie chinoise, et du Thibet*. On d'Anville's map of Tibet, he names the mountain 'Tchomour Lancma Mt',[20] a twice transliterated interpretation of Chomo Langma.

At around the same time the Tibetan cartographer monks surveyed Tibetan territories for the Qing court, a group of nuns were establishing a community in the upper Dza Rongpu (Rongbuk) Valley at the mountain's base. Their daily rituals involved prayers to the goddess, and they depended on her grace to continue living in the valley's challenging environment. As far as we know, the nuns did not write down their prayers, but we know about them from Dzatrul Ngawang Tenzin Rinpoche's writing. Dzatrul Rinpoche was a Nyingma yogi who came from a prominent family in the nearby settlement of Dingri. He moved to Dza Rongpu Valley late in the nineteenth century, and while meditating down the valley from the nuns, he experienced a vision of Guru Rinpoche encouraging him to establish a monastery there. Following the vision, he inaugurated Dza Rongpu Monastery in 1902.

Dzatrul Rinpoche's reputation as a genuine meditator and kind guide to monks, nuns, and lay villagers spread on both sides of the mountain, and he became a key figure in Tibetans' and Sherpas' religious life.[21] He wrote an autobiography describing his life at Dza Rongpu and penned a *Guide to Dza Rongpu's Sacred Sites* for the region's inhabitants. His description of the area focuses on Guru Rinpoche's sojourn at the mountain's base and his conversion of the goddess from flesh-eater to yogini, but he also acknowledges Milarepa's legacy and his relationship with the Tseringma Chenga and Miyo Langsangma. Dzatrul Rinpoche was there to greet and raise concerns about the British 'sahibs' who began visiting his valley in the 1920s and 1930s, intent on 'conquering' the world's highest mountain. He wrote of his concern about their 'back-the-front views' of reality and the pointless risks they took with their and others' safety.[22]

The British obsession with Chomolungma had begun seventy years earlier, when the Great Trigonometrical Survey of India determined in 1856 that the world's highest peak sat just outside their territory in the Nepali–Tibetan borderlands. They established the peak's height through theodolites and triangulations from hundreds of kilometres away, but it took them decades to receive permission to approach its base. In these intervening years, they established their own mythology of the mountain, embedded within imperial ambitions.

British claims that there were 'multiple names' for the mountain suggest they were not talking to the right people or looking at d'Anville's map. Most of the 'multiple names' in circulation from the 1850s were British mistakes rather than local names for the mountain. Some confused Chomolangma and her elder sister, claiming the peak's real name was Gaurishankar.[23] Another alternative name for the mountain was proffered by a group of British people living in Darjeeling, who insisted locals told them the mountain's name was 'Deodhunga'. They must have been unaware that Deodhunga (or Deo Ḍhuṅgā) means 'stones of the gods' or 'stone altars' in Nepali and is a name given to all high mountains and temples with stone altars in them.

To be fair, confusion about the mountain's name was not confined to the region's British inhabitants. When Charles Bell sought permission from the Dalai Lama's government in Lhasa for British climbers to enter Dza Rongpu Valley, no one in Lhasa knew of the mountain either. The passport the government granted the climbers reads in part, 'Minister Bell has suggested that Sahibs should be granted a pass to explore the snow mountain in Karta that he calls Chamalung.'[24]

The climbing expeditions to Dzatrul Rinpoche's valley also occasioned a discussion in the first Tibetan-language newspaper, *Melong* (*Mirror*), based in Kalimpong, about the 'proper name of the Mount Everest'. The paper's proprietor, Dorje Tharchin (1890–1976), ran a series of articles about the mountain's name from March 1933. In the first article, he was convinced that the world's highest mountain's proper name was Tonting Gyelmo, Gaurishankar. He seemed to be more confused about which mountain the British were describing than the mountain's name. After all, Tonting Gyelmo is the home of the oldest sister, Jomo Tseringma, and a much more important mountain in the region's sacred geography. What is more, from Tharchin's home in Kalimpong, Tonting Gyelmo looks higher than Chomolungma. In his very next edition of the *Melong*, however, he was less convinced. The Sherpa trade official Wang Penpa had insisted to him that the British were talking about another mountain, 'the abundantly snowy terrestrial realm of the auspicious long-life goddess, Miyo Langsangma or Chomolungma'. He had also begun to have doubts, he said, after hearing that Dzatrul Rinpoche had written about the British interest in the mountain named 'Chomolungma'.[25] He included a drawing with this second article that showed how prominent Tonting Gyelmo was in his view of the mountains and the smaller-looking Chomolungma to its right, at the back of the mountains (Figure 1.2).

These exchanges suggest that many Tibetans and Sherpas had a general image of snow mountains as special, associated the central Himalaya and the Tseringma Chenga, and Tonting Gyelmo (Gaurishankar) with the oldest sister, Jomo Tseringma. Only those who lived close to the mountain, including Sherpas like Wang Penpa, knew which specific peak the British were talking about and its association with Miyo Langsangma.

Shortly after Tharchin published his musings on the mountain's proper name, the region was thrown into decades of geopolitical turmoil that reconfigured

Figure 1.2 'The proper name of the Mount Everest', detail, 1933. Chomolungma is the smaller of the mountains in the back right of this illustration for an article by Gegen Dorje Tharchin in his Tibetan language newspaper, *Melong* (*The Mirror*) (Yul phyogs so so'i gsar 'gyur me long), 7 (1933), 27. Tharchin Collection; Series 1; C.V. Starr East Asian Library, Columbia University. Courtesy of the C.V. Starr East Asian Library, Columbia University.

international perceptions of the mountain. The Second World War, decolonisation, and the Himalaya's territorialisation within the mid-twentieth-century sovereign-state-based world order saw the goddess's abode reimagined as an international border. The border transecting the mountain not only separated two sovereign states – the Kingdom of Nepal and the People's Republic of China – but also the communist and Western spheres of influence. Dza Rongpu Monastery was razed during the Cultural Revolution, and fleeing monks carried Dzatrul Rinpoche's body across the mountain passes into Nepali territory in Khumbu, where they offered him a proper funeral.[26] Nepal and China both added the world's highest mountain to their invented nationalist traditions, renaming it accordingly.

As mentioned earlier, after geopolitics split the region, the name 'Everest' lost some of its colonial sting and became a name that connected the central Himalaya to the world beyond the nationalist Chinese and Nepali projects. Everest is not the mountain's oldest name, nor its proper name, but neither is Zhumulangma Feng nor Sagarmāthā. The region's complicated geopolitics have forestalled local efforts to decolonise the mountain's names. These kinds of renaming efforts usually come from below when empowered postcolonial local communities demand that colonial names be removed. This probably will not happen to Chomolungma soon. But perhaps the international community could make an exception to this rule and start calling this mountain by its oldest local name, Chomolungma, honouring the goddess and the people of the region who have such a long history with her. Learning to name and see the goddess would go some way to undoing Waugh's mistake and removing the stain of colonialism left behind on the mountain.

Notes

1 Ngag dbang bstan 'dzin nor bu, 'Gangs chen brgyad kyi ya gyal rdza rong phu yi gnas yig dad pa'i mgongs ldan dga' skyes dbyar gyi rnga sgra (The sound of summer's drum that delights the faithful peacocks, a guide to the sacred sites of Dza Rongpu, solitary among the eight great snow mountains)', in *Ngag dbang bstan 'dzin nor bu's gsung 'bum* (*The Collected Works of Ngagwang Tenzin*) (Kathmandu: Ngagyur Dongak Choling Monastery, 2004), pp. 401–26.

2 Nicolas Tournadre and Hiroyuki Suzuki, *The Tibetic Languages: An Introduction to the Family of Languages Derived from Old Tibetan* (Paris: LACITO, 2023).

3 Chomolungma, Chomolangma, Jomolangma, and other variants are transliterations of the name spelled *Jo mo glang ma* in Tibetan. The Sherpa community usually write 'Chomolungma', so I have followed their lead, even though it is not the most straightforward transliteration of the name. Tibetan words are spelled with many silent or

transforming letters, which makes them difficult to read in direct transliteration. I have used the most common transliterations here, but there may be others available. The Tibetan spelling of the goddess's other name is Mi g.yo glang bzang ma.

4 Carla Gianotti, 'Female Buddhist adepts in the Tibetan tradition: the twenty-four Jo Mo, disciples of Pha Dam Pa Sangs Rgyas', *Journal of Dharma Studies*, 2:1 (2019), 15–29, https://doi.org/10.1007/s42240-019-00038-x

5 Ngag dbang bstan 'dzin nor bu, 'Rdza rong phu gnas yig', p. 360.

6 Tibetan: *bya ma lung*. Charles Bell, *Portrait of a Dalai Lama: The Life and Times of the Great Thirteenth* (Boston, MA: Wisdom Publications, 1987), p. 277.

7 See also Chapter 2 by Felix de Montety and the Introduction by Hansen, Gilchrist, and Westaway in this volume.

8 Lin Chao, 'Zhumulangma de fa xian yu mingcheng (The discovery and name of Everest)', *Beijing Daxue Xuebao* (Journal of Peking University), 4 (1958), 143–63.

9 Bāburām Āchārya, 'Sagarmāthā or Jhyāmolongmā', *Sharada*, 14:8 (January 1939), republished in *Nepāli Gadya Samgraha*, Part 1 (Kathmandu: Sajha, 2030 [1973]), pp. 5–13.

10 Kamal P. Malla, 'Sagara-māthā: the linguistic conquest of Mount Everest', *Nepalese Linguistics*, 15 (1998), 19–28.

11 Hildegard Diemberger, 'When *lha lu* spirits suffer and sometimes fight back: Tibetan cosmopolitics at a time of environmental threats and climate change', in Riamsara Kuyakanon, Hildegard Diemberger, and David Sneath (eds), *Cosmopolitical Ecologies Across Asia: Places and Practices of Power in Changing Environments* (London: Routledge, 2021), p. 20, https://doi.org/10.4324/9781003036272-1

12 Katia Buffetrille, *Pèlerins, lamas et visionnaires. Sources orales et écrites sur les pèlerinages tibétains* (Vienna: Arbeitskreis für Tibetische und Buddhistische Studien Universität Wien, 2000); Andrew Quintman, 'Toward a geographic biography: Mi la ras pa in the Tibetan landscape', *Numen*, 55:4 (2008), 363–410, https://doi.org/10.1163/156852708X310509; Ruth Gamble, *Reincarnation in Tibetan Buddhism: The Third Karmapa and the Invention of a Tradition* (New York: Oxford University Press, 2018), pp. 141–7, https://doi.org/10.1093/oso/9780190690779.001.0001

13 Lewis Doney, *The Zangs Gling ma: The First Padmasambhava Biography, Two Exemplars of the Earliest Recension* (Andiast, Switzerland: IITBS GmbH, International Institute for Tibetan and Buddhist Studies, 2014).

14 Pasang Wangdu and Hildegard Diemberger, *Dba' bzhed: The Royal Narrative Concerning the Bringing of Buddha's Doctrine to Tibet* (Vienna: Österreichischen Akademie der Wissenschaften, 2000).

15 There is some argument about which of the twelve-year cycles Milarepa was born into and therefore his dates are disputed.

16 René de Nebesky-Wojkowitz, *Oracles and Demons of Tibet. The Cult and Iconography of the Tibetan Protective Deities* (The Hague: Mouton, 1956), pp. 170–230.

17 Ngag dbang bstan 'dzin nor bu, 'Rdza rong phu gnas yig', p. 360.

18 Other transliterations of this mountain's name include variations of Gang Thon Thing Gyalmo.

19 There are too many of these texts to cite here, but one collection of these texts is *bKra shis tshe ring ma'i sgrub skor sogs* (Thimphu: Kunzang Topgey, 1976).

20 Jean-Baptiste Bourguignon d'Anville, *Nouvel atlas de la Chine, de la Tartarie chinoise, et du Thibet* (Amsterdam: chez Barthelemy Vlam, 1785 [orig. 1737]).

21 Sherry B. Ortner, *High Religion: A Cultural and Political History of Sherpa Buddhism* (Princeton, NJ: Princeton University Press, 1989).

22 Ruth Gamble, 'The mountain's many faces: how geologists mistook Chomolungma for Everest', in Alison Bashford, Emily M. Kern, and Adam Bobbette (eds), *New Earth Histories: Geo Cosmologies and the Making of the Modern World* (Chicago, IL: University of Chicago Press, 2023), pp. 53–69, https://doi.org/10.7208/chicago/9780226828596-007

23 Ngag dbang bstan 'dzin nor bu, 'Bdud rtsi'i rol mtsho', in *Rnam thar 'chi med bdud rtsi'i rol mtsho* (n.p., n.d.), pp. 291a–291b.

24 This document is held by the Museum of Himalayan Mountaineering Institute, Darjeeling.

25 Dorje Tharchin, 'The proper name of the Mount Everest is', *Melong*, 7:3 (March 1933), 21. Dorje Tharchin, 'The proper name of the Mount Everest', *Melong*, 7:4 (March 1933), 27.

26 Ngawang Shedrub Tenpe Gyaltsen Rinpoche and Ven. Jamyang Wangmo, *Dharma Wheel of Great Bliss* (Kathmandu: Vajra Publications, 2008), p. 30.

2

Naming Mount Everest: mountain cartography and languages of exonymy

Felix de Montety

Numbers and names

A lithograph of 'Gaurisánkar, or Mount Everest, in the Himálaya of Nepal' for some years hung on a wall of the Alpine Club, in London. The image was painted in 1855 by the German mountaineer, geographer, and naturalist Hermann von Schlagintweit and published in 1861 after years of extraordinary and tragic travels in India and Nepal with his brothers Adolf and Robert.[1] The painting represented a barren plateau with the explorers' camp in the foreground, a deep dark valley a bit further away, a few rocky summits, and, in the distance, a series of higher snow-capped peaks dominated by an immense mountain group and its pyramid-shaped summit. Schlagintweit's Gaurisankar/Everest was later confirmed to be Makalu.[2] The painting reflected Hermann Schlagintweit's polymathic ambitions, captured early mountaineering's romantic aesthetics, and echoed one the era's great geographical controversies over the name and likeness of the world's highest peak.

Between the image's painting in 1855 and its publication in 1861, the knowledge and name of the peak was transformed by the Survey of India, whose surveyors and mathematicians measured, computed heights, named peaks, and determined that a mountain on the northern borders of Nepal was the world's highest above sea level. In 1856, the Surveyor General, Andrew Scott Waugh, proposed the name Mont Everest for this peak as a tribute to his predecessor, George Everest. The proposal was met with initial scepticism and adopted more widely from the 1860s. A number of local names for this peak were proposed and debated from 1856. These names included Chomolangma, referring to the abode of the goddess Miyo Langsangma, which climbers encountered more frequently in the early twentieth century.[3]

Why did the name Everest emerge in the first place and why was it immediately controversial? How were new names found and assessed by the scientific and mountaineering community? Can geography, history, and linguistics tell us if 'Mount Everest' will survive in the twenty-first century? This chapter examines key arguments expressed against or for 'Mount Everest' after its invention in 1856 and looks at the enduring legacy of imperial surveying, geography, philology, and mountaineering that have strengthened the use of the name until today.

Surveying and the imperial art of measurement

The idea that the Himalaya could be the highest mountain range in the world emerged at the end of the eighteenth century. The birth and rise of the name Mount Everest was intertwined with several developments, including Europe's fascination with mountains after the Enlightenment, obsessions with instrumented measurements and territorialised identities, and Britain's attempts to control its empire by collecting and ordering qualitative and quantitative data on topography, the environment, and people.[4] Observers in India wondered whether summits in the Himalaya reached higher than the Andes, then thought to be the world's highest mountains.[5] The Great Trigonometrical Survey of India was established in 1802 to map the 'Great Arc' of India in pursuit of what Matthew Edney has called a 'cartographical ideal'.[6] While India's northern frontiers attracted considerable interest from British administrators, scientists, and learned societies, the territory of Nepal remained outside colonial control and surveyors settled for long-distance observations and covert exploration to calculate the heights or learn the names of many Himalayan peaks. William Webb surveyed several prominent snow-capped peaks, including Dhaulagiri, whose height was confirmed as exceeding 8,187 metres in 1817. The mathematician and Sanskritist Henry Thomas Colebrook, then president of the Asiatick Society, declared: 'I consider the evidence to be now sufficient to authorize an unreserved declaration of the opinion, that the Himálaya is the loftiest range of Alpine mountains which has been yet noticed, its most elevated peaks greatly exceeding the highest of the Andes'.[7] Even the Andean explorer Alexander von Humboldt acquiesced in 1816 and wondered if 'behind the group of mountains of the Himalaya, there is not an even higher range'.[8]

Around 1850, the world's highest mountain remained unclear. At various times, Jomolhari, Nanda Devi, Dawalagiri, and Kangchenjunga were each

42

considered as contenders for the highest summit. In the 1840s, Andrew Waugh measured Kangchenjunga at 8,588 metres, but other heights remained to be established with certainty.[9] Humboldt and many others, though, considered Kangchenjunga probably the highest.[10]

The first British measurements of the peak that became 'Mount Everest' were made in November 1847, when John Armstrong surveyed peaks from stations situated between the Dandak and Gogra rivers with a fifteen-inch theodolite. Observations of the same mountain variously labelled 'Peak B', 'Peak γ' ('Gamma'), or 'Peak H' were made from multiple locations between 1847 and 1850 and combined under the heading 'Himalaya Peak XV'. New observations, computations on its position and height, and verifications were carried out by John Peyton, Michael Hennessey, Radhanath Sikdar, and Andrew Waugh from 1850 to 1856.[11]

The complex calculations required by observing 'Himalaya Peak XV' from great distances included adjustments for atmospheric refraction. The role of individuals in these calculations is not very clear and has been disputed. The contribution of Radhanath Sikdar to the computation of Himalayan heights was often omitted from later accounts. According to Ashish Lahiri's research in the National Archives of India, the data collected by surveyors was sent to the office of the Chief Computer Radhanath Sikdar in Calcutta, who analysed, processed, and commented on the figures before transmitting the documents to the Surveyor General in Dehra Dun, where they would be checked once again.[12] As the surveyor James Walker put it several decades later, 'the discovery of the great pinnacle was not a revelation at first sight, but the result of slow and carefully elaborated processes of induction'.[13]

The contemporary use of associating a summit (defined by its observable or measurable prominence above other forms of relief) with a proper name, precisely calculated altitude, and the authors and date of its first ascent is a well-situated practice in the longer history of humanity. Before the spread of European topographic conventions and the birth of mountaineering in the nineteenth century, the now almost undisputed idea that each summit should have a proper name was not shared by many. Geographers have since demonstrated how each culture's specific conception of space implies geographical ontologies that could be very different from the modern Western topographical categories and hierarchies that have become globally hegemonic.[14]

In many mountainous territories, names commonly referred to places on a mountain, or to a whole range or group of elevated places, rather than to individual peaks, which were only rarely climbed to their top. From the eighteenth century to the late nineteenth century, the spread of a Romantic imagination of elevated landscapes and the rise of scientific and literary discourses on the terrifying 'glacières' of the Alps and picturesque volcanoes converged in giving summits more and more importance.[15] While early modern cartographers such as the Cassini family in France emphasised rivers, resources, and human settlements in their alpine cartographies, nineteenth-century surveyors and cartographers stressed the political importance of summits, mapping each massif's peaks and inscribing their names, often in collaboration with mountaineers and alpine societies.[16] In the Alps, some geographical names were new, and privileged the personal names of daring tourists who made first ascents, or the surveyors and cartographers who produced these maps. The 'golden age of alpinism' from 1854 to 1865 was also a golden age for 'conquest place-naming', a toponymical process that simultaneously put the conquerors' names on the map and rendered invisible many non-official names and forms of local knowledge on mountains.[17]

'Mont Everest' and its discontents

Andrew Waugh announced the final values for the elevation of 'peak XV' in a letter to Henry Landor Thuillier, his Calcutta-based deputy and future successor, on 1 March 1856. 'We have for some years known that this mountain is higher than any other hitherto measured in India, and most probably it is the highest in the whole world.' Waugh was 'determined to name this noble peak of the Himalayas "Mont Everest"'. This name was an exception to the rule Waugh had been taught by his predecessor, George Everest, 'to assign to every geographical object its true local or native appellation'.

> But here is a mountain, most probably the highest in the world, without any local name that we can discover, or whose native appellation, if it has any, will not likely be ascertained before we are allowed to penetrate into Nepal and to approach close to this stupendous snowy mass. In the meantime the privilege, as well as the duty, devolves on me to assign to this lofty pinnacle of our globe, a name whereby it may be known among geographers and become a household word among civilized nations.[18]

The tendency of travellers and cartographers to name things after people from their own nation is one of the cornerstones of critical place-name studies and represents the typical cartographical imagination of European imperialism.[19] Place-naming plays a key role in the conquest, domination, and appropriation of foreign land, and geographers, anthropologists, and linguists have demonstrated how place names are originally associated with site-specific worldviews and constitute an indispensable part of any human group's relation to place and to its own unity over space and time.[20] The contemporary acknowledgement that toponymical erasure can disturb and even endanger any socio-spatial culture today makes imperial place-name erasure a moral issue, a problem of spatial and social justice which can be addressed by devoting more attention to and promoting local voices, spatial representations, and archives.[21]

It is striking that acts of toponymical erasure by explorers and cartographers were already criticised by many nineteenth-century European geographers, who believed that locally known names should be preferred not for moral but for practical reasons. To scholars like Humboldt, any geographer, lest they be deemed 'a mere maps drawer, must submit the names of rivers, lakes and mountains' to a 'sort of philological examination'.[22] In a short book on the problem of the *Philosophy of Geographical Names* published in 1851, Abraham Hume denounced the 'very objectionable' practice of British 'voyagers and travellers', who 'pass over portions of land or water previously well-known and accurately named, and apply to the places English names, which are as little known to the natives as theirs are to us. This is a fruitful source of confusion in geography'.[23] In the Himalaya, the difficulty of collecting locally known names had become a stereotypical observation in the writings of figures of exploration such as Joseph Dalton Hooker, who observed in 1854: 'To my disappointment I found that neither priest nor people knew the name of a single snowy mountain'.[24]

Waugh balanced his transgression against the rules of geographical nomenclature with an overarching argument and mitigating factors. Inventing a name was justified by the lack of knowledge of a local name, which he presented as the absence of a local name altogether rather admitting a temporary state of ignorance. The mitigating factor he highlighted to justify his choice was the idea that the new name could be temporary, and that it would mainly be used 'among civilized nations' rather than imposed on local populations. Furthermore, he suggested that the Survey of India could not be blamed for his choice, as it was Nepal's interdiction of British surveyors that prevented him from acquiring local knowledge of the peak. Throughout the second part of the nineteenth century, this argument resurfaced in justifications of 'Mount Everest', despite the fact that the Survey was not shy about using covert strategies to send staff in disguise into the Himalayas but did not employ this strategy to establish the 'native name' of the mountain.[25] Waugh's rhetoric implied that his function was not to retrieve local names; his duty was geometrical measurement of the mountains' height and positions. Under Everest and Waugh, according to Matthew Edney, 'The triangulation framework reduced all geographical data to a common and universal reference that obviated the need for any local knowledge.'[26]

Waugh's proposal divided learned circles and infuriated specialists of 'local knowledge' when it was circulated in India and Europe. Waugh's deeply personal tribute to Everest had detractors, notably the polymath and diplomat Brian Houghton Hodgson, who had been British resident in Kathmandu and became an expert in subjects from botany and languages to religion.[27] At the October 1856 meeting of the Asiatic Society of Bengal, Hodgson castigated Waugh's proposal and argued the 'nameless' peak did '*not* lack a native and ascertained name; that that is Dévadhungá, or holy hill'.[28]

Hodgson shared his objections with the Royal Asiatic Society in London to 'such incongruity as the intrusion of a purely European name amid a long series of purely Oriental names'. The mountain had Nepali and Tibetan names, and Hodgson listed the Nepali 'Deodungha', a name that soon became the main rival to 'Mount Everest'.[29] An important figure of the British Raj's 'Republic of letters', Hodgson was considered one of the foremost scholars on the Himalayas alongside the naturalist Joseph Hooker.

After Royal Asiatic Society members 'unanimously expressed their concurrence' with Hodgson's views, the arguments of Hodgson and Waugh were aired before the Royal Geographical Society in London in 1857. Waugh aimed to convince the geographers that Hodgson's names did not refer to the peak that he had identified and measured precisely, which did not have a local name. To do so, he efficiently summarised his team's surveys and enlisted the help of collaborators who concurred in contradicting Hodgson.[30] To accompany the announcement he provided a 'sketch diagram showing heights of Himalayan peaks' (Figures 2.1 and 2.2).[31]

Around this time in 1857, Waugh was also honoured by the Royal Geographical Society 'for geodetical operations, as remarkable for their extent as for their accuracy, whereby [India] has been covered by triangulation'.[32] Since Waugh was then in India, his gold medal was received on his behalf by the now London-based George Everest, whose speech conveyed the idea that the medal celebrated the Survey of India itself.[33] Without drawing a parallel with the award, George Everest also commented on Waugh's proposal for the name Mount Everest. The retired surveyor did not refuse the honour but suggested that his name might be too difficult to pronounce for non-Europeans in India. This name was apparently adequate for European publications.

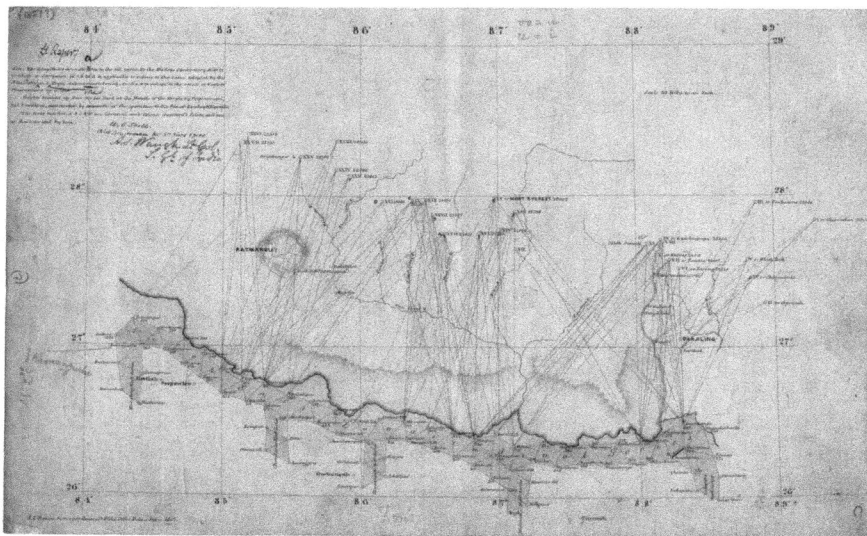

Figure 2.1 'Sketch diagram showing heights of Himalayan peaks', signed by A.S. Waugh [1858], RGS-IBG archive JMS-11-35; later published in *Proceedings of the Royal Geographical Society*, 2:2 (1858), 115. RGS Picture Library S0025738. Courtesy of the RGS-IBG.

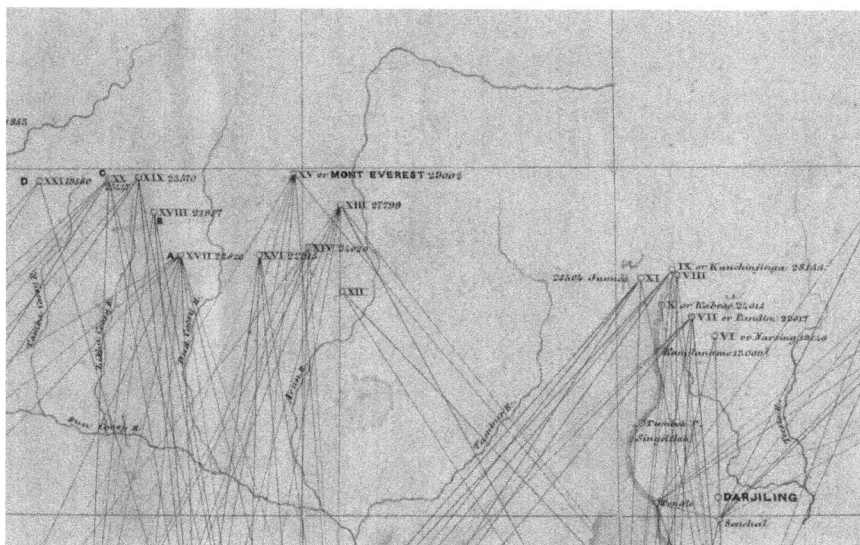

Figure 2.2 The triangulation of Mount Everest, detail. From 'Sketch diagram showing heights of Himalayan peaks', signed by A.S. Waugh [1858], RGS-IBG archive JMS-11-35; later published in *Proceedings of the Royal Geographical Society*, 2:2 (1858), 115. Courtesy of the RGS-IBG.

These remarks occurred in the context of the Indian Rebellion of 1857–58 and the Government of India Act of 1858, which effectively ended East India Company rule in India. The Survey had contributed to the Company's control of territory and may have fuelled resentment for destructive practices in the field; its activities were limited during the revolt.

The 'Mount Everest' controversy was interrupted by the uprising, but the new name was not universally embraced. On 2 October 1861, Charles Canning, Governor General since 1856 and Viceroy of India since 1858, wrote to Lord Elgin that his wife, the artist and botanist Charlotte Canning, had planned to travel to Sikkim to observe the world's highest mountain, to which he referred as 'Deodunga or Mount Everest as the Surveyors have barbarously christened it'.[34]

Philologists and statesmen were not the only ones to criticise naming practices by surveyors, from the Himalaya to the Alps. In 1857, while Waugh was battling for 'Mount Everest', John Ruskin's mountain writings were popular, tourists visited Chamonix and Zermatt, and the Alpine Club was founded in London to promote mountain exploration. By 1863, the 'Höchste Spitze' ('highest peak') of Monte Rosa became the Dufourspitze/Pointe Dufour, named after Guillaume-Henri Dufour (1787–1875), founder and first head of the Swiss Topographical Bureau (1838–65).[35] Dufourspitze on Swiss maps was criticised in a guidebook by the Alpine Club's president John Ball: 'With the highest estimate of the services of General Dufour as Director of the admirable Swiss Survey, the writer does not believe that the name of any individual can remain permanently attached to the highest peak of the second mountain in Europe.'[36]

Despite fierce opposition, Waugh's idea prevailed, as the Royal Geographical Society eventually agreed with Waugh and the Survey of India. Hodgson's credentials and assertive tone had managed to cast doubt on the appropriateness of 'Mount Everest'. In 1862, the RGS sided with the Schlagintweits' proposal for the name 'Gaurisankar'. By 1865, the RGS adopted the name Mount Everest again.

By now, the longer process of surveying and mapping had localised names such as Deodunga or Gaurisankar with summits other than Mount Everest, but this did not happen overnight. Uncertainty prevailed for some time and alternative local names for Mount Everest circulated widely in the second half of the nineteenth century.

Status quo and new ambitions

In a striking passage of *The Indian Alps and How We Crossed Them (1876)*, Elizabeth Mazuchelli recalled the moment she climbed a hill with her guides and porters and faced its highest peak. 'As we ascend still higher and emerge from behind a jutting rock that excluded it from our view, suddenly there is a loud and simultaneous exclamation of "Deodunga! Deodunga! Gaurisankar!" from my attendants, all apostrophising it in their different dialects, as the magnificent spires of Mount Everest again burst unexpectedly upon the view.' Mazuchelli added that she preferred 'the Thibetan to the English name of this glorious mountain, because the natives, who regard it with deep awe and reverence, seem to have had a fuller and deeper appreciation of it – the purest and noblest type on earth of the Almighty Architect – when they named it Deodunga'.[37]

In 1881, Sarat Chandra Das (1849–1917), a pundit working for the Survey of India, travelled across Nepal and into Tibet, and observed 'the great mountain range running from North to South, of which the culminating point is Lapchhyikang (called Mount Everest in English maps)' while also claiming that the Lap-chyi massif was dominated by Chomo Kankar, 'the grandest and loftiest of the world's mountains.'[38]

The Royal Geographical Society also debated Waugh's name for *Mont/*Mount Everest and its equivalence with 'Gaurisankar'.[39] The linguist Emil Schlagintweit, having outlived his brothers Adolf, Eduard, Hermann, and Robert, defended the family's earlier findings in debates on 'the name of the world's highest mountain' in 1888, 1890, and 1901.[40] In 1898, L.A. Waddell focused the debate on Tibetan names for these summits and mountains passes. He did not find a Tibetan name for 'Everest' but the place names and map he reproduced highlighted the extent of Tibetan geographical knowledge and the comparative limits of Western cartography.[41]

In 1903, the obstinate Douglas Freshfield reopened the 'Mount Everest' debate while Lord Curzon, then Viceroy of India, sent a surveyor to Nepal to settle the dispute. The mission mainly proved that none of the names so far suggested, including Gaurisankar, could be attested as referring to the world's highest peak. *Nature* hosted a new exchange of arguments between Freshfield and Sidney Burrard, a surveyor who defended the right of 'Mount Everest' to 'rest on our maps in peace'.[42]

The physical and intellectual difficulty of access to 'local names' remained a problem, not only in the case of Mount Everest but of the highest Himalaya or 'Transhimalaya' more generally. English geographers objected to the 'Transhimalaya' concept spearheaded by the Swedish explorer Sven Hedin. In 1907, Sidney Burrard argued that it was not necessary 'to attempt to attach an actual name to every peak', and that Western mountaineers and cartographers should 'never invent a name until its absence has become inconvenient'. In the presence of nameless Himalayan peaks, Burrard believed 'heights must be accepted to a certain extent as substitutes for names'.[43]

During the Great War, Sven Hedin seemed convinced by the Everest name: 'even if the real old native name should be found one day I the future, it would be a great mistake to try and introduce it in geography; As Mount Everest the peak will be known for ever'.[44] Hedin might have had a another reason to support the status quo: along with Everest, Humboldt, and Nikolay Prjevalski, Hedin was one of the very few people whose name was attached to a mountain by British or Russian surveys of Tibet.

The name 'Chomolangma' was first discussed at the Royal Geographical Society in May 1916. The Scottish chemist and climber Alexander Mitchell Kellas claimed that he and Charles Bruce had 'independently found' the name 'Chomo Langmo', while exploring the possibility of climbing the mountain.[45] In November 1920, Charles Bruce told the RGS that 'even if this proposed expedition finds its real name written clearly on the mountain, I hope it will take no notice, as I am sure you will agree that no name is so beautiful and suitable as Mount Everest. May the 2 feet never be cut off its 29,002!'[46]

The long-contemplated attempts to climb Mount Everest redefined the terms of the debate over its name. Tibetan passports for the first Everest expedition gave permission to travel to 'Cha-mo-lung-ma mountain' and the expedition leader, Charles Howard-Bury, concluded that 'Chomo-lungma' was the 'proper Tibetan name' for Mount Everest. Ideological patterns that excluded local names from Western geographical discourse remained enduring. Even though the first expeditions provided evidence that the local name was 'Chomolangma', most European climbers and cartographers stuck with 'Mount Everest'.

Even long-standing opponents of the imperial toponym such as Douglas Freshfield started to falter faced with the exciting prospect of a first ascent. Douglas Freshfield regretted breaking the rules of geographical nomenclature and proposed dividing the range into groups and printing the name Mount Everest, for the peak only, alongside Chomolungma, as a matter of courtesy to the Tibetan government.[47] Ironically, the next issue of the *Alpine Journal* included accounts of the Mount Everest expedition as well as ascents of 'Mount

Freshfield' in the Canadian Rocky Mountains![48] By 1924, Freshfield no longer mentioned alternative names for Mount Everest.[49]

'Chomolangma' was quickly identified but remained effectively sidelined by most British mountaineers and geographers in favour of 'Mount Everest'. Sven Hedin noted the similarity of the Tibetan name to the label for a range or summit in eighteenth-century Qing and French atlases.[50] Burrard and other alumni of the Survey of India continued to defend 'Mount Everest' out of loyalty for their organisation.[51] Twentieth-century mountaineers seem to have stuck to Mount Everest 'because it's there'. As generations always heard the imperial name, few had good reasons to spend energy arguing about the mountain's name when they could focus it on the glorious prospect of reaching its very top. While practical discussions on Himalayan nomenclature continued in specialised journals and books, most actors on the Everest expeditions showed little interest in the controversies.[52] From the 1920s to the 1950s, mountaineers kept inventing new place names on the slopes of Mount Everest.[53] In 1953, Marcel Kurz summarised that view in a publication that celebrated the hundredth anniversary of the mountain's surveying: 'Let us therefore leave the philologists to their disputes and follow, instead, the efforts of man to conquer this topmost peak.'[54]

Mountaineering and the challenges of postcoloniality?

Ironically, the problem of the world's highest place name resurfaced after the first ascent. Proposals in Britain to rename the peak included Mount Elizabeth, after the young Queen. In India, proposals included Mount Tenzing, after one of the climbers, and Mount Sikdar, after the Chief Computer in Calcutta who computed the height of the peak. Unusual names proposed in 1953 included Tenhillary, Hillarsing, and Hilltenhunt, to incorporate Edmund Hillary or John Hunt's names in the exploit.[55] Tenzing Norgay was born very close to the mountain, yet few journalists or fellow climbers showed much interest in what he called the peak. In his 1955 autobiography *Tiger of the Snows*, Tenzing noted that when he was growing up it was not Everest but Chomolungma:

> Usually Chomolungma is said to mean 'Goddess Mother of the World'. Sometimes 'Goddess Mother of the Wind'. But it did not mean either of these when I was a boy in Solo Khumbu. Then it meant 'The mountain so high no bird can fly over it'. That is what all Sherpa mothers used to tell their children – what my own mother told me – and it is the name I still like best for this mountain that I love.[56]

Later debates over mountain place names were mainly renewed by the conjunction of new eras in world politics as formally colonised countries gained independence and sovereignty over toponymy in their territories. By the 1960s, instead of 'Mount Everest', China embraced 'Qomolangma' and Nepal adopted 'Sagarmatha' as proper names for this peak. The term Sagarmāthā was invented in 1938 by Nepali historian Baburam Acharya.[57] Everest remains such a strong a myth and brand in the mountaineering community that admirers of exploratory narratives fiercely defend the Everest name and few dare defy its symbolic dominance.[58] Yet critics remain. According to William McKay Aitken, 'the vain glory of Sir George [Everest] and Sir Andrew [Waugh] will continue to haunt modern geography until "Mt. Everest" is admitted to have been a gratuitous self-serving assignation that abused the scientific credentials of the Survey'.[59]

Yet another transliteration of the Tibetan name for Mount Everest was cited by officials in the Tibetan government in exile. In 1984, Aitken, a Scottish-born writer based in India, wrote to the Dalai Lama to ask his position on the name of Mount Everest. After consulting the Library of Tibetan Works & Archives in Dharamsala, an assistant in the Dalai Lama's office replied:

> In all of the older Tibetan texts and historical documents, Everest as known to the westerners is referred to as Gang Thong Thing Gyalmo (*Gangs – mthongs – mthing – rgyal-mo*) Snow – high – blue – queen. However, among the general populace, the mountain is known by its most popular name of Gang-ri Jomolungma. The whole group of ridges forming Mount Everest is given the name Jomolungma. Whereas the Highest point (Everest) i.e. the top part is called Jomolangma.[60]

Conclusion

Although other names have received official approval since the mid-twentieth century, 'Mount Everest' remains preeminent in the imagination of the global mountaineering community. Mountain toponymy is a case study in modern mountaineering's limited interest in local knowledge and rampant blindness to political issues in the areas where climbing takes place. This blindness is made more severe by the economic context in which mountaineers try to make a living out of their exploits. From Sven Hedin to Maurice Herzog or from Reinhold Messner to Kilian Jornet, professional explorers and mountaineers often rely on book sales, film presentations, and sponsorship deals to fund their next project: the use of clearly identifiable mountain names in their books and public interventions has led most of them to favour the status quo over more progressive denominations.

Similarly, the economic context of the mountaineering industry in Nepal relies on names such as Everest to attract customers from the whole world. While Qomolangma and Sagarmatha each name the national parks in which climbers and trekkers by the thousands discover the mountain every year, most international climbers aspire to ascend 'Everest' rather than 'Chomolangma'.[61] The enduring symbolic power of Mount Everest is a form of mountain heritage that continues to limit or mediate the agency of local populations. Mount Everest is economically vital to the region and defines the impact of commercial high-altitude mountaineering as a form of *consumption of* rather than a *relation to* the mountains. The history of Mount Everest as the product of Himalayan experiences of surveying, mapping, and mountaineering shows that place names can change and reminds us that alternatives exist and can and should be debated. 'Mount Everest' is a choice. It will not necessarily last forever.

Notes

1   Hermann Schlagintweit, 'Gaurisánkar, or Mount Everest, in the Himálaya of Nepál', in *Results of a Scientific Mission in India and High Asia … Atlas of Panoramas and Views* (Leipzig: Brockhaus, 1861), figure 1, https://doi.org/10.11588/diglit.20836#0005. On the Schlagintweits, see Moritz von Brescius, *German Science in the Age of Empire: Enterprise, Opportunity and the Schlagintweit Brothers* (Cambridge: Cambridge University Press, 2019), https://doi.org/10.1017/9781108579568; Moritz von Brescius, 'Empires of opportunity: German naturalists in British India and the frictions of transnational science', *Modern Asian Studies*, 55:6 (2021), 1926–71, https://doi.org/10.1017/S0026749X19000428

2   James T. Walker, 'A last note on Mont Everest', *Proceedings of the Royal Geographical Society [RGS]*, 8:4 (1886), 259, https://doi.org/10.2307/1801364

3   See Chapter 1 by Gamble and the Introduction to this volume by Hansen, Gilchrist, and Westaway.

4   See notably Lachlan Fleetwood, *Science on the Roof of the World: Empire and the Remaking of the Himalaya* (Cambridge: Cambridge University Press, 2022); Peter H. Hansen, *The Summits of Modern Man: Mountaineering after the Enlightenment* (Cambridge, MA: Harvard University Press, 2013); Matthew Edney, *Mapping an Empire: The Geographical Construction of British India, 1765–1843* (Chicago IL: University of Chicago Press, 1997).

5   John Keay, *The Great Arc* (New York: Harper Collins, 2000), p. 35.

6   Edney, *Mapping an Empire*.

7   Henry Thomas Colebrook, 'On the height of the Himalaya Mountains', *Asiatick Researches*, 12 (1818), 254.

8   Alexander von Humboldt, *Sur l'élévation des montagnes de l'Inde* (Paris: Feugueray, 1816), p. 10.

9   Keay, *The Great Arc*, p. 163.

10 See also Jean-Christophe Bailly, Jean-Marc Besse, and Gilles Palsky, *Le Monde sur une feuille : Les tableaux comparatifs de montagnes et de fleuves dans les atlas du XIXème siècle* (Lyon: Fage, 2014), pp. 26–92.

11 R.H. Phillimore, *Historical Records of the Survey of India*, vol. 5 (Dehra Dun: Survey of India, 1968).

12 Ashish Lahiri, 'Radhanath Sikdar and the final phase of measuring Peak XV', *Indian Journal of History of Science*, 51:2.1 (2016), 283.

13 Walker, 'A last note on Mont Everest', 261.

14 See T.T. Waterman, 'The geographical names used by the Indians of the Pacific Coast', *Geographical Review*, 12:2 (1922), 175–94, https://doi.org/10.2307/208735; Yi-Fu Tuan Tuan, 'Language and the making of place: a narrative-descriptive approach', *Annals of the American Association of Geographers*, 81:4 (1991), 684–96, https://doi.org/10.1111/j.1467-8306.1991.tb01715.x; Achille Varzi, 'Introduction', *Topoi*, 20:2 (2001), 124, https://doi.org/10.1023/A:1017944405193

15 Simon Bainbridge, *Mountaineering and British Romanticism: The Literary Cultures of Climbing, 1770–1836* (Oxford: Oxford University Press, 2020).

16 Samia Ounoughi, 'Mapping in process: discourse analysis of the Alpine Club's periodicals', *Studies in Travel Writing*, 24:2 (2020), 119–30, https://doi.org/10.1080/13645145.2020.1862953; Léon Maury, *Les Noms de lieux des montagnes françaises* (Paris: Club Alpin Français, 1929).

17 See Kaisa Rautio Helander, 'Toponymic silence and Sámi place names during the growth of the Norwegian nation state', in Lawrence D. Berg and Jani Vuolteenaho (eds), *Critical Toponymies: The Contested Politics of Place Naming* (London: Routledge, 2009), pp. 253–66.

18 Royal Geographical Society (with IBG) archive: JMS-11–34; Brian Houghton Hodgson, letter to the Secretary of the Royal Asiatic Society, 27 October 1856, in 'Trigonometrical Survey of India and the discovery and naming of Mount Everest. Norton Shaw, B. H. Hodgson, et al.'; see also 'Papers relating to the Himalaya and Mount Everest', *Proceedings of the RGS*, 1 (11 May 1857), 345–7, archive.org/details/dli.pahar.0484

19 See notably Frédéric Giraut and Myriam Houssay-Holzschuch (eds), *The Politics of Place Naming: Naming the World* (London/Hoboken, NJ: ISTE/Wiley, 2022); Sergei Basik, *Encountering Toponymic Geopolitics* (Abingdon: Routledge, 2022); Gwilym Lucas Eades, *The Geography of Names: Indigenous to Post-foundational* (Abingdon: Routledge, 2017).

20 See Tuan, 'Language and the making of place'; Keith Basso, *Wisdom Sits in Places: Landscape and Language Among the Western Apache* (Albuquerque, NM: University of New Mexico Press, 1996).

21 Reuben Rose-Redwood, Derek H. Alderman, and Maoz Azaryahu, 'Geographies of toponymic inscription: new directions in critical place-name studies', *Progress in Human Geography*, 34:4 (2010), 453–70, https://doi.org/10.1177/0309132509351042; DerekH. Alderman and Joshua Inwood, 'Street naming and the politics of belonging: spatial injustices in the toponymic commemoration of Martin Luther King Jr', *Social & Cultural Geography*, 14:2 (2013), 211–33, https://doi.org/10.1080/14649365.2012.754488

22 Alexander von Humboldt, *Asie centrale* (Paris: Gide, 1843), p. 50 (my translation).

23 Abraham Hume, *Philosophy of Geographical Names* (Liverpool: Benjamin Smith, 1851), p. 27.

24 Joseph Dalton Hooker, *Himalayan Journals* (London: Ward, Lock, Bowde, 1891 [1854]), p. 260.

25 Derek Waller, *The Pundits: British Exploration of Tibet and Central Asia* (Lexington, KY: University Press of Kentucky, 1990), pp. 169–92; Kapil Raj, *Relocating Modern Science: Circulation and the Construction of Knowledge in South Asia and Europe, 1650–1900* (New York: Palgrave Macmillan, 2007), pp. 156–88.

26 Edney, *Mapping an Empire*, p. 234.

27 David M. Waterhouse, *The Origins of Himalayan Studies: Brian Houghton Hodgson in Nepal and Darjeeling, 1820–1858*(London: Routledge, 2004).

28 Brian Houghton Hodgson, 'Native name of Mount Everest', *Journal of the Asiatic Society of Bengal*, 25:5 (October 1856), 467.

29 Brian Houghton Hodgson, letter to the Secretary of the Royal Asiatic Society, 27 October 1856, in 'Trigonometrical Survey of India and the discovery and naming of Mount Everest. Norton Shaw, B. H. Hodgson, et al.': JMS-11–34, Royal Geographical Society (with IBG) archive.

30 Andrew Scott Waugh, 'On Mounts Everest and Deodanga', *Proceedings of the RGS*, 2:2 (1858), 102–15, https://doi.org/10.2307/1799335

31 'Sketch diagram showing heights of Himalayan peaks signed by A.S. Waugh'; later published as 'Map to Illustrate Col. A. S. Waugh's Paper on Mt. Everest & Deodanga', in Waugh, 'On Mounts Everest and Deodanga': JMS-11–35, Royal Geographical Society (with IBG) archive.

32 *Journal of the RGS*, 27 (1857), viii.

33 Andrew Waugh to George Everest, 29 July 1857, in 'Waugh, Lt. Col. Andrew Scott. Thos. Benny Tailyour, Andrew Scott Waugh, Lt. Col. Andrew Scott Waugh': CB4/1737 [Waugh, Lt Col Andrew Scott], Royal Geographical Society (with IBG) archive.

34 India Office Records, Mss Eur F699/1/1/2/1, letter 31 – Charles Canning to Lord Elgin, 2 October 1861, excerpt in 'Sir Andrew Scott Waugh and the naming of Everest', *Untold Lives Blog* (30 July 2020), https://web.archive.org/web/20200807225242/https://blogs.bl.uk/untoldlives/2020/07/sir-andrew-scott-waugh-and-the-naming-of-everest.html; see also British Library, India Office Records, Mss Eur F699/1/3/2/53, item 2623.

35 Arthur Fibicher, 'Dufour, Pointe', in *Dictionnaire historique de la Suisse* (2005), hls-dhs-dss.ch/fr/articles/008784/2005-11-07/ (accessed 3 September 2023). Peter H. Hansen, 'Wildest dreams of Everest and modern mountaineering', *Les Sports Modernes / La montagne: territoire du moderne?*, 1 (2023), 61–9, https://doi.org/10.33055/SPORTSMODERNES.2023.001.01.61

36 John Ball, *A Guide to the Western Alps* (London: Longman, 1863), p. 295.

37 Nina Elizabeth Mazuchelli, *The Indian Alps and How We Crossed Them* (New York: Dodd, Mead and Company, 1876), p. 366; Barbara Gates (ed.), *In Nature's Name: An Anthology of Women's Writing and Illustration, 1780–1930* (Chicago, IL: University of Chicago Press, 2002), p. 648.

38 Sarat Chandra Das, *Narrative of a Journey to Lhasa in 1881–82* (Calcutta: Bengal Secretariat Press, 1885), p. 517.

39 Douglas W. Freshfield, 'Further notes on "Mont Everest"', *Proceedings of the RGS*, 8:3 (1886), 176–88, https://doi.org/10.2307/1800965

40 Emil Schlagintweit, 'Der Name des höchsten Berges der Erde', *Dr A. Petermanns Mitteilungen aus Justus Perthes' Geographischer Anstalt*, 36 (1890), 251–2.

41 L.A. Waddell, 'The environs and native names of Mount Everest', *Geographical Journal*, 12:6 (1898), 564–9, https://doi.org/10.2307/1774275

42 Douglas W. Freshfield, 'The highest mountain in the world', *Geographical Journal*, 21:3 (1903), 294–8, https://doi.org/10.2307/1775805; Henry Wood, *Report on the Identification and Nomenclature of the Himalayan Peaks as seen from Katmandu, Nepal* (Calcutta: Office of the Superintendent, 1904); for the exchange in *Nature*, see Burrard, *Nature* (10 November 1904), 42–6, https://doi.org/10.1038/071042a0, and Freshfield, *Nature* (24 November 1904), 82, https://doi.org/10.1038/071082a0

43 Sidney Burrard, *A Sketch of the Geography and Geology of the Himalaya Mountains and Tibet* (Calcutta: Superintendent Government Printing India, 1907), p. 15.

44 Sven Hedin, *Southern Tibet*, vol. 3 (Stockholm: Lithographic Institute of the General Staff of the Swedish Army, 1917), p. 105.

45 A.M. Kellas, 'A consideration of the possibility of ascending the loftier Himalaya', *Geographical Journal*, 49:1 (1917), 47, https://doi.org/10.2307/1779778; also A.M. Kellas, 'The nomenclature of Himalaya Peaks', *Geographical Journal*, 52:4 (1918), 272–4, https://doi.org/10.2307/1779902

46 C.G. Bruce, 'Mount Everest: discussion', *Geographical Journal*, 57 (1921), 14, https://doi.org/10.2307/1781199; Craig Storti attributes these words to Francis Younghusband in Craig Storti, *The Hunt for Mount Everest* (London: John Murray, 2021), p. 45.

47 Douglas Freshfield, 'Mount Everest v. Chomolungma', *Alpine Journal*, 34 (1922), 301–2.

48 J. Monroe Thorington, 'The Freshfield group', *Alpine Journal*, 34 (1922), 387–99.

49 Douglas W. Freshfield, 'The conquest of Mount Everest', *Geographical Journal*, 63:3 (1924), 229–37, https://doi.org/10.2307/1780935

50 Sven Hedin, *Mount Everest och Andra Asiatiska Problem* (Stockholm: Andre Bonniers, 1922); on the atlas, see Mario Cams, 'Not just a Jesuit atlas of China: Qing imperial cartography and its European connections', *Imago Mundi*, 69:2 (2017), 188–201, https://doi.org/10.1080/03085694.2017.1312114

51 Sidney Burrard, *Mount Everest and Its Tibetan Names: A Review of Sir Sven Hedin's Book* (Dehra Dun: The Geodetic Branch Office, Survey of India, 1931); Sidney Burrard, 'The name of Mount Everest', *Nature*, 127 (1931), 686; J. de Graaff Hunter, 'Heights and names of Mount Everest and other peaks', *Occasional Notes of the Royal Astronomical Society*, 15:3 (1953), 37–53.

52 Geoffrey Corbett, 'The word Himalaya', *Himalayan Journal*, 1 (1929), 82–4, https://archive.org/details/dli.pahar.2410; Edwin Kempson, 'The local name of Mount Everest', in H. Ruttledge, *Everest, The Unfinished Adventure* (London: Hodder & Stoughton, 1937), pp. 285–8; Kenneth Mason, 'Karakoram nomenclature', *Geographical Journal*, 91:2 (1938), 123–52, https://doi.org/10.2307/1788003; B.L. Gulatee, 'Mount Everest – its name and height', *Himalayan Journal*, 17 (1952), https://web.archive.org/web/20220903142135/https://www.himalayanclub.org/hj/17/14/mount-everest-its-name-and-height/

53 From Mallory's 'Pumori' and 'Western Cwm' to the 'Eperon des Genevois' named by the 1952 Swiss expedition. For reactions, see Sidney Burrard, 'Geographical names in uninhabited regions and the controversy over the Mount Everest map', *Empire Survey Review*, 3:16 (1935), 66–71, https://doi.org/10.1179/sre.1935.3.16.66

54 Marcel Kurz, 'Mount Everest, a century of history', in *The Mountain World* (London: George Allen, 1953), p. 18.

55 Hansen, *Summits of Modern Man*, p. 247.

56 Tenzing Norgay and James Ramsey Ullman, *Tiger of the Snows: The Autobiography of Tenzing of Everest* (New York: Putnam, 1955), p. 20.

57 Baburam Acharya, 'Sagarmatha or Jhymolungma', *Sharada*, 4:8 (1938), 193.

58 In English-language publications, see Michael Ward, 'Review of *Sagarmatha-Mount Everest-Qomolungma*, by the National Geographic Society', *Geographical Journal*, 155:3 (1989), 433–5, https://doi.org/10.2307/635257; Michael Ward, 'The name of the world's highest peak', *Himalayan Journal*, 53 (1997), https://web.archive.org/web/20240123174610/https://www.himalayanclub.org/hj/53/3/the-name-of-the-worlds-highest-peak/; Edwin Bernbaum, 'A note on the Tibetan and Nepali names of Mount Everest', *American Alpine News*, 8:227 (1999), 25–6.

59 William McKay Aitken, 'An enquiry into the real name of Mt. Everest', in *Touching Upon the Himalaya: Excursions and Enquiries* (Delhi: The Himalayan Club/Indus Publishing, 2004), p. 122.

60 Ibid., p. 124. The reply from the Dalai Lama's office mentioned Gegen Dorje Tharcin's *Melong* as its source; for further discussion, see Ruth Gamble's chapter in this volume.

61 On the 'heritagisation' of the Himalaya, see Christophe Gauchon, 'Nommer les biens du Patrimoine mondial: processus de patrimonialisation et réinvention toponymique', *EchoGéo*, 53 (2020), 10–11, https://doi.org/10.4000/echogeo.19973; on place-naming in Nepal, see Darshan Karki and Miriam Wenner, 'What is not in a name? Toponymic ambivalence, identity, and symbolic resistance in the Nepali flatlands', *EchoGéo*, 53 (2020), journals.openedition.org/echogeo/19987

3

Re-activating the expeditionary archive

Felix Driver

This chapter is about the role that expeditionary archives have played, and could play, in histories of Himalayan exploration and mountaineering. Central to its argument is a distinction between the way the story of twentieth-century Everest expeditions has been told by those who organised them and the possibility that resources for quite different stories lie within the very archives that they created.

The idea that expeditionary collections gathered in the colonial era for one kind of project can be repurposed for another underpins much recent research across a range of disciplines including colonial history, museum anthropology, and the history of collections.[1] In many cases, for a variety of reasons, the original rationale for making these collections may no longer apply. New times bring new questions as well as new technologies, new modes of analysis and new ways of organising collections, and new approaches to engaging and sharing them. The value of colonial-era collections, in particular, may far exceed and even defy the expectations of those who founded them.

While the legacy of empire continues to weigh heavily on the way that the history of Everest expeditions has been presented, new approaches to the histories of expeditionary labour, to the infrastructure required for large-scale mountaineering projects, and to the history of cultural encounter in colonial contexts suggest new possibilities for using collections left by twentieth-century Everest expeditions in archives such as those of the Royal Geographical Society (RGS) and the Alpine Club. The era of post-imperial nostalgia, still going strong as recently as 2013 in British celebrations of the sixtieth anniversary of the 1953 ascent of Mount Everest, has given way to a much more critical and fractured vision of the history of Everest. In this context it is important to open up the archives to a wider range of scholars and practitioners, bringing with them different kinds of expertise and experience.

This chapter focuses on the uses of archives from British expeditions to Everest in the 1920s, notably those now held at the RGS in London. I begin by reflecting on the ways in which these materials have provided the basis for a different kind of history of Everest expeditions, especially the recruitment and employment of high-altitude labour. I then explore a traumatic episode – the avalanche which ended the 1922 expedition – to consider the ways in which key aspects of this history are made visible (or not) in the public record. This case highlights the ways in which historical research in colonial-era archives can suggest alternative approaches to the heritage of mountaineering. Collections-based research is by no means the only way of making Other Everests more visible, but it does offer a potentially powerful corrective to some enduring myths about exploration and mountaineering in the age of empire.

Hidden histories of mountaineering

Over the last thirty years, academic understanding of the historical context of mountaineering expeditions in the Himalayas has been transformed by the work of historians and anthropologists.[2] They have encouraged us to go beyond the stories told by climbers themselves in order to consider the wider geopolitical and cultural contexts in which feats of high-altitude climbing are planned and undertaken. This has involved making connections, on the one hand, between mountaineering and the wider politics and culture of imperial exploration, and on the other between the work done by porters for climbing expeditions and the life-worlds of Indigenous communities across the Himalayan region. By widening the scope of archival and fieldwork beyond 'official' collections such as those of the Mount Everest Committee now held at the RGS, new connections have been made and new avenues of research opened. What this means for the ways in which the official expeditionary archive itself can be re-read is the subject of this chapter.

The Everest expeditions of the 1920s were closely associated with a culture of expedition-making associated above all with the Royal Geographical Society as it evolved in the Edwardian period.[3] In combination with the Alpine Club, the Society formed the Mount Everest Committee (MEC), which was to plan all the major British expeditions to Everest between 1921 and 1953. An important part of managing these expeditions was the care and arrangement of their archives, not just for posterity (though that was important) but also for re-use in commercial, research, and educational contexts, ensuring that these collections played – and continue to play – an important role in the public life of the

Society. In this respect, the organisation of the founding archives of the MEC reflects the role of Arthur Hinks, the Secretary of the Society and also of the Committee, and the archive regime he managed at the RGS.[4]

Today, the collections of the RGS (including the Mount Everest archives) constitute a vast and diverse storehouse of national and international significance, especially for materials documenting the global histories of exploration, travel, and encounter. A number of projects – notably the Crossing Continents programme supported by the Heritage Lottery Foundation in the 2000s – have sought to use these collections to tell new stories about heritage, migration, and identity.[5] In the *Hidden Histories of Exploration* exhibition of 2009, co-curated by myself and Lowri Jones in collaboration with the RGS, the focus was turned back on the history of exploration itself, in an effort to move beyond the usual focus on the heroic successes and failures of white men. To what extent, the exhibition asked, could the expeditionary archive tell a different story, particularly concerning the role of Indigenous agency and local knowledge?[6]

'Indigenous agency' and 'local knowledge' are terms which have become almost talismanic in the academic literature on empire and exploration over the last twenty years, though they have a much longer and involved history within the disciplines of history and anthropology. By highlighting 'Indigenous agency', Lowri Jones and I were seeking to foreground the active contributions by Indigenous people and local inhabitants in the work of exploration and mountaineering, contributions which have often been obscured by the usual emphasis on expedition leaders. These manifold contributions included work in provisioning and portering; guiding and piloting; identifying and collecting; interpreting and negotiating; and sheltering and protecting. It is important to note here that all these roles were framed by wider structures and processes: while climbers and explorers might describe their dealings with local people in terms of the character or behaviour of particular individuals, the business of exploration depended on an extensive economic, political, and technological infrastructure. To put this another way, when we highlight 'agency' in this context we need to acknowledge the double-sidedness of the term: after all, the words 'agent' and 'agency' imply dependence as well as autonomy.[7] In the context of colonial-era exploration this is a vital point to make.

The other key term informing new approaches to the heritage of exploration is that of 'local knowledge'. Over the last two decades this term has been much in use, in policy circles as well as the academy, notably through challenges to the universalising and homogenising claims of modern development theory. In the context of literature on exploration this has often meant, in a nutshell, highlighting the Eurocentrism of Enlightenment scientific exploration and exposing its frequently unacknowledged reliance on more local kinds of knowledge.[8] But here it is important to enter a caveat about the pitfalls of the beguilingly attractive concept of 'local knowledge', notably in the context of travel and exploration. Especially in the context of the late nineteenth and early twentieth centuries, with intensifying interregional trade, new forms of labour migration, and new patterns of Indigenous mobility in response to the extension of colonial influence, the boundaries of the 'local' were shifting considerably. And this was exactly the combination of circumstances evident in Darjeeling during the late nineteenth and early twentieth centuries, creating the conditions for the recruitment of Sherpa labour for the first British expeditions to Mount Everest.

The Everest material used in the *Hidden Histories* exhibition was mainly from the first attempted ascent of Everest in 1922 (following the 1921 British Mount Everest reconnaissance expedition). The archives and photographs we selected from the Mount Everest Committee collection were designed to highlight the role of labour in support of expeditions, especially the geographies of recruitment. This was part of a broader argument in the exhibition about European dependence on local labour, in this case recruited in a system that owed much to precedents and procedures established in relation to military service. The exhibition thus focused on porter labour and included a photograph and archival material showing payments to the families of the 1922 porters, including documents bearing their relatives' thumbprints acknowledging payment, in lieu of signatures. The thumbprint, with its tangible and irreducibly individual trace of an embodied presence, spoke volumes, especially in an archival context where literacy is often assumed to be a precondition of self-representation.[9]

In the light of the material evidence concerning porter recruitment and the infrastructure required to mount major mountaineering expeditions in the Himalayas, the insistent emphasis on the heroic, and occasionally tragic, efforts of European climbers in popular literature, film, and photography reflects the strong hold that myths of adventurous exploration held on the public imagination for much of the twentieth century. A spectacular example is provided by a much-reproduced photographic portrait of Captain John Noel, filming on the Chang La (North Col) in early June 1922 at a height of 23,000 feet (Figure 3.1). The image shows Noel almost nonchalantly operating a Newman Sinclair camera, with its specially adapted telephoto lens. Noel had started out with the party making the third attempt on the summit and sent this photo from Base Camp to Hinks on 2 June, five days before the avalanche that ended the expedition. The accompanying letter reveals much about his awareness of the value of photography and film in promoting the expedition:

> With this letter I enclose a photograph taken at the N. Col. which shows the kinema effort of the Expedition (negative is with the others). Would you put this in the papers with the other pictures because I think it would serve to advertise our film and show that there is something of particular interest in it. This would put its value up and also arouse public interest in it. The picture shows how the Expedition has been able to carry the camera to the height of 23,000 ft and by means of the special high power telephoto apparatus to secure a picture of the climbers of the Expedition actually ascending Everest to a height of over 27,000 feet.[10]

While Noel wrote that the *expedition* had carried the camera up the mountain, what he actually meant of course was that he had employed a team of 'photographic porters' especially for the purpose of transporting and managing the equipment. True to his plan, Noel's photo was widely reproduced. It was first

Figure 3.1 'Captain Noel and kinematograph camera with large telephoto lens established on the Chang La at 23,000 feet', with Sherpa steadying a tripod (photographer unknown), 1922. Also published in *Geographical Journal*, 60:3 (1922), 218–19. RGS Picture Library S0001250. Courtesy of the RGS-IBG.

published by Hinks in the *Geographical Journal* in September 1922, before Noel's return to England, under the title 'Captain Noel and kinematograph camera with large telephoto lens established on the Chang La at 23,000 feet'.[11] The image was also used in the programme accompanying the public exhibition of Noel's film in 1922–23, the official expedition report by the expedition leader, General Charles Granville Bruce, and in fundraising events for the next expedition, including an exhibition held at the Alpine Club in January 1923. It was also reproduced in numerous advertisements for Newman Sinclair cameras.

While recognising the ideological work done by such 'heroic' images, they can sometimes provide evidence for a different kind of history. In this case, we can see another presence in this photograph, literally in the shadows: the figure of a Sherpa, his eye-protecting goggles on, steadying a tripod in the snow. The really striking thing about this iconic image, so often reproduced in books and films devoted to the history of Everest expeditions, is that the Sherpa's presence at its very centre is so rarely acknowledged, even in critical histories. Indeed, Noel himself is often credited as the author of an image created using expedition equipment and under his direction, but not actually activated by his own hands. As presented by Noel himself and by the Everest expedition more generally, this photograph had one function only and that was to picture the heroic achievement of 'kinematographing' at a record height. While remote activation of the camera was technically a possibility, there is no direct evidence of it in this case, either in the photo itself or in the expedition archives. I myself have little doubt that the image was made by the impress of a Sherpa finger on the button. This is surely the only plausible explanation for the absence of an authorial credit (in the form of initials) in the Catalogue of hundreds of Everest photographs exhibited at the Alpine Club in January 1923, the sole unattributed image.[12]

In the highly racialised world of Everest mountaineering during the 1920s, white men like Noel (and climbers such as Howard Somervell and George Mallory) could be credited as photographers, while the active role of Indigenous porters in the making of such images was rarely acknowledged. The absence of an Indigenous name in the Exhibition Catalogue, along with the title given to the image, reflects these racial hierarchies. Yet as we view the photograph today in an archive or more likely close up via a screen, the Sherpa's presence becomes obvious to our eyes. This reflects a wider truth about such expeditionary archives in which Indigenous agency is not so much erased as made *partially visible*.[13] The figure of the Sherpa crouching behind the tripod, the rings on his fingers glistening in the sun as he holds the equipment steady, can clearly be seen – but not named.

The story of the treatment of porters on Everest in the century following the first large-scale expeditions in the 1920s has been told by many historians.[14] The historical movement away from colonial conditions of labour over successive decades was slow and uneven, and shaped by a growing struggle for recognition of the achievements of Sherpa and other Indigenous peoples as high-altitude climbers. In order to understand this, one clearly needs to look beyond expeditionary archives like these to other archives (such as family and personal collections) and other methods (including ethnographic and oral history research). However, the argument of this chapter is that research, engagement, and curatorial work in metropolitan, colonial-era collections can also contribute significantly to these revisionist efforts. By this I mean work to uncover the Indigenous presence in these collections and to present it in new ways.

Such new forms of collections-based research and curation include (but are not of course limited to) exhibition design work. In the *Hidden Histories* exhibition, for example, we enlarged an album sheet of photographs of porters recruited for the 1936 expedition to almost life-size, their faces greeting visitors to the exhibition from the back wall.[15] At their original scale, in an archive box, these photos of porters with their identity tags around their necks spoke of surveillance not agency; re-scaled, the individuality of the subjects, many of them smiling at their good fortune to be selected for employment, shines through. Amongst them were the veteran expedition interpreter Karma Paul, resplendent in his Tibetan robe, directly alongside expedition leader Hugh Ruttledge; and a youthful Tenzing Norgay, seventeen years before his successful ascent of Everest in 1953. Re-scaling the image enabled the personal and social histories of labour to come more clearly into view, restoring in the eyes of our visitors the dignity and to some degree the agency of these young men. While the 'archivalness' of these images was fully evident in the form and design of the album page, their enlargement enabled these portraits to speak to the present in quite a different way.

Expeditionary archives, photographic or otherwise, can also shed light on the role of intermediaries between European climbers and Indigenous populations, both those directly employed by the expeditions and those enabling or authorising their journeys. In the case of the 1920s British expeditions, for example, these include 'fixers' like John Macdonald and his father David, British trade agent in Tibet and himself the son of a Sikkimese Lepcha woman and a Scottish planter. The elder Macdonald was fluent in Tibetan and other regional languages and played an important role in the production of several Tibetan dictionaries, glossaries, and guides.[16] The Macdonalds played a significant role supporting the 1922 Everest expedition especially through their dealings with local authorities in Tibet. While David Macdonald was literally an agent of the British interests in Tibet, other intermediaries, including interpreters, played a more ambiguous role which leaves traces in the Everest archives. Karma Paul, for example, was a Lhasa-born Tibetan educated by missionaries in Darjeeling who had a long career as an interpreter and as a sirdar (manager of the porters) on successive British Everest expeditions between 1922 and 1938. He also acted as a broker for other travellers including the influential Italian Tibetologist Giuseppe Tucci who used his services in 1948 to hire Tenzing Norgay, as well as a cook and a well-connected lama, for a trip to Lhasa.[17] Other interpreters used by the British on the 1920s expeditions included Gyalzen Kazi, member of a high-ranking Sikkimese family, and Chhetan Wangdi, who had served in the Tibetan army and for the Indian army in Egypt during the First World War. They were described by the leader of the 1921 reconnaissance expedition as 'quite invaluable': 'their tact and knowledge of Tibetan ways and customs were of the greatest use in keeping up the friendly relations established between the expedition and the Tibetans'.[18]

While the expedition archives may register the employment of intermediaries, and sometimes reveal aspects of their wider roles which made these expeditions possible, they do not of course tell their life stories. The work of interpretation requires that the fragments and traces of Indigenous agency, of the evidence of other life-worlds than those of the climbers themselves, be connected in ways that go beyond the logic of the expeditionary archive. This also requires work in other collections and other methods, and certainly greater appreciation of Indigenous languages and cultures than most of the Himalayan climbers had during this period. (Marco Pallis was a notable exception, though his engagement with Tibetan Buddhism reflected a distinctively antimodern strain in Western thought).[19]

An illustration of the gulf in understanding is provided by accounts of a famous encounter between the climbers and the monks of the Rongbuk monastery which preceded the attempted climb in May 1922. In the official narrative published by General Bruce, and also in Noel's film, the meeting is presented from the climbers' perspective as a necessary act of diplomacy, the Head Lama Zatul Rinpoche giving his blessing to the expedition. However, the publication in 1973 by Alexander Macdonald of a translated excerpt of the Rongbuk Lama's own spiritual chronicle provided an alternative account of this meeting, enabling historians such as Peter Hansen to evoke something of the Tibetan Buddhist perspective on the British incursion.[20] In this context, it is important

to acknowledge not only the role of intermediaries such as Karma Paul in negotiating what was evidently a huge cultural divide, but also the ways in which the
climbers were embedded within a colonial infrastructure that included serious
attempts to interpret and understand Tibetan worldviews. One indication of
this is the fact that an earlier translation of Zatul Rinpoche's manuscript was
undertaken by Johan Van Manen, Secretary of the Asiatic Society of Bengal,
who maintained an extensive network of Tibetan consultants in Kalimpong,
Sikkim, and Tibet during this period.[21] At some point in the 1930s, Van Manen
sent an extract to Edward Shebbeare, transport officer on the 1924 Everest
expedition, who later pasted it into the pages of his Everest journal – now in the
archives of the Alpine Club in London – describing it as 'the most interesting
part of this book'.[22]

Making visible? The story of the 1922 avalanche

The argument advanced in this chapter is that the expeditionary archive constructed by colonial-era organisations such as the Mount Everest Committee
can yield evidence of stories and perspectives that go beyond those of the climbers themselves. Sometimes this is a matter of reading evidence against the grain
of the archive, an approach which also requires us to consider what reading
'along the grain' of the archive might reveal about the systematic de-valuing
of some voices over others.[23] In this archive, evidence takes many forms, from
printed narratives and journal articles to archival photographs, diaries, and
letters, not forgetting also the material archive of equipment, instruments, and
natural history specimens. Amongst these materials, the archive of Everest
film has also begun to receive new attention, as a key means by which certain
kinds of expeditionary narrative – connecting Everest with national and indeed
imperial prestige – came to prominence. In the case of film, as with the printed
book, it is also important to go beyond the finished product to consider the
process of editing, re-editing, and indeed re-use and re-circulation. As Jan Faull
has shown in her landmark doctoral research on Everest and expeditionary
films, appreciation of the multiple forms of archival film and their constant re-
working in educational, scientific, and popular contexts is vital in this context.[24]

The restoration of Noel's 1924 film *The Epic of Everest* by the British Film
Institute, and the subsequent digitisation of the other Everest films in the RGS
collection in 2017, has added significantly to the appreciation of the role of film
in promoting particular visions of Everest.[25] Clips from the 1922 film *Climbing
Mount Everest*, showing recruitment of porters at Darjeeling, the climbers' meeting

with the Rongbuk Head Lama, and a staged climbing scene involving Sherpas, were shown as part of the 2009 *Hidden Histories* exhibition held at the RGS. In the process of reviewing the footage of the Rongbuk monastery scene for the exhibition, I noticed a fleeting detail that has stayed with me ever since: a monk carefully wrapping a small object in one of the white scarves prior to its ceremonious presentation by the Head Lama to General Bruce, leader of the expedition, through the intermediary Karma Paul. The visual evidence of wrapping and subsequent unwrapping, and of a conversation between Paul and Bruce including gestures indicating the size of the object, suggested this was a precious gift, though its presentation went unremarked in the film's sensational intertitles. In fact, the object was a small bronze Tibetan deity now in the RGS collection (Figure 3.2). Bruce himself described it as a Green Tara. Given the Green Tara's associations with the virtues of boldness and foresight in Tibetan Buddhist religious iconography, Bruce might have regarded it as a suitable gift for the leader of an expedition seeking to climb the world's highest mountain. But, as is clear from the figure's features, including multiple eyes on the feet, hands, and forehead, this is in fact a White Tara, which in Buddhist iconography represents the all-seeing vigilance of compassion and the power of healing.[26]

What this example shows is that the expeditionary archive, even as constituted by the Mount Everest Committee, takes multiple forms which may not tell a consistent story. In this case, the evidence presented in the expedition narrative and in a physical object is clearly contradictory, drawing our attention to the limits of Bruce's own understanding of the nature of the gift. Moreover, close reading of the film evidence against that of the written record suggests a further and more fundamental inconsistency, with wider ramifications for our understanding of the official narrative as presented in the film. And here the all-seeing Tara itself is a key witness. For we know from both Bruce's official report and the Rongbuk Lama's chronicle that this gift was in fact presented after the failure of the final attempt, as the expedition made its way down from the mountain, rather than – as presented in the film – on its arrival at the foot of Mount Everest. The difference might seem small, mere creative licence on Noel's part as he edited reels of footage to make his film in time for its showing in the autumn of 1922. But that would be to omit from the story the defining moment of the expedition: the avalanche on 7 June which killed seven porters as the monsoon clouds descended, bringing the expedition to an abrupt halt. What Noel presents as a crucial scene of authorisation – the granting of permission to climb Mount Everest – was actually something very different: a moment of shared mourning.

Figure 3.2 White Tara – Tibetan Buddhist goddess in the RGS Collections. This bronze Tara was presented to General C.G. Bruce by Zatul Rinpoche, Head Lama of the Rongbuk monastery, in 1922. The White Tara, representing all-seeing compassion, has seven eyes: two on her face, two on each of her hands and the soles of her feet, and one on her forehead. RGS Picture Library S0013019. Courtesy of the RGS-IBG.

The omission of the avalanche from Noel's film *Climbing Mount Everest* is a stark reminder, if any were needed, that expeditionary film is a form of creative fiction: the re-working of the evidence of actuality according to a narrative conceived and planned by Noel himself. Its absence from the film cannot be explained by technological limitations: in his letters to Hinks, Noel claimed to have filmed the track of the avalanche shortly after it took place, and even without direct footage there were many ways that he could have woven the disaster into the narrative of the film, including the use of still photographs. Nor can it be explained by a desire simply to hide news of the accident, since that news was given extensive publicity in Britain soon after it happened: a month after the event, a story appeared in *The Times*, to which all the expedition reports were syndicated, under the heading 'Avalanche on Everest: Climbers' narrow escape – seven porters killed'.[27] Further accounts of the avalanche were to be included in the public lectures of the returning climbers as well as eventually the official expedition report. In other words, its exclusion from the film must have resulted from a conscious decision about its place in the film narrative rather than any lack of ready material.

Although the Everest archives at the RGS include detailed letters from Noel to Hinks discussing the planning and editing of his film during and after the expedition, this correspondence does not shed light on the decision to exclude the avalanche from the film. However, we know from a proof copy of printed lecture notes that an early version did include a section on the avalanche, including still photographs. Noel's marginal notes indicate that this section of the film was cut, possibly in the period between the film's initial showing to members of the RGS and Alpine Club in London's Central Hall on 21 November 1922 and its gala premier at the Philharmonic Hall shortly afterwards in December. Concerning the precise rationale for this decision, the most important factor in Noel's mind would seem to be the film's intended function as a fundraiser for the next Everest expedition. While Mallory's and Irvine's deaths two years later were to be presented as a kind of martyrdom, the deaths of the seven porters in such circumstances were difficult to present as anything but a disaster, especially given that the misjudgement of the British climbers had played a significant part in the accident. The inclusion of the avalanche in the film would have been difficult to square with the claims made for the achievements of the expedition and the planning already underway for its successor.

Where the 1922 film is silent on the subject of the avalanche, the Mount Everest Committee archives do shed some light on its circumstances and the names of the porters who died. There are various accounts in surviving correspondence, including several letters from Mallory, who blamed himself for an error of judgement, a conclusion he was not alone in reaching.[28] However, much of the formal documentation of the event is concerned with evaluating the judgement of the mountaineers in the context of what was known and not known about the mountain, the physics of snow, and prevailing meteorological conditions. There is of course no account provided by the porters themselves. Only one document, as far as I know, names the men who died. Typically, this document confirms the official expedition expenditure for authorisation by the Committee in the form of a note concerning compensation to the families of the dead porters, signed by the British commissioner in Darjeeling. Here the names of six ethnic Sherpa and one Bhotia are listed: Thankay Sherpa, Sangay Sherpa, Temba Sherpa, Lhakpa Sherpa, Pasang Namgya Sherpa, Norbu Bhotia, and Pema Sherpa. Their surviving dependants, to whom payments were to be made, are recorded as living in various places in Darjeeling, Nepal, and Tibet, reflecting the regional geography of the porter remittance economy.[29] Two years later, the 1924 climbers built a cairn at the foot of Everest in memory of all those who died in all the early 1920s expeditions, including these seven porters. The cairn itself did not survive; but the photos have lasted. They document a more personal and considered act of memorialisation. Edward Shebbeare's Everest journal, mentioned above, includes a touching description of this work, done with hammer and screwdrivers: in one of its photos, Bentley Beetham is shown carving the stone to Howard Somervell's design.[30]

Further evidence concerning the avalanche can be found in published and unpublished photographs and manuscripts within the Mount Everest Committee collection at the RGS. For example, in a letter written to Hinks on 12 June 1922, five days after the avalanche, Noel reports that he had accompanied the party making a third attempt on the summit but had been forced to turn back:

> It was lucky that I decided to return owing to the softness of the snow after I had reached 22,500 (ft). The work was too heavy for carrying the cameras. My decision to descend and continue photographing the coolies and party from the foot of the Col by means of my big lens saved my life because the avalanche would have dealt hardest with me being the end of the line.[31]

Saved by the weight of his equipment, Noel claimed to have filmed the porters half an hour before the avalanche as well as its track soon after the event. Some of his best-known photographs of porters in the snow on the North Col in 1922 may in fact have been taken very shortly before the avalanche, including one published in the *Geographical Journal* of the RGS in December 1922. This was printed directly beneath a photograph of the avalanche site (under the title 'The avalanche track of June 7, below the Chang La') which Noel had sent to Hinks on 12 June (Figures 3.3 and 3.4).[32] The latter image was also reproduced a few weeks later in an article in the *Alpine Journal*, captioned 'The North Col from Camp 3', a note in brackets stating 'X = Track of Avalanche of June 7'.[33] The X, barely visible on the print, was presumably added to the negative by Noel himself. There are at least two other versions of the same image in his collection of lantern slides at the RGS, suggesting that Noel used them in public lectures.

Tracing evidence concerning the precise location and sequence of events connected with the avalanche is made more difficult due to the way that photos were archived and catalogued in the Mount Everest Committee collection and in Noel's own archives, now at the RGS. The 'creative licence' used by Noel to edit the story of the avalanche out of his film has its counterpart in the uneven

Figure 3.3 'The avalanche track of June 7, below the Chang La', 1922. Photograph by John B. Noel, published in *Geographical Journal*, 60:6 (December 1922), 416–17. RGS Picture Library S0020107. Courtesy of the RGS-IBG.

Figure 3.4 'Party resting during the ascent of the Chang La', 1922. Photograph by John B. Noel, published in *Geographical Journal*, 60:6 (December 1922), 416–17. RGS Picture Library S0001176. Courtesy of the RGS-IBG.

way that evidence concerning the disaster is presented in the archives: here the metaphor of partial visibility once more seems apt. The precise captioning of photos published in the journals of the RGS and the Alpine Club in 1922–23 ('X marks the spot') contrasts with the vague or non-existent captioning of many photos by Noel and other climbers in the RGS photo archives. In particular, the records of the 1922 avalanche site reflect little of their significance as documents of what can reasonably be described as the defining moment of the expedition. Many of the original photos on the archival cards (which provide the basis for today's digital catalogue) are untitled. And many of the titles in the online catalogue reflect later additions and amendments: for example, the RGS catalogue describes the subject of the group portrait in Figure 3.4 as 'Team members including Mallory and Sherpas at a rest stop on Everest' and this is how it now appears on the Getty Images site. Mallory's name has been added to the original caption published in the *Geographical Journal*, presumably on the basis that it adds significantly to the popular interest in, and market value of, this image. Similarly, the photo of the avalanche site at the North

Col is uncaptioned on its original archival card and unidentifiable on the RGS catalogue where it is simply titled 'Mountain landscape' along with dozens of others. The task of correcting and updating this archive is a slow process. But it does matter because our knowledge of the location of these scenes at a site of catastrophe unacknowledged in the official film record surely changes our responses to them.

Re-activating the Everest archive

In this chapter, I have presented official Mount Everest expeditionary archives as key resources for researchers interested in discovering 'other Everests'. It is important to understand something of the history of these archives in order to appreciate what they include and what they leave out; and by the same token it is often necessary to work against the grain of these collections by connecting them with other archives and other perspectives. At root, this revisionist archival work also requires an ethical commitment to the value of giving recognition to the work of many of those employed by mountaineering expeditions whose labours have often gone unacknowledged. Such recognition may come in many forms. For example, we now know that the Lepcha plant collector Rhomoo employed by the 1922 Everest expedition (whose portrait survives in the archives) was already an experienced botanist, having previously worked for commercial and colonial collectors in Sikkim, Bhutan, and Himachal Pradesh. His name has been memorialised by Edinburgh botanist Henry Noltie since the year 2000 in the naming of a type specimen of a species of Himalayan grass for the Flora of Bhutan. By incorporating Rhomoo's personal name into the taxonomic structure of Western botany, this move explicitly acknowledges the role of Indigenous labour in the development of European knowledge of Himalayan plants.[34]

The approach advocated in this chapter has some wider implications, especially for those working on the relations between history, memory, and heritage in the context of mountaineering and other kinds of expedition. For example, there is a methodological point about the value of working across different kinds of collections. By combining research on texts, manuscripts, maps, photos, films, and artefacts we can learn a lot more from this multi-dimensional archive than is sometimes assumed. For example, the two most important lessons I take from the story of the Tara gifted by Zatul Rinpoche to General Bruce in 1922 are, firstly, that while the Everest climbers did not always know what they were seeing or understand what they were given, their archives and collections may nonetheless contain evidence of Other Everests; and secondly, that by working between different types of materials it is possible to discover something new about the limitations and possibilities of these archives.

A related conclusion concerning the institutional biography of the Everest archives at the RGS is that they are significantly more complex and less coherent than many users and readers imagine. Behind what appears to be a superbly catalogued and accessible collection are multiple archives and several different modes of organisation. For example, the RGS collections include not just the official archive of the Mount Everest Committee, formed jointly by the RGS and the Alpine Club and inherited by the Mount Everest Foundation, but also numerous special collections and photographs separately donated by climbers over the years, not least by John Noel and his family. Working across these collections can produce different perspectives reflecting the divergent and sometimes competing impulses reflected in the history of British Everest expeditions. The Mount Everest Committee archive itself is of course an extraordinary resource on which all Everest historians rely. That said, nothing, to my knowledge, has been written about its origins and history.

Another wider theme emerging from this chapter on the Everest archive concerns the technology and politics of the catalogue, a key theme in contemporary museum and library studies.[35] Much more could be said about the formats of collection documentation at the RGS – for example, the untold history of the card catalogue, that powerful but now largely forgotten archival technology which during the twentieth century dominated the way such collections were managed and accessed. A few users of the RGS archives in Kensington Gore may remember how runs of index cards dominated the space of the Society's library prior to the creation of a digital catalogue and the opening of the new Foyle Reading Room in 2004. Across the building as a whole, there were in fact hundreds of thousands of cards in separate catalogues for each type of material (books, maps, photos, and so on). On my estimate, there must have been at least thirty-five different cross-referenced series of index cards. A sizeable proportion of these cards formed the basis for the digital retroconversion project twenty years ago ('Unlocking the archives'), when the information written onto these cards was manually re-keyed into a database by workers in Barbados and then Chennai, India (another Hidden History of sorts).[36] The politics to this question of the catalogue comes in the structure, language, and contents of these descriptions, and the extent to which the metadata is open to revision or fixed in the colonial language of our predecessors. Thus far this process has been managed quietly and unobtrusively by RGS collections staff, for example in the renaming of 'coolies' as porters. A more systematic and substantial project would require significant resources as well as new partnerships.

Finally, there is a larger issue raised by the case of the Everest archive about the kinds of research required to make the Indigenous presence in colonial-era collections more visible. Part of the challenge here is to connect research and engagement more closely, as the RGS has successfully done in some of its work with diaspora communities.[37] There are also significant opportunities presented by practice-based research, especially in the creative arts, in collaboration with more traditional forms of scholarship.[38] In this context, there is a good case for including exhibition design and archive curatorship in the definition of research practice. For the methods of collections management and exhibition curation can themselves be envisaged as research tools: the work of exploring, documenting, collating, selecting, arranging, and presenting a collection (for example in re-scaling and re-captioning archival photos) can itself be an integral part of the research process, enabling and developing new knowledge. What we can say about the exhibition could also be said of collections management in general. Understanding what Nicholas Thomas calls the 'museum as method' suggests that the processes of assembling, cataloguing, debating, and interpreting collections are vital forms of research practice.[39]

Notes

1 See for example Felix Driver, 'Face to face with Nain Singh: the Schlagintweit collections and their uses', in Arthur MacGregor (ed.), *Naturalists in the Field: Collecting, Recording and Preserving the Natural World from the Fifteenth to the Twenty-First Century* (Leiden: Brill, 2018), pp. 441–69; Paul Basu, 'Re-mobilising colonial collections in decolonial times: exploring the latent possibilities of N. W. Thomas's West African collections', and Luciana Martins, 'Plant artefacts then and now: reconnecting biocultural collections in Amazonia', in Felix Driver, Mark Nesbitt, and Caroline Cornish (eds), *Mobile Museums: Collections in Circulation* (London: UCL Press, 2021), pp. 21–70.

2 The work of Peter Hansen and Sherry Ortner has been pivotal: see Peter H. Hansen, 'Confetti of empire: the conquest of Everest in Nepal, India, Britain and New Zealand', *Comparative Studies in Society and History*, 42:2 (2000), 307–32, https://doi.org/10.1017/S0010417500002486; Peter H. Hansen, 'The dancing lamas of Everest: cinema, Orientalism and Anglo-Tibetan relations in the 1920s', *American Historical Review*, 101:3 (1996), 712–47, https://doi.org/10.2307/2169420; Sherry B. Ortner, *Life and Death on Mt. Everest: Sherpas and Himalayan Mountaineering* (Princeton, NJ: Princeton University Press, 1999).

3 See Hansen, 'The dancing lamas'; Felix Driver, *Geography Militant: Cultures of Exploration and Empire* (Oxford: Blackwell, 2001); Wade Davis, *Into the Silence: The Great War, Mallory, and the Conquest of Everest* (London: Bodley Head, 2011).

4   J.A. Steers, 'A.R. Hinks and the Royal Geographical Society', *Geographical Journal*, 148:1 (1982), 1–7, https://doi.org/10.2307/634237

5   Cliff Pereira and Vandana Patel, 'Terra Nova for the Royal Geographical Society (with IBG): 2007 and the Bombay Africans strand of the "Crossing Continents: Connecting Communities" project', in Laurajane Smith, et al. (eds), *Representing Enslavement and Abolition in Museums* (London: Routledge, 2011), pp. 164–74.

6   Felix Driver and Lowri Jones, *Hidden Histories of Exploration: Researching the RGS-IBG Collections* (London: RGS-IBG, 2009). https://web.archive.org/web/20240125215741/ https://issuu.com/rgs_ibg/docs/hidden_histories_of_exploration. See also Lowri Jones, 'Local knowledge and indigenous agency in the history of exploration: studies from the RGS-IBG collections' (PhD dissertation, Royal Holloway, University of London, 2010); Felix Driver, 'Hidden histories made visible? Reflections on a geographical exhibition', *Transactions, Institute of British Geographers*, 38:3 (2013), 420–35, https://doi.org/10.1111/j.1475-5661.2012.00529.x

7   This was clear from debates over the concept of agency and class during the 1970s and 1980s. See Perry Anderson, 'Agency', in *Arguments within English Marxism* (London: Verso, 1980), pp. 16–58.

8   See especially Kapil Raj, *Relocating Modern Science: Circulation and the Construction of Scientific Knowledge in South Asia and Europe* (Delhi: Permanent Black, 2006).

9   Images from these important documents were first reproduced in Stephen Venables, *Everest: Summit of Achievement* (London: Bloomsbury, 2003), p. 202.

10 John Noel to Arthur Hinks, 2 June 1922, Mount Everest Committee Archives, EE 18/3, Royal Geographical Society (with IBG) archives.

11 'The Mount Everest Expedition', *Geographical Journal*, 60:3 (1922), between pages 218 and 219, https://doi.org/10.2307/1781057

12 *Catalogue of the Exhibition of Photographs and Paintings from the Mount Everest Expedition of 1922* (London, January 1923), p. 12.

13 For this argument, see Felix Driver, 'Intermediaries and the archive of exploration', in Shino Konishi, Maria Nugent, and Tiffany Shellam (eds), *Indigenous Intermediaries: New Perspectives on Exploration Archives* (Canberra: ANU Press, 2015), pp. 11–30, https://doi.org/10.22459/II.09.2015.02

14 See for example Peter H. Hansen, 'Partners: guides and Sherpas in the Alps and Himalayas, 1850s–1950s', in Jas Elsner and Jean-Paul Rubiés (eds), *Voyages and Visions: Towards a Cultural History of Travel* (London: Reaktion, 1999), pp. 210–31.

15 Driver, 'Hidden histories made visible', 431.

16 For an excellent account of the wider networks of such intermediaries, see Emma Martin, 'Translating Tibet in the borderlands: networks, dictionaries, and knowledge production in Himalayan hill stations', *Transcultural Studies*, 7:1 (2016), 86–120, https://doi.org/10.17885/heiup.ts.23538

17 Giuseppe Tucci, *To Lhasa and Beyond: Diary of the Expedition to Tibet in the Year 1948* (Rome: Istituto Poligrafico dello Stato, 1956), pp. 12–14. Tenzing recalled Karma Paul as a key gatekeeper in the recruitment of porters: for his role on Tucci's journey to Lhasa in 1948, see Tenzing Norgay and James Ramsey Ullman, *Man of Everest: The Autobiography of Tenzing* (London: Harrap, 1955), pp. 110–24.

18 Charles Howard-Bury, 'The Mount Everest Expedition', *Geographical Journal*, 59:2 (1922), 83, https://doi.org/10.2307/1781386

19 See especially Marco Pallis, *Peaks and Lamas* (London: Cassell, 1939), part expeditionary memoir, part meditation on the traditions of Buddhist thought.

20 Alexander W. Macdonald, 'The lama and the general', *Kailash: A Journal of Himalayan Studies*, 1:3 (1973), 225–33; Hansen, 'The dancing lamas'.

21 An extended biography of Van Manen, including his relationship with consultants in the region, was published as an appendix to P.H. Pott, *Introduction to the Tibetan Collection of the National Museum of Ethnology, Leiden* (Leiden: Brill, 1951), pp. 133–65. See also Martin, 'Translating Tibet in the borderlands'; Berthe Jansen, 'Serendipity among books: the Van Manen collection', in Alexander Reeuwijk (ed.), *Voyage of Discovery: Exploring the Collections of the Asian Library of Leiden University* (Leiden: Leiden University Press, 2017), pp. 126–31. See also the Introduction to this volume by Hansen, Gilchrist, and Westaway.

22 On Shebbeare, see Jonathan Westaway, 'Thinking like a mountain: the life and career of E.O. Shebbeare', *Alpine Journal*, 122 (2018), 205–18.

23 On reading 'against' and 'along' the grain of the colonial archive, see Gyanendra Pandey, 'Voices from the edge: the struggle to write subaltern histories', in Vinayak Chaturvedi (ed.), *Mapping Subaltern Studies and the Postcolonial* (London: Verso, 2000), pp. 281–99; Ann Laura Stoler, *Along the Archival Grain: Epistemic Anxieties and Colonial Common Sense* (Princeton, NJ: Princeton University Press, 2009).

24 Janette Faull, 'Climbing Mount Everest: expeditionary film, geographical science and media culture, 1922–1953' (PhD dissertation, Royal Holloway, University of London, 2019). See also Alison Griffiths, 'Cinema in extremis: Mount Everest and the poetics of monumentality', *Film History*, 32:1 (2020), 40–71, https://doi.org/10.2979/filmhistory.32.1.02

25 John Noel (dir.), *The Epic of Everest* (UK: BFI, 2013 [orig. 1924]); John Noel (dir.), *Climbing Mount Everest* (UK: Royal Geographical Society, 1922).

26 Charles G. Bruce, *The Assault on Mount Everest* (London: Edward Arnold, 1923), pp. 78–9. For its identification as a Green Tara, see Driver and Jones, *Hidden Histories*, p. 41.

27 *The Times* (15 July 1922).

28 George Mallory to Francis Younghusband, 11 June 1922, EE 3/4 (RGS); George Mallory to Geoffrey Young, 11 June 1922, EE 3/5, Royal Geographical Society (with IBG) archives.

29 'Committee assembled to consider compensation to be given to the dependants of the men killed on the Everest Expedition', Aug 1922, EE 18/1/98, Royal Geographical Society (with IBG) archives.

30 A large print of the cairn is in the Noel collection (CHU/059), Royal Geographical Society (with IBG) archives. The photo of 'Beetham carving a stone' is in Edward Shebbeare's Everest journal at the Alpine Club.

31 John Noel to Arthur Hinks, 12 June 1922, EE 18/3, Royal Geographical Society (with IBG) archives.

32 *Geographical Journal*, 60:6 (1922), between pages 416 and 417, https://doi.org/10.2307/1781078

33 *Alpine Journal*, 34 (1923), between pages 430 and 431.

34 On Rhomoo and the Lepcha botanists, see Roland E. Cooper, '"Native collectors" of primulas', *Quarterly of the American Primrose Society*, 13:3 (1955), 98–102; Allen Elliott, 'Rhomoo Lepcha' (2013), https://web.archive.org/web/20220727191559/https://stories.rbge.org.uk/archives/4256; L. Shyamal, 'Some unsung Lepcha collectors', *Catching Flies*, 2 March 2016, https://web.archive.org/web/20240124221836/https://muscicapa.blogspot.com/2016/03/some-unsung-lepcha-collectors.html

35 Markus Krajewski, *Paper Machines: About Cards & Catalogs, 1548–1929* (Cambridge, MA: MIT Press, 2011), https://doi.org/10.7551/mitpress/9780262015899.001.0001;

Hannah Turner, *Cataloguing Culture: Legacies of Colonialism in Museum Documentation* (Vancouver, BC: UBC Press, 2020).

36 Felix Driver, Eugene Rae, and Sarah L. Evans, 'A history of the Society's collections catalogues', *Royal Geographical Society with IBG*, https://web.archive.org/web/2024013 1212330/https://www.rgs.org/research/higher-education-resources/a-history-of-the-societys-collections-catalogues

37 Pereira and Patel, 'Terra nova for the Royal Geographical Society'.

38 Of many examples of artistic interventions in the context of colonial-era collections, see Nyema Droma's exhibition at the Pitt Rivers Museum: Clare Harris, 'Creating a space for *Performing Tibetan Identities*: a curatorial commentary', *Trans-Asia Photography Review*, 9:2 (2019), https://doi.org/10.1215/215820251_9-2-202

39 Nicholas Thomas, 'The museum as method', *Museum Anthropology*, 33:1 (2010), 6–10, https://doi.org/10.1111/j.1548-1379.2010.01070.x. See also Basu, 'Re-mobilising colonial collections'; Driver, 'Intermediaries and the archive of exploration'; Martins, 'Plant artefacts then and now'.

4

The benefit of chocolate and cold tea: equipping early British Everest expeditions

Sarah Pickman

If there's one topic that seems to unite armchair, amateur, and expert mountaineers in passionate debate, it's *gear*. Where to economise on weight; pre-packing food versus foraging or buying en route; whether this or that material is more insulating or eco-friendly – all of it is up for passionate debate on websites, in periodicals, on YouTube and Instagram, and around campfires. Passions for climbing gear even spill over into our studies of past expeditions. Books like modern British adventurer Ed Stafford's *Expeditions Unpacked* illustrate some of the items carried by historic explorers and mountaineers, while *Alpinist* magazine's long-running 'Tool Users' column highlights the origins of iconic pieces of climbing kit.[1] Arguing about the merits of historical gear is fun – but what more can it tell us about the past? What can we learn by examining how the expeditions of decades or centuries prior were outfitted?

As it turns out, quite a bit. Take the British Everest expeditions of the early 1920s as an example. The Royal Geographical Society (RGS) archives hold a voluminous collection of materials related to outfitting the 1921, 1922, and 1924 Everest ventures. Correspondence related to the supplying of the 1924 expedition alone amounts to around eight hundred pages. Together, they reveal much about the social worlds that produced the expeditions.[2] Today it might be easy to look at some of the items on the packing lists – cans of quail in foie gras, Montebello champagne, formal dinner suits and hats – and dismiss them as superfluous or old-fashioned relics of a bygone era. (Who needs to carry quail for thousands of miles to eat at high altitude?) But in their own specific ways these items were considered essential at the time, an invaluable asset for keeping the climbing party in fighting shape. For example, expedition leader Lieutenant Edward Norton wrote in *The Fight for Everest: 1924* that making sure a climbing party's base camp was comfortable, including well-levelled tents and a spacious mess tent for meals, was imperative, with 'the comfort of both sahibs and porters [to be] studied in all possible arrangements: on this will largely depend fitness, and therefore possibility of success'.[3] And Norton was not alone among his contemporaries in believing that an expedition kitted out with the familiar comforts of metropolitan Britain significantly increased its chance of victory.

Taking seriously the objects – even the seemingly frivolous ones – carried by the early Everest mountaineers is the focus of this chapter. What follows is not an in-depth analysis of all the quotidian supplies from the three Everest expeditions of the 1920s, which alone would take several volumes. Rather, it will broadly discuss the 'landscape of gear' that the Everest climbers found themselves amongst in the early 1920s and use key examples from the packing lists in the RGS archives to briefly sketch the approach to the outfitting of these expeditions and the kinds of stories they can tell us. For several decades now, scholars have used the term 'material culture' to describe not only *stuff* but also what all of the processes for making, describing, and interacting with stuff tell us about the people who used it.[4] The three British Everest expeditions of the 1920s were in some ways the culmination of all the expedition-packing expertise that had accumulated in Anglophone communities since the early nineteenth century, and they also presaged the equipping of future expeditions.

More broadly, the expedition gear was connected to a new culture of adventure, as well as large, nation-spanning processes: colonialism, advances in science and medicine, the growth of Western consumer culture and advertising, British beliefs about class and status, mountaineers' expectations for life 'under canvas', and assumptions about expedition labour. These expeditions did not emerge out of a vacuum but out of the social worlds of elite Anglophone society that informed what sorts of daily rituals and forms of material and psychological comfort expeditioners came not only to desire but to expect even in extreme environments. Examining the stuff of early Everest expeditions can be one path towards telling different sorts of narratives of these ventures, collectively showing how this one mountain has long been a locus for the many permutations of consumer capitalism.

Landscapes of gear

By the turn of the twentieth century, what would now be called the 'outdoor recreation and expedition' sector of the retail world was in full bloom in Britain, continental Europe, the United States, and European settler colonies. In the early nineteenth century, explorers often purchased clothing, tents, and food from military contractors, who were the major source of material and expertise suited to travel over rough terrain. Two endeavours – war and exploration – share the word 'expedition', derived from the Latin *expeditio*, meaning 'voyage of war' or 'march'. But by the end of the nineteenth century, a plethora of more specialised outdoor gear manufacturers and retailers had begun to emerge. This change wasn't driven solely by explorers and high-altitude mountaineers – most customers of the new firms were weekend campers and hikers who liked to indulge in outdoor pursuits much closer to home – but both groups could benefit from the variety of newly available stuff.

In the early 1890s the Alpine Club, co-sponsor of the 1920s Everest expeditions, even convened a committee to evaluate the best gear for mountaineering and put together a list of recommendations for its members. The resulting report laid out what the editors felt was 'a fairly complete equipment' for both actual climbing and 'what may be useful in camp or at head quarters'.[5] What was needed at 'head quarters' was a matter of serious importance, since the Alpine Club's report stressed – as did much of the general expedition packing advice of the day – that establishing a comfortable camp was key to keeping climbers in fit shape; there was no point in unnecessarily roughing it for the sake of roughing it. This sort of expertise was even covered in the general press, such as when a popular magazine, describing a course for novice explorers at the RGS, noted how the students would learn about 'the benefit of chocolate and cold tea' and recent 'examples of the marvellous ingenuity displayed in planning and devising comforts and conveniences of every kind for men who venture into the wildest parts of the earth.'[6] Thus, the Everest climbers and their backers had a variety of items to choose from and the experience of previous climbers and explorers to draw on when making their selections.

The selection of gear for the 1921 expedition fell to the joint RGS-Alpine Club Mount Everest Committee, overseen by the Committee's secretary, geographer Arthur Hinks, along with an Equipment Committee headed by mountaineers C.F. Meade and John Percy Farrar. Given the financial climate of the post-First World War years, Hinks searched for extra funding and savings from many sources, from product discounts from retailers to licensing exclusive publication rights for books and other media.[7] Gear in 1921 came from several dozen purveyors. These included outfitter Benjamin Edgington, supplier of numerous 'Whymper' tents – named for the nineteenth-century mountaineer Edward Whymper who had originated the style based on his climbs in the Alps – as well as the Army & Navy Co-operative Society, a retailer that began as a co-operative business to supply goods to military officers and their families, which provided and packed the food.[8] Attention to even small details of packing could not be overlooked; as mountaineer Charles Granville Bruce wrote in the *Geographical Journal* in the lead-up to the voyage, they would aim to follow the example of the Duke of the Abruzzi's 1909 K2 expedition, which was 'splendidly fitted out' with 'ample porterage and the best of food – two most necessary conditions if great things are to be done well'.[9]

At the same time, Hinks worked to secure shipping discounts and the suspension of import duties in India so that the literal tons of equipment sent from Britain could arrive as cheaply as possible before the Everest team and their support personnel transported it through Tibet to the mountain. Moving this much equipment over great distances was costly and a logistical headache. Yet to make sure the expedition's equipment made it all the way, Hinks and the climbers could still rely on networks of ship, rail, and animal transportation already in place thanks to decades of British colonialism and political manoeuvring on the Indian subcontinent and in the Himalayas. Though they aimed to set foot where no humans had been before, the Everest climbers piggybacked off the established infrastructure created by the violence of colonialism. This violence included the 1903–4 invasion that opened Tibet to British political influence, an invasion led by Sir Francis Younghusband, who was, by 1921, chairman of the RGS-Alpine Club's Everest Committee.

Hidden within the extensive packing lists preserved in the RGS archives are also assumptions about *who* exactly would be transporting the Everest gear to Darjeeling, and from there to the mountain. Relying on existing avenues for hiring local labourers in colonial India and Tibet, the Everest Committee could be confident in expecting to secure all the necessary support personnel and pack animals they needed. Though in practice such arrangements did not always go according to plan, with issues ranging from recalcitrant cooks to mules that sickened and died, to yaks that bucked their loads and threw cases of gear across the ground.[10] Accounting for the dozens of local guides, porters, cooks, servants, and translators hired for the expeditions also meant accounting for more food, clothing, and sleeping supplies for these individuals. The provisions made for the local staff, though, typically differed from those allotted to the British climbers and scientists. One 1922 packing list, for example, notes that the Army & Navy Co-operative Society shipped boots, blankets, and jersey shirts designated expressly 'for coolies', a word used casually to describe the expedition's (often anonymous) local workers, and which differed from the gear recommended for the climbing party.[11]

Building on the wisdom of earlier generations of mountaineers and the surety of transporting all that was deemed necessary, with each subsequent

Figure 4.1 Voluminous baggage from the 1922 Everest expedition at Tinki Dzong, photographed by John Noel. Notes with the photograph indicate that this gear encompassed '350 yak loads – 50 coolie loads'. RGS Picture Library S0020990. Courtesy of the RGS-IBG.

expedition the British Everest climbers tailored their gear to the conditions of Chomolungma. By 1924, the men of the climbing party were receiving more explicit instructions from the Everest Committee on what to pack, and more firms were also actively writing to the Committee asking for their goods to be considered for use in exchange for the right to claim publicly that they had supplied the Everest expedition. But throughout, items that would keep the men not just in good health but equally in good spirits continued to be of paramount concern. As Norton wrote after the 1924 expedition, reflecting on more miserable days experienced just two years earlier on the same ascent: 'The difference was largely accounted for by improvements in our equipment and in the organisation of our camp, and it is by the progressive raising of the standard of comfort high on the mountain that we shall some day reach the top.'[12] Given this context, perhaps it is not surprising that items like cigarettes, portable canvas baths and washstands, and folding camp furniture were part of the outfit for men who wished to replicate certain familiar domestic experiences from home while in the field.[13] Even when commenting on the tents used on the previous expedition, Mallory wrote in 1922 that for a final climbing party of four mountaineers and four porters, three tents would be necessary to allow 'the climbers to sleep two to a tent and use the larger one for cooking: the extra tent would be worth its weight for the better chances of sleeping'.[14]

Together, the packing lists of all this *stuff* in the RGS archives give a sense of the immense amount of energy and labour – both obvious and implicit – required to research, select, organise, and transport the masses of gear. And one of the heaviest groups of items that needed to be accounted for was food.

Learning from things: food

Choosing a diet for the climbing party and support personnel was a critical part of planning for the 1920s Everest expeditions. Conventional wisdom held that mountaineering required energising foods and beverages, including tea and cocoa, as well as familiar, appealing foods to stimulate appetites that might be diminished from the effects of altitude. Here, as with other supplies, what was brought rested on a combination of the organisers' and climbers' cultural expectations, available technologies, colonial networks and labour practices, and the consumer culture of the day.

Consider the hundreds of pounds of canned food brought on each of the 1920s expeditions. Mallory himself wrote after the 1921 expedition that, with the exception of milk, 'no one will be willingly found to take tinned foods when fresh can be obtained' – though tinned milk was 'preferred by some to the local milk supplies when this could be got' on the 1921 expedition – and purchasing or hunting for fresh food along the route to Everest *was* an active part of the approach marches.[15] At the same time, the expeditions carried hundreds of cases of canned food shipped from the UK, procured from the Army & Navy Co-operative Society. Mass-produced canned food was introduced to Western consumer markets in the first half of the nineteenth century. Its manufacturers promoted the idea that the tins were a marvel of technology: with them, diners would no longer be beholden to what could be sourced locally when travelling, and familiar tastes of home would always be at hand.[16] True, canned goods did *not* always live up to their manufacturers' promises of being palatable, or even of being safe for consumption.[17] Yet in the case of the Everest missions, imported cans did allow the climbers to dine on familiar, comforting items that could not have been sourced fresh in the Himalayas, such as herring, mock turtle and

Figure 4.2 'Everest breakfast stop', 1922. Members of the 1922 Mount Everest expedition enjoy the trappings of a full meal complete with folding camp table, dishes, cutlery, and pitchers for beverages. Photograph by John Noel. RGS Picture Library S0000015. Courtesy of the RGS-IBG.

green pea soup, sausages and Heinz spaghetti, quails in foie gras, and an absolute profusion of different fruit jams and marmalades, all in tins.

Yet the Everest Committee did not always succeed in balancing the finances of the expeditions with the nutritional needs and palates of the climbers by bringing canned food. A case in point from the RGS archives concerns the Glaxo company, which supplied a crate of their condensed milk in 1921. Correspondence indicates that Glaxo's representatives hoped the expedition's members would consume the condensed milk and report on its effects at high altitudes in the official expedition report. This did not happen because, according to an unsigned reply from the RGS, 'most of the members did not like it at all' and so barely drank it.[18]

Tins, an emblem of Western industrial manufacturing prowess, could even be a vehicle for jesting at the expense of other people who had not been exposed to the same technology. The leader of the 1921 reconnaissance, Lieut.-Col. Charles Howard-Bury, related an anecdote about a local cook hired on the

1921 expedition who, having never encountered canned food before, put an entire tin of fish in a pot of boiling water to cook it, only to have the tin burst its contents. A rumour then circulated throughout the camp staff that the imported British tins were explosive, much to the delight of the climbers.[19] The hired labourers, for their part, were typically given much simpler food rations than their employers, with some allowances made for religious dietary restrictions. (Prior to the 1921 expedition Meade recommended 'nourishing and appetizing' food for support labourers, the same as would be given to British invalids.[20]) However, at times the porters also staged protest strikes over the quality and quantity of food they had been given.[21]

One category of food that appears with startling frequency on the packing lists, in both tinned and other forms, is sugary sweets and condiments. On each expedition the Everest climbers consumed jams, jellies, and fruit preserves by the crateload. Chocolate and drinking cocoa were also constants. As General Charles Granville Bruce, leader of the second and third expeditions, wrote in his 1922 account, 'We were never short of jam and chocolate', and 'the two liquid foods, cocoa and pea-soup, though not imbibed so plentifully as tea, were considered no less as the natural and fitting companions of meat on any and every occasion'.[22] Sugary foods were mountaineering staples, ones that Mallory himself considered 'import[ant] … for high climbing and marching in general'.[23] But they were also familiar table staples for Brits abroad and perhaps a comforting marker of regular routines for the climbers.

Plus, by the early twentieth century chocolate was considered not only a familiar and comforting dessert but something of a nutritious energy food. In the decades prior to the Everest expeditions, major British chocolate manufacturers like Cadbury's and J. S. Fry & Sons regularly advertised their wares with images of polar explorers and aviators they had sponsored, like Robert Falcon Scott, Fridtjof Nansen, and Lewis Alcock, to stress the nourishment chocolate gave active men. Mallory especially loved chocolate and ate it prodigiously. Mass-made chocolate was also a colonial byproduct, a comforting and tasty treat only made possible by the exploitative cacao plantations of the British Caribbean colonies and Portugal's West African colonies.[24] Just this one food item on the Everest packing lists embodied multiple, complex, globe-spanning phenomena, whether the climbers were actively aware of this or not.

The extensive provisions also hint at the elaborate systems of food packing, storage, and cooking organisation that were required for the expeditions. As hinted by Mallory and echoed by climber and scientist Bentley Beetham in *The Fight for Everest*, provisions all too often were packed into cases that could not be easily rearranged; it was inconvenient and time-consuming to find boxes with all examples of one item packed together, rather than crates with a mix of things considered part of the expedition's daily ration.[25] Beetham also stressed the cultural expectations placed on local labourers hired as cooks. Ideally, catering at base camp 'should be on a generous scale', he wrote. 'Climatic conditions are tending to debilitate the climbers; the mess should try to counteract this. Parties and individuals coming down from high altitudes should find every possible comfort at the base.'[26] Even on the march, a cook should go ahead of the party leaders on a pony, 'so that a meal may actually be ready on the arrival of the sahibs. Nothing is more trying than a long wait for food at the end of a trek.'[27]

Dressing the part

An anecdote often circulated in connection with the early Everest expeditions is that when George Bernard Shaw saw the film footage of the 1922 expedition, released commercially as *Climbing Mount Everest*, he remarked that the expedition looked like 'a picnic in Connemara [Ireland] surprised by a snow-storm'.[28] Shaw's quip, reflecting on images of the climbing party posed in tweed jackets and buttoned-up wool coats over puttees with a variety of jaunty hats, has often been interpreted to mean that the men wore garments more fit for temperate countryside than the Himalayas – that they were comically ill-prepared. Looking at these clothes from a modern vantage-point, they *do* stand in sharp contrast to the jumpsuits made of synthetic fabrics we are used to seeing on high-altitude climbers today. However, the clothing from the 1920s expeditions, like their food, illuminates the world from which these expeditions emerged.

Far from being a laughing matter, the best methods for dressing for extreme environments in the early twentieth century were topics of hot debate in medical and scientific circles.[29] The debates centred around widely available natural fibres such as wool, silk, and cotton, as synthetic fabrics like rayon were still quite novel. Often scientists and physicians even saw clothing as a vital part of British imperial logistics. Assumptions that men setting out to serve as administrators or soldiers at the farthest reaches of empire needed specific kinds of clothing to protect their bodies from unfamiliar climates were based on prevalent racial theories about how people of different races responded to heat, humidity, and sunlight. Many medical experts were especially concerned with the negative consequences of sweating too much in certain clothes. This was something they shared with climbers. Mountaineering clothes needed to be warm, yes, but also light enough not to hamper movement and able to vent perspiration. Experience from previous mountaineering and polar expeditions showed that bulky, heavy clothes that were warm but trapped sweat from strenuous activity could leave this moisture to dangerously freeze into the garments against the skin at very low temperatures.

Despite Shaw's remarks, multiple layers of wool and silk allowed Everest climbers warmth but also flexibility and ventilation and were, in this context, practical choices given the fabrics available at the time. One twenty-first-century university study replicated Mallory's garments from 1924. Using modern metrics, the study confirmed that Mallory's ensemble was likely sufficiently insulating for active climbing in good weather, though insufficient during severe winds or longer periods of inactivity, like a forced overnight camp due to stormy weather.[30]

In addition to the prevailing scientific thinking of the time, commercial interests also played a role in how the Everest expeditioners dressed. Clothing manufacturers and retailers actively solicited the Everest Committee for their patronage as early as 1921. Ultimately, the clothing firm that came to be most associated with the 1920s expeditions was Burberry. Widely known today as a luxury clothing brand, Burberry got its start outfitting sportsmen and soldiers – with its famous trench coat during the First World War – as well as explorers. In a 1921 letter, a Burberry representative wrote that they wished to 'have the honor of tendering their services' to the first Everest expedition, because they 'have had unique experience' in 'meeting the exacting conditions of such an enterprise both below and above the snow-line, when violent changes of climate and temperature have to be confronted'. Their letter notes that Burberry had outfitted a number of notable polar expeditions led by Fridtjof Nansen, Roald Amundsen, Ernest Shackleton, and Robert Falcon Scott, and remarks that the firm's experience outfitting officers during the First World War 'has further qualified us as experts in this class of work'.[31] The clothier touted as strengths the inherent quality of its goods, its connection to warfare, and sponsorship of previous expeditioners, especially polar explorers, whose feats were compared to those of mountaineers in the popular press and geographical literature.

By the 1924 expedition, the Everest Committee advised members of the climbing party to buy Burberry 'Shackleton' windproof outfits.[32] However, not everyone strictly followed the Committee's advice about clothing. George Finch, a member of the 1922 climbing party, wore a quilted, down-filled coat made of the same silk as hot air balloons that he specially commissioned from outfitter S.W. Silver & Co., a garment that presaged modern down-based outdoor clothing. Though most of the members of the 1922 party looked askance at the coat, a later document from the Everest Committee acknowledged that when Finch wore it 'on the march, in camp and at high altitudes; it was light and exceedingly warm, and he found it a complete success'.[33]

Burberry no doubt hoped for good publicity from being able to say that they had kitted out the expedition and this kind of corporate sponsorship was an accepted part of many exploratory expeditions by the 1920s. Take another example from 1924: the pharmaceutical company Burroughs, Wellcome & Co. – which had also developed a reputation for sponsoring explorers – gifted medical supplies to the Everest climbers in exchange for a letter of endorsement from medical officer Richard Hingston, which the firm reproduced in advertisements.[34] Or consider the letter from a representative of the outfitter Benjamin Edgington to the Everest Committee in 1921: 'We also note, with pleasure, that the name of our firm will be quoted as supplying to the Expedition', after the company provided tents for the climbers. This included the 'Whymper'-style and 'Mummery'-style tents that were themselves named for earlier famous mountaineers.[35] While twenty-first-century climbers often decry the 'commercialisation' of Everest as a recent development, for more than one hundred years Everest expeditions have not only been sites of heroic adventure but also a locus around which consumer capitalism and advertising have come together.[36]

The climbers in the 1920s needed to consider not only what to wear on the slopes but also what to wear on the approach to the mountain. This included proper formal attire for dinners and social functions in Darjeeling or when meeting colonial officials en route. A letter from the clothing firm Thresher & Glenny, sent to the Everest Committee to solicit the 1921 expedition's custom, recommended bringing formal clothing because 'India is a dressy place' and 'official functions call for a standard of smartness that is not met with in other tropical countries'. At the same time, they offered for sale 'light flannel shirts' as 'Native washing is somewhat rough in its methods'.[37]

Such remarks hint at the many assumptions beneath the surface held by the letter writers and the members of the Everest Committee – the necessity of meeting particular styles of dress and deportment in the field, the comfort of familiar social rituals, and assumptions about local servants who will facilitate these rituals by doing the laundry. Similar concerns were echoed by some expedition members. Norton wrote in the 1924 expedition book that 'the leader of the Expedition should take a moderately respectable coat or suit, and so eat no shame when interviewing Tibetan officials'.[38] The expeditions' leaders did not extend these concerns on attire to porters and other support personnel, who were not expected to attend official functions as representatives of an imperial nation. Instead, the expedition packing lists included items labelled 'Coolie Kit' deemed suitable for hard labour on the march and on the slope.[39]

Conclusion

The Everest packing lists that survive in the RGS archives might seem like routine, even forgettable bits of paperwork. Yet through them we get a sense of the material culture of the early British Everest expeditions, a glimpse that reveals not only the accumulated mountaineering wisdom of the early twentieth century but also many of the cultural assumptions, colonial networks, labour practices, and even scientific and medical theories that accompanied a party of British climbers venturing to the Himalayas. In particular, the climbers' desires for familiar comforts – be they foods or forms of dress or ways of thinking about labour and social time – were part and parcel of early Everest packing.

Over the last century, questions around climbers' desire for comfort on the slopes have only grown in intensity and urgency. Whose desires are respected – climbers or Sherpas? Must comfort for some necessarily entail discomfort for others? Does hauling heavy gear for wealthy clients put guides and porters at risk? Do we really need the comfort of mobile phone reception at the summit of the world's highest mountain? In an environment where trash continues to proliferate and logistically is hard to remove, what is the environmental price of packing gear for Everest?

This last question is especially important, as the environmental costs of climbing Everest may expand beyond the slopes of the Himalayas. Ubiquitous and mundane provisions like chocolate and other sugary foods, wool clothing, and a dozen other items carried by Mallory and his fellow mountaineers had baked-in environmental and labour effects related to their cultivation and processing. Today, much mountaineering equipment is made from petroleum-based plastics, and some of the most quintessential materials for climbing, such as Gore-Tex fabric, come from so-called 'forever chemicals' that take extremely long periods of time to break down.[40] Climbers have even raised concerns about the environmental cost of the bodies of deceased fellow climbers that lie on the slopes of Everest.[41] Balancing desires for humans to experience the awe of being in nature or having the opportunity to summit Chomolungma with the environmental impacts of our personal purchasing habits is a tricky line to walk or climb.

In short, the archival documents of expeditions, even the seemingly mundane ones, are not just snapshots of historical moments but testaments to ongoing processes with global consequences. Approaching these archives to consider how expeditions were outfitted, and the stories behind every supply chain and purchasing choice, can help us to cultivate new stories of Everest and of expeditions. In particular, the choice of what to bring on an Everest expedition shows how even as the climbers of the past sought to test their bodies, their mental capabilities, and their emotional stamina against the challenge of the world's tallest peak, they also naturalised certain forms of comfort on the slope, from familiar labour regimes to sugary sweet treats.

Notes

1 For example, Sarah Pickman, 'Tool users: sun protection', *Alpinist* 78 (2022), 28, https://web.archive.org/web/20240213211934/https://alpinist.com/features/tool-users-sun-protection/

2 The author thanks the archivists at the Royal Geographical Society, the team at Wiley Digital Archives, and Allegra Rosenberg for assistance navigating these materials, and Amanda Thompson, Rachael Schwabe, and Max Shron for their invaluable feedback on an early draft of this chapter.

3 Edward Felix Norton et al., *The Fight for Everest: 1924* (New York: Longmans; London: Arnold, 1925), p. 354.

4 Key foundational works on material culture include Jules David Prown, 'Mind in matter: an introduction to material culture and method', in Jules Prown, *Art as Evidence: Writings on Art and Material Culture* (New Haven, CT: Yale University Press, 2002), pp. 69–95; Arjun Appadurai (ed.), *The Social Life of Things: Commodities in Cultural Perspective* (Cambridge: Cambridge University Press, 1986); Nicholas Thomas, *Entangled Objects: Exchange, Material Culture, and Colonialism in the Pacific* (Cambridge, MA: Harvard University Press, 1991); and Bill Brown, 'Thing theory', in Bill Brown (ed.), *Things* (Chicago, IL: University of Chicago Press, 2004), pp. 1–22.

5 C.T. Dent, W.M. Conway, and J.H. Wicks, 'Report of the Special Committee on Equipment for Mountaineers', *Alpine Journal*, 15 supplement (1890–91), 1–2.

6 William Fitzgerald, 'A school for explorers', *Pearson's*, 9:3 (1903), 243.

7 Wade Davis, *Into the Silence: The Great War, Mallory, and the Conquest of Everest* (New York: Alfred A. Knopf, 2011), p. 157.

8 For more on these tents, see Mike C. Parsons and Mary Rose, *Invisible on Everest: Innovation and the Gear Makers* (Pottstown, PA: DNA Press, 2005).

9 C.G. Bruce, 'Mount Everest', *Geographical Journal*, 57:1 (1921), 1–14 (at 5), https://doi.org/10.2307/1781199

10 Anecdotes recounted by Davis, *Into the Silence*.

11 Army & Navy Co-operative Society invoice dated 27 January 1922, in 'Stores, Equipment & Transport for Everest Expeditions (1921 & 1922)', EE/8/1, Royal Geographical Society (with IBG) archives. For more on labourers of colour working in the service of white explorers, see Edward Armston-Sheret, *On the Backs of Others: Rethinking the History of*

British Geographical Exploration (Lincoln, NE: University of Nebraska Press, 2024). See also Chapter 6 by Jayeeta Sharma in this volume.

12 Norton, *Fight for Everest*, p. 107.

13 'A camp chair is a comfort in tent and for dining (the alternative being ration box)', one list circulated to the men explained. [Mount Everest Committee], 'Mount Everest Expedition. Equipment', in 'Stores and Equipment for the 1921, 1922, and 1924 Expeditions', EE/38/2, Royal Geographical Society (with IBG) archives.

14 'Notes on Equipment' by G. L. Mallory, in 'Stores and Equipment for the 1921, 1922, and 1924 Expeditions', EE/38/2, Royal Geographical Society (with IBG) archives.

15 Ibid.

16 Simon Naylor, 'Spacing the can: empire, modernity, and the globalisation of food', *Environment and Planning A: Economy and Space*, 32:9 (2000), 1625–39, https://doi.org/10.1068/a32166

17 Botulism and other illnesses from canned food were common in the nineteenth and early twentieth centuries, before improvements in canning processes.

18 Secretary, RGS, to Messrs Glaxo (unsigned), Mar. 24, 1922, in 'Trade I (Equipment, Supplies, etc.)', EE/17/1, Royal Geographical Society (with IBG) archives.

19 As related in Davis, *Into the Silence*, p. 225.

20 Members of the Expedition and of the Committee, and Francis Younghusband, 'The Mount Everest Expedition: organization and equipment', *Geographical Journal*, 57:4 (1921), 271–82, https://doi.org/10.2307/1780559

21 Sherry B. Ortner, *Life and Death on Mt. Everest: Sherpas and Himalayan Mountaineering* (Princeton, NJ: Princeton University Press, 1999), p. 80. Mallory recounted after one such incident in 1921 that the porters' own sirdar (head manager) had been stiffing them when distributing the food, but Ortner notes it's equally likely that the amount and type of food allocated for the porters had been insufficient to begin with.

22 Charles Granville Bruce, *The Assault on Mount Everest, 1922* (New York: Longmans; London: Arnold, 1923), pp. 179, 178.

23 'Notes on equipment' by G. L. Mallory, in 'Stores and Equipment for the 1921, 1922, and 1924 Expeditions', EE/38/2, Royal Geographical Society (with IBG) archives.

24 For more on this aspect of the chocolate industry in the early twentieth century, see Lowell Joseph Satre, *Chocolate on Trial: Chocolate, Slavery, and the Ethics of Business* (Athens, OH: Ohio University Press, 2005).

25 Notes on equipment' by G. L. Mallory, in 'Stores and Equipment for the 1921, 1922, and 1924 Expeditions', EE/38/2, Royal Geographical Society (with IBG) archives.

26 Bentley Beetham, 'The mess', in Norton, *Fight for Everest*, p. 368.

27 Ibid.

28 John Noel relates this anecdote in 'Photographing the epic of Everest: how the camera recorded man's battle against the highest mountain in the world', *Asia*, 27:5 (1927), 368.

29 Ryan Johnson, 'European cloth and "Tropical" skin: clothing material and British ideas of health and hygiene in tropical climates', *Bulletin of the History of Medicine*, 83:3 (Fall 2009), 530–60, https://doi.org/10.1353/bhm.0.0252

30 George Havenith, 'Benchmarking functionality of historical cold weather clothing: Robert F. Scott, Roald Amundsen, George Mallory', *Journal of Fiber Bioengineering and Informatics*, 3 (2010), 121–9, https://doi.org/10.3993/jfbi12201001

31 Burberry's Ltd to Capt. Eaton, 31 Jan 1921, in 'Trade I (Equipment, Supplies, etc.)', EE/17/1, Royal Geographical Society (with IBG) archives.

32 [Mount Everest Committee], 'Mount Everest Expedition. Equipment', in 'Stores and Equipment for the 1921, 1922, and 1924 Expeditions', EE/38/2, Royal Geographical Society (with IBG) archives.

33 Ibid.

34 Burroughs, Wellcome & Co., *The Romance of Exploration and Emergency First Aid, from Stanley to Byrd* (New York: Burroughs Wellcome & Co, 1934). Burroughs, Wellcome & Co. helped innovate product endorsements by explorers as early as the 1880s, by gifting medical supplies for one of Henry Morton Stanley's African expeditions.

35 S.W. Silver & Co. and Benjamin Edgington, Limited to Everest Equipment Committee, February 11, 1921, in 'Trade I (Equipment, Supplies, etc.)', EE/17/1, Royal Geographical Society (with IBG) archives.

36 On Everest and sponsorships from the mid-twentieth century to the 2000s, see Rachel Gross, 'Logos on Everest: commercial sponsorship of American expeditions, 1950–2000', *Enterprise & Society*, 22:4 (2021), 1067–102, https://doi.org/10.1017/eso.2020.31 and Thomas Barcham, 'Commercial sponsorship in mountaineering: a case study of the 1975 British Everest Expedition', *Sport in History*, 33:3 (2013), 333–52, https://doi.org/10.108 0/17460263.2013.826435; Peter H. Hansen, 'Commercialisation and Mount Everest in the twentieth century', in Marco Armiero, Roberta Biasillo, and Stefano Morosini (eds), *Rethinking Geographical Explorations in Extreme Environments: From the Arctic to the Mountain Tops* (London: Routledge, 2023), pp. 144–56, https://doi.org/10.4324/9781003095965-10

37 Thresher & Glenny to Secretary, RGS, Jan. 25, 1921, in 'Trade I (Equipment, Supplies, etc.)', EE/17/1, Royal Geographical Society (with IBG) archives.

38 Norton, *Fight for Everest*, p. 340.

39 'Coolie Kit', in 'Stores and Equipment for the 1921, 1922, and 1924 Expeditions', EE/38/2, Royal Geographical Society (with IBG) archives.

40 Gregory L. Simon and Peter S. Alagona, 'Beyond leave no trace', *Ethics, Place and Environment*, 12:1 (2009), 17–34, https://doi.org/10.1080/13668790902753021

41 See, for example, Alan Arnette, 'What's being done about trash (and bodies) on Everest', *Outside Online* (23 April 2019, updated 6 October 2022), https://web.archive. org/web/20240124203241/https://www.outsideonline.com/outdoor-adventure/clim bing/everest-dead-bodies-trash-removal/

5

Far-away frontiers and spiritual sanctuaries: occidental escapism in the high Himalaya

Tim Chamberlain

> My mental picture of Tibet at that time was of the vaguest, rather like an ancient news-reel, in which a scene or two dance fitfully through a fog of dots. North of the Himalaya I knew, or thought I knew, was a cold bleak land where the wind blew unceasing; a country of grey horizons meeting the sky, and mile after mile of stony plain often deep in snow. Dirty people clad in felt, and yaks, like misshapen Highland cattle, trudged across those dreary barrens. The roof of the world. And somewhere near the centre lay Lhasa, the Forbidden City.[1]

These were British explorer and travel writer John Hanbury-Tracy's preconceptions of what Tibet might be like just before he went there in 1935. His engaging travelogue, *Black River of Tibet* (1938), begins like a novel, recounting how Hanbury-Tracy met his friend Ronald Kaulback for lunch at Hanbury-Tracy's club in London's Piccadilly, where Kaulback suggested the two men undertake an expedition to explore the headwaters of the River Salween in east Tibet, a scene which is perhaps somewhat deliberately reminiscent of the opening pages of James Hilton's famous novel *Lost Horizon* (1933). Indeed, when Kaulback and Hanbury-Tracy later departed for Tibet from London's Victoria Station, Hanbury-Tracy says that 'a copy of *Lost Horizon* was shoved into my hand'.[2] Hilton's novel has shaped many people's preconceptions in the West concerning Tibet – preconceptions which have endured, perpetuated through conscious and unconscious repetition and mimicry in an erroneous attempt to instil a sense of authenticity in both fictional and factual representations of Tibet, but which instead have resulted in an imagined geography of the Himalaya as a fabled, far-away frontier.[3]

Hilton's novel, however, was based on research that he is known to have pursued in the Reading Room of the British Museum, utilising a wide range of potential source material which may have helped to inform the story and the setting of *Lost Horizon*, along with his own experiences of mountaineering in Europe.[4] The novel itself references several works relating to early Western encounters with Tibet, for example those written in the seventeenth century by Jesuit missionaries such as Antonio de Andrade and Athanasius Kircher.[5] However, contemporary source material abounded at the time Hilton was writing, particularly in the works of European explorer-adventurers such as Sven Hedin, Marc Aurel Stein, and Giuseppe Tucci.[6] Joseph Rock's lavishly illustrated articles for the *National Geographic Magazine* could possibly have provided Hilton with a vibrantly colourful source of inspiration.[7] The esoteric side of Hilton's novel very likely drew upon the religious and theosophical works of writers such as Helena Blavatsky, Alexandra David-Neel, and Nicholas Roerich.[8] The idea of 'Shangri-La' itself, as a hidden realm providing a spiritual retreat from the modern world, was first sourced by these writers from Hungarian Tibetologist Alexander Csoma de Kőrös, particularly his writings on the legend of the hidden land of Shambala.[9] However, Hilton was not the first Western fiction writer to be inspired by such material. In the 1920s, writers such as William Archer, Louise Jordan Miln, and Talbot Mundy created fantastical worlds similar to Shangri-La.[10] At this time too, actual explorers, such as Frederick Marshman Bailey (known as 'Eric') and Frank Kingdon Ward, were venturing into the deep river gorges of southeast Tibet, where they encountered stories of sacred mountains and hidden valleys known as *beyul* (*sbas yul*).[11]

In Tibetan Buddhist belief, *beyul* are sacred places of pilgrimage and refuge. Some are locatable in terms of actual physical geography while others exist in a visionary rather than a material dimension.[12] *Beyul* can be sought and revealed through spiritual practice and meditation by 'treasure finders' (*gter ston*), while others will be 'opened' only in times of great need.[13] Jacques Bacot was the first Western scholar to write about *beyul*, specifically the hidden land of Padma bkod, or 'Népémakö' in 1912.[14] Bacot encountered Tibetan refugees fleeing towards Pemako (*Padma bkod*) from brutalities committed under Chinese General Zhao Erfeng.[15] As a recognised *beyul* and as a semi-independent territory, Pemako (meaning 'hidden land arrayed like a lotus') was both a place of pilgrimage and a place of refuge which was sought out by people from neighbouring polities in times of manmade or natural calamity; hence it was viewed as a kind of paradise or promised land.[16]

Pemako was also associated with a great waterfall on the River Tsangpo which was first reported in the late nineteenth century by Kinthup, a Lepcha pundit from Sikkim working covertly for the Indian Trigonometrical Survey. Kinthup provided the inspiration and impetus for British army officer Eric Bailey to explore the region first in 1911 and again in 1913. He did so the second time with fellow army officer Henry Morshead, who was later better known as a member of the first British expeditions which set out to survey and climb Everest in 1921 and 1922.[17] However, Bailey's own travel account of this journey, specifically written for a popular audience, was not published until 1957; hence it was probably the British botanist Frank Kingdon Ward who first brought Pemako to public notice in his book *The Riddle of the Tsangpo Gorges* (1926).[18] The inaccessibility of the region again meant it became a place of refuge during the Chinese invasion of Tibet in 1950, after which Tibet was once more a closed land, and so the Tsangpo was not fully explored by outsiders until the last years of the twentieth century.[19]

Superficially, it is easy to draw a parallel between Tibetan religious beliefs concerning *beyul*, as places of sanctuary in times of trouble or as transcendental paradises to be sought out, and the Western notion of a spiritual/materialistic utopia which has become associated with Hilton's eponymous conception of 'Shangri-La', a leitmotif which has entered the lexicon of Western culture. Hilton's novel (1933) and Frank Capra's film adaptation (1937) both appeared during the interwar period; hence their immense popularity may well have been a response to global uncertainties following on from the upheaval of the First World War and the financial 'Wall Street Crash' of 1929.[20] As the novelist Graham Greene observed of the film version: 'Nothing reveals men's characters more than their Utopias ... This Utopia closely resembles a film star's luxurious estate on Beverley Hills: flirtatious pursuits through grape arbours, splashings and divings in blossomy pools under improbable waterfalls, and rich and enormous meals ... a kind of aerated idealism.'[21] Capra's *Lost Horizon* was re-released during the Second World War, suggesting it continued to provide a convivial touchstone of escapism for contemporary audiences from the everyday hardships and material scarcities of wartime.[22]

There are notable differences between the cast of characters in the book and the film, but the story is essentially the same in both iterations. An aeroplane fleeing a tumultuous revolution in Central Asia is hijacked by an unknown pilot who flies to Tibet with a group of unsuspecting Westerners on board. Soon after the plane runs out of fuel and crashes in the mountains, the pilot dies. The passengers are rescued by a group of Tibetan monks who have been expecting their arrival. They are taken to the monastery of Shangri-La, which to their surprise they find is equipped with all the modern hotel-like conveniences of Western plumbing, a vast library, music salon, dining room, and everything they could possibly desire for a comfortable life. The only condition, as they slowly come to realise, is that they should not leave the valley of Shangri-La. The novel narrates how most of the characters reconcile themselves to their situation, except for the protagonist, a British Consul named Conway, and his assistant, Mallinson.[23] Mallinson is determined to leave Shangri-La and 'return to civilization'.[24] Conway is torn between his sense of duty to accompany Mallinson and the fact that the elderly and reclusive Head Lama of the monastery has asked Conway to succeed him as the chief preceptor of Shangri-La.

The fantastical element of the storyline is heightened by Conway's discovery that the monastery is a unique repository of the world's knowledge, including lost works by composers such as Chopin, and that most of the occupants of the monastery, which includes women as well as men, are all extremely long-lived. The Head Lama, Conway discovers, was originally a Capuchin missionary, named Father Perrault, who arrived in the valley and founded the monastery in the early eighteenth century.[25] There is also a love interest, a beautiful young woman named Lo-Tsen. She was a Manchu princess, who perhaps somewhat predictably comes between Conway and Mallinson. An allusion to Lo-Tsen's dramatic ageing when they eventually leave the valley of Shangri-La at the close of the novel suggests that the esoteric secrets which Conway has learnt, and which Mallinson has disbelieved, are in fact true. The novel ends as it began, with secondary characters in conversation, recounting the hearsay of this incredible story. The last that is ever heard of Conway is his second disappearance in the foothills of the Himalaya, when he set out attempting to return to the hidden valley of Shangri-La. Whether or not Conway has been successful is left open to the reader to decide.

Tibet's mystique was derived from its characterisation as 'a forbidden land'.[26] The Tibetan government had long maintained an isolationist policy which was backed up by a nominal suzerainty under successive dynasties of Chinese emperors; this along with its geographical location on a mountainous plateau to the north of the Himalaya made it difficult for outsiders to access.[27] Since the time of Warren Hastings as Governor General, the British in neighbouring India had sought to open diplomatic relations with Tibet, seeking alternative trade routes to China; attempts which had always been unsuccessful until the British military invasion of Tibet led by Francis Younghusband in 1904.[28]

The British later obtained permission from the Tibetan government to launch a series of expeditions specifically aimed at climbing Mount Everest – then seen as 'the third pole' – during the 1920s–1930s.[29] These expeditions were the most publicised and well known of a number of military-scientific expeditions which worked to map and survey Tibet, thereby 'opening up' this unknown land to the knowledge of the wider world.[30] Several of the expedition members published their own travel accounts,[31] and two films made by John Noel, *Climbing Mount Everest* (1922) and *The Epic of Everest* (1924), gave a firsthand visual-ethnographic insight into the lives of ordinary Tibetans as well as the religious institutions of Tibetan Buddhism.[32] Noel's films showed the British climbing expeditions visiting the monastery at Rongbuk, where the climbers paid their respects to Dzatrul Rinpoche, the Head Lama, while travelling en route to Everest.[33] These films depicted Tibetan Buddhism as an archaic and notably superstitious religion.[34] This was mirrored in Hilton's conception of Shangri-La as a remote and isolated citadel of ancient learning and mystical reflection.

The mountaineer and Tibetologist Marco Pallis later wrote that: 'Sheltered behind the rampart of the Himalaya, Tibet has looked on, almost unscathed, while some of the greatest Traditions of the world have reeled under the attacks of the all-devouring monster of modernism.'[35] Similarly, many contemporary descriptions echoed the intertitle cards of Noel's films, portraying Tibet as a fossilised throwback to the feudalism of medieval Europe. It was a common cliché among Western explorers who ventured into Tibet at this time, such as the climber George Mallory, to speak of themselves walking 'off the map' and venturing 'beyond the bounds of civilization'.[36] Thomas Richards has described this phenomenon whereby Tibet became part of a fantasy of empire in which 'the British image of Tibet has preserved in the amber of myth something of Kant's basic conviction that there is a universal and essential form of knowledge' embodied in the cultural otherness which Tibet quintessentially represents.[37] Richards calls this 'a process of semioticization', exemplified by Rudyard Kipling's novel *Kim* (1901), in which the 'smooth and undifferentiated space of the old blank map became the striated and specialized space peculiar to the discipline of geography'.[38] Prefiguring Edward Said's use of the term, the French poet Victor Segalen quite literally refers to Tibet as 'l'Autre' (the Other) when describing his idealisation of Tibet as a land which represents three symbolic stages or regions: the region already travelled through, the region that will be explored, and the region which will never be reached; the third region specifically referencing Tibetan Buddhist conceptions of hidden lands, such as Poyul (*sPo yul*) and Padma bkod.[39]

There was a strong element of exoticisation from the start in depictions of Tibet, both real and fictional.[40] The early Everest expedition films of John Noel caused a diplomatic controversy when the Tibetan government raised objections to the way certain aspects of Tibetan culture as shown on celluloid might be misconstrued by outsiders.[41] However, as representations of Tibet began to proliferate during the 1930s, particularly in the form of documentary films and photographs (for example, by Frederick Spencer Chapman and Ernst Schäfer), which aimed to record the realities of life in the country, such depictions were no longer wholly unmediated by Tibetans themselves.[42] Peter Hansen describes these representations as 'examples of the intercultural construction of Tibet by Westerners and Tibetans in conversation with one another ... the product of a double vision'.[43] There were other voices too, which sought to ground fantasies of Tibet and Himalayan cultures as a kind of counterweight to the *Lost Horizon* effect.

One example is a long-forgotten novel written by a genuine British Consul named Louis Magrath King, who lived in the Sino-Tibetan borderlands between 1913 and 1922. King's novel was titled *By Tophet Flare* (1937) in the UK, and *The Warden of the Marches* (1938) in the USA. It tells a story loosely based upon incidents from King's own career. King's alter ego, Consul Brundish, is called upon by the local Chinese warlord to mediate when 'the Gate of Tibet' – the frontier town of Luchengdo (based upon Tachienlu/Dartsendo; now Kangding, Sichuan) – is threatened, first by renegade Chinese soldiers and later by the forces of a Tibetan bandit. The story is a vehicle for exploring the personality traits of different characters, something which King had already examined in a series of nonfiction articles which first appeared in *Blackwood's Magazine* before being published as a book in 1927.[44] Despite the novel's basis in reality, the style and method of storytelling used by King is reminiscent of the patriarchal language found in the King James Bible, thereby lending King's story an archaic atmosphere which helps to accentuate his rendering of Chinese and Tibetan characters as people steeped in Oriental wisdom and superstition. There are frequent references to Chinese and Tibetan proverbs, aphorisms, and Chinese philosophy; subjects in which Consul Brundish appears to be well-versed, much to the surprise and admiration of his Chinese and Tibetan associates. Aside from Brundish, there are two other European characters who have secondary but substantive roles. Both are missionaries: an English Protestant named Walter Baines, and Jean Desmoulins, a French Catholic. It seems likely these two characters were based upon real missionaries whom King knew, primarily Theodor Sørensen and Francis Goré, but also partly upon James Huston Edgar and François Doublet.

While it is my contention that King's novel was written as a counterbalance to the fantastical elements of Hilton's *Lost Horizon*, that is not to say King wholly avoids utilising such tropes in his own storytelling. In writing about Tibetan people, it is impossible for King to avoid commenting upon their religious beliefs and social customs. At one point, while fleeing from trouble, Baines finds sanctuary with a Tibetan holy man living in solitary retreat on a remote hillside. Later, Baines again comes across a group of Tibetan pilgrims making their way to Shambala. The meeting is eerily timed given that another local hermit has recently prophesied 'the end of the world' at a moment which coincides with a threat to the region posed by a Tibetan 'outlaw' named Losengdawa, which has prompted Baines to preach and circulate religious tracts in Tibetan regarding the second coming of Christ. The pilgrims invite Baines to join them on their journey to the promised land:

> Mr Baines was sorely tempted to ask where it was, this Shambala the pilgrims were going to. But he had an abhorrence of anything connected with the occult, of which there was always so much around him, amongst the Chinese as well as the Tibetans. Strange things, he was aware, happened on occasion, stranger still were believed and even, attempted. The whole thing was unhealthy even where it was not definitely uncanny, in other words – Satanic. And he had always kept himself rigidly and uncompromisingly aloof from it. It was the only way.
>
> But was not this matter of Shambala rather a question of geographical knowledge? He decided reluctantly that it was both; and the one aspect of it precluded for him the consideration of the other.[45]

At face value, this episode from King's novel appears to neatly play upon the *Lost Horizon* element of most readers' expectations, but it seems very likely that this scene was actually grounded in reality, being based upon genuine instances when Tibetans living in the Sino-Tibetan borderlands fled from the periodic uprisings and internecine conflicts between Tibetan and Chinese military forces, thereby making their way to Padma bkod, as previously noted by Bacot, Bailey, and Kingdon Ward.

A mysterious character, named Mr Mao, subsequently appears and hints that Brundish (similarly to Conway) has some sort of intuitive spiritual connection to the East. Mao states that, although Brundish is unconscious of it, he is 'on the Path'. Brundish, however, dismisses this in favour of Western pragmatism.[46] And yet the character of Brundish was based upon King, who did possess an undisclosed form of insight into the local life and culture of the peoples of the frontier among whom he was stationed. In real life, King married a Tibetan woman named Rinchen Lhamo.[47] Together they worked on a book, written by Lhamo expressly to counter misconceptions regarding Tibet which she felt the newspapers of the West were encouraging, noting that: 'It is so much easier to say what is expected than what is true, but contrary to established views.'[48]

Tibet was habitually portrayed as a static or fossilised culture, but in lived reality it was mobile and highly dynamic. Documentary films, academic articles, and popular travelogues by Western travellers were largely framed through the partiality of their own personal views as outsiders, and yet such endeavours were only made possible by the assistance of local peoples. If we look beneath the surface of texts such as King's novel and Hanbury-Tracy's travelogue, we find glimpses of Indigenous agency and the largely unseen mobilities of Himalayan cultures. What Westerners portrayed as remote and inaccessible terrain was in fact an interconnected landscape which was already well known and consciously mapped out by the polities who lived there. Hence Western outsiders actually relied, almost symbiotically, upon a network of knowledgeable and experienced Indigenes for support in fulfilling their aspirations to step 'off the map' and escape 'modern civilisation' in order to realise their search for a notionally 'unexplored' Shangri-La. These networks can be seen, albeit sometimes only fleetingly, embodied in the displaced persons seeking refuge in Padma bkod, and in brief biographical snapshots of Himalayan guides, such as those who were employed by Kaulback and Hanbury-Tracy:

> Lewa, he of the square jowl and barking voice, is a Sherpa from Nepal. He has not seen his village since he was fourteen, when he came to Darjeeling to work for Englishmen who like to climb hills, the great hills he has always lived among. A rugged character and great powers of endurance set him much in demand as a porter. He was one of the 'Tigers' of Everest. He has travelled the Himalaya from Sikkim to Kashmir, and has hauled more than one famous mountaineer up the last steps of a climb. He has been sirdar on several trips, and helped to save the remnants of the disastrous German expedition to Nanga Parbat in 1934 … Nyima Töndrup … [a Tibetan] encountered the first Everest expedition coming up from Darjeeling. Someone told him that coolie wages were three rupees a day, and he promptly signed on. He has been on one expedition or another ever since, winning high praise for dogged service. He is Lewa's shadow, and has known him for years.[49]

Men such as Lewa and Nyima Tondrup – highly skilled, knowledgeable, versatile, adaptable fixers and facilitators – were vital to European travellers. Tenzing Norgay, who famously was first to summit Everest with Edmund Hillary in 1953, and whose homeland near Everest was itself a *beyul*, was employed by Italian scholar Giuseppe Tucci on one of Tucci's Tibetan manuscript-collecting expeditions in 1948.[50] Unlike many itinerant Indigenous members of such expeditions, Tenzing's later fame enabled him to have a voice.[51] Tenzing tells us that Tucci was a difficult and exacting man: 'The other Sherpas thought I was mad to take the job, and for a while I thought so too. But in time I grew to like Professor Tucci as well as any man I have ever known.'[52] Such counterpoint views at this time, sadly, are very rare.[53] Consequently, when reading the accounts of Westerners exploring Himalayan regions – whether fictional or rooted in fact – we must aways remember that what we are seeing is only half the picture, and that picture itself was always a mutable one.

Notes

1 John Hanbury-Tracy, *Black River of Tibet* (London: Frederick Muller, 1938), p. 1.
2 Ibid., p. 7; see also Ronald Kaulback, *Salween* (London: Hodder & Stoughton, 1938).
3 Tim Chamberlain, 'Mountains and mysticism: escapism and authenticity in the cinematic exploration of the Himalaya' (forthcoming); Jim Rheingans, 'De-imagining Tibet: beyond Orientalism, reverse orientalism and other traps in the study of Himalayan histories', *Journal of the Society of Asian Humanities*, 52 (2021), 126–34, https://search.informit.org/doi/10.3316/informit.036105030734709
4 Charles Allen, *The Search for Shangri-La: A Journey into Tibetan History* (London: Abacus, 2001), pp. 39–41.
5 James Hilton, *Lost Horizon* (New York: Pocket Books, 1939 [1933]), p. 94.
6 Peter Bishop, *The Myth of Shangri-La: Tibet, Travel Writing and the Western Creation of Sacred Landscape* (Berkeley, CA: University of California Press, 1989).
7 For example: Joseph F. Rock, 'The land of the yellow lama', *National Geographic Magazine*, 47:4 (April 1925), 447–91; 'Seeking the mountains of mystery', *National Geographic Magazine*, 57:2 (February 1930), 131–85.
8 Mark Bevir, 'The west turns eastward: Madame Blavatsky and the transformation of the occult tradition', *Journal of the American Academy of Religion*, 62:3 (1994), 747–67, https://doi.org/10.1093/jaarel/LXII.3.747; Samuel Thévoz, 'On the threshold of the "Land of Marvels": Alexandra David-Neel in Sikkim and the making of global Buddhism', *Transcultural Studies*, 1 (2016), 149–86, https://doi.org/10.17885/heiup.ts.23541; James Boyd, 'In search of Shambhala? Nicholas Roerich's 1934–5 Inner Mongolian Expedition', *Inner Asia*, 14:2 (2012), 257–77, www.jstor.org/stable/24572064
9 Bernard Le Calloc'h, 'Alexander Csoma De Koros, the heroic philologist, founder of Tibetan studies in Europe', *The Tibet Journal*, 10:3 (1985), 30–41, www.jstor.org/stable/43300177; Edwin Bernbaum, *The Way to Shambala: A Search for the Mythical Kingdom Beyond the Himalayas* (New York: Anchor Books, 1980).
10 William Archer, *The Green Goddess: A Play in Four Acts* (New York: Knopf, 1921); Louise Jordan Miln, *The Green Goddess* (New York: A.L. Burt, 1922); Talbot Mundy, *Om: The Secret of Ahbor Valley* (New York: A.L. Burt, 1924).
11 F.M. Bailey, 'Exploration on the Tsangpo or Upper Brahmaputra', *Geographical Journal*, 44:4 (October 1914), 341–64, https://doi.org/10.2307/1778591; F. Kingdon Ward, 'The sacred mountain: a picturesque Tibetan pilgrimage', *The Wider World Magazine* (1911), 251–8. The sacred mountains Bailey and Kingdon Ward encountered at this time were respectively 'Kondü Putrang'/Kundu Dorsempotrang (Kun 'dus rdor sems pho brang) and 'K'a-gur-po/Ka-Kar-Po' (Kha ba dkar po).
12 Frances Garrett, Elizabeth McDougal, and Geoffrey Samuel (eds), *Hidden Lands in Himalayan Myth and History: Transformations of 'sbas yul' through Time* (Leiden: Brill, 2021), https://doi.org/10.1163/9789004437685; Toni Huber (ed.), *Sacred Spaces and Powerful Places in Tibetan Culture: A Collection of Essays* (Dharamsala: Library of Tibetan Works and Archives, 1999).

13 Franz-Karl Ehrhard, 'The role of "Treasure Discoverers" and their writings in the search for Himalayan sacred lands', *The Tibet Journal*, 19:3 (1994), 3–20, www.jstor.org/stable/43300512

14 Jacques Bacot, *Le Tibet révolté: vers Népémakö: la terre promise des tibétains* (Paris: Hachette, 1912).

15 Abdol-Hamid Sardar-Afkhami, 'The Buddha's secret gardens: end times and hidden-lands in Tibetan imagination' (PhD dissertation, Harvard University, 2001), pp. 1–2.

16 Santiago Lazcano, 'Ethnohistoric notes on the ancient Tibetan Kingdom of sPo bo and its influence on the eastern Himalayas', *Revue d'Etudes Tibétaines*, 7 (April 2005), 41–63, himalaya.socanth.cam.ac.uk/collections/journals/ret/pdf/ret_07_03.pdf

17 H.T. Morshead and F.M. Bailey, *Report on the Exploration of the North East Frontier, 1913* (Dehra Dun: The Survey of India Trigonometrical Office, 1914).

18 F.M. Bailey, *No Passport to Tibet* (London: Rupert Hart-Davis, 1957); F. Kingdon Ward, *The Riddle of the Tsangpo Gorges* (London: Edward Arnold, 1926).

19 Ian Baker, *The Heart of the World: A Journey to the Last Sacred Place* (New York: Penguin, 2004); Zhang Jimin, *The Yarlung Tsangpo Great Canyon: The Last Secret World* (Beijing: Foreign Languages Press, 2006).

20 Douwe Fokkema, *Perfect Worlds: Utopian Fiction in China and the West* (Amsterdam: Amsterdam University Press, 2011), pp. 156–62.

21 Graham Greene, '"Lost Horizon" at the Tivoli', *The Spectator*, 158:5679 (30 April 1937), 805.

22 Frank Capra (dir.), *Lost Horizon* (USA: Columbia Pictures, 1937); '"Shangri-La" brings back "Lost Horizon"', *The Hollywood Reporter*, 68:43 (29 June 1942), 3; 'Columbia's "Lost Horizon," now back in release, is clicking merrily at box offices all over the country', *The Daily Film Renter*, 17:4986 (27 September 1943), 10.

23 Names reminiscent of famous Himalayan mountaineers, Sir Martin Conway and George Mallory.

24 Hilton, *Lost Horizon*, p. 58.

25 Morshead refers to two Capuchin missionaries travelling through the Yarlung-Tsangpo valley ca. 1708, and of a mission being established in the Takpo region in 1718; see Morshead and Bailey, *Report on the Exploration*, p. 9.

26 A. Henry Savage Landor, *In The Forbidden Land: An Account of A Journey in Tibet, Capture by the Tibetan Authorities, Imprisonment, Torture, And Ultimate Release* (London: William Heinemann, 1905); Vicomte Henri D'Ollone, *In Forbidden China: The D'Ollone Mission, 1906–1909, China-Tibet-Mongolia* (London: T. Fisher Unwin, 1912); Harrison Forman, *Through Forbidden Tibet: An Adventure into the Unknown* (New York & Toronto: Longmans, Green & Co., 1935).

27 Sam Van Schiak, *Tibet: A History* (New Haven, CT: Yale University Press, 2011), pp. 143–5, 160.

28 Gordon T. Stewart, *Journeys to Empire: Enlightenment, Imperialism, and the British Encounter with Tibet, 1774–1904* (Cambridge: Cambridge University Press, 2009).

29 Alex McKay, *Tibet and the British Raj: The Frontier Cadre, 1904–1947* (Dharamsala: Library of Tibetan Works and Archives, 2009 [1997]), pp. 77–8, 136.

30 Gordon T. Stewart, 'The British reaction to the conquest of Everest', *Journal of Sport History*, 7:1 (Spring 1980), 21–39; Lachlan Fleetwood, *Science on the Roof of the World: Empire and the Remaking of the Himalaya* (Cambridge: Cambridge University Press, 2022).

31 C.G. Bruce, *The Assault on Mount Everest, 1922* (London: Edward Arnold, 1923); George Ingle Finch, *Climbing Mount Everest* (London: George Philip, 1932); Charles Howard-Bury,

Mount Everest: The Reconnaissance, 1921 (London: Edward Arnold, 1922); E.F. Norton, *The Fight for Everest: 1924* (London: Edward Arnold, 1925); Hugh Ruttledge, *Everest: The Unfinished Adventure* (London: Hodder & Stoughton, 1937); H.W. Tilman, *Mount Everest, 1938* (Cambridge: Cambridge University Press, 1948).

32 John Noel (dir.), *Climbing Mount Everest* (UK: Royal Geographical Society, 1922); John Noel (dir.), *The Epic of Everest* (UK: BFI, 2013 [orig. 1924]).

33 J.B.L. Noel, *Through Tibet to Everest* (London: Edward Arnold, 1927), pp. 138–47.

34 Donald S. Lopez Jr, *Prisoners of Shangri-La: Tibetan Buddhism and the West* (Chicago, IL: University of Chicago Press, 1998), ch. 1.

35 Marco Pallis, *Peaks and Lamas* (London: Cassell, 1946 [1939]), p. 381.

36 George Mallory to Geoffrey Winthrop Young (1921), quoted in Ed Douglas, *Himalaya: A Human History* (London: Vintage, 2021), p. 211; Ronald Kaulback, *Tibetan Trek* (London: Hodder & Stoughton, 1934), p. 270; André Guibaut, *Tibetan Venture: In the Country of the Ngolo-Setas (Second Guibaut-Liotard Expedition)* (London: Readers Union, 1949), p. 60.

37 Thomas Richards, *The Imperial Archive: Knowledge and the Fantasy of Empire* (London: Verso, 1993), p. 13.

38 Ibid., p. 14.

39 Edward Said, *Orientalism* (New York: Pantheon, 1978); John C. Stout, 'Metapoetic explorations of Tibet in Victor Segalen's Thibet and André Velter's Le Haut-Pays', *Sites*, 5:1 (2001), 63–78, https://doi.org/10.1080/10260210108456056

40 Dibyesh Anand, *Geopolitical Exotica: Tibet in Western Imagination* (Minneapolis, MN: University of Minnesota Press, 2007).

41 Peter H. Hansen, 'The dancing lamas of Everest: cinema, Orientalism, and Anglo-Tibetan Relations in the 1920s', *The American Historical Review*, 101:3 (1996), 712–47, https://doi.org/10.2307/2169420

42 Clare Harris and Tsering Shakya, *Seeing Lhasa: British Depictions of the Tibetan Capital, 1936–1947* (London: Serindia, 2003); Isrun Engelhardt (ed.), *Tibet in 1938–1939: Photographs from Ernst Schäfer's Expedition to Tibet* (Chicago, IL: Serindia, 2007).

43 Peter H. Hansen, 'Tibetan horizon: Tibet and the cinema in the early twentieth century', in Thierry Dodin and Heinz Rather (eds), *Imagining Tibet: Perception, Projections and Fantasies* (Boston MA: Wisdom Publications, 2001), pp. 105–6; see also, Samuel Thévoz, 'Visions of Tibet (1840–1910)', *Tibet Journal*, 45:1 (2020), 101–33, www.jstor.org/stable/27031092

44 Louis Magrath King, *China in Turmoil: Studies in Personality* (London: Heath Cranton, 1927).

45 Louis Magrath King, *The Warden of the Marches: A Tale of Adventure on the Chinese Frontier of Tibet* (Boston MA: Houghton Mifflin, 1938), p. 171.

46 Ibid., p. 196.

47 Tim Chamberlain, 'Books of change: a western family's writings on China, 1855–1949', *Journal of the Royal Asiatic Society China*, 75:1 (2013), 55–76, ras-china.org/ras-journal

48 Rinchen Lhamo, *We Tibetans* (London: Seeley Service, 1926), p. 95, see also pp. 6–9; another Tibetan writer similarly assisted by King's consular colleague, George Combe: Paul Sherap, *A Tibetan on Tibet: Being the Observations of Mr P. Sherap Dorje Zodba of Tachienlu* (London: Fisher Unwin, 1926).

49 Hanbury-Tracy, *Black River of Tibet*, pp. 9–10.

50 Jeremy Spoon and Lhakpa Norbu Sherpa, 'Beyul Khumbu: the Sherpa and Sagarmatha (Mount Everest) National Park and buffer zone, Nepal', in Josep-Maria Mallarach (ed.),

Protected Landscapes and Cultural and Spiritual Values: Volume 2 (Heidelberg: Kasparek Verlag, 2008), pp. 68–79.

51 Sherry B. Ortner, 'The making and self-making of "the Sherpas" in early Himalayan mountaineering', *Studies in Nepali History and Society*, 3:1 (1998), 1–34; Felix Driver, 'Hidden histories made visible? Reflections on a geographical exhibition', *Transactions of the Institute of British Geographers*, 38:3 (2013), 420–35, https://doi.org/10.1111/j.1475-5661.2012.00529.x

52 Tenzing Norgay and James Ramsey Ullman, *Man of Everest: The Autobiography of Tenzing* (London: Reprint Society, 1956), p. 111.

53 See also Ang Tharkay with Basil P. Norton, *Sherpa: The Memoir of Ang Tharkay* (Seattle, WA: Mountaineers Books, 2016 [1954]).

6

Seeing histories from the margins: an Indigenous labour force on Everest, 1921–53

Jayeeta Sharma

'The relationship between what we see and what we know is never settled.'[1]

This chapter explores 'ways of seeing' Other Everests in the labouring infrastructure of the 1921–53 British Mount Everest expeditions.[2] It juxtaposes expedition photographs of mountaineering labour with first-person published narratives from elite British mountaineers such as Brigadier-General the Honourable Charles Granville Bruce and from Indigenous Sherpa mountaineers such as Ang Tharkay and Tenzing Norgay.[3]

General Bruce, the leader of the 1922 and 1924 British Mount Everest expeditions, was deeply convinced of the value of photographs for the mountaineering endeavour: 'Sketches convey very little of the true character of the mountains; this is impossible without the help of photography.'[4] New forms of photographic equipment enabled British mountaineers of the twentieth century to produce impressive photographs that served the crucial purposes of both science and publicity. Photography was a technical and aesthetic device that enabled these mountaineer photographers to claim as truth its knowledge practices, scopic technologies, and forms of representation.[5] Historians of photography consider a photograph as a unique kind of artefact, one that is at the same time a historical document, a site of affective investment, and an aesthetic object.[6] A selection of first-person narratives from imperial and Indigenous mountaineers in dialogue with expedition photographs becomes a way to frame Indigenous histories from the mountain margins of the British Empire, and to see Other Everests.

Infrastructure and labour

Anthropologists use the concept of infrastructure to describe the forms of materials that enable exchange over space and fuel the development of diverse relationships.[7] One of those forms is the sentient, embodied labour of Indigenous humans and animals. Across the eastern Himalayas, a reliable supply of Indigenous labouring bodies was indispensable to both the production and the continuance of imperial infrastructure. This was largely due to the harsh terrain of altitude that made the provision of a modern transport network a considerable challenge. Well into the twentieth century, the embodied infrastructure of Indigenous humans and animals provided the bulk of carriage labour, especially since Himalayan geography and climate restricted the effectiveness of road and rail infrastructure.

Human labour with ethnic roots in Asia was referred to throughout the colonial period by the derogatory term 'coolie' – in British India, the Indian Ocean region, and increasingly worldwide. The term 'coolie' is believed to have originated either from a vernacular word for wages, 'kuli', or from another word that meant 'bitter labour'.[8] Over time, the use of 'coolie' acquired a specific racial sense depending on the geographical context. By the late nineteenth century, the majority of 'coolie' labourers working in the eastern Himalayas were Indigenous migrants from the borderlands of Bhutan, Nepal, Sikkim, and Tibet. They moved into British India in search of the various types of waged work that an imperial political economy had generated, especially around the mountain towns of Darjeeling and Kalimpong.[9] Geoff Childs's conceptual framework of Himalayan migrations as protracted historical processes rather than as singular events is useful to understand how such migrants constituted the embodied infrastructure of this imperial frontier, and how Sherpas became an essential part of its mountaineering endeavour.[10]

Generations of Indigenous labouring migrants took employment in every type of imperial infrastructure in the eastern Himalayas, from plantations to the military, to construction, to carriage, to expeditions. They became a recognisable working class of Himalayan 'coolies' who acquired distinct ethnic identities, as Bhutias, Paharis, Gurkhas, Nepalis, or as Sherpa and Sherpani porters. Animals accompanied many migrants, especially those who had backgrounds in nomadic pastoralism and borderlands trading networks.[11] Whether mules, donkeys, dogs, ponies, or yaks, those were animals acclimatised to altitude. Service animals such as mules, ponies, and yaks allowed their human companions to amplify the labouring services that they offered in the colonial lexicon.[12]

A considerable portion of that Indigenous labour, human and animal, was recruited into the military, exploratory, and mountaineering expeditions that ventured to ever higher altitudes of the Himalayas.

The doyen of the early British Everest expeditions, Brigadier-General Charles Bruce was the youngest son of an aristocrat whose estate was in the Welsh hills of Glamorgan.[13] His friends affectionately dubbed him the 'Mad Mountain Maniac'.[14] Bruce described how at an Alpine Club meeting of 1906, several Club members asked rhetorically: 'If the Himalaya, why not Everest?'[15] That imperial ambition to explore and attain mountain summits in the Himalayas accelerated an interest in embodied mountain infrastructure and necessitated its refinement.[16] The sentient labour of Indigenous animals and humans, as Euro-American mountaineers acknowledged, often grudgingly, was indispensable to realise that ambition. The British climbing establishment drew on existing imperial and Indigenous systems of labour mobilisation to produce the embodied and material infrastructure of these Everest expeditions.

British mountaineer George Leigh Mallory reflected in 1922 that 'The [Everest] Expedition brings to my mind's eye a view of the long mountain slopes set at intervals with groups of little tents, with loads of stores and sleeping-sacks, and with men'.[17] He produced such a view in his photograph of 'mountains and pack animals' (Figure 6.1). The photograph framed the snow-clad peaks as a backdrop for the Indigenous mules and muleteers who carried the expeditionary materials high into the mountains. He described in colourful language the necessity of those materials and, as a corollary, of the animals and humans who provided their carriage labour: 'The lack of a cooking pot, an oxygen tank, a canteen or a rope, at the right spot at the right moment, may doom the expedition'.[18]

Much of those loads consisted of the materials of the expedition's culinary infrastructure, everything from firewood, primus stoves, and fuel to stocks of food and drink.[19] Culinary infrastructure includes the facilities and technologies that connect the production and consumption of food to the human and nonhuman subjects for whom food serves as fuel. In the harsh terrain of those mountains, and especially at altitude, food and drink as fuel was both a necessity and a cherished comfort. Another British climber of the 1922 expedition, George Ingle Finch, described the sybaritic menu that the mountaineers consumed at Camp Three, after they mastered the challenge of the North Col: 'Hot tea and a tin of spaghetti' started the meal, before the appearance of 'four whole quails truffled in pate de foie gras, followed by nine sausages'.[20]

Figure 6.1 'Mountains and pack animals', 1921. Photograph by George Leigh Mallory on the 1921 Mount Everest Reconnaissance expedition. The mountain in the background is almost certainly Chomolhari in the Chumbi valley, Tibet. RGS Picture Library, S0020962. Courtesy of the RGS-IBG.

Those materials to nourish the British mountaineers travelled all the way from London to Darjeeling and Kalimpong. From that final expedition halt in British India, Indigenous humans and animals carried those loads to Everest Base Camp from the 1920s to 1953.[21] The food rations allotted to the porters and labourers were procured locally from India and carried into Tibet. The rations for the Indigenous labourers in 1953 consisted of four foods: 'atta (stone-ground whole wheat flour), rice, tsampa (Tibetan roasted barley flour), and potatoes'.[22] During the 1921 British Everest Reconnaissance expedition, its leader, Lieutenant-Colonel Charles Howard-Bury, refused to allocate anything more than such basic rations to any of the porters, even to those Sherpa porters who carried materials to the higher altitudes. Dismayed British climbers Mallory and Bullock felt obliged to sustain those Indigenous men who carried their loads high up the mountain with meat and tea supplied from their own ample allowance of food and drink.[23]

The 1921 Mount Everest Committee had tried to save money by co-opting the British Indian Army's mules and drivers to provide carriage labour all the way into the mountains. Such a cost-saving strategy failed since the army mules – which were bred for service in the Indian plains – could not cope with the rigours of altitude. At considerable trouble and expense, the expedition was forced to hire last-minute replacements. Learning from this mistake, the 1922 expedition leader, General Bruce, decided to procure an ample supply of mountain mules, yaks, and donkeys, along with their human companions, right from the start. Ponies were hired for the British mountaineers to ride as high up as they could go. Cows and cowherds provided fresh milk for tea. Bruce singled out for praise the mountain mules and drivers who provided much of the carriage labour: 'We made acquaintance with the wonderful Chumbi mule transport. These mule-men work regularly seven months in the year carrying wool from Tibet down to Kalimpong, and they thoroughly understand the art of loading and travelling the mules.'[24]

Chumbi mule transport directly linked the embodied infrastructure of that Everest expedition to the commercial infrastructure of the imperial wool trade. These mules and their drivers regularly conveyed wool from the Tibetan plateau to the Indian towns of Kalimpong and Darjeeling. Wool travelled onwards by rail from the mountain city of Darjeeling down to the port city of Calcutta, and then by ship into the British dominion of Canada.[25] Himalayan wool was transformed into the Santa Claus beards that adorned the famed Eaton department store parades in the imperial city of Toronto.[26]

Centuries before the British Empire entered those Himalayan borderlands, the embodied infrastructure of Indigenous human and animal transport had serviced the long-distance commodity trades of Asia, especially to convey staple foods such as salt and tea. During the Second World War, the Allied powers mobilised such mules and muleteers to transport essential supplies, including food and drink, to their military forces on the Burma front.[27] After the War, when the 1953 British Everest expedition embarked from Kathmandu instead of Darjeeling, the labouring animals and humans of the eastern Himalayas continued to supplement the existing transport infrastructure of Nepal so that the expedition materials might reach Everest.

Back in 1921, the efforts of the Mount Everest Reconnaissance expedition to recruit Indigenous porters bore an unfortunate resemblance to the forced labour requirements that many Indigenous elites in the Himalayas traditionally imposed on their subaltern classes. 'Every able-bodied man from the local villages is usually roped in by the civil authorities, and more or less obliged to go, nearly always against his will, certainly against the will of the majority, to carry loads up into the snows at a stated and quite inadequate remuneration, for a more or less protracted period'.[28] The 1921 expedition leader, Howard-Bury, had failed to realise that the local Jongpens (headmen) through whom he recruited carriage labour in Tibet, had taken advantage of their authority to divert to themselves the porters' remuneration. As a result, those Tibetan porters were compelled to carry the 1921 expeditionary materials for no compensation. That ill-treatment came to light only when subsequent expeditions sought to recruit Indigenous labourers locally in Tibet.[29]

General Bruce took to heart the advice of the British mountaineer and scientist Alexander Kellas to frame a well-thought-out strategy for the recruiting, employing, and provisioning of labour from the Indigenous people of the Himalayas. Kellas had combined his expertise in the fields of medicine, chemistry, and mountaineering into a body of pioneering research on the impact of altitude upon human physiology. Four years before the first British team reached Mount Everest, Kellas described the sheer dependence of a Himalayan expedition on Indigenous humans and animals. 'All tents, equipment, foodstuff etc. have generally to be carried 100 to 200 miles [...] the experienced traveller will generally use animals for a portion of the journey, if procurable.'[30] Draught animals could only go so far in altitude. 'All luggage will have to be carried by coolies, if ponies, mules, or yaks are not available, or the routes too rough for animals. After reaching the glaciers one has generally to depend upon coolie transport.'[31]

Successive Everest expedition leaders were to discover that assembling and managing that embodied infrastructure presented significant challenges. Bruce declared that the best approach was: 'Good men must be got, well clothed, well fed and trained, and above all made to take an interest in the proceedings.'[32] It remained to be seen who those good men would be.

Good men: a 'special type of coolie'

In the wake of the First World War, the modern quest for the summit became focused on Mount Everest. A complementary quest was to find a 'special type of coolie ... one who is strong and hardy and does not mind the cold and is also accustomed to live at great heights'.[33] Early testimonials from mountaineers pointed to specific ethnic groups among the Indigenous population of the Himalayas who were presumed to be particularly suited to work at altitude. In 1898, Douglas Freshfield's Kangchenjunga expedition in Sikkim relied on a multiethnic labour force that comprised a 'mixed troop of over fifty Bhootia, Lepcha, and Nepalese coolies, or porters'.[34] In the wake of an expedition to

Kabru on the Sikkim–Nepal border in 1907, Norwegian climbers Carl Wilhelm Rubenson and Ingvald Monrad Aas praised the willingness and bravery of Indigenous 'coolies, especially Nepalese Sherpas [...] We could not persuade them to be roped when loaded, but by making good steps, fixing in pegs and ropes, and helping them over difficult places there seems to be no limit to what they will surmount.'[35] Kellas was very influential in forming British opinion on the best ethnic composition of expedition labour at altitude. 'A solitary traveller, anxious to do a little easy climbing, might find it worth his while to take a few carefully selected Bhutia Nepalese with him as personal servants to any mountain region. They can be engaged at Darjeeling'.[36] When he wrote of Bhutia Nepalese, he meant Sherpas from high Himalayan communities who had migrated to Darjeeling. British attempts to employ Swiss and Italian Alpine professionals as climbing experts faded away, since they lacked local knowledge and were far more expensive than Indigenous groups from the Himalayas.[37]

The writings of General Bruce provide useful insights into a central figure of the British climbing establishment who mined years of experience in British India to champion the Gurkha soldier as the ideal sporting auxiliary for the white man at altitude. A veteran of many Welsh and Alpine summits, Bruce first undertook a Himalayan mountaineering climb in 1891 during Martin Conway's expedition to Karakoram. By the time Bruce took charge of the 1922 and 1924 British Everest expeditions, he was convinced that the Indigenous soldier migrants from Nepal who had already demonstrated sporting prowess and loyalty to their commanders were perfect candidates to support the mountaineering endeavour.

Since the mid-nineteenth century, British ethnographers and military recruiters had championed the Magar, Gurung, Limbu, and Rai ethnic groups of Nepal as the ideal 'martial races' for the British Empire.[38] Co-opted into the racial hierarchies of empire as part of Britain's divide and rule strategies, many men from those groups achieved economic and social mobility as Gurkha soldiers in the empire's military forces.[39] Bruce adopted the plural roles of military leader, mountaineer, and sports aficionado. He was dedicated to the transformation of the 'fresh caught recruits' of the 5th Gurkha regiment into modern sportsmen, through introducing them to the European sports of hill racing, track running, and mountain climbing.[40] In the 1890s, Bruce hired Alpine guide Matthias Zurbriggen at his own expense to train promising non-commissioned officers Parbir Thapa and Harkbir Thapa in snow and ice work, taking them as far as Wales and Switzerland to train with the former.[41] Bruce selected another talented soldier, Karbir Burathoki, to join the Conway expedition to Karakoram and later the Longstaff expedition to Mount Trisul.[42] Everest mountaineer George Finch warmly commended Tejbir Thapa's performance at altitude in 1922, the first Gurkha to climb to that height.[43] Impressed by those achievements, a new edition of a British military handbook added the information that sporting talent was as intrinsic to the Gurkha soldier as his aptitude for battle.[44]

Pioneering Gurkha mountaineer soldiers encountered success and tragedy. Two of Bruce's protégés died alongside British mountaineer Albert Mummery on an expedition to Nanga Parbat in 1895.[45] When seven Sherpa porters fell victim to the onslaught of an avalanche during the 1922 Everest expedition, Bruce described how their fellows mourned with a fatalistic Nepali folk saying: 'The sacrifice to the god is complete'.[46] Two more Gurkhas died after injuries on Everest in 1924.[47] Following the example of General Bruce, other military officers sought the army's permission to second regimental Gurkhas to mountaineering expeditions. Nonetheless, for that period, the rollcall of Gurkha soldiers who ventured to altitude is not long. Unlike other Indigenous migrants who depended on 'coolie' work to earn a living, those Gurkhas earned adequate compensation from British military service, including the provision of retirement pensions. They had little incentive, not even the prospect of military promotions, to risk life at altitude.

Alongside the mules and muleteers of Mallory's photograph, the embodied infrastructure of the Himalayas encompassed another set of subaltern labouring bodies who were indigenous to the Himalayan region. The photograph includes the expedition porters who carried loads of expeditionary materials on their backs into the mountains. This form of embodied infrastructure was especially important at the higher altitudes where even acclimatised mules found it hard to climb with heavy loads. While porters came from diverse Indigenous communities in the Himalayas, many were ethnic Sherpas from the Solu Khumbu region of Nepal, located immediately to the south of Mount Everest.

Sherpas were relatively recent entrants into the imperial economy of British India. For centuries they had worked as seasonal load carriers in Nepal and Tibet to supplement the meagre subsistence of mountain ecologies. According to Sherpa lore, they had relocated from eastern Tibet to the adjoining Solu Khumbu region of Nepal in the seventeenth century. There they grew barley, buckwheat, and potatoes, and pastured yaks at elevations from 3,000 to 4,000 metres.[48] Mountaineer-author Ed Douglas claims that since 1922, it became a deliberate strategy among the Sherpa porters to seek out tasks at higher altitudes. This was to prove themselves tougher and worth more financially than the other ethnic groups who laboured within the expedition's embodied infrastructure.[49] Sherry Ortner notes that it gradually became an accepted colonial precept from the 1920s that the skilled, risky, and relatively lucrative labouring jobs on Himalayan climbing expeditions should go to Sherpa men.[50] At the end of his 1934 memoir, Bruce acknowledged that in the annals of British mountaineering, his beloved Gurkhas were surpassed by that other Indigenous group from the eastern Himalayas, a group that he called the 'Sherpa Bhotias'.[51] Bruce failed to mention that, compared with Gurkha soldiers, the itinerant Sherpas faced considerable economic and social instability. Just as the imperial military had provided an opportunity for Gurkha migrants from Nepal to achieve upward mobility, mountaineering labour at altitude offered a similar prospect for ethnic Sherpas (Figure 6.2).

Figure 6.2 'Sherpa porters – Ang Tensing – Jla Kita – Kusang Sita', 1935. Photograph by L.V. Bryant on the 1935 Mount Everest expedition. RGS Picture Library, S0011147. Courtesy of the RGS-IBG.

Indigenous porters: Sherpa and Sherpani

In 1922, readers of the *Alpine Journal* who were interested in Himalayan mountaineering learnt of 'the ready adaptability of the native porters to high mountain conditions'.[52] An intriguing prediction was that 'the full powers of these natives have yet to be fathomed'.[53] By the mid-twentieth century, two Sherpa men seemed to fulfil that prediction. One was Ang Tharkay – employed on the British Everest expeditions of 1933, 1935, and 1938 as porter, sirdar, cook, and finally as a climber. The other was Tenzing Norgay, who started as an Everest porter in 1935 and became an expedition sirdar and finally a mountaineer in his own right. The British mountaineering establishment approved of such Sherpas as exemplars of a type of body that was 'strong and hardy and does not mind the cold and is also accustomed to live at great heights'.[54]

Ang Tharkay and Tenzing Norgay are the only Sherpa interlocutors of that period who produced climbing testimonies.[55] Those narratives were published, but 'plurally mediated' through the words of non-Sherpa authors and translators.[56] Ang Tharkay explained why that was the case: 'May I say I feel a bit embarrassed telling my story? [...] an unpretentious story, told simply as I find it deep within my memory, the only journal that I was able to keep, as I do not know how to read or write'.[57] In Tenzing Norgay's case, a section of his narrative was translated from spoken Hindi into English by his 'devoted friend-assistant-interpreter Rabindranath Mitra'.[58] Tenzing narrated the remainder of his 'simple story' to journalist James Ramsay Ullman 'without benefit of translation' as his English rapidly improved during months of international exposure in the aftermath of his 1953 Everest summit.[59]

Despite the 'plurally mediated' character of such narratives, first-person texts from subaltern narrators offer a rare perspective on the labouring lives and livelihoods of Indigenous high-altitude workers from the period.[60] These mediated testimonies ensure that their protagonist's motivations and experiences are in view, compared with most of their labouring peers who might appear in photographs but still remain hidden in the archive. Mediated narratives continue to provide a foundation for later generations of Indigenous narrators, including Tenzing Norgay's grandson Tashi Tenzing, to produce texts that explicitly aimed 'to remove the veil of anonymity which they [Sherpas] have worn for most of the past one hundred years'.[61]

During the 1920s and 1930s, newly coalescing networks of Sherpas and Sherpanis who laboured as porters facilitated the entry of Ang Tharkay and Tenzing Norgay into the world of climbing expeditions. About age 20,

Ang Tharkay learnt about this novel type of employment from a village comrade who had worked on British Everest expeditions. In the village of Khunde, Nim Tharkay carried 'all of his climbing equipment' and 'strutted from house to house' with vivid tales of General Bruce and the expedition. Ang Tharkay's 'imagination ran wild, when I heard his sensational descriptions of his adventures', and he felt a great desire to follow Nim Tharkay's example to join an expedition in Darjeeling.[62] Similarly, Tenzing Norgay recollected his excitement at hearing in his village from returned migrant labourers about the 'chilingna', white men who liked to travel to mountains that reached the sky and who paid well for porters to carry loads up those heights.[63]

Like the rest of Solu Khumbu's subaltern classes, both men were accustomed to carrying heavy long-distance loads for Himalayan salt traders. Sherpa men and women used that type of itinerant employment to supplement earnings from seasonal agricultural labour and rearing animals. Ang Tharkay was inspired to leave by another chance encounter after his reunion with Nim Tharkay. They had set out to buy grain at another village where they encountered a young Sherpani, a woman who had recently returned from Darjeeling. She told them a mountaineering expedition was in preparation, looking to hire Sherpa porters for Everest, and 'sirdar Gyalgen still had a few spots on his team'.[64] After a hair-raising journey to Darjeeling, Ang Tharkay and his friends reached the Planters' Club, where they learnt that the expedition had departed. He sought local jobs starting with construction, hefting loads of stones to repair the town's Victoria Hospital. Later itinerant employment included peddling contraband cigarettes and herbal medicines between the market towns of Yatung in Tibet and Kalimpong in India.[65] Ang Tharkay obtained his first portering job on a German mountaineering expedition to Kangchenjunga in 1931. Yet, in his narrative, not until he was selected by Hugh Ruttledge as a porter for the 1933 British Everest expedition and they embarked on climbing the mountain was he 'introduced to the passion of Himalayan mountain climbing'.[66]

By the 1930s, the British had assembled a core group of climbing porters. Those porters would provide carriage labour into the mountains and easily acclimatise to the higher altitudes of Everest. Sirdars such as Gyalsen and Karma Paul were asked to scout for likely candidates, with priority given to ethnic Sherpas.[67] These porters were recruited separately from the larger corps of expeditionary labour to the snow-line – the Indigenous men and women 'coolies' hired primarily to carry loads into the Tibet Himalaya to the base of Everest. This targeted strategy aimed to hire Sherpas, especially from Solu Khumbu. Such Sherpa porters were sometimes exempt from carrying loads until the expedition reached Base Camp, although that rule was not always honoured.[68] In March 1933, Ang Tharkay was one of the porters to higher elevations. He acquitted himself well. In December 1935, Major John Morris sought him out to recruit porters for the next season. The Himalayan Club bestowed the coveted Sherpa badge of 'Tiger' which had been devised by British mountaineer Harold 'Bill' Tilman.[69] By the time of the 1936 expedition, Ang Tharkay had become a sirdar, with ten porters in his charge.[70]

The preoccupation of the British climbing establishment with the ethnic identities of Indigenous hires led to Eric Shipton's notorious rejection of Tenzing Norgay in 1933. Tenzing Norgay ruefully described how he had journeyed as an 18-year-old with twelve youths from his village over the perilous mountain terrain of eastern Nepal to seek work in Darjeeling. In the town, he discarded ragged garments for a hand-me-down set of clothing from his employer, who was a Nepali milkman from the Kathmandu valley. By the time Tenzing Norgay went before Shipton and the Himalayan Club recruiters in 1933, he had also cut off his traditional Sherpa braids. His aim was to avoid looking like a rustic. Unfortunately, those were the wrong choices. The British recruiters assumed from his clothing and hairstyle that Tenzing Norgay was a Nepali plainsman, an imposter who was masquerading as a Sherpa to get preference in hiring. 'This (appearance) was all right for Darjeeling, but bad with the expedition, for they thought I was a Nepali, and they wanted only Sherpas'.[71]

After that setback, Tenzing Norgay was forced to pursue whatever work he could find. He resumed carrying for his salt trader employer in Solu Khumbu. In 1935, he returned to India for construction labour on the repairs of the St Paul's School chapel. Soon after, the Toong Soong neighbourhood of Darjeeling buzzed with the news of another Everest expedition. This time, when Tenzing Norgay set forth to interview with the Everest recruiters, he made sure that he looked like any other Sherpa man. Ironically, this involved wearing a Western-style suit. It paid off, and he was hired. Tenzing Norgay eloquently described his happiness at that job, and why it mattered: 'The wages on the expedition were 12 annas a day, which would be raised to one rupee a day for every day above snowline; so if I went, I would make more money than I ever did before.'[72] Incredibly, Tenzing Norgay and those 1935 porters still earned the same amount as the porters had done on the 1924 expedition, twelve annas a day.[73]

In 1936, Ang Tharkay received a new responsibility, to dole out food rations to the Indigenous labourers and porters. This was an annoying and demanding task, since they were perpetually hungry and 'clamoring for food'.[74]

117

When expedition leader Eric Shipton invited Ang Tharkay to join the 1938 expedition as a cook for the British mountaineers, he stipulated that Ang Tharkay had to undertake culinary training in a British imperial household. Ang Tharkay described the elaborate preparations: 'I went to Kalimpong with my wife and child to learn my new profession. I didn't know how to cook at all, and I was afraid Mrs. Odling would find me to be a hopeless student.'[75] With Mrs Odling's guidance, Ang Tharkay learnt to use all the necessary equipment, even to bake cakes and bread in a portable oven.[76] He continued to carry the same load from Base Camp up the mountain as did every other Sherpa porter.[77] Cooking over an open flame continued for decades (Figure 6.3).

Figure 6.3 'Sherpa porter tending cooking fire', 1953. Photograph by Alfred Gregory on the 1953 Mount Everest expedition. RGS Picture Library, S0001122. Courtesy of the RGS-IBG.

Since the expeditions led by General Bruce, the Mount Everest Committee had taken considerable pains to ensure that the British mountaineers were well fed. A large selection of choice food and drink was imported. A self-described epicure, Bruce took a personal interest in the expedition's choice of cooks, an essential part of the expedition's culinary infrastructure. The poor food of the 1921 expedition was notorious. To avoid a repetition, Bruce arranged in 1922 to interview candidates as soon as he arrived at Darjeeling: 'a large selection of cooks [were] ready for us to choose [...] Having fixed on the men we thought were the most likely [cooks], my cousin and I took them out into the mountains and tested them as well as we could'.[78] Given the 'great variety of bulk stores' from British food manufacturers, it was no easy task to locate local cooks who could do justice to their preparation, especially at altitude.

The food and drink for the Indigenous labour were far from adequate, according to both Ang Tharkay and Tenzing Norgay. In theory, Bruce had resolved to follow the example of the Duke of the Abruzzi's Karakoram expedition in 1909, which prioritised 'ample porterage and the best of food – two most necessary conditions if great things are to be done well'.[79] Unlike many of his peers, General Bruce had the humanity to observe: 'I have been on expeditions in which our numerous coolies slept packed together in a tent with no more cover, and lived on the lightest food; but such exposure would take it out of the strongest and best-nourished man.'[80] In practice, Bruce acknowledged that 'porters are difficult to obtain and feed'.[81] He attempted to improve the quality of tsampa and atta flour, but it is unclear if he succeeded.[82] During the 1922 and 1924 expeditions, Bruce arranged for the porters to receive an extra allowance of fresh yak meat from the Tibetan villages on the route to Base Camp, but that did not alleviate the inadequacy of the basic porter rations.[83] Ang Tharkay's and Tenzing Norgay's writings make it clear that meat was a much coveted but rarely received dietary item for the Sherpa porters. After a particularly arduous climb, an individual British mountaineer might give them food or tea from their own supply.[84] When the British mountaineers went hunting, the Sherpas hoped for a share of the game meat.[85]

The structure of porter rations remained more or less the same between 1922 and 1953. The only substantial additions to the basic porter ration were tea and sugar. These rations were in response to dicta of nutritional science that appetites shrank at altitude and a high-calorie diet was essential.[86] Not until the 1953 Everest expedition did an expedition leader introduce a meaningful change. Colonel John Hunt declared that basic porter rations would be supplemented at altitude with the surplus from British mountaineers' stores, including stores of meat.[87] That was a belated recognition that Indigenous mountaineers such as Tenzing Norgay required sufficient calories to sustain them at the highest altitudes, in the same manner as the British climbers. By contrast, each British mountaineer received a bespoke luxury box of choice foods, reserved for use at the highest camps to tempt appetite, over and above their usual elaborate meals.[88]

Work for mountaineering expeditions meant, above all, the prospect of continued employment and stable wages for Indigenous labourers. Ang Tharkay's and Tenzing Norgay's narratives demonstrate that steady work as an expedition porter was preferred over sporadic stints of poorly paid and arduous 'coolie' work available in the absence of expedition jobs. Expedition compensation was not generous, at around twelve annas a day, but it was a steady wage.[89] The increased earnings that accompanied selection for the higher altitudes on Everest might increase the wage to one rupee a day, or even to one rupee and six annas a day.[90] Such pay increases were incentives for Sherpas to go higher up the mountain. The 'brutal and dangerous life of a climber' was worthwhile to achieve some measure of economic security.[91] Unlike most British mountaineers, Sherpas did not choose to risk their lives for enjoyment or ambition. As the Dalai Lama later noted: 'Most Tibetans have to climb far too many mountain passes to have any wish to climb higher than they must'.[92]

Another contemporary porter, Ang Tsering, explained why he became an expedition porter in the 1930s: 'We went on expeditions to earn money. No one had any ambition to climb Everest'.[93] This motivation does not preclude other sentiments or, indeed, a shift in motives. Both Ang Tharkay and Tenzing Norgay expressed excitement at the adventure aspects of an Everest expedition. For those youthful adventurers, certainly, the adventure of an expedition might have been an attraction compared with the drudgery of migrant, pastoral, agrarian, or carriage labour.

Though both Ang Tharkay and Tenzing Norgay recalled the prospect of extra pay for work above the snow-line was a major attraction for Sherpas to venture to the higher altitudes, neither of these male narrators mentions that the opportunity was limited to Sherpa men. Figure 6.4 offers a significant glimpse of a Sherpani, as female labour was integral to the embodied gendered infrastructure of mountaineering expeditions, and the biases that persist. The role of the women porters was described by Hugh Ruttledge, the 1933 Everest expedition leader: 'The female Sherpas also offer their services for the ascension. They are useful for the base camps and below the height of 6,300 metres. Many of them accompany their husbands or brothers and are as enthusiastic about mountaineering as the men'.[94] Sherpani porters faced other limitations based on their gender. Weight

Figure 6.4 'Sherpani carrying a heavy load', 1953. Photograph by Charles Wylie on the 1953 Mount Everest expedition. RGS Picture Library, S0005031. Courtesy of the RGS-IBG.

limitations on loads kept female porters below the snow-line, which ensured that they remained at lower levels of wages. Sherpani porters also were ineligible for promotion to an expedition's higher paying jobs, such as sirdar or even cook. This type of gendered 'glass ceiling' in mountaineering and expeditionary labour is no surprise. Imperial households, plantations, and the military all instituted promotion opportunities for Indigenous male workers unavailable to their female counterparts.[95] The 1933 photograph of the Darjeeling marketplace by Raymond Greene, the Everest expedition doctor, shows Sherpa women vendors (Figure 6.5). The infrastructure of mountaineering expeditions also included these women at the marketplace.

Figure 6.5 Sherpa women at the marketplace in Darjeeling, India, 1933. Photograph by Raymond Greene on the 1933 Mount Everest expedition. RGS Picture Library, S0004929. Courtesy of the RGS-IBG.

The wages for expeditionary labour were typically paid as a lump sum at the end of the climbing season. Sherpas in this period had no way to send remittances from the mountains to their families. Until expedition porters returned home and were paid wages, Sherpa families subsisted on the modest earnings of their female members around Darjeeling or other locations. Indigenous women in Darjeeling before Indian independence worked at carrying loads, vending goods, or in domestic service for colonial elites.

In 1953, an American journalist who interviewed Tenzing Norgay after his Everest summit mused on the crucial role of Sherpa women. He noted that the everyday life of a Sherpa household in Darjeeling had to be balanced against the precarity of male climbing porter livelihoods: 'Sherpa women porters are seen on the streets today, carrying baskets shaped like big inverted cones or pyramids on their backs, and until Tenzing became famous, his wife, a short, strong woman who was born in Darjeeling of Sherpa parents, was often one of them'.[96]

Mountaineering expeditions to Mount Everest since the 1920s have depended on Indigenous labour, and not only on the mountain. The superstructure of reproductive, domestic, provisioning, and wage labour contributions of

Sherpani wives, daughters, and sisters was and remains part of the infrastructure of Himalayan mountaineering. The Sherpa man is difficult to see in the archives of history. The Sherpa woman is even more hidden, but still visible from the margins. Her story is yet another Other Everest.

Notes

1 See John Berger, *Ways of Seeing* (London: Penguin Books, 1972).
2 Ibid.
3 See Ang Tharkay with Basil P. Norton, *Sherpa: The Memoir of Ang Tharkay*, trans. Corinne McKay (Seattle, WA: Mountaineers Books, 2016) [original, Ang Tharkay, *Mémoires d'un Sherpa* (Paris, Amiot-Dumont, 1954)]; Tenzing Norgay and James Ramsey Ullman, *Man of Everest: The Autobiography of Tenzing Norgay* (London: George G. Harrap, 1955).
4 Charles Granville Bruce, *Twenty Years in the Himalaya* (London: Edward Arnold, 1910), p. 48.
5 See John Baptist Lucius Noel, *Through Tibet to Everest* (London: Edward Arnold, 1927); see also Michael Spender, 'Photographic surveys in the Mount Everest region', *Geographical Journal*, 88:4 (1936), 289–300, https://doi.org/10.2307/1786332
6 Kevin Coleman, Daniel James, and Jayeeta Sharma, 'Photography and work', *Radical History Review*, 132 (October 2018), 1, https://doi.org/10.1215/01636545-6942345
7 Brian Larkin, 'The politics and poetics of infrastructure', *Annual Review of Anthropology*, 42 (2013), 327, https://doi.org/10.1146/annurev-anthro-092412-155522; see Brett Frischmann, *Infrastructure: the Social Value of Shared Resources* (New York: Oxford University Press, 2012); and C.J. Calhoun, 'Infrastructure', in C.J. Calhoun (ed.), *Dictionary of Social Sciences* (Oxford: Oxford University Press, 2002), https://doi.org/10.1093/acref/9780195123715.001.0001
8 Jayeeta Sharma, *Empire's Garden: Assam and the Making of India* (Durham, NC: Duke University Press, 2011), p. 73; also see Kaushik Ghosh, 'A market for Aboriginality: primitivism and race classification in the indentured labour market of colonial India', in Gautam Bhadra, Gyan Prakash, and Susie Tharu (eds), *Subaltern Studies*, vol. 10 (Delhi: Oxford University Press, 1999), pp. 8–48.
9 See Jayeeta Sharma, 'Producing Himalayan Darjeeling: mobile people and mountain encounters', *Himalaya*, 35:2 (2016), 87–101, https://digitalcommons.macalester.edu/himalaya/vol35/iss2/12
10 Geoff Childs, 'Trans-Himalayan migrations as processes, not events: towards a theoretical framework', in Toni Huber and Stuart Blackburn (eds), *Origins and Migrations in the Extended Eastern Himalayas* (Leiden: Brill, 2012), pp. 11–32, https://doi.org/10.1163/9789004228368_003
11 Nancy E. Levine, 'A multifaceted interdependence: Tibetan pastoralists and their animals', *Études mongoles et sibériennes, centrasiatiques et tibétaines*, 50 (2019), https://doi.org/10.4000/emscat.3822; also R.B. Ekvall, *Fields on the Hoof: Nexus of Tibetan Nomadic Pastoralism* (New York: Holt, Rinehart and Winston, 1968).
12 Peter H. Hansen, 'Y is for yak', in Antoinette Burton and Renisa Mawani (eds), *Animalia: An Anti-Imperial Bestiary for Our Times* (Durham, NC: Duke University Press, 2020), pp. 213–18, https://doi.org/10.1215/9781478012818-026

13 C.G. Bruce, *Himalayan Wanderer* (London: Alexander Maclehose, 1934), p. 8. Kenneth Mason, revised by Peter H. Hansen, 'Bruce, Charles Granville (1866–1939)', *Oxford Dictionary of National Biography* (Oxford: Oxford University Press, 2004), https://doi.org/10.1093/ref:odnb/32130

14 Bruce, *Himalayan Wanderer*, p. 25.

15 Charles Granville Bruce, 'Mount Everest', *Geographical Journal*, 57:1 (1921), 2, https://doi.org/10.2307/1781199

16 See Peter H. Hansen, *The Summits of Modern Man: Mountaineering after the Enlightenment* (Cambridge, MA: Harvard University Press, 2013).

17 George Leigh Mallory, 'The first high climb', *Geographical Journal*, 60:6 (1922), 400, https://doi.org/10.2307/1781077

18 George Leigh Mallory, 'Climbing Mount Everest is work for supermen', *New York Times* (18 March 1923), https://web.archive.org/web/20231115175618/https://www.nytimes.com/1923/03/18/archives/climbing-mount-everest-is-work-for-supermen-a-member-of-former.html

19 See Jeffrey M. Pilcher, 'Culinary infrastructure: how facilities and technologies create value and meaning around food', *Global Food History*, 2:2 (2016), 105–31, https://doi.org/10.1080/20549547.2016.1214896

20 George I. Finch 'The second high climb', *Geographical Journal*, 60:6 (1922), 422, https://doi.org/10.2307/1781078

21 L.G.C.E Pugh, 'Scientific aspects of the expedition to Mount Everest, 1953', *Geographical Journal*, 120:2 (1954), 183–92, https://doi.org/10.2307/1791534

22 Ibid., 186–8.

23 Mallory, 'The first high climb', 412.

24 Charles Granville Bruce, 'Darjeeling to the Rongbuk Glacier Base Camp', *Geographical Journal*, 60:6 (1922), 387, https://doi.org/10.2307/1781075

25 Wim van Spengen, *Tibetan Border Worlds: A Geo-Historical Analysis of Trade and Traders* (London: Kegan Paul, 2000), pp. 73–85.

26 Tina Harris, 'Yak tails, Santa Claus, and transnational trade in the Himalayas', *Tibet Journal*, 39:1 (2014), 145–55, www.jstor.org/stable/43741560

27 *China/Tibet: Mule Trains Take Aid to China*, newsreel, British Paramount/Reuters (1943), youtu.be/KhHK6Kyo_9c

28 Bruce, 'Mount Everest', 6.

29 Walt Unsworth, *Everest: The Mountaineering History* (Seattle, WA: Mountaineers, 2000), p. 65.

30 A.M. Kellas, 'A consideration of the possibility of ascending the loftier Himalaya', *Geographical Journal*, 49:1 (1917), 27, https://doi.org/10.2307/1779778

31 Ibid.

32 Bruce, 'Mount Everest', 8.

33 C.K. Howard-Bury, 'The Mount Everest Expedition', *Geographical Journal*, 59:2 (1922), 83, https://doi.org/10.2307/1781386

34 Douglas W. Freshfield, 'The Sikkim Himalaya', *Scottish Geographical Magazine*, 21:4 (1905), 173, https://doi.org/10.1080/14702540508554648

35 Ian Cameron, *Mountains of the Gods* (London: Century Press, 1987), p. 154.

36 Kellas, 'A consideration of the possibility', 27.

37 Peter H. Hansen, 'Partners: guides and Sherpas in the Alps and Himalayas, 1850s–1950s', in Jas Elsner and Joan-Pau Rubies (eds), *Voyages and Visions: Towards a Cultural History of Travel* (London: Reaktion, 1999), pp. 210–31.

38 See Brian Hodgson, *On the Kocch, Bódo and Dhimál Tribes* (Calcutta: J. Thomas, 1847); Brian Hodgson, *Miscellaneous Essays Relating to Indian Subjects* (London: Trübner & Co., 1880); see also Eden Vansittart, *Notes on Goorkhas: Being a Short Account of their Country, History, Characteristics, Class, etc* (Calcutta: Superintendent of Government Printing, 1890).

39 H.R.K Gibbs, *The Gurkha Soldier* (Calcutta: Thacker, Spink & Co Ltd, 1943), p. 40; see also C.G. Morris, *Gurkhas* (Delhi: Manager of Publications for Government of India, 1933), pp. 130–1.

40 Bruce, *Himalayan Wanderer*, p. 32.

41 Ibid., p. 78.

42 Ibid., p. 104.

43 Finch 'The second high climb', 415–20.

44 Lieutenant-Colonel Eden Vansittart and Major B.U. Nicolay, *Handbooks for the Indian Army: Gurkhas* (Calcutta: Superintendent of Government Printing, 1918), pp. 140–4.

45 Ibid., p. 106.

46 Ibid., p. 276. See also Chapter 3 by Driver and Introduction to this volume by Hansen, Gilchrist, and Westaway.

47 Ed Douglas, *Tenzing: Hero of Everest* (Washington, DC: National Geographic Society, 2003), p. 10.

48 Jayeeta Sharma, 'A space that has been laboured on: mobile lives and transcultural circulation around Darjeeling and the eastern Himalayas', *Journal of Transcultural Studies*, 7:1 (2016), 81–3, https://doi.org/10.17885/heiup.ts.23539

49 Douglas, *Tenzing*, pp. 12–13.

50 Sherry B. Ortner, *Life and Death on Mt. Everest* (Princeton, NJ: Princeton University Press, 1999), pp. 80–3.

51 Bruce, *Himalayan Wanderer*, pp. 287–9.

52 J.P. Farrar, 'The Everest Expeditions. Conclusions', *Alpine Journal*, 34 (1922), 456.

53 Ibid.

54 Howard-Bury, 'The Mount Everest Expedition', 83.

55 See Ang Tharkay, *Sherpa*; Norgay and Ullman, *Man of Everest*.

56 Julie Rak, 'Mediation, then and now: Ang Tharkay's *Sherpa* and *Memoires d'un Sherpa*', *Primerjalna Književnost*, 45:3 (2022), 125–44, https://doi.org/10.3986/pkn.v45.i3.08

57 Ang Tharkay, *Sherpa*, p. 67; see Rak, 'Mediation, then and now', for discussion of Ang Tharkay's interlocutors.

58 Norgay and Ullman, *Man of Everest*, p. x.

59 Ibid.

60 Rak, 'Mediation, then and now', 125.

61 Judy Tenzing and Tashi Tenzing, *Tenzing and the Sherpas of Everest* (New Delhi: Harper Collins, 2001), p. xxi.

62 Ang Tharkay, *Sherpa*, p. 45.

63 Norgay and Ullman, *Man of Everest*, p. 21.

64 Ibid., pp. 46, 27.

65 Ibid., p. 28.

66 Ibid., p. 51.

67 Hugh Ruttledge, 'The Mount Everest Expedition, 1933', *Alpine Journal* (1933), 222.

68 Norgay and Ullman, *Man of Everest*, p. 60. In 1935, Sherpas went on strike for a day when required to carry loads from Sikkim into Tibet instead of only after they reached base camp. Eric Shipton had to arrange to hire a mule train to relieve them of those loads before the Sherpas agreed to break their strike.

69 Ang Tharkay, *Sherpa*, p. 64.
70 Ibid.
71 Norgay and Ullman, *Man of Everest*, p. 21.
72 Ibid., p. 24.
73 Douglas, *Tenzing*, p. 15.
74 Ibid., p. 65.
75 Ang Tharkay, *Sherpa*, p. 67.
76 Ibid., p. 68.
77 Ibid., p. 170.
78 Bruce, 'Darjeeling to the Rongbuk Glacier Base Camp', 386. See also Chapter 4 by Sarah Pickman in this volume.
79 Bruce, 'Mount Everest', 5.
80 Ibid.
81 Bruce, *Twenty Years in the Himalaya*, p. 133.
82 Ibid.
83 Charles Granville Bruce, *The Assault on Mount Everest, 1922* (London: Arnold, 1923), p. 52.
84 Ang Tharkay, *Sherpa*, pp. 56–7.
85 Ibid., p. 68.
86 Pugh, 'Scientific aspects of the expedition', 188.
87 Ibid.
88 Ibid.
89 Douglas, *Tenzing*, p. 15.
90 Ang Tharkay, *Sherpa*, p. 67.
91 Ibid., p. 49.
92 Tenzing and Tenzing, *Tenzing and the Sherpas*, p. xiii.
93 Douglas, *Tenzing*, p. 15.
94 Hugh Ruttledge, *Everest 1933* (London: Hodder and Stoughton, 1936), p. 150.
95 Sharma, 'A space that has been laboured on', 72–3.
96 Christopher Rand, 'The story of the first Sherpa to climb to the top of Mt. Everest', *New Yorker* (28 May 1954), https://web.archive.org/web/20240118060343/https://www.newyorker.com/magazine/1954/06/05/tenzing-of-everest

7

Women on Everest: a summit beyond

Jenny Hall

In 1975 Japanese mountaineer Junko Tabei became the first woman to summit Everest. Her achievement received global recognition at the first United Nations International Women's Year world conference and was celebrated as a symbol of women's social progress.[1] Since 1975, over seven hundred women have followed in Junko Tabei's footsteps and played an important role in the development of high-altitude mountaineering on Everest.[2] Women represent just over 11 per cent of all summiteers since 1953, and of the first fifty women who summited Everest between 1975 and 1999, 44 per cent were Asian.[3] Yet their stories are little told in the West. White male middle-class voices dominate in published records and popular culture representations of Everest.[4] This is not surprising given the history of high-altitude mountaineering as a nation-building and colonising project.[5] As mountaineering historian Walt Unsworth observed, climbing Everest 'is the story of Man's attempts to climb a very special mountain'.[6] Despite statistical studies showing that men and women have similar odds of summiting and of meeting their demise on Everest,[7] the way high-altitude mountaineering is represented in popular culture still tells a story of masculinity and extreme achievement that stubbornly resists diversity.[8]

In *False Summits*, Julie Rak makes the compelling argument that gender matters in mountaineering. She critiques the narratives of popular mountaineering literature that characterise women's – particularly Asian women's – mountaineering achievements as marked by a watershed between serious mountaineers and those pursuing stunt ascents in the wake of the commercialisation of mountaineering. Rak argues that the authenticity as climbers and role as pioneers for the first and second women to summit Everest – Junko Tabei and Pan Duo – are questioned and denied in highly influential historical accounts by Western authors such as Walt Unsworth and John Krakauer.[9] Rak shows how white, Western, and neocolonial perceptions of mountaineering infantilise, ridicule, and misrepresent the achievements of women mountaineers. For example, Unsworth relegates Junko's status and achievement to a housewife unable to climb the mountain without being dragged up by climbing Sherpa Ang Tsering, and Pan Duo is represented as the harbinger of stunt ascents.[10]

Unsurprisingly, a comprehensive history of women's achievement on Everest has yet to be written. The pervasive inequalities arising from a paucity of representation impedes recognition and understanding of women's mountaineering achievements and experiences across continents and cultures globally.[11] In Western popular culture, the story of mountaineering embeds hypermasculinity in neocolonial perceptions that perpetuate exclusion.[12] Adventure, as a form of knowledge, is materialised through a heroic masculinised body capable of suffering, bravery, strength, risk-taking, and speed, and symbolic of what a good mountaineer should be.[13]

In adventure spaces and places, the familiar trope of mountaineering heroism is governed by a hegemonic global society that subordinates difference and reinforces dominant norms.[14] Jennifer Hargreaves shows how women have been excluded from accounts of sports and female heroism. Sporting representations form part of cultural identity and memory and thus, she argues, shape popular consciousness, meanings, and the values placed upon the sporting hero.[15] In a highly commodified adventure sports industry, hegemonic masculinity is naturalised in the mountaineering hero. Delphine Moraldo's analysis of British and European mountaineering literature demonstrated that only 6 per cent of mountain autobiographies have been written by women.[16] Furthermore, the response to historical literary representations of women has often met ambivalence, their heroism defined as lesser/different, their identity essentialised, their traits feminised as healthiness, motherliness, empathy, and caring.[17]

Despite male heroism being afforded greater social importance, there is a growing recognition and a call to diversify this singular white male legacy.[18] A new wave of academic and literary publications map strategies for transformation and social justice that invite us to consider how difference intersects across multiple axes of social distinction.[19] In tandem, representations in popular culture are beginning to change perceptions and awareness of the need to challenge the dominant discourse such as Danielle Williams' Melanin Base Camp, a charitable organisation that aims to diversify the outdoors (#diversifyoutdoors).[20]

Although this chapter cannot cover the breadth of the pioneering contributions that women from the global South have made to climbing Sagarmāthā/ Chomolungma historically, it is a starting point for recognising their achievements along with a new wave of Asian women mountaineers. For example,

Samina Baig became the first Pakistani woman to summit in 2013, and actively promotes gender equality, peace, and female empowerment, like many women before her.[21] Similarly, despite political and social turmoil, Afsaneh Hesamifard and Elham Ramezani became the first Iranian women to summit Everest in 2022.[22] For these women, Sagarmāthā/Chomolungma has become a symbol of Asian women's emancipation from social, cultural, and political constraints.

This chapter explores how women, when empowered, navigate gender inequalities through pioneering women-centred approaches in high-altitude mountaineering. Analysis of memoirs and expedition accounts of and by women from the global South offers a critical reappraisal of women's contribution to climbing on Mount Everest. This perspective aims to re-balance the androcentric assumptions of mountain adventure through appreciating how women create inclusive mountaineering spaces.

The global South: climbing Sagarmāthā/Chomolungma

Since the late 1950s Asian women have navigated intersecting inequalities in mountaineering through innovating new practices and spaces to mountaineer. Although little is known of their achievements, from the 1950s onwards, pioneers such as Junko Tabei have paved the way for the next generation of women. One of the earliest and rare accounts of Asian women climbing at high altitude is recorded in 1959 when Tenzing Norgay's two daughters Nima and Pem Pem, and niece Doma joined Claude Kogan's International Women's Expedition to Cho Oyu (8,211 metres).[23] Nima set an Asian female record reaching a height of 6,400 metres, opening the door for Asian women to participate professionally as mountaineering guides.[24] In 1961, this acted as a catalyst for women to join training courses at the Himalayan Mountaineering Institute in Darjeeling and the pioneering of several Asian all-women high-altitude expedition teams.[25] This chapter now turns to explore how prominent Asian women innovate spaces to mountaineer and achieve social justice in and beyond mountaineering.

The year 2025 will mark the fiftieth anniversary of Junko Tabei becoming the first woman and thirty-eighth person to ascend Everest. Tabei's contribution to women's high-altitude mountaineering was far reaching.[26] Junko Tabei's memoir, *Honouring High Places*, is a key feminist text, offering insight into how she navigated the gendered landscape of mountaineering, creating transformational spaces for herself and a global community of women mountaineers.[27] Junko's memoir contributes new understandings of the complex intersections arising across gender, race, and class in mountaineering adventure. Hall and Miller's analysis of the memoir identifies how Tabei transcends gendered boundaries through building a network of male allies, in the 1960s and 1970s, who actively enabled access to networks, resources, and childcare that were traditionally only open to men in Japan.[28] Tabei created women-only expeditions and climbing environments, pioneering all-women high-altitude expeditions to Annapurna III and Everest, and became the first woman to climb the 'seven summits', the highest peaks on the seven continents.[29] Her influence transcended cultural and global boundaries by developing Joshi-Tohan, the first Japanese women's mountaineering club that supported women collaborating to achieve their mountaineering goals.[30]

Parallels can be drawn with approaches in the global North, with Polish mountaineer Wanda Rutkiewicz, the first European and third woman to summit Everest in 1978, who became an active feminist, creating women-only expeditions in the early 1970s, culminating in the 1982 all-Polish women climbing expedition to K2.[31] In 1995, Junko Tabei pioneered the first Women on Everest Summit conference, and invited the thirty-two women who had then successfully climbed the mountain (although not all could attend). Tabei created a women-centred transnational exchange, which New Zealand Everest summiteer Lydia Bradey welcomed: 'I found it very interesting to know that, despite our different social backgrounds, all of us share certain ideas in terms of women's role in each society.'[32] Bradey's statement evidenced how women mountaineers had become symbols of gender equality and social justice. Tabei's conference created a new women-centred way to represent and validate women mountaineers' achievements.[33] Harnessing her status as a first ascensionist, she became a leader of gender equality and challenged the prevailing and intersecting narratives of class, race, and sexism in cultural accounts of Everest.[34] Moreover, as this chapter will show, there is a global pattern of women actively working to achieve social justice for women.

Junko Tabei's first ascent was followed eleven days later by the Tibetan-Chinese woman Pan Duo (also known as Phanthog in some older accounts). Pan Duo became the first woman to climb with minimal oxygen via the northern route on the Tibetan side of the mountain.[35] The desire to make first ascents of the highest peaks evolved in the 1950s, particularly on Mount Everest, which symbolised postcolonial power and territorial and political issues in the People's Republic of China.[36] From the late 1950s, although a religiously contested landscape, both male and female Tibetan climbers featured significantly in Chinese mountaineering.[37] Tibetan women were recruited to participate in mountaineering expeditions through a state-sponsored programme organised by the Chinese Tibetan Mountaineering Association (CTMA). Pan Duo was recruited in 1958 and later selected to be one of twelve women who participated in the Chinese 1960 Mount Everest expedition. She joined a physically hard training programme of the CTMA, which enabled women from agricultural areas to escape rural poverty.[38] However, it did not guarantee that women could transcend gender inequalities on the mountainside. During the 1960 Everest expedition, as Pan Duo later told Junko Tabei, she was frustrated at being ordered to remain below 6,400 metres on Everest because above that height was 'a man's world'.[39]

Despite such prejudice, Tibetan-Chinese mountaineers like Pan Duo used mountaineering strategically to highlight political concerns relating to national minorities, religious traditions, poverty, and gender inequalities.[40] Importantly, becoming a mountaineer offered women like Pan Duo emancipation from rural poverty and Tibetan gender norms, and she was celebrated nationally for her achievements. Pan Duo was considered by the first Chinese Everest ascensionist, Gonpo, to be one of the strongest members of the 1960 Everest team.[41]

In 1974, Pan Duo was elected the Deputy Captain on a CTMA Chinese Everest mountaineering expedition, reaching the summit with eight men on 27 May 1975.[42] The race to be first female ascensionist was unknown to Tabei, who was surprised to hear of the 200-member Chinese team. Unlike the state-organised Chinese expedition, the Japanese Women's Everest Expedition (JWEE) on the Nepali side of Everest was led and implemented by an independent, all-woman team. Moreover, the mixed-gender Chinese team were recruited and trained by the Chinese state and symbolised nationhood and political power, with such high expectations they were pushed hard and ordered to 'climb ahead of the Japanese women!'[43] However, the Chinese team retreated to recover after a tragic accident, thus the race to be first woman was lost.[44] Learning of Tabei's success did not discourage Pan Duo's party: 'it greatly inspired us to resume our attack once more'.[45]

At a meeting of the first three women to summit Everest in 1979, at the invitation of mountaineer Maurice Herzog, Tabei was struck by the contrasting motivations between the women. When Herzog asked the women to explain 'Why Everest?', Tabei responded 'For myself and for my team'; Pan Duo declared 'For the Republic of China'; and Wanda Rutkiewicz expressed that it was 'For women's liberation'.[46] Undoubtedly, the motivations expressed in 1979 reflected global, national, social, and political expectations and constraints of the time. This is evidenced by Pan Duo later expressing personal and feminist sentiments, declaring that 'Regardless of the results, my success proved that we females are as outstanding as males.'[47] Although from a very different political environment, Pan Duo wanted to achieve emancipation for women, expressing that 'I did it on behalf of my 400 million Chinese sisters to prove that we women could do the same as our male companions.'[48] Despite the social, cultural, and political differences between Japan and China, such feminist principles were shared by Junko's Japanese women's mountaineering club (Joshi-Tohan) who extolled 'Go climb the Himalayas, by all means, by women alone.'[49]

This resilience and determination were shared by Indian mountaineer Bachendri Pal, who faced significant social and familial challenges; her family were strongly opposed to her becoming a mountaineer. However, this increased her determination to pursue her ambitions and empower women to access adventure opportunities. Bachendri reflected:

> When I got a job at Tata Steel, it changed people's mindset that scaling mountains can also result in a job at such a prestigious organisation as Tata Steel. Before the job offer, I was leading a lonely struggle as people wouldn't allow their daughters to talk to me and they would mock me for sitting at home despite all the education.[50]

Following Bachendri's success on Everest she was hired by Tata Steel to lead their Adventure Foundation programme that aimed to empower women in adventure sports. Bachendri is now helping women over the age of 50 to achieve their mountaineering ambitions.[51] Political change in India driven by Prime Minister Indira Gandhi was a moving force behind the first Indian expedition to Everest in 1984, 'as she aspired to see an Indian woman scale Mount Everest for the first time'.[52] As a result, Bachendri Pal became the fifth woman to climb Everest in a mixed group that included six women. Pal went on to form an 'Indo-Nepalese Women's Mount Everest Expedition' in 1993 that set a new record by helping seven women reach the summit including the youngest woman, 19-year-old Dicky Dolma.[53] Pivotal to Bachendri's success was the endorsement of her government, who sought to decolonise high-altitude mountaineering. Bachendri was honoured as a national symbol of progress and used this status to achieve social justice, playing a significant role as a campaigner and champion of women's sports.

The 1990s proved to be a significant turning point for women's high-altitude mountaineering; 1993 was an unprecedented success with fourteen women reaching the summit. Notably, Ji Hyeon-ok led in 1993 the first South Korean all-women Everest expedition, although little is known outside of Korea about her achievements. This paucity of representation is illustrated in a 1993 report in the British *Alpine Journal* which hailed Rebecca Stephens for the first ascent by a British woman but makes only a cursory nod to first ascents by women for 'Nepal and Korea'.[54] Ji was the first female mountaineer to succeed in climbing peaks above 8,000 metres without supplemental oxygen and without Sherpa assistance.[55] These achievements demonstrate the growing equality across Asia for women to pursue their mountaineering ambitions. Such pioneering spirit was shared by both Pasang Lhamu Sherpa and Lhakpa Sherpa.

The year 2023 marked the thirtieth anniversary of Pasang Lhamu Sherpa becoming the first Nepali woman to summit Everest on 22 April 1993, though she tragically died on descent.[56] Her achievement was ground-breaking for Nepali women and earned her the status of national heroine.[57] Pasang had previously made three unsuccessful attempts to climb Everest (in 1990 and twice in 1991) and on her fourth attempt reached the summit.[58] Pasang's struggle to be recognised as a mountaineer was experienced in the context of significant social and cultural constraints.[59] Born into a family of mountaineers, she had worked as a trekking guide with her father and brothers but ran away from home to avoid an arranged marriage.[60] In the 1990s social expectations in Nepal tied women to the domestic sphere as primary caregivers, who were not perceived to have a role such as mountain guide. Canadian anthropologist Susan Frohlick cites this as 'sacrificial motherhood',[61] central to a twentieth-century discourse which 'presumes that biological mothers can be the only caregivers' to children and that children's needs must come before their needs. Women who put their needs before children were considered callous and irresponsible, and cast as bad mothers. Frohlick illustrates the impact of sacrificial motherhood through the prejudicial media coverage that followed the death of British mountaineer Alison Hargreaves on K2 in 1995. Hargreaves was called selfish for leaving two small children to climb, and being a mother was viewed as incommensurable with mountaineering.[62] In contrast, such discrimination is not experienced by male mountaineers.

Defying these social norms, Pasang moved to Kathmandu to co-found one of largest Nepali trekking companies – Thamserku. Notably, she was the first Nepali woman to ascend Mont Blanc in France, and through her connections in France she was hired as a guide to the French women's 1990 Everest Expedition.[63] The expedition ended in controversy when Pasang was prevented from summiting by the French leader, Marc Batard, because he perceived her as climbing too slowly.[64] However, the first French female summiteer, Christine Janin, suggested that Batard did not want the first ascent by a French woman to be overshadowed by a Nepali woman. Janin claimed that Batard never expected Pasang to get so far, perceiving her to be only a 'housewife and mother'[65] even though her guidance had been indispensable to the expedition.[66] Facing significant intersecting racial, ethnic, class, and gendered prejudice only hardened Pasang's resolve to realise her ambition. Pasang's lack of education did not lessen her determination to convince the Nepali government to sponsor her 1993 Everest expedition, defiantly expressing that 'we are sisters of Nepal, why can't we climb?'[67] Pasang's campaign to establish the first sponsored Nepali and Nepali Women's Everest Expedition received sponsorship from the Nepali government and global brewer San Miguel.[68] This pivotal development enabled Pasang to lead a financially independent expedition, free of the constraints associated with Western renumeration. The publicity generated by the expedition inspired and created new horizons for Nepali women mountaineers.[69]

Whilst at a local level Pasang was a political pioneer for social change, seeking social and economic justice for ethnic minorities, her story is not widely appreciated globally. The transnational processes of cultural production in mountaineering remain exclusively focused on representing the achievements of wealthy white male Western mountaineers.[70] Ethnographic studies from the 1990s by Sherry Ortner and Vincanne Adams demonstrate the ambiguity of Sherpa identity as mountaineers.[71] Both scholars identify the pervasive violence of early twentieth-century representations that exoticised climbing Sherpa as a particular kind of load-bearing mountaineer possessing extraordinary endurance, strength, and willingness to be subordinated to Western service.[72] These pervasive subjectivities circulate transnationally as forms of power and cultural exchange between Western and Asian communities.[73] Susan Frohlick's analysis of Lhakpa Sherpa's climb of Everest explores how popular culture not only excludes those who do not fit the familiar white male Western heroic trope but reduces/localises their achievements at a geographical scale. Frohlick argues that Lhakpa embodied a feminised, racialised mountaineering subject, whose story, like Pasang Lhamu's, is largely unknown outside of her country due to global forces of colonialism.[74]

Ortner notes that mountaineering was an imperialist nation-building project, codified and classified through traditions of gendered heroism established within male-only clubs and governing institutions during the late 1850s. This powerful legacy continues to dominate how mountaineering is performed through masculine norms, such as risk-taking, and exhibiting manliness.[75] This hypermasculine culture pervades through expressions of bravery, strength, speed, aggression, and suffering, which are valorised in codes of practice that classify and grade the quality of mountaineering endeavours.[76] Mountaineering routes that embody danger, difficulty, technical skill, risk, and, above all, first ascents are highly prized and validated through long-established mountaineering clubs.

This is illustrated by Elizabeth Hawley's 'wry account' of Pasang Lhamu's 1993 ascent of Everest which, as Frohlick notes, denied Pasang the title of 'mountaineer'.[77] Hawley, a renowned American expat in Nepal and 'self-appointed' Himalayan expert, relied on testimony from 'disaffected' team members in her summary for the *American Alpine Journal*: 'She [Pasang] herself was not an expert mountaineer … she did she did not know how to down-climb … she was an extremely slow climber'. Hawley took umbrage at Pasang Lhamu's posthumous honours, practically 'canonized by Nepalese political leaders and the press' with an 'endless stream' of messages and memorials.[78] The Nepali prime minister's condolences for 'Pasang Lhamu Sherpa, who proved that Nepali women are also endowed with such tremendous courage', was immediately followed by Hawley's commentary: 'A street is to be named after her in Kathmandu, a city where most streets have no names.'[79] Pasang's ascent was unworthy of wider recognition for Hawley, who graded climbing by the standards of white European masculinist traditions of mountaineering.[80]

In 2000, Lhakpa Sherpa became the first Nepali woman to summit Everest and return safely. Lhakpa climbed Everest again on 23 May 2001, this time from the North Col, becoming the first Nepali woman to conquer Everest twice and second in the world to have climbed both the north and south sides.[81] Two decades later, Lhakpa Sherpa has climbed the mountain ten times, holding the women's world record for Everest summits and standing as a symbol of both national pride and transformation for women in Nepal. Following her tenth ascent of Everest in 2022, she remarked: 'I felt like I'd changed Sherpa culture, the status of Sherpa women and Nepali women. I enjoyed being outside of my home and I wanted to share that feeling with all women.'[82] She wanted to 'show the world I can do it. I want to show women who look like me that they can do it, too.'[83]

The author of a *Guardian* profile of Lhakpa in 2019 asked her readers: 'How is it that a woman with such demonstrated accomplishments and skill is without sponsorship, and must risk nearly everything to continue to climb the Himalayan mountains?'[84] The answer rests in the embeddedness of what Frohlick called 'gendered mountaineering subjectivities'[85] and the long history of Othering in mountaineering representations. For example, the dominant masculinist traditions in mountaineering narratives speak to the heroic glories of reaching the summit first.[86] In contrast, as a middle-aged woman of colour from a poor agricultural background, Lhakpa does not cut the figure of a heroic mountaineer; she is less commodifiable.[87] Nor was she the first person, or even Nepali, to do so, a factor that localises and reduces her achievement in white Western mountaineering traditions and classification.[88]

Nepali climbing Sherpa continue to be exoticised as extraordinary high-altitude porters, with unlimited endurance and skill,[89] in a pervasive narrative that localises, feminises, and subordinates them in the service of wealthy tourists.[90] Yet, as Lhakpa points out, 'If there weren't any Sherpas, … nobody could climb Everest.'[91] For Nepali women, such inequalities are compounded by gendered mountaineering subjectivities, illustrated by the fact that, before the pandemic, out of an estimated 22,000 Nepali mountain guides only 4 per cent were women,[92] which reflects the wider gender gap in tourism.[93]

Yet women such as Pasang and Lhakpa have achieved social change and created new spaces to mountaineer. For example, Lhakpa created the first all-woman climbing team for her millennium summit attempt because she wanted 'to break the stranglehold of Nepalese male mountaineering on Everest'.[94] Lhakpa was clear that she wanted to be a sponsored athlete and not a guide, and, as Frohlick argues, she understood her own power and agency through achieving successful summits, a belief widely shared by climbing Sherpa. For example, 'Babu Chirri Sherpa … once said that he climbs Everest "for the power".'[95] Lhakpa challenges the gendered category of femininity associated with being localised, traditional, and homebound in contrast to a global subject being masculine, mobile, and contemporary.[96] Lhakpa achieved a certain degree of privilege as an occasionally sponsored athlete, and she disrupts traditional global representations of women of colour through achieving national recognition. Yet the silence, acknowledged in journalist Bergman's article, demonstrates how she is marginalised, which constrains her ambitions to be supported and recognised as a world-class mountaineer.[97]

Despite these challenges, a new generation of women mountaineers in Nepal are not only proving their status as equals but also achieving recognition on a global stage, exemplified by Shailee Basnet who successfully operates trans-nationally as an entrepreneur, public speaker, comedian, and mountaineer. Shailee participated in the 2008 First Inclusive Women Sagarmāthā Expedition (FIWSE), achieving international sponsorship from the Danish government, United Nations, and Nepali government.[98] Prior to 2007, only seven Nepali women had climbed Sagarmāthā. The FIWSE was established to draw attention to the impact of climate change on the Himalayas and promote gender

136

equality.[99] The expedition challenged not only gendered boundaries but also intersecting class and racial barriers by bringing together ten Nepali women from six diverse caste and ethnic backgrounds.[100] With the message of 'unity and diversity', all ten reached the summit, making the expedition the largest and most successful women's team to climb Sagarmāthā. Importantly, the project had a decolonising agenda to reclaim the Nepali name for the mountain – Sagarmāthā.[101] For Shailee, the FIWSE project signalled a moment of social justice, by opening the door to adventure sports for Nepali women.[102]

Shailee Basnet went on to lead the formation of the first all-women Seven Summits project to climb the highest peaks on seven continents, which they successfully completed in 2014. Underpinning the project was a social justice aim to empower women and girls in Nepal, and the Seven Summits team embarked on an educational programme, visiting hundreds of schools, giving motivational speeches, and leading hikes in the Kathmandu valley. Basnet understood that after scaling Everest, people wanted to hear the team's story; so they decided to focus on their core mission of improving educational awareness, empowering women, and protecting the environment through interacting with local women and schools.[103]

Basnet and her Seven Summits team have since established charitable projects in Nepal and the US, founding a female leadership academy that helps girls and women survivors of sex-trafficking to become trekking guides.[104] Similarly, team member Maya Sherpa has also used her influence to establish a charity to support women mountaineers access employment. Maya Sherpa commented, 'Everyone dreams of traveling the world and making a name for themselves. It all came true for me. I've been to more than 20 countries. If I hadn't taken up mountaineering, I would probably be in my village living a simple life with my kids'.[105] Both Shailee and Maya have successfully navigated transnational boundaries and used their influence to achieve social justice for women in Nepal; they have been honoured by their country and been received at the White House (US) for their work supporting women.[106]

Taking these achievements further, Dawa Yangzum Sherpa is the first Asian and Nepali woman, and one of just over one hundred women worldwide, to earn mountaineering's most elite title – International Federation of Mountain Guides Association (IFMGA) certification, joining an elite group of approximately seven thousand guides, which qualifies her to guide internationally.[107] She has achieved Lhakpa's dream and is a sponsored athlete supported by the watchmaker Rolex and sports retailer The North Face (TNF). After leaving home in Rolwaling Valley in 2003, at 13 years old, as a trekking Sherpa, she moved to Kathmandu. From childhood Dawa's dream was to stand on the top of Everest, which she achieved at the age of 21. Her ambition was to follow her brothers and become a mountain guide, and through her family mountaineering connections she worked as a trekking guide and started training in 2009 with the Nepal Climbing Association. In 2010 she enrolled on a free ten-day course at the Khumbu Climbing Center (KCC), an NGO founded by acclaimed US mountaineers Jennifer Lowe-Anker and Conrad Anker. Since the 1990s and early 2000s, the significant commodification and globalisation of high-altitude climbing has transformed opportunities for mountaineers like Dawa, creating access to global mountaineering networks, media coverage, sponsorship, training, and lucrative work contracts.[108] For example, Conrad Anker talent-spotted and hired Dawa to ascend Everest, in 2012, as part of TNF-sponsored fiftieth anniversary to celebrate the first US ascent. Dawa summited alongside American climbing star and TNF-sponsored athlete Emily Harrington.[109] This endorsement undoubtedly acted as a catalyst for Dawa's career, enabling her to transcend global barriers and operate as a professional guide in the US and internationally.[110] However, Mary Anne Potts argues that part of the reason Dawa headed overseas to guide was because opportunities in her home country were still dominated by male climbing Sherpa.[111]

Instrumental to Dawa's success has been access to global mountaineering infrastructures and institutions enabling her to realise her mountaineering ambitions along with a new generation of Nepali women. In 2014, Dawa, with Pasang Lhamu Sherpa Akita and Maya Sherpa, formed the first Nepali all-women team to summit K2, attracting global media recognition and controversy.[112] Like her predecessors, Dawa has worked to influence and support other Nepali women to develop the skills to be independent mountaineers and guides through establishing a training programme for women and girls at the Khumbu Climbing Center.[113] She believes, 'During the climb, you learn so many things for your life, like patience, struggle, focus and perseverance. I think that's very important for these young women. Climbing encourages independence and allows you to get to know your body.'[114] The programme is helping athletes such as ultrarunner Rashila Tamang to advance their skills as mountaineers and guides. 'Dawa is a strong woman. She encourages women mountaineers in Nepal where they receive little support. She has set an example, she's a true role model'.[115] Nepali women are actively shaping the future of mountaineering for their countrywomen by creating women-centred spaces to learn, train, and mountaineer. Importantly, Dawa, Shailee, and Maya exemplify the first generation of Nepali women to realise their agency and successfully cross transnational boundaries to harness global resources and be recognised by the international mountaineering community.

The struggle for women's emancipation, empowerment, recognition, representation, and equality in mountaineering is shared globally, yet the challenges and transformational work of this sisterhood are largely unseen. Early parallels have been drawn with the women-centred spaces established in the global North by pioneers such as Wanda Rutkiewicz and continue in the work of accomplished American Everest summiteer Melissa Arnot-Reid establishing the Juniper Fund, which supports Nepali women and mountain workers.[116] Globally, women have used their successes and influence to become active role models, and build women-centred infrastructures to train, network, represent, climb, and protect the communities and environment in which they work. In summary, women have created their own unique spaces and practices in high-altitude mountaineering to achieve their ambitions and recognition.

Since women began mountaineering, they have formed women-centred spaces to mitigate social and political risks associated with breaking normative cultural roles and values. Many women mountaineers in the early Asian and European expeditions participated through creating women-only spaces, which helped them to negotiate social prejudice. Representationally, women remain marginalised in a highly commodified environment built on heroic white masculinities,[117] illustrated by the fact that it took nearly fifty years for an English translation of Junko Tabei's memoir to be released in the global North. Yet Junko's determination, like those who followed, worked to change the status quo, and transform opportunities for women across Asia. Their achievements call on us to take seriously issues of inclusion in spaces of mountain adventure.

Conclusion

Gender matters in creating or denying a sense of inclusion in high-altitude mountaineering.[118] By analysing women's mountaineering experiences, this chapter has showcased some of the contributions made by Asian female pioneers in the ongoing effort to re-balance representation in mountaineering adventure. Analysing the lives of women mountaineers highlights how they navigate the multi-dimensional inequalities concerning race, gender, and class. This chapter contributes new understandings of Asian women building transnational networks of support to tackle these intersecting challenges, through innovative women-centred practices, infrastructures, and camaraderie. From the very first ascent of Everest by Junko Tabei, women-centred approaches to mountaineering have provided a vital lifeline for women to achieve their goals. Women from across the globe have used their influence – politically, culturally, and socially – to forge charitable organisations that support women-only training programmes, clubs, and expeditions. Women are representing their climbing achievements through new forms of writing, publishing, public speaking, and even comedy. Importantly, women mountaineers have used their political voice beyond mountaineering to tackle issues of poverty, sex-trafficking, environmental degradation, decolonialisation, and ethnic and religious marginalisation. Women have used mountaineering to achieve social justice and change political perceptions about women's rights and gender equality at a global level, yet knowledge and representation of these achievements remain largely unseen.

Early pioneers like Junko, Pan Duo, Bachendri, and Pasang have used mountaineering as a transformative political tool to defy social norms. For example, by achieving the status of national hero in Nepal, Pasang refused to accept intersecting racial, class, and gendered inequalities, and disrupted the gendered discourse about what women could aspire to be. Her death received global attention and is now memorialised in a National Day of Mourning in Nepal. The legacy established by Pasang and Lhakpa Sherpa has paved the way for a new generation of Nepali women mountaineers, who have embraced their agency transnationally, to be recognised as equals in a highly commodified global mountaineering industry. They have mediated their identities as world-class mountaineers and political ambassadors for social justice globally.

Climbing Sherpa are beginning to change such racial and gendered inequalities. The outstanding achievements of Nirmal Purja's extraordinary record of ascending all fourteen 8,000-metre peaks in just over six months and first winter ascent of K2 with an all-Sherpa team, along with Dawa Yangzum Sherpa leading the first all-Nepali women's team to climb K2 in 2014, demonstrate there are still mountains to climb.[119] Yet we know too little of the achievements of Asian women mountaineers and few cultural texts explore the extraordinary endeavours of a contemporary generation of Asian women mountaineers. Publications such as *Honouring High Places* and films such as Nancy Svendsen's awarding-winning documentary *Pasang: In the Shadow of Everest* are beginning to change the narrative.

However, there is much work to do. If we are to re-balance the androcentric nature of mountaineering and achieve gender equality, we need to seek new ways to represent women and their achievements in mountain adventure. I call on scholars and publishers to diversify their research and publishing to address this gap in our shared cultural heritage of mountain adventure.

Notes

1 Jenny Hall and Maggie Miller, 'Troubling the silences of adventure legacies: Junko Tabei and the intersectional politics of mountaineering', in Jenny Hall, Emma Boocock, and Zoë Avner (eds), *Gender Politics and Change in Mountaineering: Moving Mountains* (Basingstoke: Palgrave Macmillan, 2023), pp. 31–50.
2 Himalayan Database (2019), https://web.archive.org/web/20230128062615/www.himalayandatabase.com/2019%20Season%20Lists/2019%20Spring%20A14.html
3 High Adventure Expeditions, 'List of women who have climbed Mount Everest', Haexpeditions.com, https://web.archive.org/web/20240122225520/https://haexpeditions.com/advice/list-of-women-who-have-climbed-mount-everest/
4 Peter H. Hansen, *The Summits of Modern Man: Mountaineering after the Enlightenment* (Cambridge, MA: Harvard University Press, 2013).
5 Caroline Schaumann, *Peak Pursuits: The Emergence of Mountaineering in the Nineteenth Century* (New Haven, CT: Yale University Press, 2020).
6 Walt Unsworth, *Everest* (London: Grafton, 1991).
7 Raymond B Huey, Richard Salisbury, Jane-Ling Wang, and Meng Mao, 'Effects of age and gender on success and death of mountaineers on Mount Everest', *Biology Letters*, 3:5 (2007), 498–500, https://doi.org/10.1098/rsbl.2007.0317
8 Julie Rak, *False Summit: Gender in Mountaineering Nonfiction* (Montreal/Kingston: McGill-Queens University Press, 2021).
9 Rak, *False Summit*; Unsworth, *Everest*; Jon Krakauer, *Into Thin Air* (London: Macmillan, 1997).
10 Unsworth, *Everest*.
11 Martin Hall and Jenny Hall (eds), *The Mountain and the Politics of Representation* (Liverpool: Liverpool University Press, 2023).
12 Jenny Hall and Katrina Myrvang Brown, 'Creating feelings of inclusion in adventure tourism: lessons from the gendered sensory and affective politics of professional mountaineering', *Annals of Tourism Research*, 97 (2022), 103505, https://doi.org/10.1016/j.annals.2022.103505; Sherry B. Ortner, *Life and Death on Mt. Everest: Sherpas and Himalayan Mountaineering* (Princeton, NJ: Princeton University Press, 1999).
13 Paul Beedie and Simon Hudson, 'Emergence of mountain-based adventure tourism', *Annals of Tourism Research*, 30:3 (2003), 625–43, https://doi.org/10.1016/S0160-7383(03)00043-4
14 R.W. Connell, 'Growing up masculine: rethinking the significance of adolescence in the making of masculinities', *Irish Journal of Sociology*, 14:2 (2005), 11–28, https://doi.org/10.1177/079160350501400202
15 Jennifer Hargreaves, *Heroines of Sport: The Politics of Difference and Identity* (London: Routledge, 2013).
16 Delphine Moraldo, 'Gender relations in French and British mountaineering: the lens of autobiographies of female mountaineers from d'Angeville (1794–1871) to Destivelle (1960–)', *Journal of Alpine Research / Revue de géographie alpine*, 101:1 (2013), 1–12, https://doi.org/10.4000/rga.2027; Connell, 'Growing up masculine'.
17 Hargreaves, *Heroines of Sport*.
18 Rachel Hunt, 'Historical geography, climbing and mountaineering: route setting for an inclusive future', *Geography Compass*, 13:4 (2019), e12423, https://doi.org/10.1111/gec3.12423

19 Hall, Boocock, and Avner, *Gender Politics and Change in Mountaineering*.
20 Danielle Williams, 'Eight amazing Asian & Pacific Islander women climbers on Instagram', *Melanin Base Camp* (31 July 2018), https://web.archive.org/web/20240122233306/https://www.melaninbasecamp.com/trip-reports/2018/7/31/eight-amazing-asian-pacific-islander-women-climbers-to-follow-on-instagram
21 Jamal Shahid, 'First Pakistani woman scales Mount Everest', *Dawn.com* (20 May 2013), https://web.archive.org/web/20240122233506/https://www.dawn.com/news/1012447/first-pakistani-woman-scales-mount-everest
22 Fatemeh Askarieh, 'How two Iranian women reached the peak of Mount Everest', *Iran Front Page* (8 June 2022), https://web.archive.org/web/20230604012852/https://ifpnews.com/iranian-women-mount-everest/
23 Vishal Rai, 'Blazing a trail to the top', *ECS Nepal*, 149 (April 2014), https://web.archive.org/web/20230608173300/https://ecs.com.np/features/blazing-a-trail-to-the-top
24 Ibid.
25 Ibid.
26 Hall and Miller, 'Troubling the silences of adventure legacies'.
27 Rak, *False Summit*; Hall and Miller, 'Troubling the silences of adventure legacies'.
28 Hall and Miller, 'Troubling the silences of adventure legacies'.
29 Ibid.
30 Ibid.
31 See Chapter 9 by Agnieszka Irena Kaczmarek in this volume.
32 Junko Tabei and Helen Y. Rolfe, *Honouring High Places: The Mountain Life of Junko Tabei* (Calgary: Rocky Mountain Books, 2017), p. 217.
33 Hall and Miller, 'Troubling the silences of adventure legacies'.
34 Ibid.
35 Brigitte Rioux, 'Ascending marginalized stories to new heights', *Ualberta.ca* (11 May 2022), https://web.archive.org/web/20230425082535/https://www.ualberta.ca/the-quad/2022/05/ascending-marginalized-stories-to-new-heights.html; Tabei and Rolfe, *Honouring High Places*.
36 Maria Luisa Nodari, 'Why do some Tibetan women climb the highest mountains? Gendering mountaineering practices on the roof of the world', *Inner Asia*, 15:2 (2013), 293–311, www.jstor.org/stable/23614926
37 Ibid.
38 Ibid.
39 Tabei and Rolfe, *Honouring High Places*, p. 210.
40 Nodari, 'Why do some Tibetan women climb'.
41 Ibid.
42 Arnold Hou, 'China's first woman on top of the world passes away', *Womenofchina.cn* (2 April 2014), https://web.archive.org/web/20160711083845/http://www.womenofchina.cn/womenofchina/html1/people/others/17/1863-1.htm
43 Tabei and Rolfe, *Honouring High Places*, p. 211.
44 Hou, 'China's first woman on top of the world passes away'.
45 Tabei and Rolfe, *Honouring High Places*, p. 211.
46 Tabei and Rolfe, *Honouring High Places*, p. 210.
47 'Pan Duo: China´s first woman on top of world', *Cctv.com* (27 September 2009), https://web.archive.org/web/20230415081736/https://www.cctv.com/english/special/tibet/20090927/104002.shtml
48 'Pan Duo: China´s first woman on top of world'.

49 Tabei and Rolfe, *Honouring High Places*, p. 69.
50 Poorvi Gupta, 'Meet legendary mountaineer Bachendri Pal – scaling new heights leading an expedition of senior women', *Herstory* (17 March 2022), https://web. archive.org/web/20230320093403/https://yourstory.com/herstory/2022/03/legen dary-mountaineer-bachendri-pal-mount-everest-new-expedition-fitat50
51 Pragati Parihar, 'Bachendri Pal: the first Indian woman to climb the Mount Everest', *Feminism in India* (25 May 2022), https://web.archive.org/web/20240123001044/ https://feminisminindia.com/2022/05/25/bachendri-pal-the-first-indian-woman-to-climb-the-mount/
52 Gupta, 'Meet legendary mountaineer Bachendri Pal'.
53 Ibid.
54 Bill O'Connor, 'Nepal 1993', *Alpine Journal*, 98 (1993), 263–6, www.alpinejournal.org.uk/Contents/Contents_1994_files/AJ%201994%20263–266%20Nepal.pdf (accessed 20 January 2023).
55 Esther Cheung, 'Korean climber lost on Himalayas' Broad Peak', *Korea JoongAng Daily* (20 July 2021), https://web.archive.org/web/20240123162106/https://koreajoon gangdaily.joins.com/2021/07/20/national/socialAffairs/Kim-hongbin-hiker-missing/ 20210720191800344.html
56 *Thamserku Our History*, https://web.archive.org/web/20240123002333/https://www. thamserkutrekking.com/about/history
57 Andrew Buncombe, 'The glass ceiling: the incredible story of a Nepali woman who climbed Mount Everest and inspired her nation', *Independent* (3 December 2017), https://web.archive.org/web/20230121141132/https://www.independent.co.uk/ arts-entertainment/films/news/nepal-woman-first-to-climb-everest-and-inspiration-pasang-lhamu-sherpa-the-glass-ceiling-a8089001.html
58 Ibid.
59 Nancy Svendsen (dir.), *Pasang: In the Shadow of Everest* (USA: Good Docs, 2022), https:// web.archive.org/web/20230203195957/https://pasangmovie.com/about-pasang-in-the-shadow-of-everest/
60 Ibid.
61 Susan Frohlick, '"Wanting the children and wanting K2": the incommensurability of motherhood and mountaineering in Britain and North America in the late twentieth century', *Gender, Place & Culture*, 13:5 (2006), 486, https://doi.org/10.1080/09663690 600858820
62 Ibid. On Hargreaves and her son, Tom Ballard, who also died climbing, see Peter H. Hansen, 'Hargreaves, Alison Jane (1962–1995), revised with Tom Ballard (1988–2019)', *Oxford Dictionary of National Biography* (Oxford University Press, online edition, 2023), https://doi.org/10.1093/ref:odnb/58208
63 Rafia Zakaria, 'Pasang Lhamu Sherpa defied societal norms to climb Mount Everest: Nepal "needed a hero"', *Washington Post* (22 April 2018), https://web.archive.org/ web/20240123004408/https://www.washingtonpost.com/gender-identity/pasang-lhamu-sherpa-defied-societal-norms-to-climb-mount-everest-nepal-needed-a-hero/
64 Ibid.
65 Ibid.
66 Ray Olson, 'Mountains to climb', *Mountain Lodges of Nepal*, https://web.archive.org/ web/20240123005614/https://mountainlodgesofnepal.com/stories/mountains-to-climb/
67 Svendsen (dir.), *Pasang: In the Shadow of Everest*.

68 Ibid.
69 Zakaria, 'Pasang Lhamu Sherpa defied societal norms'.
70 Susan Frohlick, '"Who is Lhakpa Sherpa?" Circulating subjectivities within the global/ local terrain of Himalayan mountaineering', *Social & Cultural Geography*, 5:2 (2004), 195–212, https://doi.org/10.1080/14649360410001690213
71 Ortner, *Life and Death on Mt. Everest*; Vincanne Adams, *Tigers of the Snow and Other Virtual Sherpas: An Ethnography of Himalayan Encounters* (Princeton, NJ: Princeton University Press, 1996).
72 Ibid.
73 Adams, *Tigers of the Snow and Other Virtual Sherpas*.
74 Frohlick, 'Who is Lhakpa Sherpa?'
75 C.A. Roche, 'Women climbers 1850–1900: a challenge to male hegemony?', *Sport in History*, 33:3 (2013), 236–59, https://doi.org/10.1080/17460263.2013.826437; Ortner, *Life and Death on Mt. Everest*.
76 Hall and Brown, 'Creating feelings of inclusion in adventure tourism'.
77 Frohlick, 'Who is Lhakpa Sherpa', 198.
78 Elizabeth Hawley, 'Everest first ascent by a Nepalese woman and tragedy', *American Alpine Journal*, 36 (1994), 211–13; also Elizabeth Hawley, 'Seasonal stories for the Nepalese Himalaya 1985–2014', *Himalaya Database* (2014), 134–6, https://web.archive.org/web/20230306221059/https://www.himalayandatabase.com/downloads/EAH%20Seasonal%20Stories.pdf
79 Ibid.
80 Hall and Brown, 'Creating feelings of inclusion in adventure tourism'.
81 Grayson Schaffer, 'Lhakpa Sherpa is the most successful female Everest climber of all time', *Outside Online* (10 May 2016, updated 12 May 2022), https://web.archive.org/web/20240123142633/https://www.outsideonline.com/outdoor-adventure/climbing/most-successful-female-everest-climber-all-time-housekeeper-hartford-connecticut/
82 Swaminathan Natarajan and Patrick Jackson, 'Lhakpa Sherpa: woman climbs Everest for record tenth time', *BBC News* (12 May 2022), https://web.archive.org/web/20240123143127/https://www.bbc.com/news/world-asia-61424866
83 Megan Mayhew Bergman, 'She climbed Everest nine times and set a world record – so why doesn't she have sponsors?', *Guardian* (31 October 2019), https://web.archive.org/web/20230121143130/https://www.theguardian.com/world/2019/oct/31/mount-everest-lhakpa-sherpa-climbed-nine-times-world-record
84 Ibid.
85 Frohlick, 'Who is Lhakpa Sherpa?', 199.
86 Ortner, *Life and Death on Mt. Everest*; Hansen, *Summits of Modern Man*.
87 Hall and Hall, *The Mountain and the Politics of Representation*.
88 Hall and Brown, 'Creating feelings of inclusion in adventure tourism'.
89 Frohlick, 'Who is Lhakpa Sherpa?'
90 Maggie C. Miller and Heather Mair, 'Between space and place in mountaineering: navigating risk, death, and power', *Tourism Geographies*, 22:2 (2019), 354–69, https://doi.org/10.1080/14616688.2019.1654538
91 Bergman, 'She climbed Everest nine times and set a world record'.
92 Florence Derrick, 'How women-only treks are claiming space on Everest', *Condé Nast Traveler* (20 July 2021), https://web.archive.org/web/20230513211442/https://www.cntraveler.com/story/how-women-only-treks-are-claiming-space-on-everest

93 Donna Chambers and Tijana Rakić, 'Critical considerations on gender and tourism: an introduction', *Tourism Culture & Communication*, 18:1 (2018), 1–8, https://doi.org/10.3727/109830418X15180180585112; World Economic Forum, *Global Gender Gap Report 2022*, www.weforum.org/reports/global-gender-gap-report-2022/ (accessed 26 June 2023).

94 Frohlick, 'Who is Lhakpa Sherpa?', 201.

95 Ibid., 207.

96 Ibid.

97 Bergman, 'She climbed Everest nine times and set a world record'.

98 Rai, 'Blazing a trail to the top'.

99 'UN backs over one dozen women in largest all-female Everest expedition', *UN News* (14 February 2008), https://web.archive.org/web/20230323153014/https://news.un.org/en/story/2008/02/249062

100 Sevensummitswomen.org, https://web.archive.org/web/20240123162624/http://sevensummitswomen.org/

101 Russ Pariseau (dir.), *Unity in Diversity* (Nepal: World Food Programme, 2008), https://youtu.be/zM7RQXn7Vt0?feature=shared (accessed 20 January 2024).

102 Shaileebasnet.com, https://web.archive.org/web/20240123151851/https://www.shaileebasnet.com/

103 Ibid.

104 Seven Summits Women Team, *Sevensummitswomen.org*.

105 Rai, 'Blazing a trail to the top'.

106 Shaileebasnet.com.

107 'Dawa Yangzum Sherpa: a trail-blazing Nepali mountaineer, teaching women to climb', *Rolex.com* (May 2023), https://web.archive.org/web/20240123152559/https://newsroom.rolex.com/world-of-rolex/perpetual-planet/rolex-and-exploration/rolex-and-exploration/news-10/dawa-yangzum-sherpa-a-trail-blazing-nepali-mountaineer-teaching-women-to-climb

108 Anna Callaghan, 'Smashing guiding's glass ceiling', *Outside Online* (3 April 2018; updated 12 May 2022), https://web.archive.org/web/20240123153918/https://www.outsideonline.com/outdoor-adventure/climbing/smashing-guidings-glass-ceiling/

109 Ibid.

110 'How Dawa Yangzum Sherpa became a mountaineering icon', *Gripped Magazine* (30 May 2023), https://web.archive.org/web/20240123160624/https://gripped.com/profiles/how-dawa-yangzum-sherpa-became-a-mountaineering-icon/

111 Mary Anne Potts, 'Meet the woman taking the climbing world by storm', *Redbull.com* (11 July 2017), https://web.archive.org/web/20240123154500/https://www.redbull.com/gb-en/dawa-yangzum-sherpa-mountain-climber

112 Kelly McMillan, 'Controversy over "all-female" summit of K2 – men aided climb', *National Geographic* (7 August 2014), https://web.archive.org/web/20240123155214/https://www.nationalgeographic.com/adventure/article/140807-k2-women-nepal-pakistan-mountain-summit-controversy

113 'Dawa Yangzum Sherpa'.

114 Ibid.

115 Ibid.

116 Anna Callaghan, 'The alpinist: Melissa Arnot Reid', *Outside Online* (11 Apr 2017; updated 30 June 2021), https://web.archive.org/web/20240123154125/https://www.outsideonline.com/outdoor-adventure/climbing/alpinist-melissa-arnot-reid/

117 Hall and Hall, *Mountain and the Politics of Representation*.
118 Rak, *False Summit*. See contributions by Jayetta Sharma, Anna Saroldi, Agnieszka Irena Kaczmarek, and others to this volume.
119 Among challenges that go beyond the scope of this chapter, see Anna Callaghan and Jenny Vrentas, 'For female climbers, dangers go beyond avalanches and storms', *New York Times* (31 May 2024), https://web.archive.org/web/20240531100402/https://www.nytimes.com/2024/05/31/sports/mountaineering-sexual-harassment-abuse-nims-purja.html

8

Rewriting Irvine into Everest: Audrey Salkeld and Julie Summers

Anna Saroldi

Gender in mountaineering literature

Who do you think of when you think of an alpinist? Usually, a white man. This impression is not only because of individual biases but builds on a tradition and a literature that have made this convention seem so obvious. As aptly put by sociologist Delphine Moraldo, 'codified, thought out, and told mainly by men, excellence in mountaineering was and is understood, conceived, and perceived as male'.[1] High-altitude mountaineering has been defined in key works by scholars such as Sherry Ortner, Julie Rak, and Susan Frohlick as a 'hypermasculine landscape'.[2] The relationship is reciprocal: mountaineering has also played a key role in defining masculinity in Western culture,[3] and shaped manliness from Romantic and imperial angles.[4] In mountaineering writing, a gender- and race-based opposition often emerges that separates 'real' mountaineers from women and Sherpas.[5]

A renewed interest in redressing the balance is evident by the 2020s, not just on climbing walls or among the mountains but also in how we write about and study mountaineering. A growing body of research investigates the experiences of women climbers.[6] In this book, chapters on Junko Tabei and Wanda Rutkiewicz by Jenny Hall and Agnieszka Kaczmarek examine the history of women on Everest.[7] Rather than focusing on the adventure itself, I will look at how climbing stories are transmitted and consider their importance for the consolidation of traditions in the mountaineering community. A focus on the writing and translation dynamics of mountaineering literature reveals the transnational making of this culture and highlights figures who have previously been sidelined because of their gender or their role as translators or editors.

The approach in this account is agent-oriented: rather than focusing on texts, I centre the people who made them, uncovering and sharing their stories to portray the diverse range of people behind the narrative of one of the most famous events of mountaineering history. This approach invites us to look at mountaineering books not just for what they say but for how they have been created – by whom, in what context, and with attention to how their stories have been constructed and transmitted. Why is this important? Moraldo highlights the reliance on 'male stories' in mountaineers' publications and how rare it is that women climbers write autobiographies on their achievements.[8] Across the history of mountaineering, women are few, and written traces of their exploits even fewer.

Here, I invite you to look behind the surface and explore women's presence in the telling of other stories. On the one hand, many women writing about mountaineering were still writing of male achievements, and by doing so they contributed to traditional narratives of mountaineering history and culture. In this sport, narrative is everything because any mountaineering achievement has a key phase that takes place off the mountain: the retelling of the expedition, also known as its 'debriefing'.[9] This phase is fundamental to the overall success of the climb and its reception from the rest of the community. In their writings, most of the women writers I will discuss do not openly challenge traditional gender roles – but then neither did most elite women climbers.[10] On the other hand, I argue that the presence and authority of these women writers represents an important intervention in an environment dominated by men at the level not simply of practice but also of ideology.[11] As Rak notes, the history of Everest has a specific, unparalleled weight in setting codes and goals for the community.[12] If mountaineering has been 'an activity codified and debated above all by men',[13] then it is all the more important to highlight the presence of women in this process of codifying and debating, and the importance of their agency in shaping narrative histories of one of its most important events on a mountain with more power than any other to shape the canon of mountaineering writing: Chomolungma, or Mount Everest.

Women were already present in the fabric of many male-centred Everest histories, and this chapter asks how we did not see them when they were already there. A common strategy for approaching Everest and women's history (and indeed a very important one) is to talk about Junko Tabei and other women in Everest expeditions. What interests me here, though, is the women who have written about the early Everest expeditions and their role in recovering the figure of Sandy Irvine. While Mallory and Irvine disappeared together in 1924, the name of George Mallory acquired a symbolic and heroic status in the United Kingdom and around the world. Irvine, the climbing partner in the final push for the summit, has been recentred in the conversation only decades later. This chapter focuses on Irvine's historiography and on how women historians were key to its rewriting. From a larger perspective, my research highlights a long and underexamined history of women in the mountaineering community, not only as climbers but as writers, editors, and translators who played key roles in the transmission of its narratives in the twentieth and twenty-first centuries.

I will present the examples of Audrey Salkeld and Julie Summers, who are but two of many women in Everest's history and historiography. Of course, when talking about women writing the history of Everest, another notable person is Jan Morris, who was the official journalist with the 1953 expedition and reported news of the successful summit ascent by Edmund Hillary and Tenzing Norgay.[14] Morris and many others such as Katie Ives, Elizabeth Hawley, Helen Kilness, and Jean Crenshaw are among the figures that I plan to explore in a larger project on the role of women in the making of mountaineering literature in English. Attention to nonfiction, historiography, translation, journalism, and editing allows us to search behind the scenes of mountaineering classics. Even if the genre is male dominated at surface level of its most famous climbers, this chapter contributes to writing a different history of its making, dissemination, translation, and reception.

Sandy Irvine and the 1924 Everest expedition

Andrew 'Sandy' Comyn Irvine was born on 8 April 1902, in Birkenhead, and grew up surrounded by his family. His gift for engineering and athleticism clearly emerged during his teenage years, and he rowed with Shrewsbury's winning crew at Henley's Royal Regatta in 1919. In 1921 he moved to Oxford, attending Merton College. Immediately selected to join the university boat, he rowed at the Oxford and Cambridge boat race in 1922 and 1923. In 1923, he joined the Spitsbergen expedition organised by the university. This experience was a test in many ways. Another member of the Spitsbergen team, Noel Odell, had already been selected for the 1924 Everest team, and had the opportunity to evaluate Irvine's potential for Everest. Irvine was nominated for the Everest team shortly after. In preparation for the Everest expedition, Irvine worked assiduously to improve the design of the oxygen set used in 1922. Finally, on 29 February 1924, he sailed from England, directed towards Bombay.

Sandy Irvine was only 21 years old at the time. The expedition leader, General Bruce, called him 'our splendid "experiment"', and he went from the youngest and least experienced member of the party to among the select few in a summit push: 'He rapidly ceased to be an experiment, for we soon found that with a young body he possessed a mature judgement, combined with a very remarkable handiness and adaptability as a practical working engineer.'[15] Another military officer who led the successful 1953 Everest team, John Hunt, viewed Sandy's change of status in the team as remarkable: 'it cannot have been easy, in the social and hierarchical climate of the early 1920s and in a team under military leadership, for one so young to achieve acceptance as equal'.[16] Bruce admired Irvine's stamina and Odell described him as 'mechanically-minded',[17] particularly with the oxygen sets. It was arguably for this reason that Mallory selected him as companion for the final summit attempt. After their departure, they were last seen at 12.50 pm on 8 June 1924 by Odell, who observed two 'objects' moving on what he believed to be the summit ridge, before the clouds rolled back in.[18]

During the 1930s, four more British expeditions returned to Everest, but not much more about that last climb was discovered, apart from finding, in 1933, an ice axe on the Northeast Ridge that was recognised as Irvine's by a triple-nick mark.[19] Sandy's Spitsbergen and Everest diaries were donated to Merton College in 1962, following the death of his father.[20] Herbert Carr published *The Irvine Diaries* in 1979, pointing out that 'Mallory has three biographers [...] it is only right that Irvine should have one.'[21] Yet Carr's book is not a full-length biography but rather a transcription of his diaries, with additional chapters on the Irvine family and the Irvine Travel Fund at Oxford. Until then, there had been few developments in the reconstruction of Irvine and Mallory's last climb.

That same year, 1979, Chinese climber Wang Hong Bao told Japanese expedition member Ryoten Yashimoro Hasegawa that he had seen an 'English dead' on Everest in 1975. Wang Hong Bao died in an avalanche the following day, and no one was able to ask him for more details. That 'English' body was believed to be Irvine's. After decades of conjecture and search parties to find Mallory and Irvine, the big news came in 1999: the body of George Mallory had been found by American climber Conrad Anker in an expedition team led by Eric Simonson and sponsored by the BBC and the National Geographic. Members of the 1999 search party were convinced that Irvine would be easier to find, and only understood the reality of their discovery when they recognised a personal label on Mallory's clothing.[22] This sparked renewed interest in the 1924 expedition, and several new books (on Mallory in particular) were released.[23] By this time, however, curiosity about Irvine had been brewing and it later culminated in the discovery of Irvine's remains on Everest in 2024.[24]

Audrey Salkeld

Over the twentieth century, Everest emerged as an increasingly popular subject. The surge in Everest-related content is evident in Jill Neate's bibliography of mountaineering literature, which by 1986 encompassed over a hundred Everest titles including expedition accounts, as well as anthologies, history books, poetry, and films.[25] The profusion of material transformed Everest into a specialised domain, sustaining curiosity in the unresolved 1924 mystery. In 1986, an expedition to locate Mallory's and Irvine's bodies was led by American businessman Tom Holzel. Despite meticulous planning, the expedition faced defeat due to adverse conditions.[26] A unique participant enriched the 1986 team – Audrey Salkeld (1936–2023), who was later celebrated as one of the foremost British mountaineering historians. Her prolific contributions were admired by fellow Everest biographers and historians, with Peter Gillman and Leni Gillman acclaiming her as 'the most assiduous Everest researcher of all', and aptly summarised by Ed Douglas: 'Salkeld's contribution to mountaineering history was gargantuan'.[27]

As a young adult, Audrey (née West) Salkeld had joined the Tuesday Climbing Club in London, which introduced her to local and then to wider circles of climbers. Her involvement in the club newsletter later developed into her 'People' column for *Mountain*, an influential climbing magazine. As we can see, from the beginning she had a clear focus not just on mountaineering achievements and exploits but on the individuals behind them. Salkeld's growing influence among mountaineering researchers was warmly acknowledged in the 1970s by Jill Neate, for both personal assistance and the valuable support of her library.[28] Salkeld took immense pride in her private collection of mountaineering books and materials, even describing it as 'the most comprehensive private archive in Britain on mountaineering'.[29] Her commitment to archives extended beyond her skills as collector: she was a ground-breaking researcher, and the first to study extensively the boxes on the first Everest expeditions at the Royal Geographical Society.

Salkeld's interest in the human side of climbing and writing also led her to often take part as a researcher for collaborative projects. Even when not the primary author, her voice echoed through many accounts in her role as researcher, translator, editor, or scriptwriter. Most importantly, she did the bulk of the archival research for Walt Unsworth's *Everest: A Mountaineering History* (1981 and later editions), a fundamental historical narrative that became a point of reference. Though her assistance in collaborative works, anthologies, and compilations was acknowledged, her role was not always given the promi-nence or the credit that she deserved.[30]

Unlike other translators of mountaineering literature, she had not stud-ied languages at university, but it was her passion for mountaineering history that led her to languages. She taught herself German precisely to translate books by legends of the sport such as Reinhold Messner and Kurt Diemberger. Everest was also a recurring theme in her translations, especially in Messner's *All 14 Eight-Thousanders* (1988) and *The Crystal Horizon: Everest – The First Solo Ascent* (1989), co-translated with Jill Neate. But Salkeld's prominence extended beyond being Messner's English voice and stemmed from her wider engage-ment with the mountaineering community.

Before departing for the Himalaya in 1986, Salkeld and Holzel had pre-pared a book, *The Mystery of Mallory and Irvine*, with the plan of releasing it upon their return. This title was noteworthy for including Irvine's name. The focus shifted, acknowledging that Everest's enigma was not confined solely to Mallory. This dual spotlight could partially be explained by the expectation that they would find Irvine's body (just like the search party that later found Mallory). Salkeld had contacted the Irvine family for her research, and the book gives an overview of Sandy's biography. In the chapter 'Out of the Blue', a pun referring to Sandy's 'blue' status as elite athlete at Oxford, Salkeld and Holzel go into Sandy's experience in Spitsbergen with Odell, and his trip to Mürren in Switzerland in preparation for Everest. Salkeld and Holzel understood the importance of presenting a short introduction to Irvine's life to open a window towards his motivations and goals.

Both Unsworth's and Salkeld and Holzel's Everest books speculate on the possible dynamics of the Mallory–Irvine duo, raising the still-debated question of why Mallory chose Irvine for the final summit attempt. Unsworth's book asks if this decision could have been motivated by a romantic attachment, bringing into the conversation a discussion of Mallory's bisexuality. Unsworth concluded that, even if there had been such an attachment, 'the chances are that it was entirely innocent and not reciprocated in any way'.[31] In the revised 1999 edition of their volume, Salkeld and Holzel also touch on the question, with an empha-sis on Mallory and Irvine's shared traits (such as their competitive urge and love for adventure), and also ask if there could have been physical attraction. As in the account published under Unsworth's name, they remain cautious, stating that 'there is nothing to suggest, if that were the case, that it was more than an unacknowledged sense of kinship on Mallory's part, or that it was even recog-nised by his young companion'.[32] Despite these additions, the overall focus in

Holzel and Salkeld's book remains on Mallory, his connections, and his family's reaction to his death.

The book associated with the 1986 expedition sealed Salkeld's role as Everest expert, and she could finally see her name acknowledged as coauthor. From there, she started to gain authority and became more visible and recognised in the field. In the following years, she authored, collaboratively or individually, several significant Everest books: *Last Climb: The Legendary Everest Expeditions of George Mallory* (1999, with David Breashears), *Mystery on Everest: A Photobiography of George Mallory* (2000), *Climbing Everest: Tales of Triumph and Tragedy on the World's Highest Mountain* (2003). These works, alongside the bibliography *Climbing Mount Everest* (1993, compiled with John Boyle), have stood as crucial references for researchers and the general audience.[33]

Taking part in the 1986 expedition was also a pivotal experience from a personal standpoint. Later, she would mention her excitement upon receiving the invitation: 'I'd almost given up hope of seeing the Himalaya for myself when, at the grand old age of fifty, I was invited to join a team going to look for clues to what happened to Mallory and Irvine. ... We didn't solve the 1924 mystery that year, but Everest exceeded my expectations.'[34] By taking part in that expedition, Salkeld was breaking new ground, in a personal and more public sense. From a personal perspective, she had not dared to imagine that she would be invited to Everest, as she was a historian of mountaineering rather than an elite climber. And while it is quite common for historians to retrace the steps of the subjects of their research, hers was an unusual presence in many ways. As remembered by one of her coauthors, David Breashears: 'she was a calming influence at base camp. She didn't have the ego of a lot of climbers; she didn't crave attention.'[35]

Salkeld surely knew that she did not fit the usual description of an Everest climber, but if aware of her difference, this did not stop her: 'I would be "Expedition historian". I don't think that there ever had been such a creature before and I didn't expect there to be again (although in that I was mistaken).'[36] Salkeld could not imagine it at the time, but her role would later be imitated. The expedition that found Mallory's body in 1999 also had an expedition historian, Jochen Hemmleb. Hemmleb framed himself in quite different terms (presenting himself as a climber and highlighting the similarities between himself and Mallory), but he nonetheless joined the 1999 expedition in a role that had been pioneered by Salkeld in 1986.[37]

As we have seen, Salkeld was not simply innovative and significant for her self-awareness of her distinctive position, and for her ability to carve a novel niche within the mountaineering community. She also constituted a link between generations of experts in mountaineering literature, providing an example with her writing and personal involvement in solving the 1924 mystery.

Julie Summers

Salkeld, who is remembered as a generous mentor by Gillman and Douglas, also encouraged Julie Summers, Irvine's great-niece, to pursue her interest in 'Uncle Sandy', brother of her grandmother Evelyn. Summers had then known about him for a long time, but overall her notions remained quite vague. Her interest was reignited in the late 1990s and initially mostly took the shape of extensive reading on the topic, but, despite the comprehensive bibliography on Everest, she was not able to find much on him. Holzel and Salkeld's book made the difference: 'here was a book with some real information about Uncle Sandy and now I was determined to find out more'.[38] Summers then wrote to Salkeld, who replied and told her what she could. As Summers tells us, Salkeld 'gave me the confidence and impetus to go ahead and tackle the project. "Get inside his head, Julie, I want to know what he was thinking".'[39] Salkeld's role, therefore, is key not just for the number of titles she authored and translated on the subject but also for collaborating with and supporting other women, such as Neate and Summers, in the field of mountaineering research and literature.

After receiving Salkeld's blessing, Summers started sharing her interest with her family, scouting for letters and photographs preserved by Irvine relatives. In 1999, with the discovery of Mallory's body and the surge of attention this created, it was readily apparent that not much was actually known about the other victim of June 1924. Three books were released to mark the occasion, but none was particularly revealing when it came to Sandy. Despite expecting to find Irvine's body, the official narrative of the discovery the 1999 expedition still presented Sandy Irvine as a minor figure, completely dependent on Mallory. In *Ghosts of Everest*, Irvine is repeatedly described as 'a novice' and his relationship to Mallory is even compared to that between 'the priest and his acolyte'.[40] When the climbers find a body, they are certain that it must be Irvine's, since 'it had been an article of faith that if anyone had fallen, it would have been the inexperienced Andrew Irvine'.[41] Jake Norton, climber and member of the 1999 expedition, is even reported saying that 'it had been understood that George Mallory was infallible, he didn't fall, he couldn't fall'.[42] Summers reverts this thinking: despite the fact that Sandy was an inexperienced mountaineer by comparison with Mallory, he was, for his age, a promising and already success-ful athlete, fully invested in the ascent.

Summers' biography, *Fearless on Everest*, does not focus on how Sandy Irvine died but on how he lived. As a historian and also a relative, Summers stresses that 'the memory of his life is of far more significance and interest to me than how he died'.[43] Her contribution had the advantage of bringing a family per-spective, speaking to people who had met Sandy or knew his immediate family very well. Summers had accepted Salkeld's challenge but getting in Sandy's head proved to be harder than imagined. Not many of his personal records and items from the expedition seemed to survive. Summers was able to detect that there must have been additional material on Sandy that had not been found, as she did not believe the family story that his father, William Fergusson Irvine, had destroyed evidence relating the son's participation in the expedition.[44] Summers' intuition proved to be right: a trunk was found in a family attic, con-taining letters sent during the journey and from the camps, photographs taken along the way and developed at Base Camp, as well as notes about the oxygen apparatus. This made it possible for Summers to achieve her goal of writing from Sandy's 'fresh, valid and, most importantly, personal standpoint'.[45]

Summers' work addresses all the most heated topics of the Everest debate. What happened to Mallory and Irvine during their summit attempt and why did Mallory select Irvine as climbing partner for the final push? Summers' research and careful examination of Irvine's life and aspirations allow her to move beyond what Unsworth, Holzel, and Salkeld had suggested, by looking at the relationship in closer detail. In Summers' book, Irvine is not just a very capable young man with a gift for engineering but a promising mountaineer with his own ambitions and thirst for the summit.[46] Rather than seeing Irvine as a passive recipient of other members' choices, or an object of attraction, Summers poses him as an active subject, reversing the perspective. In this case, Summers suggests that we should indeed consider that Irvine was also inter-ested in Mallory, as he knew that any chance of being selected for a summit attempt would likely depend on him.[47] Moreover, Summers shows that Mallory had considered Irvine as a potential companion for a summit attempt from early on, and that his final decision was not an impromptu one.[48] Throughout the volume, Summers partially undoes the Mallory–Irvine couple, explaining the key role played by another member of the expedition, Odell, in recruiting Irvine, and the close bond between the two.[49] She argues that Irvine and Odell's friendship was common knowledge, mentioning that they were seen as a 'well-known firm' by some of their companions, such as Norton.[50] Getting closer to

Mallory, Summers suggests, was Irvine's conscious choice, determined both by seeing in him another role model (as Odell had been) and by a strong determination to do all he could to be considered for the summit party.

In addition, Summers' research also brought new elements to the debate on Irvine and Mallory's potential attraction. Irvine's love and sex life had not been explored much to that point, as all attention was directed towards Mallory's sexuality. One of the key points in Summers' book is that Irvine had an affair with Marjory Summers, stepmother of his close friend Dick Summers (who would eventually marry Sandy's older sister Evelyn). Sandy and Dick had met while at Shrewsbury, and Dick's father was Harry Summers, a steel magnate. In 1917, Harry Summers had married for the second time, to Marjory Agnes Standish Thomson. At the time, he was 52 and she was 19, and thus much closer in age to Harry's son Dick – and to his friend Sandy. Dick often invited him to Cornist Hall, the Summers' family home in North Wales, and it was there that Sandy and Marjory met. In 1923, Summers tells us, 'the flirtation blossomed into a none-too-discreet love affair'.[51]

Sandy and Marjory did not try to hide their relationship, as she would appear with him at Henley, in London, and would even accompany him for the first part of the journey to the Arctic expedition to Spitsbergen.[52] Eventually, this relationship led to a divorce between Marjory and Harry Summers in spring 1924. In her book, Summers wonders what this relationship meant to the young Irvine, asking 'was he in love with Marjory or did he just see the affair as an entertaining diversion?' and suggesting that 'she had, if briefly, captured his heart',[53] but ultimately stressing that Irvine knew very well that 'there could never have been a future in the relationship', as ultimately 'Marjory simply wasn't the right type of girl'.[54] The relationship with Marjory, of course, does not exclude potential reciprocal attraction to Mallory, but this had never been the core question: up to that point, the suspicion had rather been that Mallory chose Irvine because he was infatuated, with no questions asked on Irvine's perspective. But analysing Irvine's relationship with Marjory and giving it prominence allows Summers to present and reframe Sandy as an embodied person with sexual and romantic feelings: not simply the object of Mallory's fascination, but a desiring subject.

In this perspective, Irvine is finally given back responsibility for his own actions: Summers' full account of his earlier years and sport career at Shrewsbury and at Oxford is important as it helps to build, little by little, a background that suggests that Irvine was fully invested in an expedition that he framed similarly to a race, a context in which his only focus would have been victory. Up to that point, the literature on the topic presented Mallory as the active public figure, the hero who captured the audience's attention. In that kind of narrative, Irvine is more private (his shyness is recurrently emphasised), a passive figure, chosen by others, whose real purpose and thirst for victory cannot match Mallory's intensity. Hemmleb, Johnson, and Simonson's book works along such binary lines, going as far as describing Mallory as 'complex' and Irvine as 'uncomplicated'.[55] The consequence of denying Sandy agency might be partially or fully blaming Mallory for Irvine's death. However, Summers' research in Irvine's diaries and correspondence led her to reach a different conclusion. The Irvine family never blamed Mallory, and she also does not hold Mallory responsible. In her opinion, 'by the time they made their final climb in the attempt to reach the summit Sandy, ever his own man, was possessed by the same determination to climb the mountain as Mallory'.[56]

Conclusion

Sandy Irvine's story is an important example of lives that fell through the cracks in the writing of Everest history, but it is not the only one. In the case of Irvine, finding extra sources allowed Summers to give us an account of Sandy that was more intimate and personal. With other deaths on Everest, such as those of seven porters in an avalanche in 1922, it is more difficult. The lack of sources should not make us forget that many different kinds of people have made and continue to make other Everest histories on the mountain or the page.

As we have seen, women are present in the fabric of mountaineering, making history in multiple roles, and are made invisible under different lenses. Their bodies are not those of the ideal climber, and their roles in writing about mountaineering are often not valued as the authors or agents of their own accounts and expeditions. Summers and Salkeld were able to bring a different kind of contribution to the mountaineering community, not by ascending new peaks but by providing access to its stories and past, retelling them and making them more widely accessible. While the role of historian may seem secondary to the dynamics of the sport, its relevance is heightened if we consider mountaineering's dependence on its history in literary and written form. As Mitchell once wrote, 'the climb is not over till the tale is told'.[57] Audrey Salkeld and Julie Summers (and Jill Neate as well) were able to carve out specific roles for themselves in the mountaineering community, representing a trend that is still relevant today.[58]

Looking back at their history and expertise is a necessary step to start to recognise the diversity of voices who wrote and established the canon of mountaineering history. Salkeld and Summers were able to make the Everest 1924 expedition not only about Mallory, to diversify the conversation around that 'last climb' and the choices and events that led to it. Writing about the history of Everest carries weight, particularly as it tackles one of the foundational mysteries in British mountaineering. Writing about Everest has been a key move for women to gain authority within the mountaineering community, in which expertise (of both the literary and practical kinds) is otherwise conceived of as male. Despite their minority position within the space of mountaineering as a practice and culture, by writing about the most famous mountain and its most famous mystery, women sealed their authority within the debate.

Of course, there are differences in their stories, in terms of class, network, and backgrounds. Audrey Salkeld was born not into a family of mountaineers but to a secretary and a builder in south London. She did not have the financial resources to go to university, attended a secretarial college, and married an architect she met at the climbing club. She became a leading voice in Everest's history, constituting a very different example from others such as Jan Morris. Other key women writers of mountaineering, including Janet Adam Smith, for instance, were often born into families of climbers and had the wealth to study languages, travel to the Alps, and make connections to get to know other members of the climbing community. In this context, what Salkeld achieved is all the more remarkable, and noticeably different from the careers of her peers. Her connections and mountaineering trips, quite unusually, came as a consequence of her research: it was through her archival work and journalism that she established connections with the climbing community and was invited to join expeditions.

Salkeld herself wrote that 'every mountaineer is an historian',[59] yet she moved on the less travelled path of historian-mountaineer. In this sense, her trajectory is different from Summers', whose discoveries were made possible by a combination of her research skills and direct relationship to Sandy Irvine, a position similar to Mallory's biographer David Robertson, who was his son-in-law. Finally, I should add that Summers' direct link to Irvine made it easier for me to start working on her. I first learned about Summers as a student at Merton College, Sandy's own college, as she is still involved with the college archive and collaborating on new initiatives on her great-uncle – and arguably it is this coincidence that drew me to focus on Irvine in the first place.[60]

Salkeld's and Summers' research is also particularly important as previous accounts had portrayed Irvine in conventionally feminine terms, as desired, chosen, and without agency, in comparison with Mallory as the incarnation and 'apex of modernist white British masculinity'.[61] By undoing the superficial description of a (too) young climber persuaded by Mallory, Salkeld and Summers recognised Irvine's intentionality, and contributed to a fuller portrait of his experience. Exploring Sandy's life is a step towards making mountaineering narratives something else than solitary heroes' quests and guides us towards a multivocal and choral dimension that, in the past twenty years, has expanded to include Sherpas, women, and non-Western climbers.

Notes

1 Delphine Moraldo, 'Women and excellence in mountaineering from the nineteenth century to the present', *The International Journal of the History of Sport*, 37:9 (2020), 727–8.

2 Sherry B. Ortner, *Life and Death on Mt. Everest: Sherpas in Himalayan Mountaineering* (Princeton, NJ: Princeton University Press, 1999); Julie Rak, *False Summit: Gender in Mountaineering Nonfiction* (Montreal/Kingston: McGill-Queen's University Press, 2021); Susan Frohlick, 'The "hypermasculine" landscape of high-altitude mountaineering', *Michigan Feminist Studies*, 14 (1999–2000), 81–104, http://hdl.handle.net/2027/spo. ark5583.0014.004

3 See Peter H. Hansen, *The Summits of Modern Man: Mountaineering after the Enlightenment* (Cambridge, MA: Harvard University Press, 2013); Victoria Robinson, *Everyday Masculinities and Extreme Sport: Male Identity and Rock Climbing* (Oxford: Berg, 2008).

4 Paul Gilchrist, 'Heroic leadership, mountain adventure and Englishness: John Hunt and Christ Bonington compared', in C. Hart (ed.), *Heroines and Heroes: Symbolism, Embodiment, Narratives & Identity* (Kingswinford, West Midlands: Midrash, 2008), pp. 247–66; Paul Gilchrist, 'Mountains, manliness and post-war recovery: C.E. Montague's "Action"', *Sport in History*, 33:3 (2013), 282–302, https://doi.org/10.1080/17460263.2013.826436; Jonathan Westaway, '"Men who can last": mountaineering endurance, the Lake District Fell records and the campaign for Everest, 1919–1924', *Sport in History*, 33:3 (2013), 303–32, https://doi.org/10.1080/17460263.2013.826438; Jonathan Westaway, '"A banner with a strange device": Longfellow's Excelsior, Alpine idealism and the transcendent in European mountaineering', in Patrick Clastres, Delphine Debons, Jean-François Pitteloud, and Grégory Quin (eds), *Gravir les Alpes du XIXe siècle à nos jours. Pratiques, émotions, imaginaires* (Rennes: Presses Universitaires de Rennes, 2021), pp. 29–37.

5 Ortner, *Life and Death on Mount Everest*; Rak, *False Summit*.

6 Jenny Hall, Emma Boocock, and Zoe Avner (eds), *Gender Politics and Change in Mountaineering: Moving Mountains* (Basingstoke: Palgrave Macmillan, 2023); Emmanuelle Tulle, 'Rising to the gender challenge in Scotland: women's embodiment of the disposition to be mountaineers', *International Review for the Sociology of Sport*, 57:8 (2022), 1301–20, https://doi.org/10.1177/1012690222107874; Jennifer Wigglesworth, 'A feminist ethnography of indoor and outdoor sport climbing and bouldering' (PhD dissertation, Queen's University, Ontario, 2021); Adele Doran, Peter Schofield, and Tiffany Low, 'Women's mountaineering: accessing participation benefits through constraint

negotiation strategies', *Leisure Studies*, 39:5 (2020), 721–35, https://doi.org/10.1080/026 14367.2020.1763439

7   See Chapters 7 and 9 by Jenny Hall and Agnieszka Kaczmarek in this volume.

8   Moraldo, 'Women and excellence in mountaineering', 729.

9   Richard G. Mitchell, *Mountain Experience: The Psychology and Sociology of Adventure* (Chicago, IL: University of Chicago Press, 1983), p. 75.

10   Moraldo, 'Women and excellence in mountaineering'.

11   Moraldo, '"There is no manlier sport in the world": how hegemonic masculinity became constitutive of excellence in mountaineering', in *Gender Politics and Change in Mountaineering*, pp. 51–70.

12   Rak, *False Summit*, p. 180.

13   Moraldo, 'Women and excellence in mountaineering', 730.

14   Jan Morris, *Coronation Everest* (London: Faber and Faber, 2003 [orig. 1958]). In a later memoir about her transition, Morris reflected on her experience on the 1953 Everest expedition, reflecting on its gendered contradictions: 'Everest taught me new meanings of maleness, and emphasized once more my own inner dichotomy'. See Jan Morris, *Conundrum* (London: Faber and Faber, 1974), p. 83.

15   E.F. Norton, *The Fight for Everest: 1924, by Lieutenant-Colonel E.F. Norton, D.S.O., and Other Members of the Expedition* (New York: Longmans, Green & Co., 1925), p. 17.

16   John Hunt, 'The Irvine diaries: Andrew Irvine and the enigma of Everest', *Geographical Journal*, 146:2 (1980), 302, https://doi.org/10.2307/632896

17   Noel E. Odell, 'In Memoriam: Andrew Comyn Irvine, 1902–1924', *Alpine Journal* (1924), 386.

18   Norton, *The Fight for Everest*, p. 102.

19   Audrey Salkeld, *People in High Places: Approaches to Tibet* (London: Jonathan Cape, 1991), p. 19.

20   Irvine's Everest diary has now been digitised and is accessible on the Digital Bodleian website, under the shelf mark Merton College MS F.3.27(b).

21   Herbert Carr, *The Irvine Diaries: Andrew Irvine and the Enigma of Everest* (Reading: Gastons-West Col Publications, 1979), pp. 15–16. Mallory's biographies include David Randall Pye, *George Leigh Mallory: A Memoir* (London: Oxford University Press, 1927); Showell Style, *Mallory of Everest* (London: Hamish Hamilton, 1967); David Robertson, *George Mallory* (London: Faber, 1969). Robertson was Mallory's son-in-law, and he had access to Mallory's family letters, then deposited at Magdalen College, Cambridge. Apparently, Sandy's father William Fergusson Irvine manifested the intention of writing a biography of his son, but this project never saw the light of day. Julie Summers, *Fearless on Everest: The Quest for Sandy Irvine* (London: Weidenfeld & Nicolson, 2000), pp. 265–6.

22   Jochen Hemmleb, Larry A. Johnson, and Eric R. Simonson, *Ghosts of Everest: The Authorized Story of the Search for Mallory & Irvine, as told to William E. Nothdurft* (London: Macmillan, 1999), p. 121.

23   The titles published after the 1999 discovery include: Conrad Anker and David Roberts, *The Lost Explorer: Finding Mallory on Mount Everest* (New York: Simon & Schuster, 1999); David Breashears and Audrey Salkeld, *Last Climb: The Legendary Everest Expedition of George Mallory* (Washington, DC: National Geographic Society, 1999); and Hemmleb, Johnson, and Simonson, *Ghosts of Everest*.

24   See Grayson Schaffer, 'Exclusive: Remains of Andrew "Sandy" Irvine believed to have been found on Everest', *National Geographic* (11 October 2024), https://www.nationalgeo graphic.com/adventure/article/sandy-irvine-body-found-everest

25 Jill Neate, *Mountaineering Literature: A Bibliography of Material Published in English* (Milnthorpe: Cicerone, 1986), p. 292.

26 Tom Holzel and Audrey Salkeld, *The Mystery of Mallory and Irvine*, rev. ed. (London: Pimlico, 1999).

27 Peter Gillman and Leni Gillman, *The Wildest Dream: Mallory, His Life and Conflicting Passion* (London: Headline, 2000), p. xv; Ed Douglas, 'Remembering Audrey Salkeld', *Climbing* (4 November 2023), https://web.archive.org/web/20240123223443/https://www.climbing.com/people/remembering-audrey-salkeld/

28 Jill Neate, *Mountaineering and Its Literature: A Descriptive Bibliography of Selected Works Published in the English Language, 1744–1976* (Harmony Hill, Cumbria: Cicerone Press, 1978), p. 4.

29 Holzel and Salkeld, *The Mystery of Mallory and Irvine*, p. 1.

30 Librarians told Peter Hansen in the late 1980s that Salkeld's contributions to the research and writing of Unsworth's book were inadequately acknowledged (personal communication). Her contribution to Unsworth's book is also mentioned by Ed Douglas, 'Remembering Audrey Salkeld', and hinted at in Matthew Bannister, 'Last Words', *BBC Sounds*, www.bbc.co.uk/sounds/play/m001sdxf. On Unsworth's 'magnum opus', see Peter H. Hansen, 'Unsworth, Walter (Walt) (1928–2017)', in *Oxford Dictionary of National Biography* (Oxford University Press, online edition, 2021), https://doi.org/10.1093/odnb/9780198614128.013.90000380378

31 Walt Unsworth, *Everest* (London: Grafton, 1991), p. 111.

32 Holzel and Salkeld, *The Mystery of Mallory and Irvine*, p. 315.

33 Breashears and Salkeld, *Last Climb*; Audrey Salkeld, *Climbing Everest: Tales of Triumph and Tragedy on the World's Highest Mountain* (Washington, DC: National Geographic Society, 2003); Audrey Salkeld and John Boyle, *Climbing Mount Everest. The Bibliography: The Literature and History of Climbing the World's Highest Mountain* (Clevedon: Sixways, 1993).

34 Salkeld, *Climbing Everest*, p. 5.

35 Douglas, 'Remembering Audrey Salkeld'.

36 Salkeld, *Climbing Everest*, p. 5.

37 See Hemmleb, Johnson, and Simonson, *Ghosts of Everest*, pp. 22–5.

38 Summers, *Fearless on Everest*, p. 9.

39 Ibid., p. 11.

40 Hemmleb, Johnson, and Simonson, *Ghosts of Everest*, pp. 24, 45.

41 Ibid., p. 123.

42 Hemmleb, Johnson, and Simonson, *Ghosts of Everest*, p. 123.

43 Summers, *Fearless on Everest*, p. 269.

44 Ibid., p. 12.

45 Ibid., p. 14.

46 Ibid., pp. 120–1.

47 Ibid., p. 173.

48 Ibid., p. 227.

49 Ibid., pp. 51, 68, 118.

50 Ibid., p. 228.

51 Ibid., p. 69.

52 Ibid., p. 73.

53 Ibid., p. 74.

54 Ibid., p. 116.

55 Hemmleb, Johnson, and Simonson, *Ghosts of Everest*, pp. 24–5.

56 Summers, *Fearless on Everest*, p. 89; see also p. 258.

57 Mitchell, *Mountain Experience*, p. 72.

58 Michal Apollo, 'There is greater gender equality in mountaineering research', *Current Issues in Tourism*, 24:22 (2021), 3121–6, https://doi.org/10.1080/13683500.2021.1880376

59 Salkeld, *People in High Places*, p. 58.

60 This contribution was written while working for the project 'Sandy Irvine: Everest 1924–2024' at Merton College, Oxford. The online exhibition and timeline related to the project are accessible at https://web.archive.org/web/20240509162638/http://www.merton.ox.ac.uk/library-and-archives/exhibitions/sandy-irvine-1924. I thank Dr Julia Walworth and Julian Reid for their support.

61 Rak, *False Summit*, p. 154.

9

Expecting hypermasculinity from a woman mountaineer: Wanda Rutkiewicz's ascent of Everest

Agnieszka Irena Kaczmarek

Culturally perceived as a masculine activity, mountaineering has always drawn more male mountaingoers than female enthusiasts. Statistics collected in different countries showcase this long-lasting tendency.[1] Despite more and more women participating in Himalayan expeditions since the 1970s and 'the mushrooming commercialization' of Everest into the twenty-first century, the gender disparities continue.[2] The Himalayan Database, which has recorded mountaineering expeditions in the Nepalese Himalaya since 1903, reveals that between 1990 and 2018 there were 40,745 visits to areas above 5,000 metres (including so-called trekking peaks). Eighty-eight per cent of recorded visits were made by men.[3] A similar ratio of gender difference was observed in the heavily publicised queue of over 220 people waiting to reach the top of Everest on 22 May 2019, which included twenty-nine women, of whom none was a mountaineering guide.[4]

Whilst social class, income, nationality, and race are important factors influencing the experience of mountaineering and ability to travel to high-altitude mountains, gender has persisted as a key category of identity, difference, and inequality within climbing and mountaineering cultures.[5] Masculinity is undoubtedly one of the dominant discourses in mountain travel accounts.[6] The image of a man conquering a mountain features in myriad narrative accounts of climbing expeditions in what literary scholar Julie Rak calls 'the well-worn white male heroic adventure story'.[7] A similar vision of male mountain conquest may be seen on screen, as programmes of mountain film festivals offer more documentaries and films about male mountaineering escapades than those that feature female protagonists.[8] The picture does not improve when we delve beyond the visual image. The qualities of hegemonic masculinity – dominant ideas about idealised male traits and identities that can be accomplished through mountaineering practices and mountaineering culture – can be found on numerous pages of mountain travel writings. These encompass depictions of male 'strength, competitiveness, assertiveness, confidence, and independence' as well as courage, risk-taking, sexual overtones, and stamina.[9] These traits can be placed within the realm of the 'hypermasculine', defined by sociologist Kirby Schroeder as 'sets of behaviours and beliefs characterized by unusually highly developed masculine forms as defined by existing cultural values'.[10] Otherwise put, hypermasculine mindsets and actions are recognised as exaggerated and excessive expressions of masculinity, seen in opposition to manifestations of femininity, which are undervalued, hidden, and erased from view. Hence, in the context of climbing, hypermasculinity may be explained as 'the glorification of danger and risk, claiming a summit' and 'overcoming extreme physical hardships' as well as violence, extraordinary physical strength, machismo, and dominance of different kinds.[11] Furthermore, as with the concepts of femininity and masculinity, hypermasculinity may be perceived differently and can take various forms in specific cultures and historical periods.

Whilst certain personality traits have been culturally codified as masculine, women mountaineers have also exhibited them since they began to scale mountains. The assertion of will has been continuously considered to be the exemplification of hegemonic masculinity; however, this inner drive to pursue further, higher, and upwards has not been the sole domain of men in mountains. It was, for instance, characteristic of Henriette d'Angeville, who climbed Mont Blanc as early as 1838, and of numerous women who have set off on high-altitude expeditions much later.[12]

By contrast, femininity, in numerous cultures, has been traditionally linked with maternity, dependency, passiveness, emotionality, gentleness, and compassion, among other qualities. As these are not the features that prevail in mountain travel accounts regardless of an author's gender, it needs to be remembered that 'there are multiple masculinities and, equally, multiple femininities within mountaineering'.[13] Thus, no one singular woman climber represents all female mountaineers' mindsets and perceptions, and different stories are narrated by men, as well. Publications on mountain experiences, memory, and representation in the 2020s provide a more nuanced consideration of bodies, affect, and emotions in mountaineering, widening our appreciation of the multiple ways of performing gender in the mountains.[14] Nevertheless, many accounts penned by female climbers show that their authors are influenced and impacted by masculinity, which turns out to be a requirement for being recognised as a high-profile mountaineer or accepted as an expedition member.[15] Wishing to find their own place in the world of the mountains dominated by men as well as questing for male recognition, female pioneer climbers represented by Henriette d'Angeville and Elizabeth le Blond 'wanted to climb *like* men', whereas prominent late twentieth-century mountaineers such as Catherine Destivelle and Alison Hargreaves aimed 'to do *better* than them', exhibiting traits regarded as masculine.[16]

Hypermasculinity has continuously been reinforced in the history of mountaineering. Since the moment when men took off to penetrate mountain environments either for scientific purposes or simply for pleasure, women have been unwelcomed in climbing teams. If they were allowed to take part in expeditions, they were wives, sisters, or close friends of male members, who usually allowed them to trek up to base camp, which was the limit of their travels. When Irene Miller, now Beardsley, was allowed to participate in Edmund Hillary's 1961 Makalu expedition, she heard that there was a possibility to move up the mountain under a given condition: 'If you want to climb with the expedition, you ought to be willing to sleep with all the men on the team.'[17] When trying to become a member of an expedition to Afghanistan in 1969, Arlene Blum was denied participation in the climb as her presence among male climbers might turn out 'to be unpleasant high on the open ice, not only in excretory situations, but in the easy masculine companionship, which is so vital a part of the joy of an expedition'.[18] Both cases highlight men's age-old social domination as well as sexism in climbing circles, which has continuously discouraged women from practising the sport.

Climbing is inseparably linked with risk-taking and attitudes to risk, responsibility, freedom, and regulation have been shaped by the asymmetries of gender power. In the 1980s and 1990s, when not accompanied by men, some women climbing together used to hear the question 'Are you alone?', asked by men concerned about their safety. To avoid the undesired attention, some women began referring to 'Bob', an imaginary figure that was supposedly giving them some advice on what moves they were to make on the wall.[19] Language can also inscribe power onto climbing landscapes, reinforcing dominant values.[20] In the 1970s, Sibylle Hechtel intended to publish an article in an *American Alpine Journal* issue and entitle it 'Walls without Balls'. Instead, its board of directors opted for 'Keeping Abreast on El Cap', which Hechtel rebuked, finally having the article released with a note 'Untitled'.[21] And even if the expression of 'conquering a mountain' is regarded as old-fashioned nowadays, it still happens that media and climbing narratives foster the theme of hypermasculinity in the verbal portrayals and photographic representations of the sport. A prominent example is that of British mountaineer Alison Hargreaves, who in 1995 reached the summit of Everest on her own and without supplementary oxygen and was praised for her ground-breaking achievement in British newspapers. However, a few months later, when she died while descending K2, the press demonised Hargreaves, a mother of two children, airing a heavy backlash against her selfishness, mountain-driven obsession, and irresponsibility. Severe critique was not voiced against Paul Nunn and Geoff Tier, fathers and mountaineers, who also died in the Karakoram a few days before Hargreaves.[22]

As a result, it has been argued that the historically conditioned marginalisation of women has led to a lack of diversity in professional mountaineering and hypermasculinity continues to pervade its culture. Women's underrepresentation in mountaineering matters. Recent research has underlined that 'the hypermasculine nature of mountaineering' considerably contributes to fewer female climbers on the slopes and walls.[23] A 2020 report found that only 5 per cent of British-registered mountain guides were women, a significant gender imbalance. Persistent barriers to personal development and social networks mean that women climbers need strategies to overcome their weak position in the mountain guide labour market.[24] Not only this, but the report also found that *how* women climbed was impacted too, with mountain guides policing their behaviours to fit with expected norms and customs. The report concluded that 'Women leaders felt that they needed to hide displays of competitiveness and are modest about their achievements, in fear that they would be perceived to be too masculine, unfeeling, hard-faced or not feminine enough'.[25]

The history of women's climbing reveals attempts to confront and challenge male mountaineering and its hypermasculine cultures (see Chapter 7). Japanese mountaineer Junko Tabei led the way in 1975 with the first female ascent of Everest. Arlene Blum's leadership of the first American ascent of Annapurna (I) in Nepal in 1978 is widely credited as a pioneering advance in women's mountaineering that inspired further all-women expeditions to high-altitude peaks. Yet there is an important Eastern European contribution to the story of Everest to acknowledge; one that both unsettles and complicates the slow advance in contesting the ideological and experiential impacts of hypermasculinity. Polish women climbers, including, among others, Halina Krüger-Syrokomska, Anna Okopińska, Anna Czerwińska, Krystyna Palmowska, and Wanda Rutkiewicz, were prominent in the 1970s and their achievements warrant close consideration in the 'Other Everests' project of bringing less well-known histories to the fore.[26]

The 1975 Polish expedition to the Gasherbrums in the Karakoram was a historic breakthrough. In the early 1970s Wanda Rutkiewicz, a natural athlete and computer engineering graduate, was gaining a reputation for her climbing deeds. She joined a Polish-Russian expedition to the Pamirs for her first high-altitude expedition in 1970, ascending Lenin Peak (7,134 metres), and this was followed by another ascent of a 7,000-metre peak, Noshaq (7,492 metres) in the Hindu Kush in 1972. Rutkiewicz was disappointed not to be selected as a member of the 1974 Polish Himalaya expedition to Lhotse. This was a severe personal blow to her as Okopińska was invited to join the team.[27] The reason for denying Rutkiewicz membership was not her lack of climbing skills and achievements but, according to Canadian mountaineering writer Bernadette McDonald, 'her excessive ambition and drive. The assumption was that she would have wanted the summit too badly, perhaps threatening the success of some male members of the team.'[28] Rutkiewicz was hurt but things improved when Polish socialist politicians indicated they were willing to sponsor women's summit attempts to garner international prestige for Poland.[29] Rutkiewicz came up with an idea of a women's expedition purposefully planned for 1975, which had been designated by the United Nations as International Women's Year.

Despite a deep sense of the team members' grievances towards leader Rutkiewicz, the expedition made history with Okopińska and Krüger-Syrokomska reaching Gasherbrum II, historically the first ascent of an eight-thousander by an independent women's team.[30] The group formed by Rutkiewicz, Alison Chadwick-Onyszkiewicz, Janusz Onyszkiewicz, and Krzysztof Zdzitowiecki reached the top of Gasherbrum III.[31] The expedition was a great success for the women involved. Since the conception of the expedition, Rutkiewicz had believed that male support would be necessary – men could facilitate communication in Muslim-oriented Pakistan and were also more experienced in the logistical organisation of large expeditions. Recalling the Gasherbrum project, Rutkiewicz even admitted, 'The girls – what can I say – had, so far, gone on expeditions acting as decorative brooches, so I was a bit worried whether they would be able to manage this expedition organizationally'.[32] In her memoir, Anna Czerwińska confirms that the women substantially contributed to its organisation,[33] and Okopińska claims that on the slopes, both men and women blazed trails.

Nevertheless, in Okopińska's view, 'the large participation of women in the success meant that the expedition to the Gasherbrums was depreciated by the male-dominated environment' in Poland.[34] Abroad, their successes on the Gasherbrums resulted in Karl Herrligkoffer's decisions to invite Rutkiewicz to his Nanga Parbat project and, later, to the German–French Mount Everest expedition of 1978.[35] Rutkiewicz was able to demonstrate her resilience, efficiency, and resourcefulness and so paved the way to high-altitude mountains for other female climbers, a route which had been blocked by male selfishness and jealousy that male climbing achievements would be eclipsed by women.[36] Details of these attitudes have emerged in English-language accounts of the 'golden age' of Polish climbing. In *Freedom Climbers* (2012), Bernadette McDonald highlights Rutkiewicz's problems with 'her not-so-friendly teammates' and 'male chauvinism' experienced on the slopes of Everest during the 1978 expedition led by Herrligkoffer.[37]

The self-depicted 'ascending machine' Wanda Rutkiewicz made history when she became the first Polish high-altitude mountaineer and the first European woman to scale Mount Everest.[38] However, as noted in her autobiographical work *Na jednej linie* [*On One Rope*] (1986) cowritten with Ewa Matuszewska, as well as other sources, the achievement was recollected by Rutkiewicz with bittersweet memories. Bearing in mind the continuous arguments that happened between the Polish climber and selected male mountaineers, Rutkiewicz confided in Herrligkoffer that she was unable to summit Everest 'with enemies', adding that the hostility she faced could drain 'the will to fight for the top, and maybe even the will to fight for life'.[39] In a 1987 interview conducted by Matuszewska, Rutkiewicz admitted: 'I've never been an equal partner in men's teams. Most brutally, I was made to feel that I am only a woman during the Mount Everest expedition'.[40]

There seem to be a few reasons why there were increased expectations of hypermasculine features from Rutkiewicz during the German–French Mount Everest expedition of 1978. Rutkiewicz joined the team with a reputation for being a high achiever. Perceived as a climber who could aspire to be a successful summiteer, she was treated as a competitor from the very beginning when in Namche Bazaar she met with Hubert Hillmaier, Sepp Mack, and Georg Ritter, regarded by the Polish climber as the mountaineers with the greatest chance of reaching the top during the expedition. After a lukewarm reception, according to Rutkiewicz's account, Hillmaier welcomed her to the group with a statement that 'Women at expeditions are nonsense',[41] which was to diminish her foregoing achievements, claiming openly she was not capable of climbing Everest from the start.

Weakened and enfeebled, Rutkiewicz went to Nepal after asking medical personnel to forget about her health checkup, which had revealed she had been suffering from anaemia. Although equipped with hematopoietic medications and supplements, she was 'feeling much worse than the male colleagues' during the first days at Everest Base Camp.[42] The drugs did not help much, and she was suffering from lack of acclimatisation and appetite, which she was trying to hide by forcing herself to eat as well as by helping to secure the safe passage through the Khumbu Icefall, a dangerous crossing on the way to the summit. In the middle of September, she also fell ill with bronchitis. The symptoms of her medical conditions and her physical weakness may not have escaped the other team members' notice, since on the way from Camp Three to the South Col, when finally acclimatised and fit to scale, she called to mind the words expressed by Sepp Mack, digesting their meaning: 'Don't even think of climbing Everest! You won't make it. Don't even try, because you'll pose a threat to the others.'[43] The reader does not know when exactly the words were stated and in what situation, a recurrent feature of Rutkiewicz's style of writing.[44] In effect, when perusing the autobiographical text, there are not many in-text, quoted word-for-word slurs ascribed to a given climber, and her verbal responses are usually missing. Given that, the chapter on the Everest ascent in *On One Rope* reveals her inner thoughts and undeniably reconstructs an atmosphere of great hostility and tension, which Rutkiewicz must have sensed during the expedition. Feeling hurt by the male team members attacking her verbally, she must have fought back, too, as among her recollections published by Reinisch, one reads: 'The problems might not have escalated so bitterly if I had had it in me to be sweeter or more diplomatic, but I'm no good at pretending and I won't sink to feminine wiles'.[45] The observation made by leader Herrligkoffer clearly illustrates the conflicts: 'On 6 September there was a falling out the like of which I had never experienced on any of my many expeditions. The root of the trouble was the perceived discrepancy between Wanda's emancipated and self-confident attitude and her inability to share tasks and burdens equally with her male colleagues. The discussion deteriorated into the most naked display of unfeeling masculine selfishness that I have ever witnessed.'[46]

According to Kurt Diemberger, at that time a participant of the French expedition that collaborated with Herrligkoffer's, the primary reason for the negative attitude towards the Polish female climber was her appointment as second deputy leader. In one of the conversations on the slopes of Everest, he once asked Rutkiewicz a rhetorical question: 'Which of our colleagues, even myself, would be delighted to be led by a woman in the mountains?', which went against conventions of mountain leadership at that time.[47] According to Rutkiewicz, besides the appointed position and her role as a cameraperson, another reason for their antagonism might be the way she behaved, bringing initiative, building relationships based on partnership, and joining discussions on which track to follow, which, in her view, was regarded as an abuse of power by the second deputy leader and 'a threat to their masculinity'.[48] Instead, she was expected 'to keep quiet' and give 'a little warmth and flirtatiousness, as well as some subordination. That would justify the fact that I'm not a man', she claimed in her autobiography.[49]

Her appointment as a cameraperson also gave rise to a few quarrels in which the expectations of hypermasculinity for the female climber fuelled the inner-group conflict. As Rutkiewicz claims in *On One Rope*, during one of the gatherings at Base Camp, the male team members of the expedition argued that the female climbers aspiring to summit Everest were obliged to carry up 'the same amount of load as men', equal to at least seventy-five kilograms.[50] Interestingly enough, in his account published in *The Himalayan Journal*, leader Herrligkoffer, with whom Rutkiewicz appeared to have a good rapport, reports that it was his decision and the minimum requirement for all would-be summiteers regardless of their gender identity was 'at least 25 kg from the Base Camp to Camp Two', which helped the mountaineers to be better acclimatised, speeded up the load transport, and made the Sherpas welcome positively the climbers' extra work.[51] Nevertheless, responsible for documenting the expedition, Rutkiewicz needed to argue for treating the three-kilogram filming equipment as part of the obligatory load. Although the other team members agreed to go with her solution, film-related issues remained the area of acrimonious disputes. When walking up to Camp Three on 29 September, Rutkiewicz left the tent with a view to capturing the expedition on film, which she failed to do due to the severe weather conditions, as noted in *On One Rope*. The following day Sigi Hupfauer scolded her for failing to shoot film footage: 'You are nothing, such a little, not great, Wanda!', words regarded by Rutkiewicz as an attempt to disparage her climbing competencies.[52]

Although known for her physical strength, Rutkiewicz knew she was not able to compete with male climbers. Once she asked rhetorically: 'How can women's climbing ever win proper respect when every woman on every mixed expedition is continuously judged by the men, and driven to prove herself better than them?'[53] In an interview when questioned if it was meaningful for her that she was better than men, she denied and voiced her opinion that the best female climber would always be worse than her male counterpart.[54] On the slopes of Everest, in a conversation with Diemberger, when trying to grasp the reasons for the resurfacing antagonisms, Rutkiewicz admitted she did not perceive herself as a competitor to Sigi Hupfauer, Hubert Hillmaier, Sepp Mack, or Georg Ritter, who belonged to the group of the strongest mountaineers on the expedition team.[55]

A woman of driving ambition, Rutkiewicz was determined to achieve her goal of standing on top of Everest. During the expedition, she consciously took risks, including descending the mountain on her own and climbing through the constantly moving Khumbu Icefall without a safety rope. 'If I'm playing with death, I clearly need it. I love nature and risk; they are part of my life' are the motto words that open the 2017 biography by Anna Kamińska, summing up her life concisely.[56] Combative as well as resilient, Rutkiewicz was resolved to compete for her chance for the summit attempt. When a favourable weather window finally emerged, Herrligkoffer decided to make the whole team work for the two strongest mountaineers, Hans Engl and Sepp Mack, so as to facilitate their climb to the summit, a decision Rutkiewicz did not like. When it was finally agreed that the other members of the team could summit Everest as well, on the eve of her ascent, Rutkiewicz admitted: 'The action I am awaiting removes fear. I like this feeling. I think that's one of the reasons why I climb'; and in another fragment we read, 'in the middle of danger I feel safe'. Rutkiewicz did not share her mother's faith; it was not prayers that gave her inner strength and determination but climbing logic.[57] When asked in an interview about her motivation for mountain-going, she enumerated five main reasons, firstly mentioning mountains themselves, and secondly, climbing 'for sport … I am interested in records',[58] which was in line with her liking for challenges. In a 1990 documentary, when recollecting her attitude to nature during the 1978 Everest expedition, Rutkiewicz asserts that at that time a mountain was her opponent and she aimed to conquer a mountain, being 'a bit like a real conqueror'. Her way of thinking later changed, she adds, as Rutkiewicz sought to cement her international reputation by becoming the first woman to scale the world's fourteen highest peaks. Stopped by her death on Kangchenjunga in 1992, her unfinished project, 'The Caravan to Dreams', was aimed at climbing the eight-thousanders missing from her list of successful ascents in a little more than a year.[59]

In the mountains, Rutkiewicz was regarded as a tough personality: tough on herself and on her climbing companions. During the Everest expedition, when expecting hypermasculinity from herself, she sometimes expected a similar attitude from German Marianne Walter, another female climber on the team, who went to the Himalaya with her spouse Josef Walter. When together on the slopes of Everest, Rutkiewicz criticised Marianne Walter – who later became the first female summiteer of Shishapangma (8,027 metres) in 1983, with no supplemental oxygen – for a lack of self-reliance, regarding her as a woman completely dependent on her husband in the mountains. She had initially perceived Walter as a would-be partner in a potential women's summit team and later expressed disappointment at her passivity and lack of independence.[60] 'Marianne did not take any initiative on this expedition; she did not take part in the discussions. Her husband did it for her. And that's probably why her presence was indulgently tolerated by her colleagues. Since she was unable to move on her own even on a glacier, she was no match for them.'[61] Rutkiewicz even admits that she laughed at Josef Walter's thoughtfulness towards his wife, although she felt jealous of the attentiveness Marianne Walter received from her spouse. To put it another way, being independent, full of initiative and plans for the ascent, and involved in the discussion, Rutkiewicz perceived herself as Walter's flipside, thereby identifying with the features regarded as the embodiment of masculinity, not femininity. Interestingly, Rutkiewicz asserts that without the verbal aggression vented by her male colleagues, she would be capable of exhibiting the features traditionally ascribed to women – that is, being compassionate and attentive to others' needs and suffering,[62] visibly the feelings that Josef Walter expressed on Everest towards his wife.

In a 2007 documentary, climber and film director Anna T. Pietraszek quotes Rutkiewicz, who shared with her that during the expedition she was told by her German colleagues that her role was to help Marianne Walter, their 'representative', reach the summit.[63] When it was known that the German female climber would not be able to get to the top, Rutkiewicz, as Pietraszek recounts, refused to bring Walter back to Base Camp, because that would also mean no chance for her to attempt to scale the world's highest mountain, a sequence of events that are missing in *On One Rope*, her autobiographical account.

With high expectations of hypermasculinity from the male team members as well as her own expectations of other people and herself, Rutkiewicz also showed the feminine side of her nature when ascending Everest. She found the courage to talk about fear when male climbers rather avoided the subject. In one of the accounts recalling her earliest impressions of the climb, she spoke of being apprehensive of losing balance due to the narrowness of the ridge from the lower South Summit to the main peak of Everest.[64] Filming her colleagues scaling the perilous Hillary Step, she was 'behind alone', which made her feel uncomfortable: 'Loneliness at 8,000 meters is rather unpleasant', she remarked, summarising the climb.[65] In a narrative written for Herrligkoffer, Rutkiewicz also made a comment on fear and loneliness, being most fearful that she 'might fall down and no one would even notice that' and recollecting that 'Somewhere inside it feels strange to be so completely alone at this height'.[66] *On One Rope* contains more passages in which Rutkiewicz admits being fearful for different reasons. She reveals that she was apprehensive of the route from Camp Two to Camp One, afraid of walking close to the Nuptse wall, which Rutkiewicz found more difficult than ascending the summit of Everest.[67] Loaded up on antibiotics, she was afraid of ascending to the next camp and of a relapse of her bronchitis. In 1989, when asked if she frequently felt fear, she replied: 'Of course, I'm scared almost all the time. I'm simply a coward',[68] a mind-boggling response given after ascending K2 in 1986 and before launching the project 'The Caravan to Dreams'.

A greatly controversial figure, arousing extreme emotions and opinions, Wanda Rutkiewicz was a peculiar combination of femininity and masculinity, who followed hypermasculine patterns of behaviour, being tough on herself and those in her surroundings. She spoke against the binary division into feminine and masculine features, arguing for women's ability to be precise, decisive, and consistent, as well as for their capacity to think logically by putting aside then-negatively perceived emotionality.[69] On the Everest expedition of 1978, she refused to take the stereotypical position designated for a woman and was courageous in expressing her fear of being alone on the steep edge of Everest's summit. She demanded independence in action and discussion from her female colleague on the team and exhibited the same personality traits when arguing with male mountaineers.

Thus, in the interviews, articles, and her story about the 1978 climb, it is possible to perceive Rutkiewicz as a woman who embodied a mountaineer with a hybrid identity, not binary; who did different genders, not just one, when on the move.[70] Those men climbers on the slopes of Everest were extremely annoyed by her attitude;[71] those in Poland who were jealous of her successful ascent saw red; and Andrzej Zawada, a legendary Polish expedition leader, who at that time was trying to receive a permit to climb Everest in winter, commented on Rutkiewicz's achievement: 'I said not to send a bloody woman to Everest'.[72] Contrary to these men's expectations, the Polish climber summited Everest. Rutkiewicz confronted the pervasive sexist attitudes of her colleagues and compatriots in blazing a trail to the top of Everest and earned an international reputation as a resilient though stubborn and egotistical climber who remained also stubbornly in the mould of the hypermasculine mountaineer as she broke gender barriers in high-altitude mountaineering.

Notes

1 Michal Apollo, Joanna Mostowska, Agnieszka Legut, Kamil Maciuk, and Dallen J. Timothy, 'Gender differences in competitive adventure sports tourism', *Journal of Outdoor Recreation and Tourism*, 42 (2023), 1–5, https://doi.org/10.1016/j.jort.2022.100604; Emmanuelle Tulle, 'Rising to the gender challenge in Scotland: women's embodiment of the disposition to be mountaineers', *International Review for the Sociology of Sport*, 57:8 (2022), 1301–20, https://doi.org/10.1177/10126902221078748

2 Maurice Isserman and Stewart Weaver, *Fallen Giants: A History of Himalayan Mountaineering from the Age of Empire to the Age of Extremes* (New Haven, CT: Yale University Press, 2008), p. 423; Jon Krakauer, *Into Thin Air* (New York: Anchor Books, 1999), p. 26.

3 Michal Apollo, 'There is greater gender equality in mountaineering research', *Current Issues in Tourism*, 24:22 (2021), 3121–6, https://doi.org/10.1080/13683500.2021.1880376

4 Jenny Hall and Katrina Myrvang Brown, 'Creating feelings of inclusion in adventure tourism: lessons from the gendered sensory and affective politics of professional mountaineering', *Annals of Tourism Research*, 97 (2022), 1–12, https://doi.org/10.1016/j.annals.2022.103505

5 Dúnlaith Bird, 'Travel writing and gender', in Carl Thompson (ed.), *The Routledge Companion to Travel Writing* (Abingdon: Routledge, 2016), p. 35.

6 Delphine Moraldo, 'Gender relations in French and British mountaineering: the lens of autobiographies of female mountaineers, from d'Angeville (1794–1871) to Destivelle (1960–)', *Journal of Alpine Research/Revue de géographie alpine*, 101:1 (2013), 1–12, https://doi.org/10.4000/rga.2027

7 Julie Rak, *False Summit: Gender in Mountaineering Nonfiction* (Montreal/Kingston: McGill-Queen's University Press, 2021), p. 6.

8 Susan Frohlick, '"That playfulness of white masculinity": mediating masculinities and adventure at mountain film festivals', *Tourist Studies*, 5:2 (2005), 175–93, https://doi.org/10.1177/1468797605066926; Peter L. Bayers, 'Yosemite climbing films and the regeneration of white masculinity in the American West', in Susan Bernardin (ed.), *The Routledge Companion to Gender and the American West* (London: Routledge, 2022), pp. 70–82.

9 Vikki Krane quoted in Gill Pomfret and Adele Doran, 'Gender and mountaineering tourism', in Ghazali Musa, James Higham, and Anna Thompson-Carr (eds), *Mountaineering Tourism* (Abingdon: Routledge, 2015), pp. 138–55; Susan Frohlick, 'The "hypermasculine" landscape of high-altitude mountaineering', *Michigan Feminist Studies: Masculinities*, 14 (1999–2000), https://hdl.handle.net/2027/spo.ark5583.0014.004. Many thanks to Emerson Case and Rebecca Penrose from California State University Bakersfield for their help in accessing sources.

10 Kirby Schroeder, 'Hypermasculinity', in Michael Kimmel and Amy Aronson (eds), *Men and Masculinities: A Social, Cultural, and Historical Encyclopedia* (Santa Barbara, CA: ABC-CLIO, 2004), pp. 417–18.

11 Tulle, 'Rising to the gender challenge', 1303.

12 Peter H. Hansen, *The Summits of Modern Man: Mountaineering after the Enlightenment* (Cambridge, MA: Harvard University Press, 2013), p. 173.

13 Pomfret and Doran, 'Gender and mountaineering tourism', p. 143; Frohlick, 'The "hypermasculine" landscape'.

14 Martin Hall and Jenny Hall (eds), *The Mountain and the Politics of Representation* (Liverpool: Liverpool University Press, 2023).

15 Delphine Moraldo, 'Women and excellence in mountaineering from the nineteenth century to the present', *The International Journal of the History of Sport*, 37:9 (2020), 727–47, https://doi.org/10.1080/09523367.2020.1819250

16 Moraldo, 'Gender relations', 7.

17 Arlene Blum, *Annapurna: A Woman's Place* (San Francisco, CA: Sierra Club Books, 1998), p. xviii.

18 A letter from the expedition leader quoted in Blum, *Annapurna*, p. xvii.

19 David Mazel (ed.), *Mountaineering Women: Stories by Early Climbers* (College Station, TX: Texas A&M University Press, 1994), pp. 13–14.

20 Joseph Taylor, 'Mapping adventure: a historical geography of Yosemite Valley climbing landscapes', *Journal of Historical Geography*, 32:1 (2006), 190–219, https://doi.org/10.1016/j.jhg.2004.09.002

21 Sibylle C. Hechtel, 'Walls without balls', in Mikel Vause (ed.), *Rock and Roses: Mountaineering Essays by Some of the World's Best Women Climbers of the 20th Century* (La Crescenta, CA: Mountain N'Air Books, 1999), p. 45.

22 Paul Gilchrist, '"Motherhood, ambition and risk": mediating the sporting hero/ine in Conservative Britain', *Media, Culture and Society*, 29:3 (2007), 395–414, https://doi.org/10.1177/0163443707076182

23 Tulle, 'Rising to the gender challenge', 1302.

24 Jenny Hall and Adele Doran, *Researching Women in Mountaineering, United Kingdom, 2020* (York: St John University, 2020), p. 2.

25 Ibid., p. 5.

26 Wanda Rutkiewicz (ed.), *Zdobycie Gasherbrumów* [*Ascending Gasherbrums*] (Warsaw: Sport i Turystyka, 1979).

27 Rutkiewicz in a 1989 TV interview '100 pytań do … Wanda Rutkiewicz' [100 questions to… Wanda Rutkiewicz], hosted by Anna Grzeszczuk-Gałązka, www.youtube.com/watch?v=yT3GoHIhvLM (accessed 26 August 2023).

28 Bernadette McDonald, *Freedom Climbers* (Sheffield: Vertebrate Publishing, 2012), p. 40.

29 Anna Czerwińska, interviewed by Łukasz Długowski, 'Lodowi wojownicy boją się kobiet' [Ice warriors are afraid of women], *Wyborcza* (28 March 2014), https://wyborcza.pl/magazyn/7,124059,15706696,lodowi-wojownicy-boja-sie-kobiet.html (accessed 19 October 2023).

30 Janusz Kurczab, *Polskie Himalaje: Część 4. Panie w górach* [*The Polish Himalaya: Part 4. Ladies in the Mountains*] (Warsaw: Agora, 2008), p. 47.

31 Ibid., p. 46.

32 Wanda Rutkiewicz and Barbara Rusowicz, *Wszystko o Wandzie Rutkiewicz; wywiad rzeka Barbary Rusowicz* [*Everything about Wanda Rutkiewicz: An Extended Interview by Barbara Rusowicz*] (Toruń: Comer & Ekolog, 1992), p. 79.

33 Anna Czerwińska and Roman Gołędowski, *GórFanka: Moje ABC w skale i lodzie* [*GórFanka: My ABC in Rock and Ice*] (Warsaw: Annapurna, 2013), pp. 203–4.

34 Okopińska quoted in Olga Przybyłowicz, '45 lat temu Polki Krueger-Syrokomska [*sic*] i Okopińska jako pierwsze na świecie weszły na ośmiotysięcznik' [45 years ago, Polish women Krueger-Syrokomska and Okopińska were the first in the world to climb an eight-thousander] (12 August 2020). https://web.archive.org/web/20200925202045/https://sport.interia.pl/aktualnosci-sportowe/news-45-lat-temu-polki-krueger-syrokomska-i-okopinska-jako-pierws,nId,4665417

35 Wanda Rutkiewicz and Ewa Matuszewska, *Na jednej linie* [*On One Rope*] (Warsaw: Iskry, 2010), p. 145.

36 Leszek Cichy in a documentary, Marek Kłosowicz (dir.), *Karawana marzeń* [*Caravan of Dreams*] (Poland: TVN, 2007), www.youtube.com/watch?v=rjh4fZgvAJs (accessed 12 August 2023).

37 McDonald, *Freedom Climbers*, pp. 64–5.

38 Interestingly, as noticed by Julie Rak, George Mallory in *Climbing Everest* speaks of his body as 'machine', too. Julie Rak, 'Because it is there? Mount Everest, masculinity, and the body of George Mallory', *The International Journal of the History of Sport*, 38:2–3 (2021), 159, https://doi.org/10.1080/09523367.2020.1854738

39 Rutkiewicz and Matuszewska, *Na jednej linie* [*On One Rope*], p. 178. All the quoted fragments derived from Polish-language sources have been translated by the author of the chapter. Many thanks to Marta Knight with whom the translations were consulted.

40 Wanda Rutkiewicz, interviewed by Ewa Matuszewska, 'Kobiecość kontrolowana' [Controlled femininity], *Uroda*, May 1987, in Ewa Matuszewska (ed.), *Uciec jak najwyżej: nie dokończone życie Wandy Rutkiewicz* [*Escaping to the Highest: The Unfinished Life of Wanda Rutkiewicz*] (Warsaw: Iskry, 2007), pp. 142–8.

41 Rutkiewicz and Matuszewska, *Na jednej linie* [*On One Rope*], p. 166.

42 Ibid., p. 170.

43 Ibid., p. 193.

44 Agnieszka Kaczmarek, 'Wanda Rutkiewicz and Ewa Matuszewska: deliberations on the auto/biographical *Na jednej linie* [*On One Rope*]', in Hall and Hall, *The Mountain and the Politics of Representation*, pp. 169–88.

45 Rutkiewicz quoted in Gertrude Reinisch, *Wanda Rutkiewicz: A Caravan of Dreams*, translated by Dieter Pevsner (Ross-on-Wye: Carreg, 2000), p. 44.

46 Karl M. Herrligkoffer quoted in Reinisch, *Wanda Rutkiewicz*, p. 44.

47 K. Diemberger quoted in Rutkiewicz and Matuszewska, *Na jednej linie* [*On One Rope*], p. 179.

48 Rutkiewicz quoted in Reinisch, *Wanda Rutkiewicz*, p. 44.

49 Rutkiewicz and Matuszewska, *Na jednej linie* [*On One Rope*], pp. 166, 176.

50 Ibid., p. 172.

51 Karl M. Herrligkoffer, 'The German-French Mount Everest expedition, 1978', *The Himalayan Journal*, 36 (1980), https://web.archive.org/web/20231231090518/www.himalayanclub.org/hj/36/7/the-german-french-mount-everest-expedition-1978/

52 Rutkiewicz and Matuszewska, *Na jednej linie* [*On One Rope*], p. 177.

53 Rutkiewicz quoted in Reinisch, *Wanda Rutkiewicz*, p. 44.

54 Rutkiewicz in '100 pytań do … Wanda Rutkiewicz' [100 questions to … Wanda Rutkiewicz].

55 Rutkiewicz and Matuszewska, *Na jednej linie* [*On One Rope*], p. 178.

56 Anna Kamińska, *Wanda. Opowieść o sile życia i śmierci* [*Wanda: A Story about the Power of Life and Death*] (Kraków: Wydawnictwo Literackie, 2017).

57 Rutkiewicz and Matuszewska, *Na jednej linie* [*On One Rope*], pp. 195–6; Rutkiewicz and Rusowicz, *Wszystko o Wandzie Rutkiewicz* [*Everything about Wanda Rutkiewicz*], pp. 20–1.

58 Rutkiewicz in '100 pytań do … Wanda Rutkiewicz' [100 questions to … Wanda Rutkiewicz].

59 Rutkiewicz in *Ślady na śniegu* [*Footprints in the Snow*], a documentary directed by Waldemar Heflich (Interpress Film, 1990).

60 Rutkiewicz and Matuszewska, *Na jednej linie* [*On One Rope*], p. 171.

61 Ibid., p. 181.

62 Ibid., p. 182.

63 Anna T. Pietraszek in Marek Kłosowicz (dir.), *Karawana marzeń* [*Caravan of Dreams*].
64 'Polish woman atop Mt. Everest', *Polish Facts on File*, 390 (1978), 11. Many thanks to Monika Nyczanka for finding this article.
65 Ibid.
66 Wanda Rutkiewicz, 'Mój Everest' [My Everest], originally in Karl M. Herrligkoffer (ed.), *Mount Everest ohne Sauerstoff. Mit authentischen Berichten von 9 Gipfelbezwingern* [*Mount Everest Without Oxygen. With Authentic Reports from 9 Summiteers*] (Bamberg: Bayerische Verlagsanstalt, 1979), pp. 70–82. Translated from German by Józef Nyka and published in *Biblioteczka Historyczna Głosu Seniora* [*The Historical Little Library of the Senior's Voice*], 12 (2003), https://web.archive.org/web/20211203222402/http://nyka.home.pl/bibl_his/pl_ascii/12.htm
67 Rutkiewicz and Matuszewska, *Na jednej linie* [*On One Rope*], pp. 173–4.
68 Rutkiewicz in '100 pytań do … Wanda Rutkiewicz' [100 questions to… Wanda Rutkiewicz].
69 Rutkiewicz in Matuszewska, 'Kobiecość kontrolowana' [Controlled femininity], p. 144.
70 Dúnlaith Bird, 'Gender', in Charles Forsdick, Zoë Kinsley, and Kathryn Walchester (eds), *Keywords for Travel Writing Studies: A Critical Glossary* (London: Anthem Press, 2019), pp. 99–101.
71 Sylwia Dec-Pustelnik, 'Kobieta na dachu świata, czyli kilka słów o historii oraz wizerunku medialnym Wandy Rutkiewicz' [A woman on the world's roof, or a few words about the history and media image of Wanda Rutkiewicz], *Dziennikarstwo i Media*, 10 (2018), 31, https://doi.org/10.19195/2082-8322.10.2
72 Kamińska, *Wanda*, p. 267.

10

The 'Slovenian' Everest 1979: a small nation and the highest mountain in the world

Peter Mikša and Matija Zorn

On 13 May 1979, Andrej Štremfelj and Nejc Zaplotnik became the first Slovenes and Yugoslavs to climb the highest mountain in the world.[1] 'Tone, we are at the summit! We are sitting by the Chinese tripod, and we don't know what to do now', they radioed to Base Camp on that historic occasion.[2] They reached the summit after forty-five days, climbing in extreme cold and strong winds up the demanding West Ridge Direct, the most difficult route on Everest at that time. The ascent represented the success of the twenty-five-member Yugoslav team, twenty-one of whom were Slovenes. The vast majority of Yugoslav ascents before the breakup of Yugoslavia were made by Slovenian mountaineers. Yugoslavian ascents solidified the reputation of Slovenian mountaineers during the 1975 ascent of the South Face of Makalu (8,481 metres), the world's fifth-highest mountain, and the 1979 ascent of Everest's West Ridge. The Everest ascent in 1979 was considered the crown jewel of Yugoslav alpinism and established Slovenian alpinism as among the best in the world for almost half a century.[3]

The wealth of experience from earlier Himalayan expeditions was critical to this success on Everest and other peaks. Few sports in Slovenia have a richer history than alpinism, which has been a strong unifying element for Slovenian nationalism since the beginning of the twentieth century.[4] This remained the case after the creation of Yugoslavia in 1918 and its transformation into a socialist federal republic after 1945. The wave of ascents of 8,000-metre peaks in the 1950s bypassed both Slovenia and Yugoslavia. The first Yugoslav Himalayan expedition took place in 1960 after almost all the highest Himalayan peaks had been climbed. The 1960s and 1970s were the most fruitful period for multimember Yugoslav expeditions, which left their mark on mountains around the world. In addition to expeditions to Makalu, Gasherbrum I, and Everest, climbers from Yugoslavia also went to the Caucasus, Pamirs, Hindu Kush, Andes, and so on.[5] By the 1990s, Slovenian climbers applied new approaches and methods to high-level alpinism and realised the vision of Aleš Kunaver (1935–84), who led several Himalayan expeditions and said of Slovenia's belated start climbing in the Himalayas: 'If you want to catch a missed train, you have to outrun it.'[6]

This chapter focuses on the 1979 Everest expedition, and the environment in which Yugoslav and Slovenian mountaineering operated. The Yugoslav political system at the time was fairly closed but never turned down large expeditions to mountains in foreign countries. On the contrary, climbers received generous support so that Yugoslavia could show the world during the Cold War that it was autonomous and successful with its own political and ideological activity.[7] Slovenes became the leading force in Yugoslav alpinism, and Yugoslav expeditions made up for the late start with extraordinary successes on difficult and unclimbed routes on Everest, other 8,000-metre peaks ('eight-thousanders'), as well as lower mountains.

Slovenia's path to the Himalayas

The Yugoslav expedition to the West Ridge of Everest was typical of the large national climbing teams of the 1970s, with experienced alpinists and strong logistical support from Sherpas that allowed for multiple attempts by a roped team to reach the top. In the 1980s, the large teams were replaced by smaller so-called pocket expeditions, whose members climbed in alpine style. These decades also saw climbers of other nationalities summit all fourteen eight-thousanders, with some ascents made solo or without supplemental oxygen. Slovenes developed an intense focus on summiting eight-thousanders and making first ascents in the world's highest mountains.

A series of expeditions to the Himalayas all bore the official name of 'Yugoslav Alpinist Himalayan Expedition' (JAHO in the Slovene acronym). These expeditions took place in the 1960s and 1970s (see Table 10.1).[8] The first expedition, JAHO I, was organised in 1960 to Trisul (7,120 metres). Today, it is hard to imagine the kind of problems faced by both the expedition organisers and participants, even before departure. Materials were unknown: tents started with the selection of the fabric; shoes with the leather-tanning techniques; backpacks with straps and buckles. For down clothing, everything had to be selected, from fabric to down insulation to the appropriate tailoring. Where local factories could not produce something, dedicated supporters stepped in and taught themselves how to do it. During the preparations, the participants showed exceptional amateur enthusiasm. Only the most unusual materials for

179

Table 10.1   Yugoslav Alpinist Himalayan Expeditions, 1960–79

Organisation	Year	Mountain
JAHO I	1960	Ascents of Trisul (7,120 metres)
JAHO II	1965	Attempts on Kangbachen (7,902 metres)[i]
JAHO III	1969	Ascents of Annapurna II (7,937 metres) and Annapurna IV (7,540 metres)
JAHO IV	1972	Attempts on South Face of Makalu (8,463 metres)[ii]
JAHO V	1974	Ascents of Kangbachen (7,902 metres)
JAHO VI	1975	First ascent of South Face of Makalu (8,463 metres)
PZS	1977	First ascent of southwestern ridge of Gasherbrum I (8,068 metres)[iii]
JAHO VII	1979	First ascent of West Ridge Direct on Everest (8,848 metres)

Notes:
[i] Cf. Tone Škarja, *Slovenians in Himalaya* (Ljubljana: Planinska zveza Slovenije, 2004).
[ii] Peter Mikša and Urban Golob, *Zgodovina slovenskega alpinizma* [*History of Slovenian Alpinism*] (Ljubljana: Friko, 2013), p. 87.
[iii] Peter Mikša, 'The mountains that wrote them: Slovenians climbing and writing about eight-thousand-metre peaks', *Slavica Tergestina*, 28:1 (2022), 158.

that time had to be imported from abroad: nylon fabric and thread, zippers, gas cartridges, and some climbing gear.

The unclimbed South Face of Makalu (8,463 metres) became the goal for the ascent of an eight-thousander in the 1970s. In 1972, the summit attempt on Makalu by JAHO IV was unsuccessful, but expedition members crossed the 8,000-metre mark and demonstrated that an ascent via the South Face was possible.[9] In 1975, Yugoslav alpinists returned in JAHO VI, and seven members of the expedition succeeded in this first ascent along the South Face route to the summit of Makalu. Marjan Manfreda reached the summit without the use of supplemental oxygen, a world altitude record at the time.[10] This was the first eight-thousander in Slovenian and Yugoslav alpinism and an impetus for subsequent exploits.

In 1977, an expedition of Slovenian alpinists went to Gasherbrum I in the Karakoram. This expedition was organised not by the official JAHO but by two sections of Slovene alpine clubs affiliated with the Alpine Association of Slovenia (PZS in the Slovene abbreviation), an umbrella mountaineering organisation. The PZS lacked previous experience in planning Himalayan expeditions; nevertheless, the success of this expedition surpassed the efforts of organisations with longer traditions and significantly greater resources at their disposal. The 1977 climbers included the barely 20-year-old Andrej Štremfelj and Nejc Zaplotnik. Their first ascent of the southwestern ridge of Gasherbrum I (8,068 metres) represented the second Slovenian ascent of an eight-thousander.[11] An idea that seemed utopian, brash, and even impossible to Slovenian climbers a few years earlier – ascents of eight-thousanders by a new route – became reality on the first attempt. The climax of Yugoslav Himalayanism followed in the form of 'Everest 79'.

Towards the top of the world: Everest Expedition 79

Even today, a more tempting goal is difficult to imagine for any alpinist than standing on the very top of the world. How important this goal was from a state, national, and personal point of view in the 1970s can be easily understood from the reports, as well as from the recording taken when Andrej Štremfelj and Nejc Zaplotnik in 1979 became the first Yugoslavs/Slovenes to stand on top of Everest. 'Victory, victory!' echoed from the radio stations at Base Camp, where they were following the ascent. JAHO VII, under the leadership of Tone Škarja, succeeded in making this first ascent on what was quickly dubbed the Yugoslav route. This represented a new milestone and in fact the pinnacle of Yugoslav and Slovenian alpinism.[12]

The route along the West Ridge of Everest was only the fifth route to the highest mountain in the world, and even today, with around twenty routes to the summit, it is among the most difficult. Its extended length, exposure to the wind, and great technical difficulty, especially on the upper part of the mountain, make it extremely challenging to climb. Despite numerous attempts, only two expeditions have managed to repeat it in more than forty years. All of this makes it an extremely attractive route to climb. Reinhold Messner has described it as the most difficult of all routes to the summit of the world's highest mountain, and this assessment likely still holds true today.[13]

The idea of climbing Everest first took shape in the offices and minds of offi-cials of the PZS in the early 1970s. Everest first appeared as a topic at the meet-ings of the PZS Commission for Expeditions to Foreign Mountains (KOTG in the Slovene abbreviation), which was in charge of organising all expeditions abroad, in 1973, when Yugoslav alpinists did not yet have much experience in the Himalayas.[14] In 1974, the KOTG began more serious preparations for Everest and established contacts with China and Nepal:[15] 'We were negotiating with the Chinese regarding a joint expedition along the North Face of Everest, but the Nepalese approved our ascent to the summit for the spring of 1979.'[16] The wheels of diplomacy, and especially Chinese bureaucracy,[17] turned slowly and a lot of time was required for any kind of reply, and the decision as to where the Yugoslav expedition would mount its assault on the summit shifted to Nepal and the West Face or West Ridge.

From 1975 to the end of 1978, serious preparations were made for the expedition, which PZS called 'Everest 79'. The preparations involved extraordinary efforts, as KOTG members did most of the work themselves in the afternoons after work and during weekends, holidays, and vacations. In 1978, they also made a scouting expedition to the base of Everest, where they took a closer look at the mountain and possible points of approach. The goal of the expedition was certainly ambitious. They wanted to reach the top of the world via the West Ridge. From Base Camp, which stood on the Khumbu Glacier at an altitude of 5,350 metres, rises the 700-metre-high wall to the Lho La col, over which the mountaineers extended a cable so that they could transfer all their equipment to the col. The col is followed by the few-hundred-metres-high West Face, which continues into a 2,500-metre-long ridge with exposure to high winds, ending with the beginning of the steep part of the summit pyramid of Everest.

The first challenge KOTG tried to meet was to have alpinism reclassified as a team sport within the framework of Yugoslav sports. Although it was regarded as a sport, it did not qualify as a team sport, which would have offered certain benefits to climbers, such as exemption from military service and paid leave from work.[18] Expedition members were unable to resolve this problem, so they had to rely on the benevolence of their superiors to approve several months of leave.

The next challenge was the purchase of equipment since the climbers had to supply it themselves. They made use of all the contacts they had from previous expeditions and asked various producers from across Yugoslavia if they would be willing to participate in the expedition by either donating or selling their products at a reduced price. The response, especially from Slovenian companies, was truly exceptional. For example, food was provided by well-known food companies such as Žito, Eta, Droga, Kolinska, Mlinotest, and others.[19] Electrical equipment was provided by Iskra, and Intereuropa and other logistics services helped with certain transportation needs. Where possible, the members of the expedition therefore used the flagship companies of Yugoslav (mostly Slovenian) industry to equip them with as much equipment as possible, although some did need to be imported.[20]

This involved primarily specialised climbing gear and oxygen apparatus, both from France.[21] The supply of equipment came with some interesting stories. Several different Yugoslav companies were engaged in the preparation of the tents. Induplati sewed the tents, and another company offered its plastic products for their construction, but they were only able to do this after the alpinists themselves had provided a design for these tents, since until then no company in Yugoslavia had manufactured them.[22] Andrej Štremfelj recalls this as follows:

> At that time, we had the best equipment that Yugoslav industry at the time could make. Tents from Induplati, boots from Alpina and down gear were outstanding. We were the first to have windsuits made from imported Gore-Tex. Even so, we were quite poorly equipped compared to foreign expeditions at the time, for example, English and German. We were dressed in flannel shirts and breeches; we wore homemade gloves with primitive canvas covering. We wore the same type of covering over our shoes. Our crampons were attached with straps. In short, every hiker I meet today in the mountains in winter is better equipped than we were back then.[23]

The Yugoslav umbrella mountaineering organisation, the Alpine Association of Yugoslavia (PZJ in the Slovene abbreviation), contributed to the difficult organising conditions. Although it was committed to financing the expedition, it left the work of making the actual arrangements to the PZS. From the very beginning, communication with the PZJ was poor, as they were unwilling or unable to intervene when problems arose with customs and slow to transfer the necessary money and foreign currency to the PZS account, which was absolutely necessary to pay for the contracts that expedition members had agreed with suppliers.[24] In July 1978, at a meeting of the PZJ presidency, the credibility of the PZS and its financial transparency in organising were even called into question.[25] The PZJ later settled its obligations, but not entirely, so that the PZS had to contribute money from its budget just before departure to ensure that the expedition could even make it to the Himalayas.[26] They managed to enlist support from the President of Yugoslavia, Josip Broz Tito, who agreed to honorary patronage; this opened many a door both at home and abroad.

The selection of members took place in three rounds. Candidates had to send the history of their ascents to the KOTG and satisfy certain criteria prepared by the selection committee. Tone Škarja (1937–2020) remembered it as follows:

> First we sent out a call for applications, then the Commission for Expeditions to Foreign Mountains selected those who met the basic criteria for consideration. Then we had to narrow that down to a shortlist, which was basically a pretty thankless job, because we had to reject many people. We had the help of a psychologist, who based on various tests made suggestions as to who would be compatible with whom. The climbing teams formed in this way were sent onto the mountain by turns.[27]

The Everest 79 expedition comprised twenty-one Slovenes, two Croats, and two Bosnians among the climbers and team doctors.[28] Due to the great public interest in the expedition, journalists from the main Slovenian newspaper *Delo* and the public broadcaster Radio-Television of Ljubljana, as well as their radio operators and cameramen, also took part, bringing the total to thirty-one participants in the expedition.[29]

'How far have our guys got to on Everest?'

The expedition lasted for more than four months, from the end of February to the beginning of June, and offered something that, according to Andrej Štremfelj, is no longer possible today:

> For today's generation of alpinists, the duration of the expedition is unimaginable. We were in and above Base Camp for two months, and just getting to Base Camp took three weeks. News from home travelled by post to Kathmandu, from there by plane to Lukla and on by letter carrier to Base Camp. But these contacts with family have been preserved to this day, as we wrote letters to each other, whereas today's electronic and text messages quickly disappear.[30]

The expedition set off for the Himalayas on 28 February by Air India, the only airline that offered a flight from Yugoslavia to India, specifically to New Delhi.[31] After arrival, the team soon left for Kathmandu, the capital of Nepal, but complications intervened even before departure. On 27 February, Edvard Kardelj, formerly the highest and most influential Slovenian politician, and for many decades the second most powerful man in Yugoslavia after Tito, died. Back then, days of official mourning were declared upon the death of leading politicians, so there was a good chance that the equipment would not be sent on time. Fortunately, mourning was broken long enough for the equipment to be loaded and flown to India. The greatest problems were encountered on the India–Nepal border. Customs refused to allow the equipment to cross, and Nepal's Ministry of Tourism delayed issuing a permit to climb the West Ridge, which is close to the border with China. By 10 March, customs and climbing permit issues had been sorted out. A small group with essential equipment flew by helicopter to the foot of Everest to begin setting up Base Camp, while the others began a trek that would take just over two weeks.

All the most important daily and weekly newspapers in Yugoslavia regularly reported on the progress of the expedition. There was great interest in what was happening on the mountain throughout Yugoslavia – even the women selling produce at the market in the country's capital, Belgrade, asked daily, 'How far have our guys got to on Everest?'[32] All of Yugoslavia was expecting success, which put enormous pressure on the climbers. The expedition leader, Tone Škarja, felt this most keenly: 'It would have been a real national disaster if we failed. But there was no direct pressure, it was something we created ourselves.'[33]

From late March to early April, expedition members set up equipment on the slope between Base Camp and the edge of the Lho La col. They installed a hand-operated 200-metre-long winch to haul around six tonnes of equipment and food. Camp One, called Alpina after one of their sponsors, accommodated around forty persons and was set up at an elevation of 6,050 metres. All the high-altitude camps were named after the companies that had supplied equipment.[34] The rock and ice wall above the col (with a climbing difficulty of IV) was equipped with fixed ropes, and a second high-altitude camp, called Induplati and accommodating twelve people, was set up at 6,770 metres.[35] From 14 to 18 April, supplies were laid in at the third high-altitude camp, Rašica, also accommodating twelve, at an altitude of 7,170 metres. Camp Four, Krka, at an altitude of 7,520 metres, was set up on 27 April at the end of a 2,500-metre-long ridge where the American route from 1963 crosses over. Camp Five, Energoinvest, was set up at an altitude of 8,120 metres only on 9 May.[36] Storms and extreme winds caused great problems and made it impossible to fully equip the route above 8,000 metres. Equipment was slow to arrive due to the long distance to Base Camp.

Since the expedition was of great national importance for the country, the political authorities in Belgrade expected the climbers to reach the summit on one of the important dates for the Yugoslav regime: Labour Day (1 May), Victory Day (9 May), or perhaps Youth Day (25 May), when the birthday of Josip Broz Tito, the President of Yugoslavia, was celebrated. These desires and hints, of course, expressed the mentality of socialist planning at the time and were based on complete ignorance of alpinism and Himalayan conditions. The mountain had its own laws and 'plans'.[37]

Summiting

Once Camp Five was established, the expedition zeroed in on reaching the summit. The first two attempts were not successful. First up were Marjan Manfreda (Marjon) and Viki Grošelj, who had also set up Camp Five. A day later (10 May), they found their path blocked by a thirty-metre overhanging chimney. The only way forward was to climb through it. Marjon led the pitch with Grošelj belaying, since his oxygen valve was not working properly. During the climb, Marjon slipped and realised that to successfully climb through this extremely demanding pitch – a rating of V+ at an altitude of 8,200 metres – he would have to remove both his oxygen cylinder and his gloves and climb with his bare hands. It took him almost two hours of climbing to cover thirty metres before he could attach a fixed rope, which made it possible to climb to the top. But the price of climbing and setting up protection along this key stretch of the West Ridge was high for Marjon, and Viki Grošelj also paid for his patient belaying in the frigid shade below. To open the way for others to follow, Marjon had frostbite on his hands that later required amputation of several fingers, while Grošelj's feet were frostbitten while belaying in the snow.[38]

The next climbing pair were Roman Robas and Dušan Podbevšek, on 12 May, but they chose the wrong passages above 'Marjon's' chimney and ended up at a peak along the West Ridge (8,320 metres) from which it was no longer possible to continue towards the main summit. Later the same day, they did find a way forward, but due to lack of time they had to turn around at an altitude of 8,300 metres.[39]

On 13 May, Nejc Zaplotnik, Andrej Štremfelj, and Marko Štremfelj made their summit bid, but Marko had to turn back due to a faulty valve on his oxygen cylinder. The remaining pair advanced without any problems and at around 11 am announced to the camp that they would probably reach the top in about three hours.[40] At 1.51 pm Nepali time they did indeed find themselves on the top of the world, after more than a month of strenuous effort on the mountain. 'We hugged and patted each other on the back, then Nejc turned on the radio transmitter and spoke the famous words: "Tone [Škarja], we are at the summit!"', recalled Andrej Štremfelj.[41] Before descending, Štremfelj took a photograph of Zaplotnik attaching a Yugoslavian flag to the Chinese tripod on the summit (Figure 10.1). They descended together along the American route on the West Ridge and reached their Camp Four in the late evening hours.

Two days later, Stane Belak, Croat Stipe Božić, and Ang Phu, the sirdar or leader of the expedition Sherpas, also reached the summit. Ang Phu became the first person to climb Everest twice along two different routes, having reached the summit with an Austrian expedition on the Southeast Ridge in 1978. After setting out from the highest camp, the trio did not completely follow the West Ridge but traversed into the Hornbein Couloir, which they had also used to reach the summit. On the way down, the three got stuck. Night overtook them,

Figure 10.1 Nejc Zaplotnik on the summit of Everest in 1979. Image: © Andrej Štremfelj, courtesy of Peter Mikša.

a storm was raging, and the radio receiver also failed. Exhausted, out of oxygen, and lacking bivouac gear, they barely survived the night at 8,300 metres in the Hornbein Couloir. Out of concern for their colleagues, the next morning the third team, consisting of Borut Bergant, Ivč Kotnik, and Vanja Matijevec, set out to rescue them instead of making a bid for the summit themselves. While meeting his friends who were rushing to their aid, Ang Phu slipped and fell 2,000 metres down the West Face to his death. The expedition was over.[42]

Ang Phu was considered the most respected climber among the expedition members. His death shocked everyone. During the months they worked together on the mountain, they had become very close. The Sherpa team, under his tutelage, was extremely well tuned and very helpful to the expedition. The smiles and joy of reaching the summit were replaced by gloom and harsh reality. The return to base was therefore rather sad; even more than the physical exhaustion, there was the psychological turmoil. One of the members said in tears: 'he will be no more! I've already held him ...'. On their departure, the members of the Yugoslav expedition honoured Ang Phu with a neat little chorten in his memory.[43]

The expedition's achievements were remarkable despite Ang Phu's tragic death. The West Ridge route was unique by running from Base Camp to the summit completely within Nepal. The expedition assumed that by avoiding the dangerous Khumbu Icefall used by most expeditions to reach the Western Cwm and Southeast Ridge, the Yugoslav route would be considered safer and more attractive. This was not the case, as the technical difficulty of the West Ridge is very high on the upper part of the mountain. The death of Ang Phu clearly demonstrated the dangers.

The expedition reached the summit of Everest due to a well-studied route, thorough preparation, and superb training, but above all due to unconditional solidarity with one another and excellent co-operation with the Sherpas. 'At that time, the ascent of one team to the summit was a success for the entire expedition. We worked all for one, one for all. It was definitely the most harmonious and purest expedition I've ever led', recalled Tone Škarja. 'We all lived and breathed for Everest, we all wanted the summit and failure was simply not an option.'[44] After their return, the team became national heroes in Yugoslavia and Slovenia.

Other Slovenian Everests

The 13 May 1979 ascent established the Yugoslav route along the Everest West Ridge, a new route on the highest mountain in the world. Yugoslavia was the fourth country to climb Everest along a new route. Slovene alpinists shaped this success and continued the tradition after Slovenia achieved its independence from Yugoslavia in 1991. Since the Piolets d'Or were established in 1992, Slovenes have received ten awards, including two for lifetime achievement. Despite the late start, Slovenes not only caught up with the missed Himalayan train but secured a first-class seat.

Three later Slovene ascents of Everest were noteworthy. In 1990, Marija and Andrej Štremfelj became the first married couple to reach the summit together. Marija Štremfelj was the first Slovenian woman and thirteenth woman to ascend Everest. In 1997, Pavle Kozjek reached the summit of Everest from the north without the use of supplemental oxygen, the only Slovene to do so to date. On 7 October 2000, Davo Karničar accomplished perhaps the most significant of these later feats, the first ski descent from the summit to Base Camp. Karničar's continuous descent on skis from the summit of Everest to Base Camp, 3,500 metres below, took over four hours. Overall, nineteen Slovenes have summited Everest by three different routes.[45]

Another Everest legacy from 1979 may be even more enduring – the Slovene initiative to open the first mountaineering school for Nepali mountain guides at Manang, near Annapurna. In the 1960s, Aleš Kunaver made a short film about Sherpas and noticed on Annapurna that some Sherpas did not know how to tie crampons or use an ice axe. He resolved to build a school to teach climbing skills and safety so that Nepalis could become guides and not just porters or cooks. He recalled: 'The Sherpas are known for their resilience and stamina, but they don't have the skills to climb on steep walls. This lack of knowledge is dangerous. They should be trained.'[46] With support from Yugoslav and Slovene agencies – and a deadline to spend solidarity funds before the end of 1979 – Kunaver had a choice: climb Everest or build the school. 'Everest is a goal, and Manang is a mission! The expedition is completed at the end, but the school is permanent.'[47] The school that Kunaver built at Manang opened for climbing classes in November 1979. The mountaineering school was officially turned over to the Nepal Mountaineering Association in 1980, and Slovenian alpinists and doctors continued to serve as instructors or volunteers until 2013. Since then, the Manang Mountaineering School has been operated and taught exclusively by Nepalis. 'The school in Manang helped many locals make an easier living, saved many lives on Himalayan walls, and made life in villages at the foot of the world's highest mountains much more pleasant. It has become the cradle of a new era, not just for the people from the area but for the whole of Nepal where tourism has become the leading industry.'[48]

Notes

1 Acknowledgement: the work was supported by the Slovenian Research and Innovation Agency through core research programmes 'The Slovene History' (P6-0235) and 'The Geography of Slovenia' (P6-0101).
2 Tone Škarja, 'Jugoslovani četrti s svojo smerjo na Mount Everestu' [Yugoslavs fourth with their route on Mount Everest], *Delo* (2 July 1979), 14.
3 Peter Mikša and Urban Golob, *Zgodovina slovenskega alpinizma* [*History of Slovenian Alpinism*] (Ljubljana: Friko, 2013); Peter Mikša and Kornelija Ajlec, *Slovenian Mountaineering* (Ljubljana: Planinska zveza Slovenije, 2015).
4 Mikša and Golob, *Zgodovina slovenskega alpinizma*, p. 99.
5 Peter Mikša and Jure Čokl, 'Slovensko osvajanje osemtisočakov [Slovenian ascents of eight-thousanders] (1975–1995)', *Zgodovinski časopis*, 76:3/4 (2022), 510–32.
6 Ibid., 527.

7 Peter Mikša, 'Od gore do simbola: Triglav in njegova vloga pri Slovencih' [From mountain to symbol: Mount Triglav and its role among Slovenes], *Geografija v šoli*, 29:2 (2021), 6–7; Peter Mikša and Matija Zorn, 'Nacionalni boj za gore in slovenska identiteta' [National struggle for the mountains and Slovenian identity], *Časopis za zgodovino in narodopisje*, 92:1 (2021), 67–88.

8 Mikša and Golob, *Zgodovina slovenskega alpinizma*; Mikša and Ajlec, *Slovenian Mountaineering*.

9 Mikša and Golob, *Zgodovina slovenskega alpinizma*, p. 97.

10 Ibid., p. 97.

11 Peter Mikša, 'The mountains that wrote them: Slovenians climbing and writing about eight-thousand-metre peaks / Góry, które ich napisały. Słoweńcy wspinający się na i piszący o ośmiotysięcznikach', *Slavica Tergestina: European Slavic Studies Journal*, 28 (2022), 152–74, 158, https://doi.org/10.13137/2283-5482/33711

12 Tone Škarja, 'Odprave v tuja gorstva – Himalaja' [Expeditions to foreign mountains – the Himalayas], in Božidar Lavrič (ed), *Planinski zbornik: ob 110-letnici Slovenskega planinskega društva in Planinske zveze Slovenije* (Ljubljana: Planinska zveza Slovenije, 2003), pp. 268–9; cf. Tone Škarja, *Slovenci v Himalaji* [*Slovenians in Himalaya*] (Ljubljana: Planinska zveza Slovenije, 2004).

13 Andrej Štremfelj, *Na vrh sveta: od prvih pristopov do najvišjih sten* [*To the Top of the World: From the First Approaches to the Highest Faces*] (Ljubljana: Mladinska knjiga, 1992), pp. 74–5; Dušica Kunaver, *Od Triglava do treh vrhov sveta* [*From Triglav to Three World Summits*] (Ljubljana: Didakta, 1994), pp. 211–14.

14 Viki Grošelj, *Velikani Himalaje* [*Giants of the Himalayas*] (Ljubljana: Planinska zveza Slovenije, 2013), p. 53.

15 Archives of the Republic of Slovenia, Ljubljana, SI AS 1176 Alpine Association of Slovenia, Report on the Yugoslav expedition to Mount Everest in the spring of 1979, box 2.

16 Ibid.

17 Tone Škarja, 'Everest', in Marjan Krušič (ed.), *Na vrh sveta: Jugoslovanske odprave od Trisula do Everesta* (Ljubljana: Mladinska knjiga, 1979), p. 217.

18 Ibid.

19 Archives of the Republic of Slovenia, Ljubljana, SI AS 1176 Alpine Association of Slovenia, 'Everest 79' campaign, box 38.

20 Ibid.

21 Ibid.

22 Ibid.

23 Ibid.

24 Špela Ankele, '"Bilo je nezemeljsko lepo – kot da vrh sega v vesolje": Slovenci na Everestu' ['It was unearthly beautiful – as if the summit reached into outer space': Slovenes on Everest], *Delo* (4 January 2012), 22.

25 Archives of the Republic of Slovenia, Ljubljana, SI AS 1176 Alpine Association of Slovenia, 'Everest 79' campaign, box 38.

26 Ibid.

27 Janez Dekleva and Franci Savenc, 'Zahodni greben je najdaljša smer na najvišjo goro sveta' [The West Ridge is the longest route on the world's highest mountain], *Delo – Sobotna priloga* (12 May 1979), 26.

28 Tina Horvat, 'Ni jih poklical Tito, ampak sam Everest' [It wasn't Tito calling, but Everest itself], *Slovenske novice* (26 Febraury 2019), 8. Climbing members: Slovenes Zvone Andrejčič, Stane Belak, Borut Bergant, Viktor Grošelj, Tomaž Jamnik, Stane Klemenc,

Franc Knez, Ivan Kotnik, Marjan Manfreda, Štefan Marenče, Vanja Matijevec, Dušan Podbevšek, Bojan Pollak, Roman Robas, Tone Škarja, Andrej Štremfelj, Marko Štremfelj, Igor Tekavčič (doctor), Evgen Vavken (doctor), Nejc Zaplotnik, and Jože Zupan, as well Croats Stipe Božić and Vladimir Mesarić and Bosnians Muhamed Gafić and Mohamed Šišić.

29 They were Marjan Raztresen (*Delo* journalist), Slavko Vajt (television cameraman), Matevž Culiberg (radio operator), Slavko Šetina (radio operator), Rade Kovačević (correspondent), and Franc Novinc (painter). Tone Škarja, *Everest* (Ljubljana: Mladinska knjiga, 1981), pp. 299–314.

30 Ibid.

31 Ankele, 'Bilo je nezemeljsko lepo', 22.

32 Marjan Raztresen, 'Prvi raport "Himalajcev" po dveh dneh čakanja' [First report from the 'Himalayans' after two days of waiting], *Delo* (2 March 1979), 13.

33 Mikša and Golob, *Zgodovina slovenskega alpinizma*, p. 104.

34 Horvat, 'Ni jih poklical Tito'.

35 Škarja, 'Jugoslovani četrti', 14.

36 Ibid., 14.

37 Ibid., 14.

38 Mikša and Golob, *Zgodovina slovenskega alpinizma*, p. 107.

39 Ibid.

40 Škarja, 'Jugoslovani četrti', 14.

41 Ibid., 14.

42 Andrej Štremfelj, 'Ko na vrhu ne veš, kaj bi: Everest med prvim vzponom in slovensko smerjo po Zahodnem grebenu leta 1979' [When you don't know what to do at the top: Everest during the first ascent and the Slovenian route along the West Ridge in 1979], *I-gore*, 1:2 (2003), 10.

43 Andrej Štremfelj, *Kristali sreče: avtobiografija alpinista* [Crystals of Happiness: Autobiography of an Alpinist] (Kranj: Založništvo N. Štremfelj, 2022), pp. 225–6.

44 Štremfelj, *Na vrh sveta*, pp. 74–5.

45 Slovenes who have summited Everest: Andrej Štremfelj, Nejc Zaplotnik, Stane Belak, Viki Grošelj, Marija Štremfelj, Janez Jeglič, Franc Pepevnik, Pavle Kozjek, Franc Oderlap, Viki Mlinar, Marko Lihteneker, Roman Benet, Davo Karničar, Tadej Golob, Matej Flis, Gregor Lačen, Tomaž Jakofčič, Tomaž Rotar, and Andrej Gradišnik.

46 Aleš Kunaver in Dušica Kunaver, 'Naučimo jih loviti ribe! = Let's teach them how to fish!', in Mojca Volkar Trobevšek (eds), *Z znanjem do zvezd: slovenska šola za nepalske gorske vodnike = Knowledge to Reach for the Stars: The Slovenian School for Nepalese Mountain Guides* (Ljubljana: Planinska zveza Slovenije, 2022), p. 66.

47 'Slovenska alpinistična šola za nepalske gorske vodnike v Manangu' [Slovenian mountaineering school for Nepalese mountain guides in Manang], https://web.archive.org/web/20240123221656/https://ales.kunaver.com/sola-v-manangu/

48 Kunaver and Kunaver, 'Naučimo jih loviti ribe!', p. 89.

11

Reclaiming Everest: discontents, disasters, and the making of a Nepali mountain

Ian Bellows

Over the past decade, Mount Everest has endured a series of disasters and disruptive incidents. In 2013, a violent confrontation between high-altitude workers (HAWs) and professional mountaineers rocked the climbing community. The following year, a deadly avalanche in the Khumbu Icefall sparked protests and unrest that ended the climbing season. Unprecedented resistance and activism among HAWs brought renewed scrutiny to the structural inequities inherent to commercial mountaineering in the Himalaya and powered the rise of Nepali companies and mountaineers who have increasingly become the Everest industry's prime movers. The changing face of Everest reflects a series of profound transformations reshaping contemporary alpinism in Nepal including growing professionalisation, proliferation of local expedition operators, and the emergence of an indigenous Nepali sport-climbing tradition.

These developments have been celebrated both in Nepal and among some in the international climbing community as an Indigenous reclamation of Everest, and Himalayan mountaineering as a whole, after decades of marginalisation and exploitation. But what exactly does it mean to 'reclaim' a mountain like Everest, and how have Indigenous Himalayan peoples' attempts to do so marked critical junctures in Everest's history? In this chapter, I trace the evolving nature of Indigenous resistance and reclamation through three critical eras: the expeditionary period from the 1920s through the 1970s, the commercial era culminating in the tumultuous 2013 and 2014 Everest seasons, and the rapid development of Nepali alpinism during the past decade. I demonstrate that protests and growing assertiveness in the 2010s are the latest episodes in a century-long struggle for respect and better working conditions and reflect a continuous negotiation with foreign mountaineers over power and control.[1] While this advocacy has yielded significant gains, I also argue that these transformations have left the foundational mountaineering modality and moral economy of

Everest relatively unchanged. Even as a rising generation of Nepali expedition operators, guides, and alpinists have increasingly supplanted those from other countries, there has been scant progress towards addressing the long-standing questions of workers' rights, environmental protection, and sustainability they inherited.

This chapter is primarily based upon archival research and analysis of contemporaneous news reports and media depictions of Everest and Himalayan mountaineering, with an emphasis on the writings and perspectives of Indigenous Himalayan individuals. I also reference interviews I conducted over ten months of field research in Nepal between 2014 and 2016.

Development of Indigenous high-altitude labour in the Nepal Himalaya

The involvement of Indigenous Himalayan peoples in mountaineering began by 1891, when four Gurkha soldiers joined a British expedition to the Karakoram.[2] With the expansion of market economies into the Nepal Himalaya, wage labour became an important livelihood adaptation to the shifting political-economic conditions in remote mountain regions.[3] By the mid-nineteenth century, ethnic Sherpa men from Nepal's Solukhumbu region established a pattern of circular migration to Darjeeling in British India seeking seasonal employment as 'coolies' on construction, exploration, and survey projects and eventually on mountaineering expeditions.[4] The first British Everest expeditions in 1921, 1922, and 1924 recruited hundreds of porters from this and other local Indigenous communities to support the siege-style assaults that characterised early attempts on Himalayan peaks. Indigenous peoples were also Everest's first victims; the deaths of seven Sherpa porters in an avalanche ended the 1922 British expedition.[5]

A succession of international expeditions to Everest and other Himalayan peaks from the 1920s to the 1950s provided steady employment opportunities. The term 'Sherpa' came to refer to any Indigenous HAW due to the high proportion of ethnic Sherpa involved in high-altitude work during the expeditionary period, but HAWs from many ethnic groups distinguished themselves through their strength, stamina, and supposed physiological adaptation to high altitude. Expedition accounts from the era speak glowingly of their good humour, selflessness, heroism, and loyalty.[6] Chroniclers also noted their passivity, aversion to conflict, and apparent nonchalance towards mortality, behaviour attributed to their Buddhist religious beliefs.[7] This characterisation became central to Everest's mythologising project and made them ideal companions in the pursuit of Himalayan greatness, well suited to the physical rigours of mountaineering and to supporting the imperial summit ambitions of their employers.

Despite the idealised portrayal of HAWs in mountaineering literature and the popular imagination, strikes and other acts of resistance occurred regularly during the expeditionary period as HAWs became more assertive in response to inequitable treatment. Resistance reached a crescendo in the post-war era from the 1950s to the early 1970s, when expeditions were organised along militaristic lines and HAWs often felt that leaders treated them as inferiors within strictly racialised and classed hierarchies. Conflict arose on the 1953 British and the 1963 American expeditions due to unequal provision of equipment and oxygen and especially the perceived refusal of some foreign team members to equally share in expedition hardships and hazards.[8] In 1972, a German expedition failed to bring enough equipment for the team's HAWs, who responded by striking. Leader Karl Herrligkoffer was forced to return to Europe to retrieve the equipment in 'perhaps the most extreme instance of sahib defeat on record'.[9]

Despite frequent conflict on early expeditions, high-altitude labour played a critical role in creating economic opportunity and social mobility for some Indigenous Himalayan people. Foremost among them was Tenzing Norgay, who achieved the first ascent of Everest with Edmund Hillary on the 1953 British expedition. By the time expedition leader John Hunt recruited him Norgay had already been to Everest six times, including reaching a then-record altitude of about 8,600 metres on the 1952 Swiss expedition with Raymond Lambert.[10] Norgay's ascent of Everest made him the first internationally famous mountaineer from a Himalayan nation; Hunt wrote that Norgay had 'established himself not only as the foremost climber of his race but as a mountaineer of world standing'.[11] Despite achieving considerable celebrity and being showered with decorations including Britain's George Medal, Norgay tellingly stated in his ghostwritten autobiography that being considered a full expedition member – rather than support staff – on the 1952 Swiss expedition was 'the greatest honour that had ever been paid me'.[12]

Norgay is mostly remembered today as Hillary's loyal companion, a humble man with a wide smile who was content to let his accomplishments speak for themselves. In Nepal and his adopted homeland of India, his ascent was deeply significant and he became an icon of South Asian achievement.[13] Norgay climbed little after Everest, but he remained active in the development of

Himalayan mountaineering and HAW advocacy. He became the Director of Field Training at the Himalayan Mountaineering Institute in Darjeeling upon its founding in 1954.[14] He also chaired the Sherpa Association, 'a sort of employment agency and labour union for expedition Sherpas, trying to get a higher wage scale than that set by the Himalayan Club [the British-run HAW recruitment bureau] and better compensation for men who are injured and the families of those who are killed'.[15] As the centre of Himalayan climbing shifted to Kathmandu, Sherpa founded the Himalayan Society there around 1961 with similar objectives.[16]

These groups seemingly brought about few changes. Nevertheless, they reflected a new level of political consciousness around reimagining Himalayan mountaineering. The desire for better pay, improved working conditions, and recognition would remain top priorities for HAWs in the following decades, as Norgay's son Jamling Tenzing Norgay emphasised in 2001:

> The Sherpa don't greatly mind that foreigners take the glory and credit for successful ascents. Most Sherpas want to be paid well, ideally with a bonus, because their principal desire is to provide for their families and bring improvements to their villages. They do appreciate, however, fair treatment and personal acknowledgement.[17]

Resistance and the changing face of Everest 2013–14

Between the late 1970s and early 1990s, Everest climbing transitioned from national expeditions to an era of commercial mountaineering and individual record-chasing. Commercial climbing was innovative because it allows wealthy individuals to pay to be guided to the summit of mountains like Everest, but the social relations and technical infrastructure that enable it changed little from the expeditionary period. On Nepal's South Col route, Icefall Doctors from the semi-governmental Sagarmatha Pollution Control Committee establish the route between Base Camp and Camp Two, setting thousands of metres of fixed ropes and placing dozens of ladders in the Khumbu Icefall that allow climbers to navigate crevasses and other hazards.[18] An ad hoc team of HAWs then sets the route from Camp Two to the summit. Over several weeks or months, teams use this infrastructure to establish a series of successively higher camps before making a final summit attempt. Carrying equipment to Base Camp, setting fixed ropes, establishing high camps, and escorting clients to the summit requires a massive labour input, and expeditions employ thousands of low-altitude porters and hundreds of HAWs each season.[19] Expedition operators, guides, clients, and HAWs themselves universally acknowledge that commercial operations on Everest would be impossible without these essential workers.

While all Himalayan climbing involves inherent risk, high-altitude work requires and often incentivises HAWs to spend significant time in hazardous terrain and conditions. Companies pay HAWs bonuses for carrying loads through the Icefall, so many make a dozen rotations in a season compared to two to four for guides and clients.[20] Unsurprisingly, objective hazards like avalanches and rockfall cause most HAW fatalities, although falls, exposure, and altitude illness also account for many deaths.[21] Between 1922 and 2023, at least 125 HAWs died on Everest[22] and hundreds more have been left disabled.[23] Despite being one of the world's most dangerous occupations, many HAWs believe the financial rewards of high-altitude work justify the risk; depending on experience they can earn about USD 4,000 to 6,000 in a season before bonuses, many times the average annual Nepali income of about USD 600.[24] However, these earnings are a pittance compared with Nepal's USD 700-million-a-year tourism industry[25] and the USD 3 million to 4 million in annual permit revenues the government of Nepal earns from mountaineering.[26]

On 27 April 2013, violence between HAWs and international climbers threatened to derail the Everest season. The incident began when professional mountaineers Ueli Steck and Simone Moro along with photographer Jonathan Griffith ascended the Lhotse Face above Camp Two. They bypassed the HAWs setting the route by climbing quickly in alpine style, violating a community agreement not to disturb the rope-fixing team and causing the HAWs to lose face. Both groups accused the other of kicking ice down onto its members, and when the rope-fixing team demanded that the climbers descend, Moro's profane response in Nepali was broadcast over a hot radio microphone. Over a hundred angry HAWs met the trio when they returned to Camp Two, some of whom started throwing rocks while others punched and kicked Steck and Moro, injuring them. Only the intervention of international guides prevented further escalation.[27]

The so-called 'Everest brawl' was caught on video by a documentary film crew and made mainstream media headlines. It shocked the climbing world and renewed debates about power, access, and how even elite climbers quietly depend on HAW support and commercial climbing infrastructure. 'Climbing Everest is so big now, with so much money involved, and the Sherpas are not stupid … they want to take over the business and kick out the westerners', claimed Steck.[28] For their part, the HAWs were incensed that Steck, Moro, and Griffith placed others at risk by climbing and by Moro's disrespectful

use of profanity.[29] Tashi Sherpa, an HAW for American expedition operator International Mountain Guides, offered further insight into the HAWs'
response: 'The resentment was always there … we are the ones who, despite
the risks and hazards, make sure that all is well on Everest. This is our life, our
livelihood … But this incident was waiting to happen, and it will happen again
as long as Sherpas are humiliated.'[30]

Following the incident, climbing proceeded without further disruption.
However, simmering tensions flared again the next year, when a historic disaster sparked protests that devolved into boycotts and threats that ended the
climbing season. On the morning of 18 April 2014, over a hundred HAWs
ascended the Icefall carrying supplies to the high camps of thirty-eight teams.
At approximately 6.30 am, a serac (block of glacial ice) weighing an estimated
64,000 tons collapsed onto the route, killing sixteen HAWs and injuring nine
others. The disaster was the deadliest single incident for HAWs and the deadliest day on Everest up to that point.[31]

Even before the initial shock and grief at the disaster subsided, unrest began
brewing in Base Camp. Mourning turned to anger when the government
announced that it would pay about USD 400 to the families of the deceased,
an amount HAWs considered insultingly low. On 20 April, a group of sirdars[32] met with government liaison officers and presented them with a thirteen-
point charter that demanded doubling the life insurance requirement to about
USD 22,000, mandating disability insurance coverage of about USD 10,000,
a funeral stipend, a relief and education fund financed by permit royalties, and
other changes.[33] After sirdar Pasang Bhote read the charter to the hundreds
of assembled HAWs and international mountaineers, an HAW in the crowd
said: 'If company owners don't pressure the government to uphold our rights,
we will … Sherpas deserve greater respect. Without Sherpas on the mountain,
there is no Nepal.'[34] Another HAW implicitly called for respecting the dead
by not climbing that year. Bhote then asked, 'Do you want to continue or not
continue?' to which the crowd responded, 'Yeah, we don't want to continue!'
The 274 HAWs signing the charter promised further protests if their demands
were not met.[35]

Before Nepal's Ministry of Culture, Tourism and Civil Aviation could
respond, 400 to 500 HAWs held a memorial *pujā* (religious ceremony) on
22 April to offer prayers and eulogies for the dead. Calls for a work stoppage
became explicit, with one mourner declaring, 'We should cancel this year, and
in this we should unite.'[36] Someone also allegedly shouted, 'If anybody goes
up, we might break their leg with an ice axe!' After the *pujā*, rumours spread

197

warning that any attempt to continue climbing would be met with violence.[37] While the veracity of the rumours is unknown, the teams that had not already cancelled their climbs did so out of concern for the safety of their staff and clients. Their departure marked the de facto end of the season.

The 2014 disaster had far-reaching consequences beyond the tragic human toll. There was a widespread feeling that the season's events changed Everest forever, but international mountaineers, HAWs, and observers wondered precisely what sort of inflection point the season represented. The season's abrupt end caused massive financial losses for expedition operators and clients who had paid them tens of thousands of dollars for the chance to summit Everest, leaving many disillusioned and angry despite grieving with their HAWs. After the disaster Russell Brice, owner of New Zealand-based Himalayan Experience, told his staff, 'Yes, we had one avalanche. Unfortunately, it killed a lot of people. That's no reason to stop the expedition.'[38] In the past climbing had always resumed following HAW deaths, so the unprecedented labour stoppage and threats fuelled speculation that the protests were orchestrated by a handful of 'hotheads', 'militant Sherpa', or Maoist agitators who exploited the tragedy for political gain. 'Before it was always friendly, smiley Sherpa, always helping', Brice noted ruefully.[39] Commentators quickly connected the protests to the brawl the year before and to a series of other alleged acts of insubordination and intimidation on Himalayan peaks like Manaslu in the preceding few years.[40] Relations between HAWs and international mountaineers deteriorated to the point that some climbers began describing themselves as 'hostages' of an 'Everest mafia'.[41]

Contrary to these perceptions, support for the protests was seemingly both broad-based and spontaneous as HAWs leveraged the international media spotlight following the disaster. While HAWs succeeded in drawing attention to dangerous working conditions and poor labour protections, their demands for policy reforms yielded few concrete gains. The government pledged to increase the life insurance requirement to about USD 15,000[42] and create a welfare fund for HAWs,[43] but it never implemented these changes and failed to respond to the thirteen-point charter's other demands. Beyond this, the disaster's enduring legacy is one of unrest, ill will, and a lost season that put hundreds of HAWs out of work. Some Nepali guides I spoke with worried that the events of 2013 and 2014 damaged Nepal's reputation and made Everest a less attractive destination by introducing new risks and volatility. These fears proved unfounded as Nepal and China issued Everest permits to at least 558 climbers in 2015, setting a new record.[44]

From sahibs to Sherpas: the making of a Nepali mountain

While the 2013 brawl and 2014 protests surprised many international observers and mountaineers, they continued a historic pattern of resistance and advocacy by HAWs. They also came against the backdrop of profound transformations already underway in Nepali alpinism, and further accelerated the professionalisation of Nepal's climbing industry, the proliferation of Nepali expedition operators, and the emergence of a homegrown sport-climbing tradition.

The wide availability of low-cost, high-quality mountaineering training has powered the development of Nepali alpinism. International guides and mountaineers started training programmes like the Khumbu Climbing Center to improve technical proficiency, empower frontline workers, and give back to the people and communities that enabled their Himalayan climbing aspirations.[45] Newer programmes, including those offered by the Nepal Mountaineering Association, reflect the industry's growing capacity to perpetuate itself. These programmes build foundational skills and create professional development pathways to advanced training and certification. As of 2022, seventy Nepali nationals have become International Federation of Mountain Guides Associations (IFMGA) guides, the highest internationally recognised, skill-based mountaineering credential, and dozens more are currently pursuing certification.[46]

Guiding – leading expeditions and working directly with clients as opposed to serving as expedition support staff – has created considerable opportunities for Nepali mountaineers. It is now common to find Nepali nationals and expatriates guiding not only on Everest and other Himalayan peaks but on mountains worldwide like Kilimanjaro, Aconcagua, Denali, or Mount Rainier. Some now guide for the outfitters who once hired them as sirdars or lower-ranking HAWs, while others have established their own companies to meet exploding demand for guided Himalayan expeditions. Nepali law has long required international guide services to contract with in-country companies to manage logistics and staffing, but hundreds of local expedition operators now operate independently. According to Nepali guides, by 2016 over two hundred Nepali-owned companies offered mountaineering trips and over fifty ran expeditions on 8,000-metre peaks, numbers that have increased each year. Nepali expedition operators primarily compete on cost; by not employing expensive foreign guides and minimising overheads, some offer Everest climbs for USD 30,000 or less, significantly undercutting international operators which typically charge USD 60,000 or more.[47] This advantage has enabled Nepali companies to capture an ever-growing share of the Everest market; 2014 was the first year that more international clients climbed Everest with Nepal-based expedition operators than international companies.[48]

The combination of experience and professionalisation has also driven the development of an emergent Nepali sport-climbing movement, one that reflects a series of generational, aspirational, and demographic shifts. Veteran Nepali mountaineers like Kami Rita Sherpa, a sirdar for United States–based Alpine Ascents International who has summited Everest a record thirty times, view climbing as a dangerous livelihood that allows them to build generational wealth and provide for their families. They climb so that their children do not have to, and so that they can eventually give up mountaineering to retire comfortably in Kathmandu or pursue new life possibilities abroad.[49] Conversely, a rising generation of Nepali alpinists, guides, and HAWs view mountaineering as a means to embrace their Himalayan inheritance and become the lead authors of the next chapter of climbing in Nepal. Their ranks – now composed mainly of Sherpa from Rolwaling, Makalu, and Kangchenjunga and those of other ethnicities, rather than Sherpa from Solukhumbu who once dominated Himalayan mountaineering[50] – increasingly reflect Nepal's pluralistic society. With increased diversity have come fresh ideas and new ambitions.

Since 2014, Nepali climbers have accomplished several notable mountaineering firsts, including two of the most significant achievements in modern alpinism. In 2015, mountaineers Nima Tenji Sherpa, Tashi Sherpa, and Dawa Gyalje Sherpa made three first ascents of 6,000-metre peaks in Rolwaling Valley, the first known instance of an all-Nepali team undertaking first ascents in their own country. Explaining the trio's motivations Dawa Gyalje said:

> We are hoping, as young climbers, to take climbing in Nepal to a new level … All of us have climbed much bigger mountains but always with foreign climbers. We want to show that we are not just porters on the mountain, climbing only for our livelihood, but we are interested in climbing because we enjoy it, too.[51]

In 2019, Nirmal Purja, an ethnic Magar and British Brigade of Gurkhas veteran, summited the fourteen 8,000-metre peaks in just six months and six days, besting the previous record by over seven years. In 2021, during a lull in commercial Himalayan expeditions due to the COVID-19 pandemic, Purja led a team of expert Nepali alpinists to make the first winter ascent of K2.[52]

Mountaineering accomplishments like these have attracted international attention and transformed Nepali climbers from mostly unheralded expedition support staff to sponsored athletes, bestselling authors, and celebrity guides. This transition is exemplified by the meteoric ascent of Purja, who has become the most recognisable Nepali mountaineer since Tenzing Norgay. An alpinist tailor-made for the social media age, Purja chronicled his achievements in his book *Beyond Possible* and Netflix documentary *14 Peaks*. He then capitalised on his notoriety to establish Elite Exped, the company through which he offers guided Everest climbs to Qatari royalty, influencers, and other notables.[53] Purja's brash, unapologetic style and tireless dedication to his personal brand propelled his rise to fame and enable him to advocate for Nepali mountaineers who have long toiled in obscurity. 'I'm the face of these people, bro', Purja told a *GQ* reporter, punctuating his response with an expletive. 'I'm their hope now.'[54] His rise to prominence has also been clouded by controversies including allegations of sexual misconduct.[55] With Purja as its polarising frontman, Nepali alpinism is defined today by bravado, hustle, self-promotion, and an unprecedented ability for Himalayan people to tell their stories in their own unfiltered voices.

These developments have upended many of the economic and social relations that historically defined the Everest paradigm. In particular, rising education, affluence, and cosmopolitanism among Nepali climbers have unsettled traditional portrayals of the 'Sherpa' as simple mountain people compelled to work in the mountains due to poverty. But beyond Nepali companies claiming a greater market share, few substantive changes to Everest's core mountaineering modality and underlying moral economy have emerged after a decade of increased local influence. Most local companies follow the established model of large-scale, full-service expeditions, substituting Nepali guides for international ones but otherwise leaving the existing sociotechnical infrastructure that undergirds the commercial system relatively intact. The extent to which rank-and-file HAWs have benefited from this change is not clear, and many within the industry question whether their participation in mountaineering is as voluntary or aspirational as the well-placed Nepali expedition operators and mountaineers who employ them.

Additionally, the absence of meaningful government oversight, slim margins, and fierce competition that define the Everest industry create considerable incentives to cut corners and skirt the few existing labour and environmental regulations. Nepali and international mountaineers believe that newer budget companies – many of which seem willing to accept underqualified clients, hire staff with a lower level of training and experience, and use substandard equipment in return for gaining a foothold in a crowded market – are responsible for some of the worst violations. The proliferation of local operators and cut-rate 'logistics services' on Everest has created jobs and expanded industry capacity, but questionable operating practices by some companies lower safety margins, contribute to an already overcrowded mountain, and make it difficult for others to maintain high professional standards.

Despite persistent calls for reform from both within and outside of the Everest industry, in the absence of further government regulation, market demand, or initiative from the private sector there seems to be little incentive to alter the current commercial system. Individual companies, INGOs, and other entities are responsible for the few incremental changes that have occurred. Purja's Elite Exped began paying its top guides up to USD 70,000 to close the pay gap with international climb leaders.[56] Government-mandated insurance coverage remains inadequate – policies pay about USD 11,000 for death, about USD 3,000 for injury, and about USD 5,000 for rescues[57] – so charities like the United States–based Juniper Fund have emerged to support families of HAWs injured and killed in the mountains.[58] Other frequently discussed changes, like requiring clients to have a minimum level of mountaineering experience before attempting Everest, have either attracted little consensus or the government has repeatedly delayed their implementation.

The lack of substantive reform to date raises profound questions about the long-term sustainability of the current Everest paradigm. In a broad sense, it is unclear how an inherently risky activity like climbing Everest might be made acceptably 'safe' regardless of the measures implemented, and whether this is even a desirable goal when much of Everest's appeal lies in the danger and excess involved in climbing it.[59] It also raises questions regarding what ethical and moral responsibilities, if any, an Indigenous 'reclamation' of an iconic, sacred, and lucrative resource like Everest should entail. Further change will likely remain elusive as long as mountaineers are willing to pay to climb Everest and leading expedition operators and alpinists – international and Nepali – continue to benefit from the current system. The stubborn resilience of the Everest industry amidst continual crises makes it difficult to imagine a scenario that would finally compel its practitioners to confront its most problematic structural features.

Conclusion

The 2013 brawl and 2014 disaster on Everest marked a critical inflection point in Himalayan mountaineering. In both cases, HAWs seized on historical moments to draw attention to long-standing grievances and advocate for greater rights within the current commercial mountaineering system, continuing a century of struggle for respect and better working conditions on the world's highest mountains. Over the past decade, Nepali expedition operators, guides, and alpinists have embarked on a remarkable effort to reclaim Everest and Himalayan mountaineering, transforming climbing from a livelihood into an increasingly aspirational pursuit. Nepali climbers have achieved long-sought global recognition for mountaineering accomplishments and Nepal-based companies have claimed a growing share of the commercial mountaineering market on peaks like Everest. However, the lack of substantive changes to the underlying economics of Everest climbing and lack of progress in addressing entrenched structural inequities highlight the difficulty of enacting change in a self-regulating industry that continues to significantly benefit its key Nepali and international stakeholders.

Notes

1 For a thorough history, see Bernadette McDonald, *Alpine Rising: Sherpas, Baltis, and the Triumph of Local Climbers in the Greater Ranges* (Seattle, WA: Mountaineers Books, 2024).

2 Maurice Isserman and Stewart Weaver, *Fallen Giants: A History of Himalayan Mountaineering from the Age of Empire to the Age of Extremes* (New Haven, CT: Yale University Press, 2008), p. 39.

3 Tom Fricke, 'Introduction: Human Ecology in the Himalaya', *Human Ecology* 17:2 (1989), 131–45, https://doi.org/10.1007/BF00889710

4 Sherry B. Ortner, *Life and Death on Mt. Everest: Sherpas and Himalayan Mountaineering* (Princeton, NJ: Princeton University Press, 1999), p. 12; see also Chapter 6 by Jayeeta Sharma in this volume.

5 Isserman and Weaver, *Fallen Giants*, p. 115.

6 Ortner, *Life and Death on Mt. Everest*, pp. 58–67.

7 Ibid., pp. 135–42.

8 Ibid., pp. 154–62.

9 Ibid., p. 159. Until the 1970s, HAWs used the term 'sahib' – Hindi for 'boss' or 'master' – to address or refer to any foreign mountaineer (ibid., p. 5).

10 Tenzing Norgay and James Ramsey Ullman, *Tiger of the Snows: The Autobiography of Tenzing of Everest* (New York: Putnam, 1955), pp. 159, 207.

11 John Hunt, *The Ascent of Everest* (London: Hodder & Stoughton, 1953), pp. 60–1.

12 Norgay and Ullman, *Tiger of the Snows*, p. 177.

13 Peter H. Hansen, 'Confetti of empire: the conquest of Everest in Nepal, India, Britain, and New Zealand', *Comparative Studies in Society and History*, 42:2 (2000), 307–32, https://doi.org/10.1017/S0010417500002486

14 Isserman and Weaver, *Fallen Giants*, p. 298.

15 Norgay and Ullman, *Tiger of the Snows*, p. 121.

16 Ortner, *Life and Death on Mt. Everest*, p. 156.

17 Jamling Tenzing Norgay and Broughton Coburn, *Touching My Father's Soul: A Sherpa's Journey to the Top of Everest* (Thorndike, ME: Thorndike Press, 2001), p. 190.

18 Grayson Schaffer, 'Everest's darkest year', *Outside Online* (8 July 2014), https://web.archive.org/web/20161114084454/https://www.outsideonline.com/1924596/everests-darkest-year

19 Bhadra Sharma and Mujib Mashal, '"I see no future": Sherpas leave the job they made famous', *New York Times* (7 May 2023), https://web.archive.org/web/20230507070603/ https://www.nytimes.com/2023/05/07/world/asia/sherpas-everest.html

20 Grayson Schaffer, 'The disposable man: a western history of Sherpas on Everest', *Outside Online* (10 July 2013), https://web.archive.org/web/20150406020709/https://www. outsideonline.com/1928326/disposable-man-western-history-sherpas-everest

21 Paul G. Firth, et al., 'Mortality on Mount Everest, 1921–2006: descriptive study', *BMJ*, 337:a7684 (2008), 1430–3, https://doi.org/10.1136/bmj.a2654

22 Alan Arnette, 'Everest 2023: season summary – deadliest in history', *Alanarnette.com* (2 June 2023), https://web.archive.org/web/20230602192939/https://www.alanarnette. com/blog/2023/06/02/everest-2023-season-summary-deadest-in-history/

23 Schaffer, 'The disposable man'.

24 Ibid.; Sharma and Mashal, 'I see no future'.

25 'Nepal tourism may take 5 years to recover', *Nepali Times* (8 September 2020), https:// web.archive.org/web/20200918120234/https://www.nepalitimes.com/latest/nepal-tourism-may-take-5-years-to-recover/

26 Schaffer, 'The disposable man'.

27 Ibid.

28 Tim Neville, 'Brawl on Everest: Ueli Steck's story', *Outside Online* (2 May 2013), https://web.archive.org/web/20210921084337/https://www.outsideonline.com/out door-adventure/climbing/brawl-everest-ueli-stecks-story/

29 Deepak Adhikari, 'The Everest brawl: a Sherpa's tale', *Outside Online* (13 August 2013), https://web.archive.org/web/20150408172047/https://www.outsideonline.com/192 9351/everest-brawl-sherpas-tale

30 Ibid.

31 Schaffer, 'Everest's darkest year'.

32 The sirdar (from Hindi *sardār*, 'leader') is the seniormost local staff member and HAW foreman on an expedition. See also Chapter 12 by Young Hoon Oh in this volume for additional terms.

33 Schaffer, 'Everest's darkest year.'

34 Jennifer Peedom (dir.), *Sherpa* (Australia: Felix Media, 2015).

35 Schaffer, 'Everest's darkest year'.

36 Peedom, *Sherpa.*

37 Schaffer, 'Everest's darkest year'.

38 Peedom, *Sherpa.*

39 Ibid.

40 Alan Arnette, 'Everest 2014: season summary – a Nepal tragedy', *Alanarnette.com* (9 June 2014), https://web.archive.org/web/20140625053439/https://www.alanarnette. com/blog/2014/06/09/everest-2014-season-summary-nepal-tragedy/

41 Schaffer, 'Everest's darkest year'.

42 Ibid.

43 Sharma and Mashal, "I see no future'.

44 Alan Arnette, 'Everest 2015: season summary – summits don't matter', *Alanarnette.com* (6 May 2015), https://web.archive.org/web/20150528220207/https://www.alanarnette. com/blog/2015/05/06/everest-2015-season-summary-summits-dont-matter-2/

45 Freddie Wilkinson, 'The Khumbu Climbing Center: in the footsteps of Hillary and Norgay', *National Geographic* (15 March 2012), https://web.archive.org/web/20210

509100821/https://www.nationalgeographic.com/adventure/article/sherpas-khumbu-climbing-center. See also Chapter 10 by Mikša and Zorn in this volume.

46 Nepal National Mountain Guide Association, 'IFMGA Mountain Guides', Nnmga.org, https://web.archive.org/web/20230505201936/https://www.nnmga.org/international-guides/

47 Alan Arnette, 'Sherpas are taking control of climbing in Nepal', *Outside Online* (20 November 2015), https://web.archive.org/web/20151122171814/https://www.outsideonline.com/2036831/sherpas-are-taking-control-climbing-nepal

48 Arnette, 'Everest 2014: Season summary'.

49 Sharma and Mashal, 'I see no future'.

50 Ibid.

51 Stewart M. Green, 'Sherpa and American teams climb first ascents in Rolwaling Himal', *Alpinist* (9 November 2015), https://web.archive.org/web/20151116182848/https://www.alpinist.com/doc/web15y/newswire-sherpa-americans-climb-first-ascents-rolwaling-himal

52 Grayson Schaffer, 'The controversial king of hardcore climbing', *GQ Sports* (19 January 2023), https://web.archive.org/web/20230130134805/https://www.gq.com/story/nims-purja-profile

53 Ibid.

54 Ibid.

55 Anna Callaghan and Jenny Vrentas, 'For female climbers, dangers go beyond avalanches and storms', *New York Times* (31 May 2024), https://web.archive.org/web/20240531100402/https://www.nytimes.com/2024/05/31/sports/mountaineering-sexual-harassment-abuse-nims-purja.html

56 Schaffer, 'The controversial king of hardcore climbing'.

57 Sharma and Mashal, 'I see no future'.

58 Schaffer, 'The disposable man'.

59 Elizabeth Mazzolini, 'Food, waste, and judgment on Mount Everest', *Cultural Critique*, 76 (2010), 1–27, https://doi.org/10.1353/cul.2010.a402867

12

Sherpa's Everest and expedition conglomerate

Young Hoon Oh

On an early morning in May 2013, I was jugging on the rope fixed over the iced section of Lhotse Face, at around 7,000 metres. Camp Three, perched in the middle of the sheer wall, was in sight. Over a dozen climbers were ascending at a crawl on the same rope. I could proceed at my own pace, fortunately. Almost exactly a year earlier, I was stuck in the middle of crowds progressing much more slowly than I wished at a similar location. A photo of that scene made a *National Geographic* spectacle and international headlines. Yet the photo could not convey the confluence of miscommunication, distrust, ethnic and racial politics among the expedition organisers, and institutional failures that caused the traffic jam leading to six casualties.

Then, a voice from the expedition manager resounded through the radio attached to my rucksack. 'Namaskar, this is Mingma Sherpa from Seven Summit Treks. There is one sick member in the Lhotse Camp Four now. Please, if you're available go for him and bring him down. I'll pay 1,500 dollars. Again, there is a sick member …' The urgency was felt from the rush in his voice. The manager had arrived at Base Camp by helicopter a few days before this series of summit attempts to oversee and control the movement of his company's group – the largest in Base Camp with over thirty members, climbers who paid to join the team. Talking in Nepali via the pan-Sherpa radio channel, Mingma was communicating with the several dozen climbing Sherpas from any group scattered beyond Camp Three. Early that morning, an unsuccessful longline rescue had attempted to reach the Southeast Asian man who for three days had been unable to move himself. Approaching the end of the season, though, those climbing Sherpas high on the mountain were, perhaps with no exception, too busy or exhausted. The reward Mingma offered seemed too modest to quit their own immediate challenges.

The scene of a dying climber also cannot convey the untold processes that might help understand why no aid eventually reached him. This chapter attempts to make sense of the grid of relations that constitute the current practices of climbing a Himalayan peak; the invisible hands that prescribe directions, movements, and goals of climbing bodies. Based on my two years of ethnographic research from 2012 to 2014, when I joined nine expeditions, as well as another month in 2018 for extensive interviews, I will describe the ways in which insiders are variously positioned in the industry of Himalayan mountaineering. Yes, the sport is an industry and should be seen as such if one wishes to track its century of evolution. The industrial practices are best described as an assemblage of neoliberalism, neocolonialism, ethnic politics, and individuals' struggles to move through those contextualising factors.

A brief history of Himalayan mountaineering from the Sherpa's point of view

The epitome of Himalayan mountaineering's historical development is the creation of a division of labour. The growth and sophistication of this division of labour centres on the rise of Sherpas in the whole series of expedition tasks. During the first decade of the twentieth century, a few Sherpas from Darjeeling outcompeted workers from other ethnic/caste groups hired on a few expeditions, such as the Norwegian expedition to Kabru in 1907. Their exceptionally positive demeanour as well as outstanding physical capacity were noted in scientific terms by the Scottish chemist Alexander Kellas during his own expeditions in the 1910s, and garnered the interest of climbers who wished to prove they had arrived at the final stage of human evolution by reaching the highest point on earth.

The Sherpas hired for Himalayan expeditions understood well why they were chosen. They asked for special treatment, such as an exemption from carrying loads to the mountain and higher salaries than lowland porters. They formed a separate group within an expedition. An internal hierarchy developed, where an experienced Sherpa was appointed to oversee expedition chores, such as hiring the rest of the workforce and purchasing food and miscellaneous local materials. He was named sirdar, a word of Persian origin appropriated by the British colonialists to mean a local janissary in Egypt and elsewhere.

Sherpas took increasingly important roles on climbing expeditions. Over time, this created a highly stratified division of labour in Himalayan mountaineering. The division of labour was brought about by three conditions. First, the modus operandi of Himalayan expeditions became increasingly sophisticated. Nearly all necessary knowledge and skills – in terms of logistics, expedition organisation, climbing gear, route details, tactics, techniques, and so on – are devised, analysed, and shared with others so they could climb successfully any of the available peaks. Many of these diversified tasks were gradually placed on the shoulders of employees. Second, local assistance in many of the matters beyond climbing itself has always been crucial across all the active areas for Himalayan mountaineering in Nepal, Pakistan, India, and China. These matters include dealing with bureaucracy, customs clearance, lowland logistics, local transactions, and employee management. Legal, linguistic, and cultural hurdles make it very hard if not impossible for foreign nationals to organise an expedition without local assistance in these countries.

Last but not least, the upsurge of climbing individualism, especially since the mid-1960s after national teams completed the race to make first ascents of all fourteen peaks over 8,000 metres, has deepened the division of labour in Himalayan mountaineering. Mainstream mountaineering discourses throughout Western countries – in climbing magazines, club meetings and bulletins, international gatherings, award ceremonies, and so on – conceive of climbing and mountaineering essentially as a man-versus-mountain affair. From this perspective, everything a mountain climber undergoes between home and the moment of actual climbing is a mere prelude, outside the focal point of the climb (man versus mountain) that gives the journey its meaning. As a result, the term 'expedition' has lost some of its earlier usage, other than the sense of mountaineering in a remote place. This changing perspective accelerated the development of a climbing industry that facilitates nearly everything up to the very act of climbing. Clients may focus solely on conditioning during travel, the trek, or the stay at base camp, and are free from physical or mental hassles related to expedition management. One might even say that the current high standard of elite mountaineering on even the most remote Himalayan peak has been made possible by the firm establishment of comprehensive outfitter services.

This colonial background and historical development of the division of labour in Himalayan mountaineering has led to the institutionalisation of the office of sirdar under new labels. The various tasks once managed by the Sherpa leader have been systematised into the job of an agency staffed in Kathmandu. Tourism agencies that currently play the most significant part in Himalayan mountaineering originated via two routes. On the one hand, as early as the 1950s tour companies in London, New York, and San Francisco pioneered group trekking in Nepal. On the other, mountaineering expeditions organised by climbers had to be facilitated or even reorganised in Kathmandu due to the large need for labour and materials for the venture. The dual location of expedition organisation – expeditions conceived and financed elsewhere that still must be completed, facilitated, and organised in Kathmandu – continued to be the main form for most Himalayan expeditions until around the middle of 2010s.

In the early 1990s, a few competent Western guides – notably Thor Kieser, Rob Hall, Scott Fischer, and Anatoli Boukreev – began selling guiding services for Himalayan giants as well. During the first decade of the 2000s, some experienced Sherpa climbers began recruiting international clients with their own guiding companies. The year 2012 marked another historic moment of this century-long transformative development of Himalayan mountaineering. On the Nepali side of Everest, the largest guided group was organised, for the first time, not by a Western mountaineer/outfitter but by a company based in Kathmandu, namely Seven Summit Treks.

Employment positions in Himalayan mountaineering expedition

The secret for their business success is really no secret. The cost of climbing with Seven Summit Treks was obviously competitive. While describing the market changes in the 2010s, Pasang Tenji Sherpa, the managing director of Pioneer Adventure Trek, founded in 2017, complained that the business practices of the previous dual system were extractive.

> Their [the Western companies'] price is expensive. It's because the Europeans get the money while they don't give much to the Nepali offices. This is unfair! Once everyone arrives in Nepal, the office and local guides do all the works. The European guides go only up to basecamp. While remaining there, they just tell and order and yet don't really do anything. Why on earth should you pay to them?

For a guided Everest climb, the newer agencies like Seven Summit Treks and Pioneer Adventure Trek charge a similar rate of around USD 35,000 per person, certainly a bargain price compared with previous climbing companies. More importantly, their fee schedule is never fixed. In 2013, I met one client on Everest who had paid a mere USD 14,000 after a series of discounts. The key reason for their success was not simply the cheaper price but rather the high level of resiliency bolstered by hospitality practices associated with the characteristics of Sherpa entrepreneurs and guides. Their resilient approach seems also to have played a part in expanding their role as guides across the Himalayan belt and beyond.

Questions arise: how is this exceptional business resiliency possible, and who, or which parts of an industrial division of labour, must bear the risk of loss or failure to sustain such resiliency? Answers may be found in the social relationships that link the participants. The century-long development of the division of labour in Himalayan expeditions resulted in multitudes of task positions. As of the 2010s, the positions are typically team guide, base camp manager, climbing Sherpa, trekking Sherpa, kitchen staff, and porter.

Team guide

Also called group leader, this position is sometimes erroneously referred to by outsiders as sirdar. Ordinarily, the leader of the climbing Sherpas takes the role of team guide as well. The team guide oversees all on-site tasks involving the expedition and administers the daily communications with clients. He (almost always male) makes most important decisions, such as the scheduling of expedition progression and hiring workers on the spot. Most importantly, he commands expedition finances, paying for hotels, food, salary, tips, and other field expenditures, often without a receipt. For this reason, the managing director invariably assigns the title of team guide to the one who is not only among the most experienced and well-reputed but is also among those closest to him.

Base camp manager

This is one of the positions built into the newer form of expedition that I call expedition conglomerate. In an expedition conglomerate, a complex pyramidal governance of staff provides services to a large number of clients, which may consist of multiple sub-groups or simply separate individuals, all jointly sharing facilities for fixed-rope climbing and enjoyable base-camp experiences. From around the early 2010s, the Everest Base Camp in Nepal began transforming from a place for climbing preparation and passive rest to a place for active revitalisation and new experiences through entertainment, socialising, distant communication, and sponsor advertisement. The base camp manager oversees various facilities that enable enjoyable base camp experiences, such as the bakery, wine bar, dancing hall, helicopter logistics, medical support, and wireless communication. It might not always be clear and obvious whether the team guide or the base camp manager is the most authoritative office in an expedition, which can lead to disputes, as their influence will depend on the number of personnel that each has under their charge.

Climbing Sherpa

This is a technical term for those commonly called simply Sherpa and used mostly within the agency only. In the government paperwork they are referred to as climbing guides. In Pakistan, the bureaucratic title for a similar position is high altitude porter, or HAP, although a HAP is generally not in charge of guiding. A climbing Sherpa is required to perform a variety of tasks on the expedition: fixing rope on the route, setting up and breaking down tents, carrying food, gear, fuel, and virtually all supplies needed on the mountain up and down, and escorting a client in the summit push. In the case of Everest's spring season, climbing Sherpas normally accompany paired clients during the three-day period of the summit attempt, and they initiate their escort from Camp Four, Camp Three, or infrequently Camp Two, depending on the clients' condition. During the critical period in the expedition, larger groups often send to the highest camp 'extra Sherpas' not paired with any client, perhaps those in apprenticeship, so that they may respond to any call for unexpected demands high on the mountain.

Trekking Sherpa

Unless the client uses helicopter transportation to arrive at or leave base camp, an expedition involves periods of hiking for several days as the base camps are in remote places. In these periods, an expedition moves in a way similar to an ordinary trekking group. One of the differences is that on an expedition, trekking guides are mostly staffed with ethnic Sherpas, who indeed constitute a minority in the trekking industry. Among over two thousand registered tourism agencies in Nepal, the few that specialise in organising expeditions to 8,000-metre peaks, and currently thrive, are mostly run by ethnic Sherpas. For the task of trekking guiding on the expedition, agency managers often hire junior or retired Sherpa climbers.

Kitchen staff

By definition, one of the functions of an expedition is to sustain itself, and therefore food production is one of its crucial tasks. A kitchen is a sub-institution in the organisation of every Himalayan mountaineering expedition; its staff consists of one cook and two or three kitchen helpers. In the case of Everest (on both the north and south sides), a kitchen facility is established at Camp Two (circa 6,400 metres) as well. An expedition cook may specialise in Korean food, Chinese food, Indian food, or 'Western' food, while all will be able to prepare Nepali dishes as well. Kitchen helpers, customarily called kitchen boys, are in charge of fetching water or ice, boiling water, washing the dishes, serving food to clients, and so on. Kitchen employment is considered menial, and the staff usually consists of ethnically non-Sherpa.

Porter

While the positions described so far are those hired directly by the agency in Kathmandu, porters are among those who are hired locally by the team guide. The former, 'primary' employees may sometimes be called Sherpa as a collective, signifying their elevated status in the tourism industry, while the porters must not, as they are considered subsidiary employees. Although the daily wage that porters receive may be slightly better than those of other primary employees on an expedition, especially in Khumbu due to its chronic inflation, porters will be excluded from expeditionary benefits, such as meals, tents, and shoes for snow. Since a large number of porters needs to be hired at once for a single expedition, it is important for the agency manager to maintain solid connections with a local contact person, be they a hotel owner or a porter leader. This regionally powerful individual will prearrange the staff before the expedition arrives at the departure point, such as Lukla (2,860 metres) for Everest and other peaks in Khumbu.

A caravan of yak or *Jopkyo* (a yak-cow crossbreed) may also be an option for transporting the tons of luggage. This option is cheaper but comes with a few shortcomings, such as their relative unavailability, the possibility of luggage being damaged, and the relative inability to modify daily schedules due to different movement patterns from human groups. In the late 2010s, in order to reduce transportation costs, a few agencies that owned helicopters began flying luggage directly to base camps. This provoked the local authorities in Khumbu to ban the practice in 2023.

From this brief overview of the division of expedition labour emplaced in the 2010s, an internal hierarchy is obvious, but it is never static, as it weaves the various individuals into an organic body that resiliently functions to fulfil the constantly changing needs of mountaineering tourists. How, then, is the hierarchy maintained? What ties connect them and also allow them to dissociate? If wages dictate responsibilities, then in what ways are the wages calculated and paid?

Wage practices on the mountain

On average, climbing Sherpa earn significantly more than most other ordinary labourers in Nepal. In 2013, the official monthly salary for the four staff of one Kathmandu-based expedition agency spanned from NPR 9,000 to NPR 14,000 (USD 100–160). In the same year, Everest's climbing Sherpas earned USD 2,000–7,000 for three months of work. How could they make this much in comparison with others in Nepal? And why is there such a large range in climbing Sherpas' income schedule? As will soon become obvious, the wage structure is neither straightforward nor conclusive. There are multiple sources from which climbing Sherpa earn income through expedition participation. In general, climbing Sherpa earn compensation from the following six categories: daily wage, equipment fee, carry bonus, summit bonus, tip, and payments for by-work.

Daily wage

This wage is calculated based on the dates from and to Kathmandu. Although most primary employees normally begin their respective tasks in Kathmandu several weeks before the expedition actually embarks, their labour in this period is not counted for the wage. The duration of an Everest expedition for the employees is usually fifty to sixty days in total. The rate for daily wage will follow an identical scale for every position within an agency, while the rates vary between different agencies. In 2013, the daily wage was NPR 500–800 (USD 5.6–8.9) across Everest expeditions.

Equipment fee

This payment originated from the custom devised during the 1920s British Everest expeditions, when Sherpas began to be hired systematically.

To maximally utilise labour-power across glacial terrain, the British mountain-eers not only celebrated the perceived usefulness of Sherpas but also brought and distributed clothing, shoes, ice axes, and other specialised gear. As expedi-tions returned, some experienced Sherpas joined with gear from previous expe-ditions and were given money instead. Similarly, today the equipment fee is generally regarded simply as a distinct part of the salary. A novice Sherpa could opt to spend this portion of money to purchase some essential gear. Agencies fulfil the historical obligation to equip their Sherpas properly and may guar-antee purchases with this payment long before they receive the actual salary. The amount of equipment fee also varies depending on the agency. In 2013, the median was around USD 1,500 while the smallest I heard of was USD 800, followed by grunts.

Carry bonus

Though called a bonus, this is not technically awarded as a 'bonus' but rather paid as compensation for labour performed, on an ascending scale. The calcu-lation is based on the sections and total weights one has accomplished carrying. The carry bonus system is not universally practised in Himalayan mountain-eering but put in place where two market logics are met. For one, there must be large numbers of labourers and workloads, large enough so laissez-faire operations may take place. For the other, uncertainty must be eliminated so anyone who desires may go for the bonus. Throughout the 2010s, the carry bonus system was in place regularly in the spring on Everest and autumn on Manaslu, and occasionally in the spring season on Makalu. Except for these well-populated slopes, on other Himalayan mountains climbing Sherpas usu-ally work together with clients at a fixed rate.

In my sample from Seven Summit Treks throughout the 2010s, the spring Everest season rate for one *bari* (fifteen kilograms of luggage) from Base Camp to Camp Two was USD 55; from Camp Two to Camp Four was USD 120. A 'double *bari*' is also attainable. Across agencies there was a wide disparity, such that the rate could vary from USD 80 to 500 for carrying a *bari* from Base Camp to Camp Four. Since it is not permitted to carry for an expedition other than one's own, the fee schedules would be reported with begrudging and gripes in the secluded circles of Sherpas.

A closer look at the custom of carry bonus reveals some of the ways in which the Sherpas are obliged to one another along the expedition hierarchy. The team guide or a camp manager is in charge of recording the number and

Figure 12.1 Camp manager (in the middle) recording the number of oxygen canisters to be carried by each climbing Sherpa, at Camp Two of Mount Everest, 3 May 2013. Image: © Young Hoon Oh.

weight of loads carried by each climbing Sherpa. An act of deception may take place, meanwhile, on the part of either the field recorder, the agency manager, or both. It is an open secret that the managing directors of many agencies pay their employees a smaller share of the salary than promised, if they pay at all. The amount of the embezzled portion is considered the price for patronage, or *zindak* in Sherpa, in that a powerful person gives favours to those among his closest associates, such as the more remunerative opportunities in an expedition. Supposing this to occur, the camp manager poised in between might want to give favours to those he wishes to build a close relationship with by recording higher load-carrying amounts more than the Sherpa actually took.

Summit bonus

This segment of salary could make a big difference in the end. Unless the client pays this directly, as they sometimes do, the agency will pay this bonus to climbing Sherpas who successfully reach the summit together with their clients. The amount varies remarkably depending on the agency and the mountain.

At Seven Summit Treks, Everest's summit bonus was USD 1,000 in 2012 and USD 1,500 in 2019. For Manaslu, it was about USD 300 to 500.

It is important to note that a climbing Sherpa's personal competence in climbing and guiding rarely registers as a crucial factor for a successful summit. Whether or not the Sherpa–client pair summits is mostly due to the fitness of the client. In turn, the decision of who pairs with whom falls onto the shoulders of the team guide. The team guide often enjoys the highest chance of reaching the top by assigning to himself the client who is seemingly the most fit. Hence, the amount of summit bonus, total income, and reputation seldom reflect climbing Sherpas' levels of fitness or effort, but these are, rather, more or less manifestations of their social capital.

Tips

Tipping is widespread across a variety of interpersonal economic practices in Nepal, regardless of tourist involvement. For several days of labour, a day's wage might be given additionally as a tip. The practice of tipping in Nepal originates from the South Asian practice of *dan*, or charitable donation. *Dan* differs from the practice of aggressive individualism that engenders the custom of tipping in other contexts. In US restaurants, for example, the size of the tip is considered a customer's measurement of the quantity and quality of the service provided by the attendant. Across South Asia, the practice of *dan* contains the structure of ethics in which the relationship between the donor and the receiver matters most. Not only is the donor's generosity acknowledged, by receiving, but the receiver's generosity is also acknowledged since, thanks to the receiver, the donor now obtains an opportunity to build up good karma. In this scheme, tipping is regarded as a practice of goodwill, a sign of good nature, with a relational capacity for both the tipper and the tipped. In 2012, for example, a Chinese climber bailed at Camp Four of Everest with no summit, and tipped USD 2,500 to her climbing Sherpa, nonetheless. This occasion was shared and retold many times among the circle of Sherpas, mostly praising her perceived good nature.

Payments from by-work

While expedition employment is the major type of economic contract on Himalayan mountains such as Everest, a variety of other transactions may take place at nearly every part of the mountain. A wide range of by-work, such as the rescue mission I reported earlier in the chapter, are usually available throughout each season. The following three cases of oxygen bottles, trash, and bodies illustrate additional sources of income for climbing Sherpas and other employees on the mountain.

The first example is to collect and sell used oxygen bottles. In the last three decades, the standard oxygen tank used in Himalayan mountaineering is the one produced by the Russian company Poisk. A brand-new Poisk bottle weighs 4.4 kilograms and a used-up one 2.9 kilograms. Though the practice is illegal and unreliable, empty tanks are commonly collected from the mountains for refilling, reselling, and re-use. A larger agency may own the refilling facility at its garage. At Everest Base Camp in 2013, one empty bottle was purchased at NPR 1,000–8,000 (USD 11–89). In Kathmandu, the price goes up to around USD 150. A refilled bottle is sold at USD 350, whereas the new one – and a refilled one that looks brand-new – costs over USD 400. Since the bottles are highly valued, climbing Sherpas at Camp Four usually pick up and carry abandoned canisters, often instead of their portion of camp materials. At Base Camp, climbing Sherpas will hide the bottles they have collected if they want to sell them to an agency manager or businessperson who purchases at a price higher than their own manager.

Secondly, the rationalised absurdity in comparing the value of what to bring down from high on the mountain is also evident at the clean-up campaigns. One of the media fantasies in the twenty-first century imagines Everest as a sewer of human debris, both symbolically and literally. Cleaning up the imperial symbol of willpower, reiterated as a publicity project once in a while since the 1980s, may therefore register as a heroic act in an era many perceive as disgraced. In 2013, the governments of India and Nepal jointly launched a similar initiative, where carrying one kilogram of garbage collected from Camp Four and down to Camp Two was paid NPR 1,000 (USD 11). The carry bonus rate for one *bari* (15 kilograms) for the same section was USD 100, driving some climbing Sherpas to bring garbage instead of expedition luggage. One Sherpa rightly carped, 'Trash is more expensive than equipment!' On an idle day, a Camp Two kitchen helper left his workplace to join the lucrative task, to the anger of his boss.

Finally, rescuing an endangered person or retrieving a dead body high on the mountain – dangerous and taxing operations – is also well-paid by-work that is available intermittently. In 2013, a party of nine transported a corpse from Camp Four to Camp Two at the wage of USD 900 each. One of the participants later complained after he learned that the task's leader, who sum-moned the personnel and received the total fee from the client to distribute as

Table 12.1   *Detailed hypothetical income for a climbing Sherpa from an Everest expedition*

Equipment fee	USD 1,500
Daily wage (NPR 600 × 50 days)	USD 333
Carry bonus 55 × 5 *bari* (BC to C2) + 120 × 2 *bari* (C2 to C4)	USD 515
Summit bonus	USD 1,500
Tip	USD 500
Oxygen canisters 50 × 2 pcs	USD 100
In total	**USD 4,448**
Patronage embezzlement	−10%
Expected income	**USD 4,003.20**

promised, embezzled USD 300 from his share of the wage. The *zindak* patronage might have been the rationale for the embezzlement, but the one who complained was not ethnically Sherpa and the embezzling was done furtively. If *zindak* still serves as a useful principle for a minority to gain limited opportunities, more often than not it is appropriated to exploit or to endorse malpractices on the marketised mountain slopes.

In 2018, Mingma Sherpa of Seven Summit Treks told me that climbing Sherpa in general earned about USD 4,000 from an Everest expedition. My own estimation roughly concurs, as shown in Table 12.1.

Yet the *de jure* income that goes into the worker's pocket may still diverge far from the *de facto* salary in both Mingma's and my own estimations. The precarity of capitalism is paramount amid the social, global, and environmental uncertainties inherent in the Himalayan mountaineering industry. The ice avalanche in 2014, the Gorkha earthquake in 2015, and the COVID-19 pandemic in 2020–21 all hit the industry hard. The industry has also been quickly transformed by the aggressive strategies of newer agencies. There is essentially no insurance or other backup resources for the companies themselves, providing further incentive for their owners to extract profit as much as possible, to benefit fully from the unrestrained economic liberalism cultivated on the cosmopolitan mountains.

Contemporary patterns of climbing Everest

A few conclusions may be drawn from the observations above regarding the division of labour, the salary schedule, and the associated practices surrounding mountaineering expeditions to Himalayan giants such as Everest. These illustrate how climbing Sherpa became a lucrative profession and how Sherpas have managed to create and monopolise the related business sectors.

These direct further attention to the underlying economic and social relationships through which Everest climbing has been patterned.

First, the twin principles of ethnicity and social belonging enable many male members of Sherpa communities to secure the mountain slopes as a place of boon and fame. This should not be a surprise, for the same principles are at work in many other areas of Nepali society as a whole. Although popular aphorisms such as 'the death zone' or 'conquistadors of the useless' might preach a differing view, Himalayan mountaineering is not an exception. Perhaps only from this angle may one track the evolution of climbing on Everest over the last century, the period when no description can do justice without weighing the collective efforts of Sherpa communities in materialising the feat.

Second, the economic liberalism and neoliberalism that remain unchecked in a country infamous for corruption and weak governance have had critical effects on nearly every aspect of the mountaineering industry, seemingly converting some undertakings into profitable games of chance. I am not sure what grounds can justify or defend the failed call to offer financial incentives for a mountain rescue which opened this chapter. Yet the popular perception of mountaineering decisions as the straightforward effects of personal ethics and psychology ignores the crucial role played by multitudes of social channels and historical contingencies that bring together hundreds of men and women to share the slopes of Everest. To move beyond the criminalisation or heroisation of Himalayan mountaineering requires attention to grids of relations that permit individuals to function systematically high on the mountain.

Lastly, acknowledging that forms of Himalayan mountaineering are constantly in transformation, the marketisation that created the expedition conglomerate on Everest is perhaps the dominant force in constituting contemporary forms of mountaineering worldwide. The tasks that Sherpas established and have performed on Himalayan slopes for the past century squarely complement the practices that climbers and mountaineers from elsewhere increasingly consider insignificant or less meaningful achievements. Perhaps the odds on the Himalayan mountains have their equivalents in contested economic, social, and ethical relations in the vertical realms across the globe.

Note

This chapter is drawn mostly from my own fieldwork mentioned in the text. More observations are available from my doctoral dissertation, *Sherpa Intercultural Experiences in Himalayan Mountaineering*. For historical and sociological discussions, I relied on various writings and scholarly works. Notable sources include Ian Mitchell and George Rodway on Kellas's selective hiring of Sherpas in the 1910s; E.F. Norton detailing the systemic employment of Sherpas in the 1920s; and Anatoli Boukreev's vignettes of the rise of guided Himalayan mountaineering expeditions in the 1990s. Essays edited by Joanna Pfaff-Czarnecka and Gérard Toffin present the politics of belonging in Nepali society, and Madhusudan Subedi notes widespread malpractices derived from social connections and multiple identities practices.

References

Boukreev, Anatoli. *Above the Clouds: The Diaries of a High-Altitude Mountaineer.* New York: St. Martin's Griffin, 2001.

Mitchell, Ian R. and George W. Rodway. *Prelude to Everest: Alexander Kellas, Himalayan Mountaineer.* Edinburgh: Luath, 2011.

Norton, Edward Felix. *The Fight for Everest: 1924.* New York; London: Longmans; Arnold, 1925.

Oh, Young Hoon. 'Sherpa intercultural experiences in Himalayan mountaineering: a pragmatic phenomenological perspective'. PhD dissertation, University of California, Riverside, 2016.

Pfaff-Czarnecka, Joanna and Gérard Toffin. *The Politics of Belonging in the Himalayas: Local Attachments and Boundary Dynamics.* New Delhi: SAGE, 2011.

Subedi, Madhusudan. 'Afno Manchhe: unequal access to public resources and institutions in Nepal', *Dhaulagiri Journal of Sociology and Anthropology,* 8 (2014), 55–86, https://doi.org/10.3126/dsaj.v8i0.10722

13

The numbers game on Mount Everest: new 'lows' on the world's highest mountain

Pradeep Bashyal and Ankit Babu Adhikari

The 2023 pre-monsoon expedition season on Mount Everest concluded in the last week of May. Everest Base Camp was deserted again as the last lot of Sherpas pulled down the remaining tents and returned home. Slowly a peace came over the mountain, following months of frenetic activity on Everest. Some outfitters and guides left Base Camp and moved on to Kathmandu to celebrate the seventieth anniversary of the first successful ascent of Mount Everest.

A few weeks later, a drone took off and hovered in the sky above Everest's death zone at over 8,000 metres, in an attempt to locate a Malaysian climber who had gone missing during an expedition. In the eternal vastness and silence of the deserted post-expedition mountain, the drone carefully scanned the surface of the mountain – zooming in and out and moving up, down, right, and left. The missing climber was nowhere to be seen, but the visual data that the drone returned with took everyone by surprise. Camp Four on the South Col, at 8,000 metres the last rest point on the way up to the summit of Everest, was still crowded with colourful rows of upright tents – not one, not two, but dozens of abandoned tents, as if the footage was taken during the middle of the expedition season.

The tents are only the most visible manifestation of the problem of consumer waste on the mountain. For every tent there is an unaccounted load of packaged food inside the tent. There are mattresses, empty oxygen tanks, trash, ropes, batteries, torchlights, plastic waste, and human excrement that nobody is ever going to carry down. In all likelihood, the tents will be torn apart and blown away by winter storms, or crushed beneath accumulations of snow, but the remains of plastic and aluminium will never decompose. Next year, climbers will return to Everest again; new tents will be set up over the grave of older ones, and the cycle will perpetuate itself.

Despite routine cleaning efforts led by Nepali authorities, including the Nepal Army and charities, concern over alarming amounts of waste on Everest is increasing every year.[1] The waste removal attempts are often limited to lower camps and are easily overrun by the Western consumer lifestyles on the mountain, which are creating a waste stream that exceeds the authorities' capacity to deal with it.

The more the merrier?

In 2023 the government of Nepal issued a record high number of 478 Everest climbing permits. With a ratio of 1.5 Sherpa guides and porters to every climber, nearly 1,000 people made an attempt on the summit in 2023, with a success rate of about 60 per cent. The number of climbers and guides on the mountain has been growing by the year. In 2012, the number of permits issued stood at 315. This represents a 51 per cent increase in permits issued in the last decade. This excludes three zero-summit years – in 2014 due to an avalanche at the Khumbu Icefall which killed sixteen Sherpas; in 2015 due to the 7.9 magnitude earthquake and avalanche that swept the Everest Base Camp killing fourteen (with deaths among climbers, base camp staff, and trekkers); and in 2020 due to the global COVID-19 pandemic.

Table 13.1   People on the summit of Everest (Nepal side), 2010–23

Year	Client success	Sherpa success	Total success	Permits	Deaths
2010	170	296	466		0
2011	165	113	278		
2012	174	219	393	315	6
2013	242	336	578		6
2014	0	0	6*	341	16
2015	0	0	0	357	14*
2016	197	254	451	292	5
2017	199	227	426	388	6
2018	262	298	560	346	5
2019	280	364	644	381	9
2020	0	0	0	0	0
2021	182	277	459	409	2
2022	240	399	639	323	3
2023	268	391	659	478	18
2024	287	470	757	421	8

Note:
* After the 2014 avalanche closed the climbing route, a Chinese mountaineer and Sherpa team landed a helicopter at Camp 2, a summit that remains controversial. The 2015 earthquake caused 19 deaths at Everest Base Camp, including 5 people in Base Camp as trekkers and 14 people on climbing permits, noted above.
Source: Nepal's Department of Tourism, Nepal Mountaineering Association, AlanArnette.com

Nepal is one of the poorest countries on earth, where about one-quarter of the national revenue comes from remittances sent by about five million Nepali citizens working as migrant labourers in the Gulf, in India, and elsewhere. Revenue generated through tourism, including Everest expeditions, is a major source of national income. In 2023, the Nepal Ministry of Tourism charged a royalty fee of USD 11,000 for each Everest climbing permit. This yearly increase in the number of permits issued has increased the Nepal government's foreign exchange revenue. In 2023, the Nepal government made USD 5.5 million from Everest climbing permits issued for the pre-monsoon expedition season. Fees from Everest climbing permits combined with other tourism revenues contribute nearly 10 per cent of Nepal's national GDP.

The growth of tourist numbers on Everest has transformed the lives of Sherpas. The greater the number of climbers, the higher the number of jobs for Sherpas. More climbers mean more customers for the businesses of Everest region, which include small teahouses, hotels, and lodges on the way from Lukla to Everest Base Camp. Tourists fly to Lukla's short takeoff and landing (STOL) airport from Nepal's capital, Kathmandu. From Lukla, Everest Base Camp is a one-week trek through the Sherpa villages of Phakding, Namche, Khumjung, Tengboche/Phortse, Pangboche, and Dingboche, among others. During an expedition season, while most Sherpa men get employed as porters, yak transporters, and guides, the women run teahouses, small restaurants, and lodges along the trekking route.[2] The majority of Sherpas involved in mountaineering expeditions as high-altitude porters or guides earn up to about USD 5,000 a year. Nepal's national GDP per capita is just a little over USD 1,000, so the income of Sherpas involved in mountaineering is generally considered to be attractive. Mountaineering income has enabled Sherpas in the Solu Khumbu region to dominate labour hierarchies in the tourist industry, invest in businesses, and often maintain a comfortable lifestyle in the mountain villages where the cost of living is significantly higher than other areas of the country. Transportation costs often exceed the per-unit cost of an item as many goods must be transported by helicopter and expensive yak caravans.

Sherpas and other Indigenous Nepali entrepreneurs have also begun to successfully compete with Western outfitters for access to lucrative markets for trekking, mountaineering, and adventure tourism in Nepal. Less than a decade ago, adventure tourism on Everest was still mostly dominated by foreign-owned and foreign-run expedition companies, with only a handful of native Nepali companies in the marketplace. Nepali companies consistently struggled to win the trust of clients and compete with better capitalised foreign competitors who had access to global networks and resources.

There has been a long history of Sherpa entrepreneurs in the mountaineering and adventure tourism industry of the region. Since the 1960s and 1970s, well before the beginning of commercial mountaineering expeditions, one influential Sherpa family from the village of Khumjung had already begun to recognise the importance of Western mountaineering expeditions for the economy and development of the region. Konjo Chumbi Sherpa, who was friends with Tenzing Norgay growing up together in Khumjung, had accompanied Sir Edmund Hillary on a world tour in 1960, exhibiting what was believed to be the skull of a yeti from Khumjung. Konjo Chumbi's engagement with Western mountaineers and experience of travel outside the region cemented his leadership and influence in the Everest region. Konjo Chumbi became the undisputed 'go-to' local support for international Everest expeditions following the first successful British expedition of 1953 and he managed the logistics for the 1963 American Everest expedition.

Konjo Chumbi's son, Ang Tshering, later went on to build on his family's legacy in trekking and mountaineering, launching a company called Asian Trekking in the early 1980s. When foreign-owned commercial Everest expeditions started taking off in the 1990s, Ang Tshering's Asian Trekking was a homegrown competitor, slowly and steadily carving out a prosperous future for the entire Sherpa community. Ang Tshering has trained and employed hundreds of Sherpas from the Nepali mountain regions of Khumbu (Everest), Makalu, and Rolwaling and a large number of these Sherpas later established their own companies that would begin to challenge the foreign dominance of commercial expedition outfitting in Nepal. According to Ang Tshering, 'Establishing the dominance of Nepali people in mountaineering has taken long years of patience. However, we Sherpa people always had it in us, as we were in clear advantage of the terrain and mountain operations. We may not have been smart businesspeople from the very beginning, but we always had a dominance when it came to managing business in the mountains.'[3]

Seven Summit Treks, one of today's major commercial expedition outfitters in global mountaineering, is run by a protégé of Ang Tshering's who worked at Asian Trekking. Mingma Sherpa is the eldest of three brothers who have turned their company into a global business. Seven Summit Treks currently employs hundreds of Sherpas simultaneously in different mountains throughout the world – from Everest to Antarctica.

Tendi Sherpa's company, Tag Nepal, also a spinoff from Ang Tshering's Asian Trekking, is another successful Sherpa-run business that has developed a lucrative commercial niche catering to wealthy clients from all over the world. Tendi's company charges over USD 200,000 per client for expeditions to climb Mount Everest. An internationally certified mountain guide himself, Tendi is in high demand globally. His lifestyle is increasingly that of an international businessman, so much so that even his close friends must go through his yearly calendar sometimes to make a dinner appointment.

'After all, the success was waiting for us all the time', said Tashi Lhakpa Sherpa, one of the three brothers running Seven Summit Treks. 'We are the people of the mountains, and we have always been the first choice when it comes to climbing. With all the latest technologies, our genetic abilities, and expertise built through training and experience, there is nothing that can stop us from playing the offense.'

The economic impact of the Everest industry is huge, and the success of Indigenous Nepali entrepreneurs means that revenue is increasingly staying in Nepal. The combination of royalties for Everest climbing permits, commercial outfitters' fees ranging from USD 35,000 to over USD 200,000, insurance and rescue work, and the earnings of small businesses in the Everest region is said to contribute over USD 300 million annually to Nepal's USD 46 billion economy.[4]

The more the scarier

Out of all the attempts made at reaching the summit of Everest in 2023, about 60 per cent were successful. While some aborted their mission for different reasons, for some there was no way back home. Between 13 and 26 May 2023, a total of twelve confirmed deaths were recorded on Everest. Five climbers were also reported missing, presumed dead by authorities, bringing the death toll to seventeen in 2023, a record high number.[5] As in previous years, most of these deaths occurred above 8,000 metres between Camp Four on the South Col and the summit – an area also often referred to as the 'death zone', where lack of oxygen and extremes of altitude, terrain, and weather present huge objective risks to mountaineers.[6]

To die on Everest does not necessarily take a disaster or an avalanche. According to Tendi Sherpa, the seasoned climber and internationally certified mountain guide who has climbed Everest fifteen times, seemingly trivial things can kill someone on Everest: a fall whilst unclipping from fixed lines or starting out too late in the day on your summit push. Most Western mountaineers who die on Everest die descending from the summit. Determined to reach the summit, they succumb to fatigue or high-altitude pulmonary edema (HAPE) on their way back down in the death zone. Prolonged inactivity quickly leads to hypothermia and death.

High-altitude guides have to monitor and carefully assess their clients' capabilities. According to Tendi Sherpa, 'Often times, clients tend not to communicate how hard they are struggling to keep up with the climb as their only goal is to reach to the summit. They are scared the guide might abort their mission if they present themselves as weak. It is the job of a guide to continuously assess the performance of the client, how much water the client is drinking, his/her breathing pattern, rhythm and pace, appetite, among many other attributes.' He added, 'A guide is also responsible to clinically regulate the amount of supplementary oxygen intake of a client. Supplementary oxygen is never enough, and if a climber consumes much of that in easier parts already, they are very much likely to fall short of the life-saving gas when in death zone where they need it the most.'

The increasing number of aspirant climbers on Everest has led to overcrowding on the route up the mountain and notorious 'traffic jams' at critical bottlenecks on the route. Every year, the push to the summit of Everest is determined by narrow weather windows during mid-May, marked by a significant decrease in northbound windspeeds, which drop to 20–30 km/hour from their usual 150–200 km/hour during the rest of the year.[7] Climbers naturally aim for their summit push during these narrow windows. This has resulted in harrowing traffic jams, especially above 8,000 metres, and the phenomenon of 'blue sky deaths' where mountaineering clients spend too long waiting to both ascend and descend at altitude as everyone seeks to exploit the narrow window of stable weather conditions.

As the numbers increase on Everest, more and more inexperienced clients are drawn to the mountain by the promises from adventure travel outfitters guaranteeing clients a successful summit bid. 'When this mix of competent and less-competent climbers queue up in narrow tracks of death zone, there is bound to be some collateral damage, as the risk is same for everyone at the edge of life and death, and the mountain does not know who is experienced and who is not', said Tendi Sherpa. When an inexperienced climber struggles to keep up, they block the route for everyone behind them on the fixed lines. If someone sits down to rest while climbing down from the summit, it increases the risks for everyone behind them as every second counts in the descent.

To be safe, climbers should be back at Camp Four on the South Col by noon to avoid increasing windspeeds during the second half of the day. When there is an accident in the death zone, climbers must be rescued. This means that other clients must often wait until the track is cleared, significantly draining their oxygen and energy levels.

Overcrowding on Everest has become a source of contention, with many mountaineers criticising the problems with the business model of commercial expeditions on Everest. A *Washington Post* article in 2017 quoted one climber saying, 'it's become a walk in the park',[8] after the increase of traffic on Everest following the gap due to the 2014 and 2015 disasters. The climbing permits issued in 2014 and 2015 were carried forward and piled up in these years. The 'walk in the park' label was evidence of this skyrocketing number of climbers. One *New York Times* headline in 2019 read: 'It was like a zoo…',[9] referring to the then all-time high in Everest numbers. While overcrowding on Everest has alarmed many, for some operating climbing businesses on Everest, it's all normal. In an article covering a notorious 2019 Everest traffic jam, a Nepali climbing company owner was quoted as normalising traffic jams on Everest: 'climbing Everest is like attaining highest pilgrimage' and the line of climbers 'is just like waiting for your turn outside a temple'.[10] In stark contrast to the rising concerns of safety and littering on Everest due to increasing numbers every year, these remarks show the capitalist mindset of the climbing business, where the numbers tend to supersede its side effects.

The growth in the number of commercial clients on Everest has been facilitated by an increasingly diverse range of commercial outfitters offering expeditions at different price points for a range of consumers. In the spring of 2023, there were forty-four teams on Everest, all with their own different ways of operating. Their clients represented many different nationalities and different walks of life – some were rich and willing to pay a premium to be comfortable on the mountain. The current Everest business model relies on customer satisfaction and increasingly seeks to replicate Western standards of living on the mountain. Companies aim to keep their customers happy. They secure more business for the future by competing with other commercial outfitters on levels of comfort, luxury, and amenity on the mountain.[11]

Based on how much a climber is willing to pay, the commercial expedition outfitter segregates their clients into different categories. The 'A-listers' get assigned a greater number of Sherpas; they are provided with an unlimited supply of bottled oxygen, which they can consume at any pressure they are comfortable with right from the base camp. For 'A-listers' paying the highest fees, their stay at the base camp replicates many of the comforts and amenities experienced by the privileged leisure classes of the world. There are imported luxury tents and dorms, fully insulated and with expensive furniture inside – king-size beds, heated mattresses and blankets, carpets, sofas, and tables. Kitchens are staffed by foreign 5-star chefs, putting together elaborate, multicourse meals. There are late-night DJ parties, karaoke, drinking, and dancing. Whilst it is not possible to retain all these base camp luxuries in the higher camps, the expedition companies do all they can to make the Sherpa porters carry every last bit of luxury to the highest point possible. Luxury dorms, extra food and oxygen bottles, and luxury mattresses, follow their wealthy clients up as high as Camp Two at 6,400 metres. During pre-acclimatisation rotations up to the higher camps of Everest, some of the richer clients have the choice to take a break before their final summit push. After they are well acclimatised and have completed their rotation exercises, they can board a helicopter at Camp Two, fly back to Kathmandu, rest for a few days in the comfort of a 5-star hotel, and when the window for the summit push opens, fly back to Camp Two and resume the expedition.

Sherpas have expressed concerns about the noise of helicopter traffic triggering avalanches. Until the 2010s, helicopters would avoid flying above Base Camp unless there was an urgent need for a rescue in one of the higher camps but now there is increasing aviation traffic up and down the Khumbu Icefall catering to the needs of a new breed of adventure tourists.

So, what's wrong with all this if someone is willing to pay for these services? Well, the problems are manifold. Let's start with the supply of additional Sherpa guides and porters. The greater the number of people thronging Everest, the higher the chances of overcrowding on the mountain, and the greater the amount of waste produced. For every three times a client goes up and down the mountain between the higher camps on Everest during acclimatisation rotations and the final summit push, a climbing Sherpa has to go up and down that same route thirty times, carrying supplies and fixing tents, increasing their exposure to the objective dangers of the route. The additional climbing Sherpas assigned to 'A-list' clients are a form of conspicuous consumption that makes little difference to a client's ability to acclimatise. Commenting on the problematic overtourism on Everest and the mismanagement of the numbers of clients trying to climb Everest, the mountaineer Reinhold Messner, in an interview with the *Diplomat* magazine, said, 'this is not alpinism. This is tourism. People are buying the possibility to go up the piste on Everest.'[12]

Adventure tourists contribute to the problems on the mountain by insisting on replicating Western levels of consumption. 'People just take way too much of food', Tendi Sherpa told the authors. 'As a climber, you should know, and if you are a company, you should tell your client that their appetite is going to plummet as they go higher up in the mountain. You don't feel like eating anything, and all you can really do is soup, chocolates, and wafers, no matter what you may have in your backpack. You are not going to carry any of that all the way back to base camp. You'll just dump it somewhere on the snow.'

The same goes for tents, mattresses, and any other excess items many climbers insist on taking with them. After summit, tired climbers start dumping their things on the way. Many don't bother to take down their tents, or pack things away at Camp Four. 'Ideally, the less you take the better, as anything extra is just going to stay up there and gradually eat up the mountain you love so much', Tendi said. 'But these are principles, and nobody seems to care about them in today's competitive era.'

The cost of everything

When Kuntal Joisher from Mumbai, India, decided to reach the summit of Mount Everest in 2010, the first thing he did was quit his job as a software developer in Los Angeles. Joisher hoped to be the first vegan to summit Everest. Without any prior mountaineering experience, Kuntal put together a meticulous diet and training plan. He hiked every week, meditated every day for several hours, and was determined to develop the mental strength to enable him to climb Everest. He was so focused on his dream that he convinced his wife to defer their plan for having a baby. Joisher immersed himself in his Everest project and did his best to not think of anything else but his goal. 'I remember at some point I became totally selfish for my Everest dream, and lost all empathy towards even my family', Joisher recalls.

It took Joisher four years, including successful ascents of other 8,000-metre peaks, to finally realise he was ready for Everest in 2014. He had to wait another two years as disastrous avalanches and earthquakes struck Everest in 2014 and 2015. Finally, in 2016, Joisher stood on top of the world. He had hired Mingma Tenzi, one of the strongest Sherpa guides, later known for his historic winter ascent of K2 in 2021 as part of a team with Nimsdai Purja and Mingma G. 'Mingma Tenzi is one of the best Sherpas I have ever known, and I knew I was in safe hands', Joisher said. 'However, with all the years of preparation, I had come to realize that I would be on my own, that I should wear my crampons myself, and I must myself undertake all responsibilities of my safety. It was an equal partnership with Mingma, and he had made it clear from the very beginning.'

Many commercial clients are far less prepared than Kuntal Joisher, with stories circulating of people arriving at Everest Base Camp being unable to put on their own crampons. And not all Sherpas or commercial mountaineering companies would insist like Mingma on making their clients realise the value of shared ownership and shared responsibility in climbing, which might be seen as undermining the current business model on Everest. Kuntal's experience of individual responsibility as a climber and his fortunate encounter with Sherpas like Mingma Tenzi challenge the popular 'customer is always right' model, where most climbers are entirely dependent upon Sherpas, and overlook their part of the job.

A successful climber with two Everest summits from both North and South routes today, Joisher often gets asked about how to go about climbing Everest. The majority of these questions begin with the basic queries about the cost of climbing the mountain and naive questions about how easy or how hard climbing Everest is. 'I am surprised by how easily the value of Everest and mountaineering are undermined by a majority of climbers', he said. 'What took me years of patience and spiritual awakening is so casually reduced to money, and it only enrages me at times.'

In the age of globalisation, reducing the number of climbers is easier said than done. Nevertheless, a part of the problem with increasing overtourism could be balanced with the sense of integrity and individual responsibility in climbing that climbers like Kuntal Joisher advocate for. Mountain archiver and writer Alan Arnette identifies Kuntal as a person of courage, conviction, and integrity.[13]

The commercial approach to adventure tourism on Everest has led to much criticism from traditional mountaineers, who have called out some of the irresponsible attitudes to risk and client safety exhibited by some of the commercial outfitters on Everest. Companies sometimes make rash promises to their clients, guaranteeing that they will get them to the summit. The traditional values of alpinism, encompassing spiritual and aesthetic bonding with the mountains and care for nature, have been replaced on Everest by an aggressively commercial culture of adventure tourism that sells a particular form of consumer lifestyle.

The Sherpa community, who work as porters and guides on Everest, often bear most of the risk in climbing the mountain and often bear the brunt of the blame when things go wrong. 'Sherpas' lives have been treated as expendable. If anything goes wrong, the blame always comes to the Sherpas', Joisher said.

Sherpas are an easy target for clients and companies when things go wrong. 'Everyone else is […] blaming a Sherpa guy – "you left your client…", "you didn't take care of your client" … "you should have done this or that" – as if everything is their responsibility', according to Kuntal Joisher.

An innovation the government of Nepal thinks can address the concerns about overcrowding on Everest is to increase the summit royalty fee from USD 11,000 to USD 15,000. Although there has not been an official decision yet, the increased price is expected to come into effect from 2025, according to an official at the Nepal Department of Tourism, who spoke with the authors. The government is also working on creating a team of liaison officers, who will spend time at the base camp throughout a climbing season and maintain scrutiny over expedition operations. The tourism department official said this will ensure implementation of environmental and tourism regulations – for example, monitoring everything that is being ferried up and ensuring that everything is removed from the mountain during the descent. As of now, the designated liaison officers aren't required to stay throughout a climbing season to monitor all mountaineering expeditions.

There is currently a regulation for mandatory retrieval of eight kilograms of human waste from above base camp per expedition, which only a handful of climbers have been following. The government is also planning to take stern measures for effective implementation of the provision of mandatory waste management responsibilities to be undertaken by expedition companies. Many suggest that the government officials regulating expeditions from base camp should use digital scanning systems to monitor what's being taken up and eventually brought down.

Since 2013, the government of Nepal has been introducing new climbing rules every year in an attempt to regulate activity on the mountain. In 2023 a new requirement was made for all climbers to disclose if they were planning on attempting a record on Everest, a rule that had previously been instituted in 2013 with little success. The government also suggested the idea that there should be a deployment of the Nepali Armed Forces stationed at Everest Base Camp. The government has also suggested enacting a law that would require a climber wanting to climb Everest to have first summited other 6,000-metre or 7,000-metre peaks in Nepal, a rule that the Chinese authorities apply when climbing the mountain from the north. This would supposedly reduce climbing numbers on Everest by about half, but without affecting the government's revenue, as climbers would still need to pay for permits to climb other smaller mountains in Nepal before climbing Everest.

Above Base Camp, a lot of these regulatory efforts fall apart. For example, it is best practice for climbers to abort their mission to the summit after 13:00 hours, as winds get stronger later in the afternoon. But many inexperienced climbers don't even know that time is an important factor in climbing. Similarly, even though rules prohibit solo climbing, these rules are sometimes ignored.

Sherpa high-altitude guides often talk about solutions to the problems they experience on Everest. Phurba Tashi Sherpa, also known as the Everest Yak, suggests establishing a Sherpa-led corps of guides to regulate climbing up to Camp Four. He previously held the world record for the highest number of Everest summits, with Apa Sherpa, at twenty-one ascents, a figure later surpassed by other climbing Sherpas. According to Phurba Tashi, Sherpas are the only ones who can stay at Camp Four and work on behalf of the government and on behalf of the mountain. A similar solution was piloted when the 2008 Beijing Olympic torch was being taken to the summit of Everest. To avoid any potential anti-Chinese protests by Tibetan activists, the government of Nepal deployed members of the armed forces up to Camp Two on Everest. 'That was a very good example, but if you want to ensure strict monitoring of climbing norms and regulations, there are no better people than Sherpas, whom the government can permanently rely upon', Phurba Tashi added.

Tendi Sherpa echoes Phurba Tashi, arguing for an effective monitoring mechanism at higher camps on Everest. 'Everything boils down to the numbers, and with haywire government management, it's getting crazier every year', he said. With his technical expertise, international experience, passion for climbing, and deep love for the mountains, Tendi believes there should not be more than 300 to 400 climbers including both clients and Sherpas on Everest throughout the popular spring season. He takes a pause, and corrects his number, 'I would say 200 is an ideal number, and not more than 50 in the death zone at a time.'

Despite the solutions suggested by Tendi and Phurba Tashi, in the highly polarised and politicised society of Nepal, with political affiliates of different political parties even within Nepal's mountaineering community, barely any practical solutions have made it onto the law books. The current silence around sensitive issues like limiting the number of climbing permits shows how apathetic the government of Nepal is in seeking to address the problems of overtourism on Everest. Any attempt to limit numbers on Everest is deemed to threaten to reduce a major source of foreign tourist revenue. At the individual level, the government authorities who the authors spoke with do sound responsible, and they are committed to gradually addressing the issue of overtourism. However, from a broader viewpoint, in a complicated industry mired in political mess, the individual willingness of a few people in authority is barely enough to correct things that have gone wrong over decades.

Notes

1 'Mountain Clean-up Campaign 2023 collects over 35 tons of waste from Mt Everest, other peaks', *Himalayan Times Online* (7 June 2023), https://web.archive.org/web/20240124010933/https://thehimalayantimes.com/nepal/mountain-clean-up-campaign-2023-collects-over-35-tons-of-waste-from-mt-everest-other-peaks

2 For more on Sherpa women and men as climbers and guides in this period, see Chapters 7, 11, and 12 by Jenny Hall, Ian Bellows, and Young Hoon Oh in this volume.

3 Pradeep Bashyal and Ankit Babu Adhikari, *Sherpa: Stories of Life and Death from the Forgotten Guardians of Everest* (London: Octopus, 2022). Interviews by the authors for this longer project are the source of many quotations in this chapter.

4 Pablo Robles, 'Unfreezing the Everest economy', *Bloomberg* (20 November 2020), https://web.archive.org/web/20201201095703/https://www.bloomberg.com/graphics/2020-everest-reopening-sherpa-supply-chain/

5 Hannah Ellis-Pedersen, 'Climate change to blame for up to 17 deaths on Mount Everest, experts say', *Guardian* (30 May 2023), https://web.archive.org/web/20240110200157/https://www.theguardian.com/world/2023/may/30/climate-change-to-blame-for-up-to-17-deaths-on-mount-everest-experts-say

6 Bashyal and Adhikari, *Sherpa*.

7 Pradeep Bashyal, 'Demystifying Everest: what it's really like to climb the world's tallest mountain', *The Diplomat* (10 May 2017), https://web.archive.org/web/20171007220843/https://thediplomat.com/2017/05/demystifying-everest/

8 Pradeep Bashyal, and Annie Gowen, 'Mount Everest is so crowded this year, there is a risk of "traffic jams"', *Washington Post* (3 May 2017), https://web.archive.org/web/20230326112410/https://www.washingtonpost.com/world/mount-everest-is-so-crowded-this-year-there-are-traffic-jams/2017/05/03/7b4f4fe6-2f3c-11e7-a335-fa0ae1940305_story.html

9 Kai Schultz, Jeffrey Gettleman, Mujib Mashal, and Bhadra Sharma, '"It was like a zoo": death on an unruly, overcrowded Everest', *New York Times* (26 May 2019), https://web.archive.org/web/20240120093921/https://www.nytimes.com/2019/05/26/world/asia/mount-everest-deaths.html

10 Ankit Adhikari and Joanna Slater, 'How Mount Everest's popularity turned fatal', *Washington Post* (27 May 2019), https://web.archive.org/web/20240124192212/https://www.washingtonpost.com/world/how-mount-everests-popularity-turned-fatal/2019/05/27/eea7d2b4-806c-11e9-9a67-a687ca99fb3d_story.html

11 Shankar Dahal, 'Mt Everest in business class', *Nepali Times* (25 May 2022), https://web.archive.org/web/20240124191940/https://nepalitimes.com/banner/mt-everest-in-business-class

12 Saransh Sehgal, 'Reinhold Messner on the future of climbing Mount Everest', *Diplomat* (19 April 2017), https://web.archive.org/web/20180313093012/https://thediplomat.com/2017/04/reinhold-messner-on-the-future-of-climbing-mount-everest/

13 Alan Arnette, 'Everest 2018: Interview with Kuntal Joisher – integrity in motion', Alanarnette.com (2018), https://web.archive.org/web/20240124165425/https://www.alanarnette.com/blog/2018/04/02/everest-2018-interview-with-kuntal-joisher-integrity-in-motion/

14

Digital media on Everest: practices, imaginations, and futures

Jolynna Sinanan

On 6 May 2011, British alpine and high-altitude climber Kenton Cool posted 'Everest summit no 9! 1st tweet from the top of the world thanks to a weak 3G signal & the awesome Samsung Galaxy S2 handset! @samsunguk' to Twitter. At the time, the emerging competitive smartphone market was dominated by Apple and Blackberry, but Samsung was a sponsor for Cool's expedition, where product placement and social media platform Twitter provided key modes of publicity approaching the commercial climb.[1] However, Cool was not the first person to post to social media from the top of Everest.

On 15 October 2010, Boulder, Colorado-based polar adventurer Eric Larsen posted 'Everest summit!' to Twitter, using an adapted version of a satellite phone, by then a well-established communications technology amongst high-altitude mountaineers. Larsen used a DeLorme PN-60W in his endeavour to be first to reach the 'three poles' – the North and South Poles and the summit of Everest – in the same year. This unit had a special attachment priced around USD 550 and did not depend on mobile phone coverage. His device was, according to its press release, 'the first handheld GPS navigation device capable of sending customised text messages'.[2]

Across the 2010s, both adventurers cultivated social media profiles that attracted thousands more followers to their profiles on Instagram, the image-sharing social media platform, than to profiles on Twitter. In 2023, as Eric Larsen prepared for an expedition as a commercial guide leading clients to the North Pole, his Instagram profile described him as 'First and only person to go to the South Pole, North Pole & top of Everest in one year. Expedition Guide. Colorectal cancer survivor'. More details were available in links in his profile. In May 2023, Kenton Cool reached the top of Everest for the seventeenth time, setting a record for the most Everest summits by a non-Nepali person. Leading up to his summit push from Base Camp, Cool posted video updates to Instagram.[3]

Everest history is inseparable from a history of mediatisation. The first summit by Sir Edmund Hillary and Tenzing Norgay on 29 May 1953 preceded the televised coronation of Queen Elizabeth II by four days. The strategy and speed of *Times* correspondent Jan Morris (then James Morris) to ensure these key moments of the twentieth century would be inextricably linked in British history is well documented.[4] Technologies of visual cultures remain influential in shaping how Everest is perceived, and the values attached to the mountain. Elizabeth Mazzolini describes how the size of Mount Everest has confounded the predominantly Western imagination, situating it in the tradition of the sublime – natural phenomena of scale beyond human comprehension and control. She then argues that visual technologies have played a role in reducing the mountain to a conceivable and therefore commodifiable experience: 'visual culture surrounding Mount Everest has rendered Mount Everest's significance increasingly abstract, light, and portable by constructing subjects in relation to the mountain's extreme enormity'.[5]

Most of the global population's encounter with Everest is through book and screen. Take, for example, the film depictions of the 1996 disaster told in Jon Krakauer's bestseller *Into Thin Air*. *Everest*, a 2015 film, completed a trifecta with a television programme and landmark IMAX film.[6] Such films continue a trajectory of the interrelationships between film and Everest that contribute to the most famous constructions of Everest as 'the commercialisation of risk', 'selling adventure', and 'made for Hollywood disaster'.[7] The role of media was inextricable from the early Everest expeditions and solidified narratives of Western conquest. The filmmaker and photographer Captain John Noel's cinematic depictions of the early Everest expeditions in the 1920s made remarkable use of media technologies but were not without controversy.[8] *The Conquest of Everest* film in 1953 linked the coronation and conquest in its opening scenes and in tours of the UK.[9] Photography exhibitions like 'Everest through the Lens' at the Royal Geographic Society shared images previously not seen by the public.[10] The history of the mediatisation of Everest creates commercial and technological entanglements of sponsorship, production, marketing, distribution, and exhibition that have shaped scientific and cultural perceptions of the mountain.

This chapter argues that these many constructions of Everest are being reinforced as well as challenged through the digital practices of mountaineers and trekkers, as well as those who live in the region or work seasonally in the tourist industry. As the opening examples of posting to social media from the summit suggest, the latest moment in Everest's media history is characterised by digital media and the development of mobile phone infrastructure in the Khumbu region. This chapter provides a brief overview of digital media and Everest in the first ten years of its unfolding and draws on insights that have emerged from ethnographic fieldwork, which has noted and investigated these features.

Between 2017 and 2019, I conducted participant observation and interviews during fieldwork visits of three to four weeks in Kathmandu and the towns of Lukla and Namche along the Everest Base Camp Trek, with guides, porters, managers of guest and porter accommodation houses, and trekkers. Digital infrastructure, data, and Wi-Fi were newly available through mobile phones and this phase of the research focused on mobile media and mobile livelihoods. Khumbu Sherpa have been associated with Everest mountaineering as the Indigenous inhabitants of the region. As the mountaineering and trekking tourism industry expanded, more of the population of the workforce of cooks and porters were from the Tamang and Rai ethnic groups from the lower hills surrounding the Solukhumbu, who have historically been at the economic peripheries of Nepali society.[11] Several participants in my continuing study are Tamang and Rai, who work seasonally in Solukhumbu. My ethnographic fieldwork practice drew on Nina Nyberg Sørensen and Karen Fog Olwig's notion of mobile livelihoods, which takes material and infrastructural conditions of work together with the immaterial conditions: the social relationships, emotional connections, and individual and collective imaginations that these livelihoods imply. Mobile livelihoods consider 'the ways that social knowledge is produced by affiliations with different relationships in wider spatial contexts' in the movements involved with making a living.[12]

This phase of the study examined the role of mobile media, especially smartphones and to a lesser extent laptops (participants did not typically use tablets), in the tourist encounter – how mobile media shapes the meanings of Everest for tourists and how it is imbricated in the routine practices of mobile workers. Insights gained from the first phase of the research revealed the ways in which digital visual communication became part of strategies for securing further work with trekking clients[13] and the role of digital media within contested imaginations of Everest in relation to social and economic change associated with working in regional tourism.[14]

My earlier study on mobile media and mobile livelihoods in Everest tourism has become incorporated into my ongoing wider research to develop a long-term ethnography examining the 'Everest economy'. Upon returning to Nepal in 2023, I attempted to resume my research documenting digital practices in relation to social change over time. Participants expressed that they were not interested in discussing digital media and smartphone practices as the years of the pandemic had rendered them largely dependent on digital devices for social connections and entertainment. Instead, guides were more enthusiastic to reflect upon how tourism had changed within the wider context of Nepal, to speculate on the implications for the future in relation to climate change, and to consider their aspirations for continued work. Several participants in the study were introduced to the tourism industry by their father or uncles who were working with international trekking agencies as cooks. They worked seasonally throughout the year to complement income from farming activities in their villages.

One network of participants who are currently working as trekking guides and guides for mountains under 7,000 metres are from Jiri, which has a significant connection to Everest mountaineering history. Prior to the building of Lukla airport, Everest treks and expeditions would depart from Jiri. Swiss mountaineering companies, for example, were instrumental in the town's development, providing resources for schools, medical facilities, and mountaineering training, which provided work and an introduction to Everest tourism. My longer-term ethnography examines social and cultural continuities and changes in the Everest economy related to the emergence and growth of the tourism industry over the past fifty years, across three generations of workers in trekking and mountaineering. This chapter presents insights from fieldwork visits across the wider study and the names of all participants referred to have been anonymised in the chapter.

Digital media at the top of the world

Two mobile service providers (the national network NCell and Everestlink) now service the Solukhumbu region. Residents and proprietors of accommodation along the Everest Base Camp Trek can subscribe to internet connection annually so guests and workers can connect with Wi-Fi. Connectivity up to 3,800 metres in the town of Namche is fast and reliable, provided by three towers whose reach spans 93 kilometres each. Tourism in the area has been lucrative, which has led to investment in new and reliable electricity infrastructure. Electrical support is more consistent than what is available in Lukla and Kathmandu, due to hasty upgrades with lower-quality units during reconstruction after the 2015 earthquake. Above Namche, internet service provider Everestlink, founded by Tsering Sherpa, provides connectivity with two hundred hotspots deployed in over forty villages, where residents can purchase fixed-price internet plans and guests can access internet connectivity through preloaded internet packages on SIM cards.

Remote regions generally receive less investment in telecommunications infrastructures as investments are not perceived to earn returns due to low population density.[15] Indigenous populations are more likely to be the main inhabitants of remote areas and are more likely to experience the impacts of digital inequalities. Indigenous populations situated in countries in the global South are further impacted by interrelated structural inequalities that compound constraints related to digital technologies such as cost, access, and literacies. Prior to smartphones and mobile data, internet connectivity remained sparse in remote regions. The availability of mobile data on smartphones has shifted the emphasis from access and digital literacies to practices – the kinds of usage and their meanings.[16]

The emergence of digital connectivity and infrastructures in Solukhumbu is largely due to the co-operation between state and private entities in reconstruction efforts following the earthquake, and motivation to restore and enhance confidence in safety for increasing numbers of adventure tourists. Mobile communications infrastructure has been more suitable for complex mountainous geographies.[17] The context of disaster recovery and the motivation for lucrative tourism have arguably 'brought' digital infrastructure to the Solukhumbu region. The unfolding practices of digital media use, the values they reflect, and the power dynamics associated with them are part of this historical legacy.

#Everest, global visibility, and regional populations

Contemporary tourism work in Solukhumbu is largely divided along lines of class and ethnicity. These categories should be understood not as defined by essentialist and biologically determined factors but rather as having emerged historically, according to regional geographies and habitation.[18] The Everest tourism industry has grown exponentially since the 1960s with the emergence of tourism as counterculture and the appeal of Nepal for providing imaginary escapes from the malaise of twentieth-century capitalism in the West.[19] As the inhabitants of Solukhumbu, the Sherpa population has led the development and ownership of tourist infrastructure, supported by Nepali government policies (for building permits are offered at lower cost to populations indigenous to the region). The workforce of guides and porters in the early years of Everest tourism was almost exclusively Sherpa.[20]

During the 1990s, Sherpa provided most high-altitude guides and porters, and owned, managed, and maintained accommodation along the Everest Base Camp Trek. Many of the anthropological studies and journalistic and travel accounts of this period note economic and cultural changes to Sherpa populations in Solukhumbu.[21] Popular and regional narratives lament the loss of the authenticity of Sherpa culture and a traditional way of life, from aspirations to attain global goods to desires to migrate to 'Western' countries.[22] However, through the intergenerational wealth acquired by Sherpa working in the tourist industry, many have migrated to Kathmandu or abroad to attain higher levels of education and economic opportunities.

Originating from Pharak in the southern Everest region, anthropologist Pasang Yangjee Sherpa has documented Sherpa populations in the region and diaspora in relation to climate change and Indigenous knowledge. She observes that tourism on routes on the Everest Base Camp Trek has contributed to significant economic and social change.[23] Infrastructure and commercial activity are more visible in villages along routes on the trek than in those off-route. Households on-route have been engaged in commercial activities related to tourism, some for three generations, in occupations as farmers, herders, hotel owners, cooks, and shop keepers. Sherpa diasporas remain active in engaging with the Solukhumbu region through various cultural expressions and means, including commentating on social media. In her study of Sherpa diaspora in New York, Pasang Yangjee Sherpa describes how Sherpa migrants form community groups that continue traditions from their regional origins: carrying out funeral rites involving lamas, developing community centres as places of worship and for other religious functions, promoting cultural heritage and language learning.[24]

Through social media practices, guides and porters from Sherpa populations and other ethnic groups from outside of the region have been active in constructing narratives of their experiences of work, making observations on environmental change, and displaying aspects of cultural heritage. The affordances of Instagram and Facebook, for example, facilitate documenting treks through posting mountainscapes, describing aspects of daily life on treks, and sharing images of and with clients at scenic landmarks. Guides in the ongoing study do not necessarily desire to advocate that Nepali mountaineers and expedition support crews continue to play the role they have done historically nor to challenge British narratives of 'heroic' figures.[25] They do create narratives that amplify the visibility of their work and expertise in trekking and mountaineering tourism through everyday digital practices.

Dorjae, for example, was a guide in his mid-thirties when we met in 2018. He has over twenty years' experience with international trekking companies and now works for two Nepali companies, with whom he prefers to lead small groups of clients. As Dorjae explained, now that his children have grown up and are more financially independent, he can reduce the number of clients he works with. His aim is to work with three groups per year, leading the Annapurna Circuit or Everest Base Camp Trek. If they have an average two-week itinerary, and if he charges USD 1,000 per person in a group of two or three (which is relatively low compared with the average USD 2,000 per person asked by an international trekking company), then he can live between Kathmandu and his village near Jiri very comfortably for the year. After the earthquake in 2015, trekking tourism began to recover in 2017, which Dorjae described as having 'good business'. He supplemented working with companies with two return clients who had contacted him on Facebook Messenger. On this platform, they chatted about an itinerary and suitable budget, and the clients returned for different trekking itineraries with small groups of friends. His next ambition was to create a website to which he could direct his word-of-mouth clients. He had a webpage in progress that listed the itineraries he offered as well as an 'About' page with a short biography. The website described his experience but did not contain his personal story or where he had come from.

I enquired as to why he did not say anything about himself on his website, especially as we had spoken to a few young guides during the visit who discussed the importance of personal branding and creating a personal story a client felt they could connect with. Dorjae explained, 'People who come to Everest expect their guide to be a Sherpa. Sherpa are more famous with trekking and mountaineering and people expect they will trek with them, learn about their local culture. Sherpa is the brand for Everest, so I don't want to say too much that I am Tamang. It's not that I am ashamed or not proud, but I don't think clients are so interested if I am not Sherpa.'

In other discussions, Dorjae and other guides emphasised that although they might be from different ethnic groups, they 'are all Nepali'. Considering their social media practices, Dorjae, another guide, and a porter he works with post images that reflect aspects of their lives outside of work. Dorjae's Facebook timeline includes images with his trekking clients, but also return visits to his home village near Jiri. In these images, he poses with his older brothers in front of their home with small farming fields in the background or with friends active in local political party meetings in front of the party's advertising posters.

Similarly, Dorjae's colleague Bal, a guide with the same company as Dorjae, posts images with family members and friends at events at his community temple and sites of Buddhist significance. Bal described the different images on his timeline as acknowledging his peers but also generating interest from his international clients, who he has befriended on Facebook. 'I don't take too many photos, but if it is a nice event, I will share it and tag my friends. Some clients also "like" the photos and they will comment or message me to ask what is happening. So, I can tell them it is a puja (prayers), or it is a celebration for the Buddha's birthday, or something like that, and they learn a bit about my culture as well.'

These brief examples speak to themes related to identity and the commodification of culture that can emerge as part of the growth of the tourist industry. First, Dorjae's and Bal's assertions reflect crises in Nepal's experience of the Maoist insurgencies of the 1990s and government aims to build a unified Nepali state.[26] While disparities and inequalities in Nepali society run deep along the lines of ethnicity and caste, the economic opportunities of tourism provide some means for marginalised populations to attain upward mobility. Second, they reflect a more complex relationship between cultural identity and ethnicity within the history of Everest tourism. Anthropologist Shae Frydenlund examines the ways in which 'passing for Sherpa' became part of the negotiation of ethnicity in the labour dynamics of Everest tourism. In her study of non-Sherpa trekking industry workers, she observed a tendency to actively promote oneself as being Sherpa, or, if mistaken for being Sherpa by other Nepalis or Western foreigners, not correcting and asserting their ethnic identity.[27] While Sherpa have been historically associated with Everest mountaineering, they have also been more favourably positioned in Nepali society by legal and economic codes that classified and ranked the different ethnic groups.[28] Frydenlund argues that 'passing for Sherpa' becomes a means to counter these positionings as migrant labourers and outsiders within Nepal's political economy and mountain industry.[29] The guides in her study are slightly older (aged over 50) than the cohort I reflect upon in this chapter. Nevertheless, there is scope to suggest that a longitudinal study of mountain industry workers that considers social, economic, and technological change will identify changing forms of agency in the negotiation of ethnic identity in the Everest industry.

These changes near Everest also speak to trends in the commodification of identity in tourism more broadly. Kalyan Bhandari argues that Nepal in the years after the abolition of the monarchy is undergoing changes in how it is marketed as a destination to tourists.[30] In the mid to late twentieth century, Nepal was often depicted as an exotic kingdom in the sacred Himalaya, a mystical Shangri-La untouched by the modern world, imagery that resonates in earlier expedition films.[31] Following the abolition of the monarchy and the 2015 constitution that established Nepal as a Federal Democratic Republic, Nepal could no longer market itself as a distinctive kingdom or rely on royal patronage for the conservation of natural sites and resources.[32] Cultural and leisure (adventure) tourism became points of emphasis in tourist marketing, ahead of pilgrimage tourism. Guides in my study emphasise that their expertise, experience, and hospitality are consistent with what tourists expect from trekking or mountaineering as part of adventure tourism.

Comparative scholarship on tourism in the global South (formerly referred to as developing countries) has established that in emergent liberal economies promoting and marketing countries and their peoples is critical for attracting foreign investment. Anthropologist Thomas Carter draws on his extended field-work in Cuba to argue that constructing and maintaining imaginations of places and the bodies that inhabit them become inseparable from the growth of the tourist industry. Spaces within Havana, for example, are deliberately marketed as fulfilling foreign desires and commodify illusions of Cuba as a Caribbean island of exotic and erotic Afro-Cuban bodies and culture.[33] Thomas Klak and Garth Myers further argue that tourism is linked to wider economic strategies, where states seek to attract foreign investment in manufacturing through aggressively promoting and selling their countries and people as politically stable sources of cheap labour, with natives friendly to investors and mass audiences.[34]

Consider another example from Solukhumbu. Arun, who was 22 years old in 2019, has worked as a porter for different Nepali trekking companies since he was 18. He has a high-school education and comes from an agricultural household in a village two days' walk below Lukla, where he usually meets trekking groups. When he works for a larger group (twelve to fifteen people), he sometimes takes the bus to Kathmandu and assists the allocated guide with activities in the days prior to the trek. The most typical day trips are to Swayambhu Mahachaitya, the most sacred Buddhist temple in Kathmandu, and Shree Pashupatinath, the most sacred Hindu temple and cremation site. He then flies to Lukla with the group. Porters often come from lower-income families, where they enter a hierarchy of porter work. The least educated and skilled porters usually carry goods and produce flown from Kathmandu to accommodation and services along the Everest Base Camp Trek for the lowest wages. Porters who have a high-school education and speak some English find work for trekking companies where they may advance to training as an assistant guide. Trekking porters can carry up to forty kilograms (eighty-eight pounds) a day to meet their trekking group at the end of the day's itinerary. Many porters stay in porter accommodation attached to the trekkers' guesthouse or in separate facilities. These are usually small, with one large sleeping area and an attached kitchen and dining area. Meals are basic but substantial, and alcohol and cigarettes are sold in most porter accommodation lodges.

The most important amenity in porter accommodation is fast and reliable Wi-Fi. Larger towns and villages along the trek have snooker houses and bars for porters to socialise as they may arrive at their destination several hours before their group. In smaller villages at higher altitude, there is little activity for porters except 'killing time' on their phones, chatting with friends, browsing Facebook, Instagram, or TikTok, or watching YouTube. Porter work and their digital practices resemble Xinyuan Wang's findings in her ethnography of rural-to-urban migrants in China.[35] Factory workers in industrial towns are attracted to the financial opportunities outside of rural villages and the ability to live more independently from their family. Though the living conditions for factory workers might be small spaces with multiple young people, smartphones provide a unique opportunity to experience privacy. That is, they can chat in private with friends and peers with whom they would like to develop romantic relationships, whereas face-to-face socialising is usually in the presence of extended family or other people who know them. Similarly, time spent with other young people implies they are not restricted to their family or wider family networks and can form friendships based on autonomy, on their own terms.

Arun's work as a porter introduced him to forms of mobility that he might not have had in his village. He enjoys nights out with friends in Kathmandu and travels by plane more than many of his peers. He is slowly learning English through interactions with trekking clients. He created his Facebook profile in 2016, the only platform he posts to, and uses Facebook Messenger as his only messaging app. Arun's profile image was taken in the newly renovated Tribhuvan International Airport. He is posing wearing trekking clothing, the logo of the Nepali trekking company he works for clearly visible on his T-shirt, and he is holding his boarding pass to Lukla. His cover image is a landscape taken from Kala Patthar, the highest destination before Everest Base Camp on most trekking itineraries, with Everest squarely in the middle of the image. Arun's posts have changed steadily over the years. Images from his late teens, when he first started working as a porter, show him hanging out with friends, posing mid-karate move, or standing next to upmarket cars, all wearing iconic US rock band T-shirts and sporting fashionable haircuts. His later posts show him maturing into his profession in the tourist industry, with images from treks, wearing full trekking gear and sunglasses and posing with clients or with spectacular mountain backgrounds.

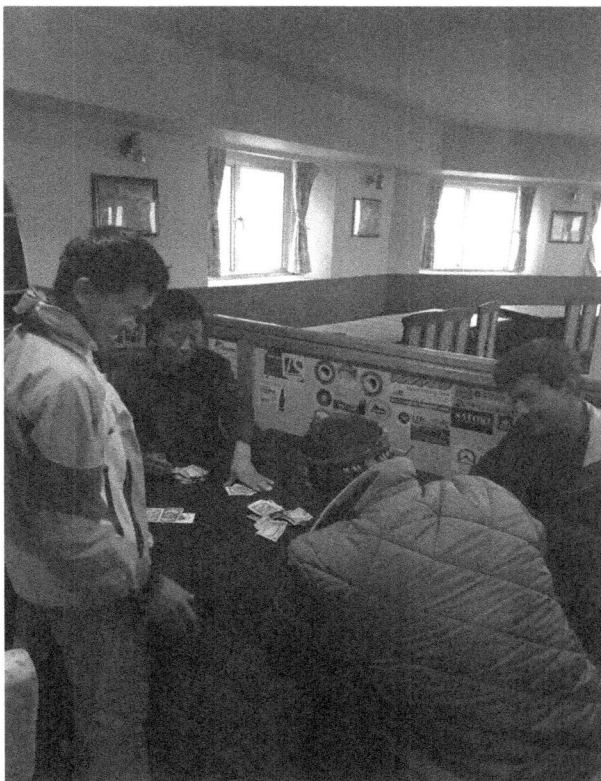

Figure 14.1 Porters playing cards after arriving at guesthouse in Dingboche, Solu Khumbu, Nepal. Image: © Jolynna Sinanan.

Conversations with Arun substantiate and contextualise his forms of self-presentation on Facebook. When he spoke about his aspirations for the future, Arun described how he was working as a porter because the income was better than what he could generate in his village, but he hoped to start working as an assistant guide, improve his English, become a certified guide, and eventually start his own trekking company. He hoped to make enough income to travel abroad to Singapore and then to countries in Europe. Several porters I encountered between the ages of 18 and 25 expressed aspirations akin to achieving a Western middle-class income and global mobility. Urban youth in Kathmandu have been able to access affordable English classes in schools and afterschool classes in English since the boom in TESOL (Teaching English to Speakers of Other Languages) classes in the late 1990s and early 2000s which also contributed to tourism and development in Nepal. Such English classes are not as available in rural areas, where many porters have come from.[36] Porter work in trekking tourism has become a means to meet aspirations for global mobility and achieve a middle-class lifestyle.

As well as the regional inflections of meeting aspirations through trekking work, Arun's experience further resonates with trends in sport tourism and global mobility, where digital media has played a significant role. Sociologist Holly Thorpe identifies two repercussions of digital media for sport cultures. First, the distinction between media producers and media consumers collapses. Previously, sport cultures were subject to image making and dissemination based on broadcast industry models through commercial sport films and magazines. With digital media, though, participants overwhelmingly contribute to textual and visual representations of their cultures through new media technologies and use of social media to disseminate and circulate content. And second, user-driven social media platforms contribute to global imaginaries of action sport cultures through circulation of spectacular images of sport-tourism destinations and desirable transnational careers.[37]

Within these wider processes of change, the digital practices adopted in adventure sport tourism cultures offer unique experiences in how the use of digital media by participants is informed by the attitudes, values, and social background of their guides. Notably, Arun's reflections on smartphone filming and photography differ from Dorjae's and Bal's, arguably along the lines of intergenerational digital practices. Arun describes the kind of photos that trekking clients (particularly those under the age of 25) aspire to take – posing on ledges, sometimes in minimal or fashionable clothing at Base Camp (for some women, bikini shots) – to post on Instagram. He is used to taking these kinds of images with clients, and sometimes he poses with them. While Dorjae and Bal adhere to requests from clients to take more spectacular or eye-catching images, they don't actively encourage them for reasons they explain as risk taking, compromising safety, and being 'disrespectful' to the cultures of the region and to other trekkers and guides.

Gender and education levels also play a role in the types of work that populations from outside of Solukhumbu could embark upon in the tourist industry. Porters' accommodation lodges are largely run by women from Rai ethnic groups. They usually come from lower-income families with livelihoods from agriculture, with a high-school education but little to no English or complex skills. Migrating seasonally for work allows for a more lucrative income with the skills they have acquired at home through gendered divisions of labour. Managing porters' accommodation lodges involves daily cooking, cleaning, and basic shopkeeping. The work is decent, and many form ongoing collegial relationships with guides who integrate them into networks of exchange of goods and information to further opportunities. Women as young as 18 can work seasonally for a few years and then move to their home villages for marriage. Porter houses are highly masculine environments, but young women largely describe living and working conditions as safe and secure. Porters are respectful and if they behave inappropriately, their behaviour is berated by peers and senior guides. Given the highly networked nature of employment where guides and trekking companies will employ the same porters seasonally, social reputation as hard working, reliable, and conducting oneself appropriately on a trek is valued by employers and adhered to by porters.

In contrast to the ways male porters cultivate social media profiles of masculinity, professional identity, and aspirations for global mobility, young women's digital practices while away from home focus on leisure, entertainment, and maintaining friendships and relationships. Rita, for example, was running a small porter house off the main road from the entrance into the town of Namche at age 20 in 2019, her third year running the lodge. Her 18-year-old sister joined her with the intention that they would return home after the season, but Rita would then stay in the village as she was engaged, and her sister would continue to work in the lodge. Scrolling through her timeline on Facebook on her phone, Rita explained that she spends a lot of time on her phone playing games or watching YouTube but doesn't post while she is away from home. She looks at posts of her friends and cousins and leaves comments in the form of a GIF or sticker. She says that because she is working, there is nothing to post about. Photos from her time at home during off-seasons show her with her sisters or friends dressed for religious festivals, or against landscapes in the village. She is often tagged in images of other relatives or with babies who are her nieces, nephews, or second cousins. Now she is married herself, her images are almost entirely of family: she posts images of herself with her husband, and with their baby who is a year old. Rita's posts are reflective of differences in posting between genders of the same peer group, where men cultivate a professional image and aspirations outside of the home, and women cultivate respectability and domesticity along cultural ideals of womanhood.[38]

Conclusion

This chapter has presented insights from my unfolding ethnography of the Everest economy and has focused on trends in digital practices in the initial years of the development of digital infrastructures in Solukhumbu. Digital images taken by trekking and mountaineering tourists tend to conform to visual tropes that are popular on social media platforms, emphasising personal journey and adventure, themes that are long-standing in Everest narratives. Further, tourists come to Nepal to find 'their own mass-mediated image-memories' shaped by decades of popular culture.[39]

Digital practices of populations working in the Everest tourism industry reflect complementary as well as competing interests. The brief illustrations presented in this chapter capture the ways in which workers navigate professional identity, through reproducing popular narratives of Everest as adventure through digital images. However, these images are also reflective of individual and collective aspirations for the future. These aspirations are inextricable from cultural and gendered values that have been shaped regionally and historically, but they should also be understood generationally. This chapter has emphasised that guides witnessed the rapid growth of the tourist industry alongside social, economic, and political change in Nepal at the turn of the twenty-first century, and their experiences negotiated identity and the valorisation of regional heritage and culture.

Ethnographic fieldwork in Solukhumbu reveals the routines, structural conditions, and relationships that provide context which cannot be ascertained by examining visual posts alone. Guides and porters in the study did not claim to seek fame and notoriety through their social media posts (many have at most a couple of hundred friends or followers), though some explained they hoped posting would generate further income or document memorable experiences on treks. Furthermore, their posts display affiliations with different structural relationships (kinship, political engagement, religious significance) but do not assert desires for collective action based on their role as Everest tourism workers. Such findings complement other ethnographic studies such as those by Shae Frydenlund, who discusses the motivations behind 'passing for Sherpa', and Jase Wilson and Katherine Dashper on the consequences of precarious livelihoods on collective action on behalf of high-altitude mountaineering tourist workers.[40] Guides and porters express aspirations for livelihoods, recognition for expertise and regional knowledge, and intergenerational mobility in ways that are consistent with studies of Himalayan hubs as sites of social and cultural encounters which intertwine different forms of work as associated with ethnic categories.[41] The digital infrastructures implemented in the 2010s and 2020s, and the practices that followed, provide the technologically mediated opportunities for

248

regional populations to express perspectives to counter those that historically have been perpetuated by cinema and broadcast media.

Notes

1 Mark Brown, 'Is Kenton Cool really the first to tweet from Everest?', *Wired* (18 May 2011), https://web.archive.org/web/20240126173811/https://www.wired.com/2011/05/kenton-cool-first-everest-tweet/

2 Lars Gesing, 'Eric Larsen: the long way to tweeting atop Mount Everest', *CU Independent* (14 February 2014), https://web.archive.org/web/20240126180636/https://www.cuindependent.com/2014/02/14/eric-larsen-talk/

3 On Instagram, see www.instagram.com/elexplore/; www.instagram.com/kentoncool/.

4 Jan Morris, *Coronation Everest* (London: Faber and Faber, 1958).

5 Elizabeth Mazzolini, *The Everest Effect: Nature, Culture, Ideology* (Tuscaloosa, AL: University of Alabama Press, 2015), p. 96.

6 David Breashears and Greg MacGillivray (dirs), *Everest* (USA: Miramax, 1998); Robert Markowitz (dir.), *Into Thin Air: Death on Everest* (USA: Columbia Tristar, 1997); Baltasar Kormákur (dir.), *Everest* (USA: Universal, 2015).

7 Catherine Palmer, '"Shit happens": the selling of risk in extreme sport', *Australian Journal of Anthropology*, 13:3 (2002), 323–36, https://doi.org/10.1111/j.1835-9310.2002.tb00213.x

8 Peter H. Hansen, 'The dancing lamas of Everest: cinema, Orientalism, and Anglo-Tibetan relations in the 1920s', *The American Historical Review*, 101:3 (1996), 712–47; https://doi.org/10.2307/2169420; Alison Griffiths, 'Cinema in extremis: Mount Everest and the poetics of monumentality', *Film History: An International Journal*, 32:1 (2020), 40–71, https://doi.org/10.2979/filmhistory.32.1.02; Janette Faull, 'Climbing Mount Everest: expeditionary film, geographical science and media culture, 1922–1953' (PhD dissertation, Royal Holloway, University of London, 2019). Faull presents a comprehensive historical study of Everest expedition films in the first half of the twentieth century.

9 Peter H. Hansen, 'Coronation Everest: the Empire and Commonwealth in the "second Elizabethan age"', in Stuart Ward (ed.), *British Culture and the End of Empire* (Manchester: Manchester University Press, 2001), pp. 57–72, https://doi.org/10.7765/9781526119629.00009

10 'Everest through the lens', Rgs.org, https://web.archive.org/web/20240126232215/https://www.rgs.org/our-collections/stories-from-our-collections/online-exhibitions/everest-through-the-lens; see also Chapter 3 by Felix Driver in this volume.

11 Sanjay Nepal, 'Tourism and remote mountain settlements: spatial and temporal development of tourist infrastructure in the Mt Everest region, Nepal', *Tourism Geographies*, 7:2 (2005), 205–27, https://doi.org/10.1080/14616680500072471; Shae Frydenlund, 'Situationally Sherpa: race, ethnicity, and the labour geography of the Everest industry', *Journal of Cultural Geography*, 36:1 (2019), 1–22, https://doi.org/10.1080/08873631.2018.1516601

12 Nina Nyberg Sørensen and Karen Fog Olwig (eds), *Work and Migration: Life and Livelihoods in a Globalizing World* (London: Routledge, 2002), p. 10.

13 Jolynna Sinanan, '#Everest: visual economies of leisure and labour in the tourist encounter', in Elisabetta Costa, Patricia G. Lange, Nell Haynes, and Jolynna Sinanan (eds), *The*

Routledge Companion to Media Anthropology (London: Routledge, 2022), pp. 247–59, https://doi.org/10.4324/9781003175605-24

14 Jolynna Sinanan, 'Everest, Everestland, #Everest: a case for a composite visual ethnographic approach', *Visual Anthropology*, 35:3 (2022), 272–86, https://doi.org/10.1080/08949468.2022.2094187

15 Laura Evelyn Dyson, 'Framing the Indigenous mobile revolution', in Laurel Evelyn Dyson, Stephen Grant, and Max Hendricks (eds), *Indigenous People and Mobile Technologies* (New York: Routledge, 2016), p. 8.

16 Jonathan Donner, *After Access: Inclusion, Development, and a More Mobile Internet* (Cambridge, MA: MIT Press, 2015), https://doi.org/10.7551/mitpress/9740.003.0001

17 Sojen Pradhan and Gyanendra Bajracharya, 'Socio-economic impacts on the adoption of mobile phones by the major Indigenous nationalities of Nepal', in Dyson, Grant and Hendricks (eds), *Indigenous People*, p. 227.

18 John Whelpton, *A History of Nepal* (Cambridge: Cambridge University Press, 2005).

19 Mark Liechty, *Far Out: Countercultural Seekers and the Tourist Encounter in Nepal* (Chicago, IL: University of Chicago Press, 2017).

20 See also chapters 11 and 12 by Ian Bellows and Young Hoon Oh in this volume.

21 Sherry B. Ortner, *Life and Death on Mt. Everest: Sherpas and Himalayan Mountaineering* (Princeton NJ: Princeton University Press, 2001).

22 L.R. Loland, 'Commons of identity: Sherpa identity management', *Dhaulagiri Journal of Sociology and Anthropology*, 1 (2005), 176–92; Y. Mu, S. Nepal, and P. Lai, 'Tourism and sacred landscape in Sagarmatha (Mt Everest) National Park, Nepal', in Michael A. Di Giovine and Jaeyeon Choe (eds), *Pilgrimage Beyond the Officially Sacred: Understanding the Geographies of Religion and Spirituality in Sacred Travel* (London: Routledge, 2020), pp. 82–9.

23 Pasang Sherpa, 'Climate change, perceptions and social heterogeneity in Pharak, Mount Everest region of Nepal', *Human Organization*, 73:2 (2014), 153–61, https://doi.org/10.17730/humo.73.2.94q43152111733t6

24 Pasang Yangjee Sherpa, 'Sustaining Sherpa language and culture in New York', *Book 2.0*, 9:1–2 (2019), 19–29, https://doi.org/10.1386/btwo_00003_1

25 Paul Gilchrist, 'Motherhood, ambition and risk: mediating the sporting hero/ine in Conservative Britain', *Media, Culture & Society*, 29:3 (2007), 395–414, https://doi.org/10.1177/0163443707076182

26 Whelpton, *A History of Nepal*.

27 Frydenlund, 'Situationally Sherpa'.

28 Whelpton, *A History of Nepal*; D. Gellner, 'Caste, ethnicity and inequality in Nepal', *Economic and Political Weekly*, 42:20 (2007), 1823–8.

29 Frydenlund, 'Situationally Sherpa', 4, 13, attributes religious discrimination to an 1854 legal code in Nepal, revised in 1963, with legacies that remain.

30 Kalyan Bhandari, 'Tourism in Nepal: post-monarchy challenges', *Journal of Tourism and Cultural Change*, 8:1–2 (2010), 69–83, https://doi.org/10.1080/14766825.2010.491917

31 See Chapter 5 by Tim Chamberlain in this volume.

32 Bhandari, 'Tourism in Nepal', 70.

33 Thomas F. Carter, 'Of spectacular phantasmal desire: tourism and the Cuban state's complicity in the commodification of its citizens', *Leisure Studies*, 27:3 (2008), 241–57, https://doi.org/10.1080/02614360802018806

34 T. Klak and G. Myers, 'How states sell their countries and their people', in Thomas Klak (ed.), *Globalization and Neoliberalism: The Caribbean Context* (Lanham, MD: Rowman & Littlefield, 1998), pp. 87–109.

35 Xinyuan Wang, *Social Media in Industrial China* (London: UCL Press, 2016), https://doi.org/10.14324/111.9781910634646

36 B.K. Khadka, 'Development of ELT in Nepal: an overview', *Journal of NELTA*, 27:1–2 (2022), 124–40.

37 Holly Thorpe, *Transnational Mobilities in Action Sport Cultures* (Basingstoke: Palgrave, 2014), p. 71.

38 Daniel Miller and Jolynna Sinanan, *Visualising Facebook* (London: UCL Press, 2017), https://doi.org/10.14324/111.9781911307402

39 Liechty, *Far Out*, p. 320.

40 Frydenlund, 'Situationally Sherpa'; Jase Wilson and Katherine Dashper, 'In the shadow of the mountain: the crisis of precarious livelihoods in high altitude mountaineering tourism', *Journal of Sustainable Tourism*, 31:10 (2023), 2270–90, https://doi.org/10.1080/09669582.2022.2108038

41 Jayeeta Sharma, 'Producing Himalayan Darjeeling: mobile people and mountain encounters', *Himalaya*, 35:2 (2016), 87–101, digitalcommons.macalester.edu/himalaya/vol35/iss2/12

15

Thin ice, thin air

Yvonne Reddick

A boom like a thunderclap. The mountain itself is detonating. '*Avalanche!*' cries Hem Raj.

Snow surges down the side of Nuptse. It rushes like water, fanning out over grey rock. Clouds of spindrift fume above it. Hem Raj, Prem, Anna, Kristin, Melissa, and I are standing on the ridge of the Khumbu Glacier's moraine. We're on the opposite side of the valley. Safe. But there's a knot of tension in my neck. I always thought the melting of the mountains would be slow: ice lost in millimetres, rivers creeping and encroaching. This is violent.

In the distance, there's a village of yellow and white tents, perched on the ice itself: Everest Base Camp, the high point of our trek. We can only see the top-most pinnacle of Everest from this angle, but we're standing right on its rocky root-system. A scarf of wind-driven snow spools from the mountain's forehead.

The tents of Base Camp stand on the living Khumbu Glacier. Beyond the camp, there's the Khumbu Icefall, often described as the most treacherous section of the ascent from the south. And the biggest risks aren't borne by wealthy clients who pay to take their chance at the summit. They're taken by Sherpa mountaineers, who fix the lines of ascent and place ladders across the crevasses. By Sherpa porters who must cross the icefall again and again to stock the high camps with supplies. Sixteen Sherpas died in 2014, when an enormous ice tower collapsed. The glacier bristles with crevasses and seracs. I watch four tiny figures, stark against the white ice, setting out for the ascent.

I imagined that the summit of Everest would shine with snow, but it's sombre, grey, stolid. Its huge shoulder blade stretches out westwards. While Nuptse resembles the white sails and graceful mast of a boat, and Ama Dablam's glacier-pendant sparkles, Everest appears hulking. In 1921, when Mallory first glimpsed it, he called the mountain 'a prodigious white fang, excrescent from the jaw of the world'. Writing the following year, he perceived its face as 'cold and white'; in the same letter, he detailed the avalanche that killed seven porters assisting his expedition. Jon Krakauer described first setting eyes on the 'ink-black wedge of the summit pyramid' in his account of the 1996 Everest disaster, *Into Thin Air*. Authors' contexts and preoccupations colour their accounts of the mountain – Krakauer's Everest is sombre because he writes in the wake of eight deaths. But as I stand at the mountain's foot, almost exactly a hundred years after Mallory's second expedition, the mountain appears stark and dark and bare because it is losing its ice.

I've never climbed Everest, and probably never will. But I sometimes try to imagine my lungs straining, heart hammering, head swimming in sparse air. I read Ian Serraillier's poem *Everest Climbed* at school, and ever since, I have wanted to see the mountain that Nepalis call Sagarmatha, the Sky Goddess. When I look at maps, I try to pick out the Western Cwm, the West Shoulder, the South Col, and North Col. *Cwm* is Welsh and *col* is Alpine French: names from lower ranges far away, mapped incongruously onto the loftiest of heights. How this mountain possesses people. And there are all those who died, too soon, too young. Their sky burials in high cold and rare air. Most of them are still up there. If I did attempt to reach the summit, my odds of joining the dead would be – what? Is it still as many as one in fourteen? And in one of the more ghoulish actions of climate change, the mountain glaciers are giving up their dead. Up at Camp One, a climber's hand emerges from the ice. I thought of what the Swiss writer, environmentalist, and alpinist Maurice Chappaz wrote about the way bodies are preserved in the crypt of crevasses: *A son sees his father again, younger than him*. My father always wanted to trek to Base Camp. What wouldn't I give to see his face again.

The ice is alive. You hear it groan, shift, and settle. To the east of the gravelly path leading to Base Camp, the glacier stretches out, smudged with grey debris. Pools of blue or grey water break through the rubble of boulders and rock flour on its surface. There are cigarette butts and coconut cookie wrappers and empty Coke bottles and yak shit on the broad, gravelly trail. I pass a porter carrying an empty jerrycan of fuel down in a wicker basket. This morning, as we hiked, Kristin played 'Fire Song' by the folk singer Jessica Willis Fisher through her portable speakers:

The smoke is filling up the room
can you smell the kerosene?

An enormous lump of granite stands at the entrance to the camp, daubed with 'Everest Base Camp' and scrawled with tourists' names. A rusty oil drum serves as a bin, labelled 'Transported by Sagarmatha Pollution Control Committee'. The path curves right, and we step from gritty moraine onto debris-covered glacial ice. The trail perches on the edge of an enormous meltwater crater. Snow penitents – spires of ice resembling white-shrouded figures in pointed hats – spike up from its edge. But they are so thin that the sun shines through them. *The sky's about to cave… the moon is black as coal*, goes the song.

Row upon row of tents are perched on the gravelly glacier: white geodesic domes, rectangular sleeping quarters in high-vis yellow or highlighter orange.

Three men come stomping down the rough path in knee-high mountaineering boots. Hem Raj confers in Nepali with their leader: 'They've come from Camp Two', he explains to us. 'Well done!' we respond. These alpinists will climb up to each of the four camps in turn, acclimatising to the brutal altitude before they push for the summit.

A Russian mountaineer stumbles past, badly sunburnt, sporting a Seven Summits Club softshell. He mutters a gruff 'Zdraste!' His Sherpa leader wears a harness that clinks with jumars and karabiners: the gear climbers need to attach themselves to the mountain on fixed lines.

'Namaste!' Hem greets him.

'Well done!' we say.

The Russian climber looks spent. He trips on the moraine, staggers, regains his footing, and dives into an orange tent.

Meltwater burbles into a channel, mixing with plastic wrappers and green-brown smears of yak dung. Pedestals of ice support great mushroom-caps of rock. These are glacier tables: rocks which cast shadows that prevent the ice immediately underneath them from melting. Some of the raised boulders have skeins of prayer flags draped around them. As I approach the nearest one, grains of rock loosen and skitter down to its foot.

Climbers report seeing the ice bulging up under their tents, and crevasses yawning open while they sleep.

The Khumbu Glacier is the second longest in Nepal, but it is shrinking by thirty metres per year. Base Camp is lower than it was for Hillary and Tensing. The village of climbers' tents may soon be moved lower down the mountain, where there is no permanent ice.

Glaciers store memories of places and their pasts. Ice cores taken from Everest reveal that the last hundred years have been the hottest in two millennia. And glaciers can literally disappear into thin air. The heat of the sun transforms them straight from solid to vapour, bypassing the liquid stage: a process called sublimation. As I pause at the point where gravel gives way to naked ice, I think about the strangeness of this. So many people have written about mountains as sublime – inspiring an awe tinged with fear – but the mountain cryosphere is delicate and vulnerable. Sublimation is the main way the South Col Glacier, higher up Everest, loses ice. Its snowpack has dwindled, and its black ice is bared to the sun. It may be gone in a few decades. Ten years before I hiked to Base Camp, veteran Everest mountaineer Apa Sherpa described the world's highest peak as having more 'bare rock' than when he first climbed it, causing dangerous rock falls.

And it's too late now, Jessica Willis Fisher sang from the speakers this morning.
Look up, look up,
the flames are getting higher.

Despite the cold, the sun is overpowering; I can feel it burning my cheeks and the nape of my neck.

I ask Hem Raj, our trek leader, about changes he's seen. 'I've been coming here for fifteen years,' he tells me, 'and each time the ponds on the glacier get bigger. The mountains are melting. The glaciers are melting, and some of the lakes are disappearing. When a glacier melts, the mud and rocks go into the lake, and it gets smaller and smaller until it is gone. Landslides are becoming worse – people died in a bad one in 2017. And as global warming increases, the landslides come more often. It's a problem all over the world', he continues. 'Nepal may lose the mountains, but when the glaciers here melt, cities near the coast will sink into the sea.'

There's a twist of unease in the pit of my stomach. I'm under no illusion about the part I've played in this. I'm from a wealthy country, I've flown here, I've got oil on my hands. I look at a meltwater pond and remember the puddles of aviation fuel on the runway at Lukla, the mineral stink of petroleum. Some people here may even benefit from climate change – warmer weather means that crops flourish in regions where they never grew before. But the greatest beneficiaries of climate change are the ones who have worked hardest to hide or deny it: fossil fuel companies.

I walk back towards the glacier's snout, to the edge of a huge sunken bowl in the ice, where the ground drops away. A slope of damp, unstable gravel. It reminds me of the Great Stone Chute on Skye. The slope hangs above a great cauldron in the glacier. A curving stream scours and rushes below. Icicle columns overhang its lip. The water churns down into this sinkhole – a moulin, I guess. I inch down, using the sides of my boots for traction, but I lose my footing, stumble, and slither half a metre on my bottom. A French trekker, camera in hand, is trudging up from the edge: 'You can take your bag off and walk more easily.' I smile. 'Thank you.'

I creep as close as I dare to the sinkhole and stand on the brim. I look down into the frigid water. If I fell in, the stream would whirl me down the glacier's freezing gullet, to its stony bed. I'm standing on rock that the glacier has ground to powder, and I know that beneath my boot soles, the ice splits and slips and liquefies. The water's roar overwhelms my hearing. I stand there, giddy with altitude, my neck and ears blistered by the sun, and look down into the churn of meltwater. I'm balanced on the brink of a tipping point.

16

Everests on stage: contemporary theatre's contribution to decolonising the mountain

Jonathan Pitches

For most people, transporting the highest mountain on Earth on to the boards of a stage sounds like folly. What can the theatre offer the cultural record of Chomolungma / Sagarmatha / Everest that hasn't already been achieved in literature, music, photography, or film? Its pragmatic limitations – auditorium size, stage dimensions, fly-tower height, scene dock access – are surely constraining enough to thwart the most concentrated efforts, before one contemplates the aesthetics of recreating the extremities of the death zone using haze and tungsten light.[1] Yet the dramatic record of Everest is rich, extensive, and long-lived. Indeed, there is a substantial repertoire of staged renditions of the mountain, spanning at least the same hundred years as the film record – from John Noel's *Epic of Everest* (1924) to Nirmal Purja's *14 Peaks: Nothing Is Impossible* (2021).[2] In the theatre, a parallel century of creative activity covers the full political spectrum and range of genres: a fascist tribute to Mussolini, Vitaliano Brancati's *Everest* (1928); a surreal, psychoanalytical verse drama, Auden and Isherwood's *Ascent of F6* (1937);[3] a highly fictionalised account of the 1960 Chinese expedition to Everest staged at the Shanghai People's Art Theatre, *Zhumulangma* (1962); a 'delectably loony' romantic skit by Arthur Kopit, *The Conquest of Everest* (1971);[4] and an operatic translation of the fateful 1996 expedition, *Everest* composed by Joby Talbot and Gene Sheer,[5] premiering in Dallas in 2015 with a concert staging at the Barbican in London in 2023. All in all, a desk-based survey of staged works dedicated to Everest yielded twenty-five pieces, with dramatic interest in the mountain demonstrably increasing since the 1990s.[6]

How to make sense of this history of Everests on stage? What does a theatre historiography of the mountain reveal, to complement and/or challenge other historiographies? Are there developments in decolonial thinking in the Everest theatre record which parallel other disciplines in mountain studies? And what can be learnt from a close reading of some of the theatrical experiments of the late 2010s and early 2020s? In this chapter, using the centenary of the 1924 Mount Everest expedition as a catalyst for reflection, I want to focus on the last half-decade of staging Everest in the theatre, asking what, if anything, these performances tell us about the changing symbolic significance of Everest in the contemporary world. I draw on newly conducted interviews with four artists (Matt Kambic, Carmen Nasr, Gary Winters, and Gregg Whelan)[7] as well as an analysis of their stagings of Everest. How do these works differ from earlier expressions of triumphalism, conquest, and occupation, ones at play in Brancati, the Shanghai Art Theatre, and Isherwood and Auden in variegated ways?

Brancati was a Sicilian dramatist and poet who aligned himself clearly with Mussolini's Blackshirts at the beginning of his career, before distancing himself from fascism from the middle of the 1930s. Brancati's *Everest* is firmly in the former period. Although little has been written about the play, its first performance is notorious for prompting a chorus of (very brave) disapproval. At a time when it was forbidden to criticise Mussolini, Brancati's concluding image drew derision and outrage from its audience – an illuminated bust of Il Duce embedded into the fabric of the mountain, Mount Rushmore-style. The negative reaction was such that it led the poet Trilussa[8] to proclaim Brancati a genius, although his tongue may have been in his cheek. Soon after, the playwright signalled his movement away from Mussolini with a companion piece, *The Old Man in Boots* – 'a work which dismantles *Everest*'.[9]

At the other end of the political continuum, the propagandist *Zhumulangma* testifies to the extent to which theatre was seen as an effective means of communicating socialist macro-narratives in the young state of the People's Republic of China. As Maggie Greene has pointed out, the Shanghai People's Art Theatre production, based on the first successful ascent of Everest from the north in 1960,[10] was part of a wider cultural crusade in this decade which sought to connect mountaineering success with the socialist cause. 'The actors performing the play', she tells us, 'were both acting out mountaineering for audiences, and – just like the expedition itself – performing a politically perfect, noble and modern vision of Chinese socialism'.[11] Heroism expressed on the slopes of the mountain, became capital in the hands of the actors to inspire domestic audiences towards collective pride and commitment to Mao's communism.

Auden and Isherwood's *The Ascent of F6* is much more difficult to interpret, though it still grapples with tropes of empire.[12] Ostensibly an allegorical play, with F6 constructed as a mythic peak, Abbie Garrington's scholarship suggests that there is little doubt as to the identity of the titular mountain. The barely veiled reference to the local name for the peak 'Chormopuloda';[13] the affinities between the protagonist Michael Ransom and the historic figure of George Mallory; and the wordplay between F6 and the pre-Everest code name 'Peak XV', all point, she argues, to the inspiration for Auden and Isherwood's collaboration to be Everest.[14] At times impenetrable, and seemingly unstageable, *F6* plays out many of the colonial debates about mountaineering and its implicated relationship with empire. Ransom-Mallory as British hero is tasked by the Colonial Office with securing the first ascent of F6, beating its imperial rival (the fictional Ostnia) to the summit, and thus cementing Britain's political credibility along with its ongoing occupation of Sudoland (another dramatic construct). The concluding image, however, hardly endorses Ransom as imperial hero: he dies on the summit in a Freudian embrace with his mother, she who had previously persuaded him to climb F6 as 'the greatest climber in the world' with 'the power to stand alone'.[15]

Three Everests on stage

If *The Ascent of F6* exposed some of the fractures in dramatic formulations of Everest-as-conquest as early as 1936, how does the most recent dramatic output of the twenty-first century refresh the cultural record of the world's highest peak? In this section, split into three subsections, I draw on interview testimony, primary source analysis, and wider contextual research to consider in finer detail the motivations, challenges, and dramaturgical approaches taken by four selected theatre artists to stage their versions of Everest in the period 2018–22.

Beyond their contemporaneity and variety of style, there is no overarching or guiding principle determining my choice; I do not wish to imply, or start to construct, a new canon of Everest dramas. Instead, this small sample should serve as a paradigm of the ways in which Western contemporary theatre has engaged with the history, culture, and geopolitics of the world's highest mountain, using varied means to render Everest's cultural complexity, contradictory reception, and historical density with a lightness of touch which belies its rigour and import.

The Sherpa and the Beekeeper: Summit on Everest, by Matt Kambic

Constructed as a vibrant series of imagined dialogues between Tenzing Norgay (the Sherpa of the title, of course) and Edmund Hillary (the beekeeper), Matt Kambic's two-hander treats the summit of Everest as the platform for decades of speculative conversation between the two first ascensionists. His starting point is the controversy over which of the two stood on the summit first – Hillary (ironically a New Zealander, and not British born), or Tenzing, who had already been near the summit in 1952, proving his status, in expedition leader John Hunt's assessment, as a 'mountaineer of world standing'.[16] While the summit plateau of the mountain remains constantly under their feet, Tenzing (played by Jericho Nicodemus) and Hillary (Cameron Smith) transform over the three acts of the play. From the hotly contested moment summiting on 29 May 1953, through dark reflections on unwanted celebrity years later, to a final section, again after an undisclosed passage of time, where the now-seasoned icons of mountaineering history meet once more, surrounded by 'detritus: discarded oxygen tanks and other bits of gear'.[17] In this last act, both climbers weigh the impact of their success, literally taking the long view on the environmental damage and increase in footfall after 1953, partly occasioned by the development of Lukla airport,[18] a project funded and overseen by Hillary:

Figure 16.1 *The Sherpa and the Beekeeper* at Meteor Theatre, Hamilton, Aotearoa/New Zealand, 25 May 2022. Image: © Matt Kambic.

Hillary: It opened up a gusher of tourists, marching in with their empty stomachs and candy wrappers, and ill manners, right into the heart of your homeland. In droves, like fattened-up sheep.

They're down there right now, below us.

Not all, unwelcome, you know that. But so many, too many, so fast. I should've thought that out.

Tenzing: (*squinting to see*) They are so small from up here.[19]

The play concludes with a rapid return to the time and conditions of Act One, set just metres away from the summit point. Teasing the audience, US-born writer Kambic orders a blackout just before the two reach the summit, thus preserving the so-called mystery of who reached the top first. It was, says Kambic in my interview with him, 'the lovely wrinkle of getting them ready to go up and the audience anticipating "we'll finally see who *did* step up there first" and then just cutting it'.[20] Resisting the noise around 'who got there first', Kambic aimed to 'get the Hillary and Tenzing that the public knows […] and then just say it really doesn't matter, it didn't matter in the end and you're not going to find out anyway [*laughs*]'.[21]

Kambic's reticence to contribute to seventy years of often-internecine speculation about whose boots first reached the top of Everest is ironically not reflected in his two characters' attitudes. From the moment they have summited, marked on stage by Hillary taking the famous photograph of Norgay holding his ice pick aloft with flags attached, the two climbers exchange good-humoured claims to being the first:

Tenzing: I say, first, Hillary second. Hillary say first, Tenzing second. No, good. We both together.[22]

This is Kambic's key dramatic ploy – to position the two individuals as emblems of the wider geopolitical storm and contested histories which emerged on the international stage following the successful expedition, a storm charged with the rhetoric of empire. As Hillary declares before they descend in Act One: 'And here you and I are; a Colonial and a Nepalese. That might surprise the Queen. She might have been happier if her two wards, Tom and Charles[23] had made it up here two days ago'.[24]

Accurate and well-researched history is drip-fed through the fictional dialogues of Tenzing and Hillary, sometimes to the detriment of narrative momentum.[25] Although Acts Two and Three are entirely imagined, Kambic was motivated by a desire to treat the legacy of the two climbers accurately and respectfully: 'I wanted to bring Everest, Hillary and Tenzing to the audience in as authentic a manner as I could, especially for the First Act', [26] he states, a function of his scholarly immersion in Himalayan histories since reading Maurice Herzog's *Annapurna* as a boy. This spirit of authenticity extends as far as the stage design – a bold and simple attempt to pluck the topmost section of Everest from Nepal/China and transport it unscathed to the theatre in Hamilton, New Zealand. Originally, Kambic 'wanted to build the summit [so that it was] identical to the geophysical Mount Everest summit'[27] but compromised slightly to allow for spatial dynamics and height differences which aren't a feature of the very top of Everest to be explored in the play. Nevertheless, the play exploits the geographical realities of the summit, playing with the border between China and Nepal that bisects the mountaintop and helping the audience visualise its striking liminality:

> *Hillary steps up to access the very summit and runs his finger in a line across the top. The line separates he and Tenzing, who stands on the opposite side of the peak (in Tibet).*
> **Hillary:** I am in Nepal, you're in Tibet.
> **Tenzing:** Summit of Everest separates two countries. Now two men. [28]

This simple visualisation, which surfaces again later in the play when the two climbers drop their stove in Nepal and it falls into the neighbouring country, says much about the affordances theatre offers to the discourse of mountain studies. In a few seconds of stage time, decades of debate and dispute are crystallised: the right to claim ownership of a sacred Mountain; the stratified status games played by both the British and Indian governments to claim national victory and divide the collective achievement of Tenzing and Hillary; the class and cultural divisions between Sherpa and Explorer; and perhaps more philosophically the disconnect between the virgin white snow and untrampled territory we see on stage and the images many of us have when we think of Everest today: fixed-rope queues, graveyards of frozen climbers, and piles of empty oxygen cannisters. For Kambic, this capacity for a single stage image to speak volumes was a given, the opportunity to humanise the wider socio-cultural complexity of Everest enticing:

> It was quickly apparent that I could take Hillary and Tenzing, guys with good hearts, down to earth, and present some of these larger issues and the way as you say how we relook at stuff in history that occurred [...] I wanted to remind myself and the audience that it was *the climb* that made all the rest of this happen and anchor it back into the reality of that day.[29]

The Climbers, by Carmen Nasr

Where historical fidelity and geographical verisimilitude were drivers for Kambic, British Lebanese writer Carmen Nasr has constructed what she terms 'a fever-dream' with *The Climbers* – a neoexpressionist and slippery whodunnit where 'the higher the altitude of the scene, the more unreliable the truth is'.[30] This device, to implicate the audience in a parallel journey of altitude sickness and confusion, leads to a sparse and disjointed dramaturgy – a controlled 'mess-iness', Nasr calls it.[31] Two acts hold a total of twenty-seven scenes, the majority demarcated by their height above sea level (it is only the choric interventions of Tshering, the guide, that are placeless). Resisting blackouts between scenes, Nasr calls instead for 'shifts' from one scene to the next: 'It's sort of a shift in memory,' she observes, 'a shift in Yasmin's [the central female climber's] mind, I guess, or a shift in feeling or place'.[32] Billed as an 'offering to the creative team',[33] the term suggests that dramatic fluidity and momentum exceed any need for spatial specificity. In marked contrast to *The Sherpa and the Beekeeper*, place is experienced kaleidoscopically: from a camp just below the summit (26,000 feet) to a hotel room in a Nepali valley (4,600 feet); from Base Camp

Figure 16.2 *The Climbers*, premiering at the Theatre by the Lake, Keswick, UK, 17 June 2022. Image: © The Other Richard.

(17,700 feet), back to the hotel and on to a comfortable rural dwelling in the south of England (115 feet). Dizzy from these rapid location shifts, we reach relative stability with Tshering's first chorus, zooming out to provide a bird's-eye view:

> **Tshering:** People arrive here with their story already written out in their head, but just like the mountain's history was overwritten by the Europeans, nature re-writes the stories the climbers bring with them, and they quickly find out that things never go to plan.[34]

The casual reference to unplanned occurrences is an oblique allusion to the tragedy at the centre of the play: Yasmin's partner Charlie's death high up on 'The Mountain' (the name Everest is never explicitly used in the play). But in this second of five choruses, Tshering, the only local, Indigenous voice in the play,[35] also aligns Eurocentric history-making – the act of appropriating the mountain as Everest rather than Chomolungma or Sagarmatha (names used in Tibet or Nepal)[36] – with a cognate European arrogance in mountaineering prowess. Assuming control, he pointedly observes through language and nomenclature, partial histories of claimed ownership, or narratives of expeditionary immortality that the most fundamental shadow cast by potential outcomes is fatality.

Indeed, alternative versions of history are both the stimulus for and the dramatic pivot of *The Climbers*. Reading John Krakauer's *Into Thin Air* (1997) alongside Anatoli Boukreev's *The Climb* (1997), Nasr became fascinated by the contrasting versions of the same 1996 tragedy: 'these are two published books by two very well-respected climbers who are saying different things and remembering it differently', she notes.[37] That realisation sparked an extensive research process, taking her to Herzog's *Annapurna* (again), to Himalayan ghost stories, the documentary film *Sherpa* (2015), and other 'rabbit holey' investigations into subjects as diverse as Kathmandu and karaoke. This detective work is embodied in the character of Connie, a private investigator working for the mother of the lost climber Charlie. Connie is well aware of the vagaries of memory, particularly when cognitive function is compromised by altitude and grief:

> **Connie:** I understand that this is all very upsetting. But memories they fade and change, it's important we talk as early as we can, when the truth is still within our reach.[38]

Despite her best efforts to ascertain a single truth, ostensibly motivated to secure closure for Charlie's mother, several parallel versions of the tragedy emerge: Charlie 'fell for miles', accidently slipping down the mountain;

he was lost in a storm, separating him and Yasmin from Tshering, their guide; Tshering willingly left Charlie solely to Yasmin's care; Charlie is still alive and using his satellite phone to ring his mother at night; Yasmin pushed Charlie in a deadly marital row; Charlie (either alone or not) met his end slowly under a ledge with no fall. These anomalies are summed up simply by the other female climber, Gwen, speaking to the PI: 'Can I give you some advice, from a hardened climber? There's no such thing as truth up there'.[39]

This may be true at the level of the character but constructing a rationale and logic for the cast remains a crucial part of the creative process, as Nasr put it: 'you do have to explain yourself to a room of actors because they are, like, "why" and "what?"' [40] In the final image of the play, as with *The Sherpa and the Beekeeper* one of rich and layered complexity, Charlie and Yasmin are together in his last moments. The atmosphere is other-worldly, 'glittery', different to or beyond the other versions of Charlie's death witnessed earlier; arguably – perhaps – more definitive. A physically fit Yasmin is tarrying briefly but according to a pact struck between the couple, the stronger must leave the weak behind if one should get into trouble. They dance in the shimmering snow to the strains of a karaoke tune, before (in the staged version) Yasmin leaves her partner to his fate, stripped now of her protective gear, climbing up the ladder to a new life.[41]

Describing in prose this multi-sensorial theatrical moment is unavoidably reductive but even in the two dimensions of a written chapter the layered meanings should come through. Nasr's final scene offers several things at once: a thought-provoking take on the individualism of modern tourist-climbing, where walking past a dying fellow human being is pragmatically normalised; a haunting vision of a mountain's blend of beauty and suffering, the weather both deadly and desirable, enhanced through the effects of extreme altitude; a pointed reminder of the senselessness of it all, the addition of yet another frozen body unable to be airlifted to the morgue. And an existential prompt, in one spectator's eyes 'about the inevitability that every partnership must end, and one will always leave the other behind, no matter what'.[42]

On Everest, by Lone Twin

Originally conceived as a final degree show piece for the BA Performance Writing at Dartington College of Arts in 1997, Gary Winters and Gregg Whelan's *On Everest* has had several outings since, the latest at stage@leeds in the University of Leeds in 2018.[43] The 1997 show was the first time Winters and Whelan worked collectively as Lone Twin, initiating a long-standing and critically acclaimed repertoire of performance pieces with task-oriented, endurance-based self-referentiality and mock heroism as common ingredients. In David Williams and Carl Lavery's tight phrasing, Lone Twin has an enduring 'interest in manufacturing simple structures for complex conversational outcomes'.[44]

In *On Everest*, that simple structure is nothing less than the performed climbing of Everest in front of an audience – achieved by the walking of a line of white gaffer tape on the floor, measuring 1/400th of the height of the mountain. In Whelan's words, the attraction was the idea 'of a studio that [...] conceptually went uphill. But there was no physical manifestation of that other than how you would behave in the space.'[45] Winters does the walking – 400 traverses of the stage – while Whelan delivers an academic paper, also titled *On Everest*, spending much of his time in a paddling pool full of polystyrene beads.

Needless to say, we are in very different territory from the heightened stage poetics of *The Climbers* or the faithful Socratic dialogues of *The Sherpa and the Beekeeper*. Indeed, inaccuracy and invention are framed as fundamentals from the outset, and some of the information, Gregg tells us at the top of the show,

Figure 16.3 Lone Twin's *On Everest*, stage@leeds, 22 March 2018. Image: © Jonathan Pitches.

Figure 16.4 Lone Twin's *On Everest*, stage@leeds, 22 March 2018. Image: © Jonathan Pitches.

'is a bit shaky'.[46] Nevertheless, *On Everest* is the product of a similar dedication to research[47] and draws on cognate ideas, particularly in relation to the effects of altitude and the relationship between hypoxia and nostalgia – 'climbers identifying that [while] they should be self-monitoring or thinking about what's happening to them physically' the lack of oxygen instead makes for an out-of-body feeling of 'nostalgia or melancholy'.[48] This discovery led Whelan to focus on Everest 'the poster mountain of all mountains'[49] and to the central device: the pivot between the events on stage and past historical endeavours, 'myths, legends and fibs about this place'.[50]

Place here is essentially plural – the place of Everest, of the original Studio 11 in Dartington in 1997, of stage@leeds in 2018, of the act of performance-making as place-making for this theatrical company being asked 'to write, to fold, one space into another'.[51] For Lone Twin, this does not mean the transplantation of a recognisable mountain feature – Kambic's summit of Everest, for instance – rather a perspective that values the 'imaginary' and 'dreamt' aspects of place as much as its physical realities.[52] *On Everest* explores that concept in stark, simple terms – an expansive, largely empty stage space, demarcated by the white line of tape and punctuated by three cheap paddling pools – 'little islands' in Winter's words,[53] the smallest housing an office fan. There are no grand scenic gestures to Everest but little indications, wrought with the artificiality of the stage: a pile of white polystyrene beads, shaped into the smallest of summits, wind gusting from the fan, a bear suit aping a yeti. Constructed as a lecture delivered by Whelan, broken down into sixty chapters (some which exist purely as titles), Winters gets on with the job in hand, hiking the equivalent of the five and a half miles of Everest on the flat in the background. Artifice constantly rubs shoulders with the very real in *On Everest*, a signature of the company's oeuvre since 1997.

Though melancholy and nostalgia were the driving first ideas, the piece is light in tone, humorous, and beguilingly unserious about itself. Summiting success is by no means guaranteed as they wrote two possible endings. The doubt hanging over the feat – a nod to the attraction and emotionalism of live sport – is part of the fun for Whelan and Winters. Any whiff of heroism associated with endurance or walking five-and-a-half miles in an hour, sometimes in a shaggy bear suit, is sharply undercut by the suit itself and by the duplication of endings:

> I think for all of us a very emotional moment. We have come a long way, and what's more, we have come a long way together. It is hard to know exactly what to say at a time like this, I'm sure – and I know it's true of Gary and myself – that our thoughts are by and large, a little bit muddled and confused, but nevertheless, charged with a great sensation of achievement, or perhaps its opposite.[54]

These are the words for *both* Chapter 58, 'On not quite making it' *and* Chapter 60, 'On the summit', although a live audience may not be aware of these parallels. Viewed together in the performance script, the conflation of success and failure returns us to the artifice of the piece: 'Whatever happens it's still just the last 5 minutes of the show', Whelan notes, 'and it needs to deliver a certain thing for the "showness" to end'.[55]

But in the context of this chapter and the different approaches to conquest and heroism that we have seen, both conclusions to *On Everest* quietly question the notion of achievement itself. Climbing Everest is an accomplishment, 'or perhaps its opposite'. This gentle jibe is heightened by the final joke of the performance – a reminder to the audience that 'we' means all of us, and that collectively we now need to descend 'and find our own ways down'.[56] For some, this command might chime with the theme of abandonment seen in *The Climbers*. For Lone Twin, this is a playful extension of the contract they have struck with their audience, the co-operative 'endeavour'. Our quotidian existences in the days after the play are thus fused with the residue of *On Everest* – 'it's a flip of one of the first ideas in the piece about the effects of altitude sickness [...] You're in everyday life, but we are putting you on the mountain [...] you are walking down it in a conceptual way, but you're actually going through these places in your life'.[57]

Conclusion

Kambic, Nasr, and Whelan and Winters came to their respective Everest projects with very different motivations. But, speaking to each of them, their common conviction is in the value of rigorous research, drawing on and critically evaluating some of the vast literature dedicated to the world's highest mountain. At some stage in the process, that research had to stop – none of them aimed to produce a documentary – and it is down to the shrewd judgement of an artist when to set aside inspiring extant literature to carve out what Nasr calls a new 'space of imagination'.[58] The iterative relationship between imaginative theatrical thinking and existing research on the Himalayas is important. It suggests that the many stage versions of Everest should not be isolated from other contemporary work in mountain studies. Dramatic art is part of that interdisciplinary field, whether the creatives in this chapter see themselves embedded in it or not.

As such, it is perhaps unsurprising that this chapter has identified similar revisionary and decolonial agendas at work in the stage record of Everest, a parallel distrust of historic simplifications, misrepresentations, and appropriations. For Kambic, that revisionary urge is reflected in the extended thought experiment he stages – Hillary and Tenzing engaged in an enlightened and impossible dialogue, separated at the summit from their cultural histories, and blessed with all the benefits of hindsight. For Nasr, it is in the solipsism of the Western tourist-climber, sharply contrasted with the unromanticised wisdom of the Nepali guide, Tshering, a business-savvy custodian of the mountain. And for Whelan and Winters, the self-aware mockery of their own immersion in tropes of masculinity and endurance means that we never take them too seriously: 'We say we like stiff-upper-lipness, and we're sort of driving that, and trying to skewer that' at the same time.[59] As the sensitive and complex process

269

of revisiting monolithic histories gathers apace, there is something to be said for the agility theatre has in striking such a double-edged critique – a view from the wings, at once implicated and dislocated.

Notes

1 Haze is an atmospheric effect used in the theatre in conjunction with light, a mist which stays suspended for sometimes long periods in the air to provide definition to the lighting.

2 John Noel (dir.), *Epic of Everest* (UK: BFI, 2013 [orig. 1924]); Torquil Jones (dir.), *14 Peaks: Nothing is Impossible* (USA: Netflix, 2021).

3 Vitaliano Brancati, *Everest: mito in un atto* (Catania: Studio editoriale moderno, 1931); W.H. Auden and Christopher Isherwood, *Ascent of F6* (London: Faber and Faber, 1936).

4 Arthur Kopit, *The Day the Whores Came Out to Play Tennis & Other Plays* (London: Samuel French, 1993), a collection of one-act plays, with contents detailed in: https://web.archive.org/web/20230320090659/https://store.bizbooks.net/daythewhorescameout toplaytennis.aspx

5 Joby Talbot (composer), *Everest: opera in one act* (London: Chester Music, 2017).

6 Fifteen of the twenty-five plays, musicals, and operas were written and/or performed after 2010. The preliminary research for the survey, as well as transcriptions of the interviews, was undertaken by Dr Ceri Pitches, postdoctoral researcher in the School of Performance and Cultural Industries, University of Leeds. Without this pivotal research, this chapter would not have been possible.

7 I am indebted to all four artists for their generosity and insights. Full transcripts of the interviews conducted for this chapter are hosted on the *Performing Mountains* website: https://web.archive.org/web/20240123174831/https://performing-mountains.leeds.ac.uk/newwritingandinterviews/

8 Real name: Carlo Alberto Camillo Salustri.

9 Interview with Corrado Sofia in Jeffrey T. Schnapp, *Staging Fascism: 18 BL and the Theater of Masses for Masses* (Stanford, CA: Stanford University Press, 1996), p. 166.

10 The first ascent of Everest from the north in 1960 was made by a mixed Chinese and Tibetan team of climbers, following in the footsteps of Mallory and Irvine. It was subject to much scrutiny and some unseemly Western scepticism at the time but is now largely recognised as genuine.

11 Maggie Greene, 'Performing socialism at altitude: Chinese expeditions to Mount Everest, 1958–1968', *Performance Research*, 24:2 (2019), 63–72, 68, https://doi.org/10.1080/13528165.2019.1624030

12 Isherwood himself likened its form to a 'mad rugby scrum', quoted in Lawrence Normand, 'Modernity and Orientalism in W. H. Auden and Christopher Isherwood's The Ascent of F6', *Modern Philology*, 108:4 (2011), 542, https://doi.org/10.1086/660366

13 Auden and Isherwood, *Ascent of F6*, p. 31.

14 Abbie Garrington, 'What does a modernist mountain mean? Auden and Isherwood's *The Ascent of F6*', *Critical Quarterly*, 55:2 (2013), 26–49, https://doi.org/10.1111/criq.12043. There are other possible genealogies of F6, it should be noted, including potential mappings to the Pamirs and Karakoram. Auden's brother John took part in the Karakoram surveys in the 1930s – thanks to Jonathan Westaway for pointing this out.

15 Auden and Isherwood, *Ascent of F6*, pp. 45, 47. While much has been made of Auden and Isherwood's time in Berlin as being influential on their theatre writing, Breon Mitchell suggests an Ibsenite influence to the conclusion of *F6* is more likely, specifically from *Peer Gynt*. Breon Mitchell, 'W. H. Auden and Christopher Isherwood: The "German Influence"', *Oxford German Studies*, 1:1 (1966), 163–72, https://doi.org/10.1179/ogs.1966.1.1.163

16 John Hunt, *The Ascent of Everest* (London: Hodder and Stoughton, 1953), p. 61.

17 Matt Kambic, *The Sherpa and the Beekeeper – Summit on Everest* (2022), 20. All quotations are from the unpublished manuscript generously shared with me by the author.

18 Lukla airport, a short flight from Kathmandu, opened in 1964 and is reputedly the most dangerous airport in the world, with a poor safety record.

19 *The Sherpa and the Beekeeper*, 33.

20 Interview with the author, 24 February 2023.

21 Ibid.

22 *The Sherpa and the Beekeeper*, 5.

23 Tom Bourdillon and Charles Evans. Both men were forced back on 26 May 1953, less than 100 metres from the summit, due to problems with Evans' oxygen supply.

24 *The Sherpa and the Beekeeper*, 7.

25 For instance, in Act 2 scene 1, where Hillary narrates back to Tenzing the latter's climbing career in documentary detail.

26 Interview with the author, 24 February 2023.

27 Ibid.

28 *The Sherpa and the Beekeeper*, 6.

29 Interview with the author, 24 February 2023.

30 Carmen Nasr, *The Climbers* (London: Nick Hern Books, 2022), p. 4.

31 Interview with the author, 10 March 2023.

32 Ibid.

33 Ibid.

34 *The Climbers*, p. 19.

35 Nasr clearly agonised over the representation of the Sherpa community in the play: 'either you leave that voice out, or you include that voice, and if I'm going to be driven by fear, then that's gonna silence that character and all the stories I was reading on Everest, people from the Sherpa community were there. They're there, you know, in all of the different stories. So I thought, No, there has to be a character.' Interview with the author, 10 March 2023.

36 Sam Ellis, '"No name intelligible to civilised men:" hidden voices in Mount Everest's nomenclature', *Charleston Hub*, https://web.archive.org/web/20240123174437/https://www.charleston-hub.com/2022/09/no-name-intelligible-to-civilised-men-hidden-voices-in-mount-everests-nomenclature/. See also the Introduction by Hansen, Gilchrist, and Westaway, and Chapters 1 and 2 by Ruth Gamble and Felix de Montety in this volume.

37 Interview with the author, 10 March 2023.

38 Nasr, *The Climbers*, p. 8.

39 Nasr, *The Climbers*, p. 37.

40 Interview with the author, 10 March 2023.

41 Nasr, *The Climbers*, pp. 72–3. In the published version the play ends with the couple dancing.

42 Interview with the author, 10 March 2023. The spectator was Jonathan Westaway.

43 To date, *On Everest* has been performed at Dartington College of Arts (1997), the ICA in London (1997), Nottingham Expo (1997), Glasgow CCA (2000), Bristol's Arnolfini

(2006), and stage@leeds (2018). An edition of 150 bespoke scripts of the piece is produced for each performance, with subtle adaptations. My quotations are from the stage@leeds version.

44 David Williams and Carl Lavery (eds), *Good Luck Everybody: Lone Twin – Journeys, Performances, Conversations* (Aberystwyth: Performance Research Books, 2011), p. 22.

45 Interview with the author, 31 March 2023.

46 Lone Twin, *On Everest* (Leeds, 2018), 6.

47 For example: 'place-based, spatial theory, arts practice, philosophy, critical thinking, literature, and looking at contemporary ethnography, anthropology, cultural geography'. Gregg Whelan interview with the author, 31 March 2023.

48 Interview with the author, 31 March 2023.

49 Ibid.

50 Lone Twin, *On Everest*, 6.

51 Gregg Whelan, 'Here we are, let's go: Dartington College of Arts, 14 June 1997, Studio 11, 6:30 pm. A revision of Lone Twin's *On Everest*', *Theatre, Dance and Performance Training*, 9:3 (2018), 431–44, 436, https://doi.org/10.1080/19443927.2018.1503615

52 Ibid.

53 Interview with the author, 31 March 2023.

54 Lone Twin, *On Everest*, 26, 28.

55 Interview with the author, 31 March 2023.

56 Lone Twin, *On Everest*, 26.

57 Interview with the author, 31 March 2023.

58 Interview with the author, 10 March 2023.

59 Interview with the author, 31 March 2023.

Bibliography

Each chapter in *Other Everests* includes full citations including archival sources in chapter endnotes. This bibliography includes all sources cited in the work apart from archival sources and was prepared by Peter Hansen.

This bibliography will be permanently available and Open Access at www.manchester hive.com and at https://digital.wpi.edu/collections/everests

Bibliography

'Ascents – Spring 2019'. *The Himalayan Database*, (2019). https://web.archive.org/web/20230128062615/www.himalayandatabase.com/2019%20Season%20Lists/2019%20Spring%20A14.html.

bKra shis tshe ring ma'i sgrub skor sogs. Thimphu: Kunzang Topgey, 1976. https://library.bdrc.io/show/bdr:WA30292.

'Columbia's "Lost Horizon," now back in release, is clicking merrily at box offices all over the country'. *Daily Film Renter*, 17:4986 (27 September 1943), 10.

'Dawa Yangzum Sherpa: A trail-blazing Nepali mountaineer, teaching women to climb'. *Newsroom.rolex.com*, (May 2023). https://web.archive.org/web/20240123152559/https://newsroom.rolex.com/world-of-rolex/perpetual-planet/rolex-and-exploration/rolex-and-exploration/news-10/dawa-yangzum-sherpa-a-trail-blazing-nepali-mountaineer-teaching-women-to-climb.

'How Dawa Yangzum Sherpa became a mountaineering icon'. *Gripped Magazine*, (30 May 2023). https://web.archive.org/web/20240123160624/https://gripped.com/profiles/how-dawa-yangzum-sherpa-became-a-mountaineering-icon/.

'Lama of the Rongbuk Monastery. Printed diary. Visit of the Mount Everest Expeditions'. *Statesman*, (1 January 1931).

'Most days, it's not so crowded on My Everest'. *Nepali Times*, (28 May 2019). https://web.archive.org/web/20230315101306/https://nepalitimes.com/here-now/most-days-it-s-not-so-crowded-on-mt-everest.

'The Mount Everest expedition'. *Geographical Journal*, 60:3 (1922), 218–9. https://doi.org/10.2307/1781057.

'Mountain Clean-up Campaign 2023 collects over 35 tons of waste from Mt Everest, other peaks'. *The Himalayan Times*, (7 June 2023). https://web.archive.org/web/20240124010

Bibliography

933/https://thehimalayantimes.com/nepal/mountain-clean-up-campaign-2023-col lects-over-35-tons-of-waste-from-mt-everest-other-peaks.

'Nepal tourism may take 5 years to recover'. *Nepali Times*, (8 September 2020). https://web. archive.org/web/20200918120234/https://www.nepalitimes.com/latest/nepal-touri sm-may-take-5-years-to-recover/.

Nepālī-gadya-saṅgraha. Kāṭhamāḍauṃ: Sājhā Prakāśana, 2030 [1973].

'Pan Duo: China's first woman on top of world'. *Cctv.com*, (27 September 2009). https:// web.archive.org/web/20230415081736/https://www.cctv.com/english/special/ tibet/20090927/104002.shtml.

'"Shangri-La" brings back "Lost Horizon"'. *Hollywood Reporter*, 68:43 (29 June 1942), 3.

Slovenska alpinistična šola za nepalske gorske vodnike v Manangu [Slovenian mountaineering school for Nepalese mountain guides in Manang]. 2014, https://web.archive.org/web/20240123221656/ https://ales.kunaver.com/sola-v-manangu/.

'UN backs over one dozen women in largest all-female Everest expedition'. *UN News*, (14 February 2008). https://web.archive.org/web/20230323153014/https://news. un.org/en/story/2008/02/249062.

Yul phyogs so so 'i gsar 'gyur me loṅ = Tibet Mirror. https://clio.columbia.edu/catalog/6981643

Ācārya, Bāburāma, Shreekrishna Acharya, and Madhav Acharya. *China Tibet and Nepal: Historical account of Nepal's relationship with neighbours in the north.* Kathmandu: China Study Center, 2018.

Āchārya, Bāburām. 'Sagarmāthā or Jhyāmolongmā'. *Sharada*, 14:8 (January 1939), 193.

———. 'Sagarmāthā or Jhyāmolongmā.' In *Nepālī gadya saṅgraha*. Kathmandu: Sājhā Prakāśana, 2030 [1973], pp. 5–13.

Adams, Vincanne. *Tigers of the Snow and Other Virtual Sherpas: An Ethnography of Himalayan Encounters.* Princeton, NJ: Princeton University Press, 1996.

Adhikari, Ankit, and Joanna Slater. 'How Mount Everest's popularity turned fatal'. *Washington Post* (27 May 2019). https://web.archive.org/web/20240124192212/https://www. washingtonpost.com/world/how-mount-everests-popularity-turned-fatal/2019/05/27/ eea7d2b4-806c-11e9-9a67-a687ca99fb3d_story.html.

Adhikari, Ankit Babu, and Pradeep Bashyal. *Sherpa: Stories of Life and Death from the Forgotten Guardians of Everest.* London: Octopus Publishing, 2022.

Adhikari, Deepak. 'The Everest brawl: a Sherpa's tale'. *Outside Online*, (13 August 2013). https://web.archive.org/web/20150408172047/https://www.outsideonline.com/192 9351/everest-brawl-sherpas-tale.

Aitken, William McKay. 'An enquiry into the real name of Mt. Everest'. In *Touching Upon the Himalaya: Excursions and Enquiries*. Delhi: The Himalayan Club/Indus Publishing, 2004, pp. 122–4.

Alderman, Derek H., and Joshua Inwood. 'Street naming and the politics of belonging: spatial injustices in the toponymic commemoration of Martin Luther King Jr'. *Social & Cultural Geography*, 14:2 (2013), 211–33. https://doi.org/10.1080/14649365.2012.754488.

Aljančič, Janez, and Andrej Štremfelj. *Na vrhovih sveta: od prvih pristopov do najvišjih sten [To the top of the world: From the first approaches to the highest faces].* Zbirka Slovenija. Ljubljana: Zal. Mladinska knjiga, 1992.

Allen, Charles. *The Search for Shangri-La: A Journey into Tibetan History.* London: Abacus, 2000.

Anand, Dibyesh. *Geopolitical Exotica: Tibet in Western Imagination.* Minneapolis, MN: University of Minnesota Press, 2007.

Anderson, Perry. 'Agency.' In *Arguments within English Marxism*. London: Verso, 1980, pp. 16–58.

Bibliography

Ankele, Špela. '"Bilo je nezemeljsko lepo – kot da vrh sega v vesolje": Slovenci na Everestu ['"It was unearthly beautiful – as if the summit reached into outer space": Slovenes on Everest]'. *Delo*, (4 January 2012), 22.

Anker, Conrad, and David Roberts. *The Lost Explorer: Finding Mallory on Mount Everest*. New York: Simon & Schuster, 1999.

Apollo, Michal. 'There is greater gender equality in mountaineering research'. *Current Issues in Tourism*, 24:22 (2021), 3121–6. https://doi.org/10.1080/13683500.2021.1880376.

Apollo, Michal, Joanna Mostowska, Agnieszka Legut, Kamil Maciuk, and Dallen J. Timothy. 'Gender differences in competitive adventure sports tourism'. *Journal of Outdoor Recreation and Tourism*, 42 (2023), 100604. https://doi.org/10.1016/j.jort.2022.100604.

Appadurai, Arjun. *The Social Life of Things: Commodities in Cultural Perspective*. Cambridge: Cambridge University Press, 1986.

Archer, William. *The Green Goddess: A Play in Four Acts*. New York: Knopf, 1921.

Armston-Sheret, Edward. *On the Backs of Others: Rethinking the History of British Geographical Exploration*. Lincoln, NE: University of Nebraska Press, 2024.

Arnette, Alan. 'Everest 2014: Season summary – a Nepal tragedy'. *Alanarnette.com* (9 June 2014). https://web.archive.org/web/20140625053439/https://www.alanarnette.com/blog/2014/06/09/everest-2014-season-summary-nepal-tragedy/.

———. 'Everest 2015: Season summary – Summits don't matter'. *Alanarnette.com*, (6 May 2015). https://web.archive.org/web/20150528220207/https://www.alanarnette.com/blog/2015/05/06/everest-2015-season-summary-summits-dont-matter-2/.

———. 'Everest 2018: Interview with Kuntal Joisher-Integrity in motion'. *Alanarnette.com*, (2 April 2018). https://web.archive.org/web/20240124165425/https://www.alanarnette.com/blog/2018/04/02/everest-2018-interview-with-kuntal-joisher-integrity-in-motion/.

———. 'Everest 2023: Season dummary – deadliest in history'. *Alanarnette.com*, (2 June 2023). https://web.archive.org/web/20230602192939/https://www.alanarnette.com/blog/2023/06/02/everest-2023-season-summary-deadest-in-history/.

———. 'Sherpas are taking control of climbing in Nepal'. *Outside Online*, (20 November 2015). https://web.archive.org/web/20151122171814/https://www.outsideonline.com/2036831/sherpas-are-taking-control-climbing-nepal.

———. 'What's being done about trash (and bodies) on Everest'. *Outside Online*, (23 Apr 2019), Updated 6 Oct 2022. https://web.archive.org/web/20240124203241/https://www.outsideonline.com/outdoor-adventure/climbing/everest-dead-bodies-trash-removal/.

Askarieh, Fatemeh. 'How two Iranian women reached the peak of Mount Everest'. (8 June 2022). https://web.archive.org/web/20230604012852/https://ifpnews.com/iranian-women-mount-everest/#:~:text=Afsaneh%20Hesamifard%20and%20Elham%20Ramezani,sits%20in%20the%20Himalayan%20heights.

Auden, W. H., and Christopher Isherwood. *The Ascent of F6: A Tragedy in Two Acts*. London: Faber & Faber, 1936.

Bacot, Jacques. *Le Tibet révolté. Vers Népémakö, la terre promise des tibétains*. Paris: Hachette, 1912.

Bailey, F. M. 'Exploration on the Tsangpo or Upper Brahmaputra'. *Geographical Journal*, 44:4 (1914), 341–60. https://doi.org/10.2307/1778591.

———. *No Passport to Tibet*. London: Hart-Davis, 1957.

Bailly, Jean-Christophe, Jean-Marc Besse, and Gilles Palsky. *Le monde sur une feuille: les tableaux comparatifs de montagnes et de fleuves dans les atlas du XIXe siècle*. Lyon: Fage, 2014.

Bibliography

Bainbridge, Simon. *Mountaineering and British Romanticism: The Literary Cultures of Climbing, 1770–1836*. Oxford: Oxford University Press, 2020. https://doi.org/10.1093/oso/9780198857891.001.0001.

Baker, Ian. *The Heart of the World: A Journey to Tibet's Lost Paradise*. New York: Penguin, 2004.

Ball, John. *A Guide to the Western Alps*. London: Longman, 1863.

Bannister, Matthew. *Last Word, BBC Sounds*. 2023. http://www.bbc.co.uk/sounds/play/m001sdxf.

Barcham, Thomas. 'Commercial sponsorship in mountaineering: a case study of the 1975 British Everest Expedition'. *Sport in History*, 33:3 (2013), 333–52. https://doi.org/10.1080/17460263.2013.826435.

Bashyal, Pradeep. 'Demystifying Everest: What it's really like to climb the world's tallest mountain'. *The Diplomat*, (10 May 2017). https://web.archive.org/web/20171007220843/https://thediplomat.com/2017/05/demystifying-everest/.

Bashyal, Pradeep, and Annie Gowen. 'Mount Everest is so crowded this year, there is a risk of "traffic jams"'. *Washington Post*, (3 May 2017). https://web.archive.org/web/20230326112410/https://www.washingtonpost.com/world/mount-everest-is-so-crowded-this-year-there-are-traffic-jams/2017/05/03/7b4f4fe6-2f3c-11e7-a335-fa0ae1940305_story.html.

Basik, Sergei. *Encountering Toponymic Geopolitics: Place names as a political instrument in the post-Soviet states*. New York: Routledge, 2023. https://doi.org/10.4324/9781003293057.

Basnet, Shailee. *shaileebasnet.com*. 2023, accessed 20 Jan 2024, https://web.archive.org/web/20240123151851/https://www.shaileebasnet.com/.

Basso, Keith H. *Wisdom sits in places: Landscape and language among the Western Apache*. Albuquerque, NM: University of New Mexico Press, 1996.

Basu, Paul. 'Re-mobilising colonial collections in decolonial times exploring the latent possibilities of N.W. Thomas's West African collections.' In Felix Driver, Mark Nesbitt and Caroline Cornish (eds), *Mobile Museums*. Collections in circulation: UCL Press, 2021, pp. 44–70. https://doi.org/10.2307/j.ctv18kc0px.9.

Bayers, Peter L. 'Yosemite climbing films and the regeneration of white masculinity in the American West.' In Susan Bernardin (ed.), *Routledge Companion to Gender and the American West*. Routledge, 2022, pp. 70–82. https://doi.org/10.4324/9781351174282-7.

Beedie, Paul, and Simon Hudson. 'Emergence of mountain-based adventure tourism'. *Annals of Tourism Research*, 30:3 (2003), 625–43. https://doi.org/10.1016/S0160-7383(03)00043-4.

Bell, Charles Alfred. *Portrait of a Dalai Lama: A Biography of the Great Thirteenth*. Boston, MA: Wisdom,1987.

Berger, John. *Ways of Seeing*. London: Penguin, 1972.

Bergman, Megan Mayhew. 'She climbed Everest nine times and set a world record – so why doesn't she have sponsors?'. *Guardian*, (31 Oct 2019). https://web.archive.org/web/20230121143130/https://www.theguardian.com/world/2019/oct/31/mount-everest-lhakpa-sherpa-climbed-nine-times-world-record.

Bernbaum, Edwin. 'A note on the Tibetan and Nepali names of Mount Everest'. *American Alpine News*, 8:227 (1999), 25–6.

———. *Sacred Mountains of the World*. 2nd ed. Cambridge: Cambridge University Press, 2022. https://doi.org/10.1017/9781108873307.

———. *The Way to Shambhala: A Search for the Mythical Kingdom Beyond the Himalayas*. Garden City, NY: Anchor Books, 1980.

Bibliography

Bevir, Mark. 'The West turns eastward: Madame Blavatsky and the transformation of the occult tradition'. *Journal of the American Academy of Religion*, 62:3 (Fall 1994), 747–68. https://doi.org/10.1093/jaarel/LXII.3.747.

Bhabha, Homi K. 'The Other question'. *Screen*, 24:6 (1983), 18–36. https://doi.org/10.1093/screen/24.6.18.

Bhandari, Kalyan. 'Tourism in Nepal: Post-monarchy challenges'. *Journal of Tourism and Cultural Change*, 8:1–2 (2010), 69–83. https://doi.org/10.1080/14766825.2010.491917.

Bhutia, Kikee Doma. '"A world where many worlds fit": Understanding cosmopolitics through narratives of possessions and spirit invocation among the Lhopos (Bhutia) in Sikkim'. *Narrative Culture*, 8:2 (2021), 263–80. https://doi.org/10.13110/narrcult.8.2.0263.

Bird, Dúnlaith. 'Gender.' In Charles Forsdick, Zoë Kinsley and Kathryn Walchester (eds), *Keywords for Travel Writing Studies: A Critical Glossary*. London: Anthem Press, 2019.

Bishop, Peter. *The Myth of Shangri-La: Tibet, Travel Writing, and the Western Creation of Sacred Landscape*. Berkeley, CA: University of California Press, 1989.

Blum, Arlene. *Annapurna, A Woman's Place*. San Francisco, CA: Sierra Club Books, 1980.

Boukreev, Anatoli, and Linda Wylie. *Above the Clouds: The Diaries of a High-altitude Mountaineer*. New York: St. Martin's Press, 2001.

Bourguignon d'Anville, Jean-Baptiste. *Nouvel atlas de la Chine, de la Tartarie Chinoise, et du Thibet*. Amsterdam: Barthelemy Vlam, 1785.

Boyd, James. 'In search of Shambhala? Nicholas Roerich's 1934–5 Inner Mongolian Expedition'. *Inner Asia*, 14:2 (2012), 257–77. https://doi.org/10.1163/22105018-90000004.

Brancati, Vitaliano, and Telesio Interlandi. *Everest: mito in un atto*. Catania: Studio editoriale moderno Catania, 1931.

Breashears, David, and Greg MacGillivray (dir.). *Everest*. United States: Miramax, 1998.

Breashears, David, and Audrey Salkeld. *Last Climb: The Legendary Everest Expeditions of George Mallory*. Washington, DC: National Geographic Society, 1999.

Brown, Bill. 'Thing theory.' In *Things*. Chicago, IL: University of Chicago Press, 2004.

Brown, Mark. 'Is Kenton Cool really the first to Tweet from Everest?'. *Wired*, (18 May 2011). https://web.archive.org/web/20240126173811/https://www.wired.com/2011/05/kenton-cool-first-everest-tweet/.

Bruce, Charles Granville. *The Assault on Mount Everest, 1922*. London: Edward Arnold, 1923.

———. 'Darjeeling to the Rongbuk Glacier Base Camp'. *Geographical Journal*, 60:6 (1922), 385–94. https://doi.org/10.2307/1781075.

———. *Himalayan Wanderer*. London: A. Maclehose, 1934.

———. 'Mount Everest'. *Geographical Journal*, 57:1 (1921), 1–14. https://doi.org/10.2307/1781199.

Buffetrille, Katia. *Pèlerins, lamas et visionnaires: sources orales et écrites sur les pèlerinages tibétains*. Wien: Arbeitskreis für Tibetische und Buddhistische Studien, Universität Wein, 2000.

Buncombe, Andrew. 'The glass ceiling: the incredible story of a Nepali woman who climbed Mount Everest and inspired her nation'. *Independent* (3 December 2017). https://web.archive.org/web/20230121141132/https://www.independent.co.uk/arts-entertainment/films/news/nepal-woman-first-to-climb-everest-and-inspiration-pasang-lhamu-sherpa-the-glass-ceiling-a8089001.html.

Burrard, Sidney Gerald. 'Geographical names in uninhabited regions and the controversy over the Mount Everest map'. *Empire Survey Review*, 3:16 (1935), 66–71. https://doi.org/10.1179/sre.1935.3.16.66.

———. *Mount Everest and its Tibetan names. A review of Sir Sven Hedin's book*. Dehra Dun: Geodetic Branch Office, Survey of India, 1931.

———. 'Mount Everest: The story of a long controversy'. *Nature*, 71:1828 (1904), 42–6. https://doi.org/10.1038/071042a0.

———. 'The name of Mount Everest'. *Nature*, 127:3209 (1931), 686. https://doi.org/10.1038/127686a0.

Burrard, Sidney Gerald and H. H. Hayden. *A Sketch of the Geography and Geology of the Himalaya Mountains and Tibet*. Calcutta: Superintendent government printing, India, 1907.

Burrard, Sidney Gerald, H. H. Hayden, and A. M. Heron. *A Sketch of the Geography and Geology of the Himalaya Mountains and Tibet*. 2nd, rev. ed. Delhi: Manager of Publications, 1933.

Burroughs Wellcome and Co. *The Romance of Exploration and Emergency First-aid from Stanley to Byrd*. New York: Burroughs Wellcome & Co., 1934.

Calhoun, Craig J. 'Infrastructure.' In Craig J. Calhoun (ed.), *Dictionary of the social sciences*. New York: Oxford University Press, 2002.

Callaghan, Anna. 'The alpinist: Melissa Arnot Reid'. *Outside Online*, (11 Apr 2017), Updated 30 June 2021. https://web.archive.org/web/20240123154125/https://www.outsideonline.com/outdoor-adventure/climbing/alpinist-melissa-arnot-reid/.

———. 'Smashing guiding's glass ceiling'. *Outside Online*, (3 April 2018), Updated 12 May 2022. https://web.archive.org/web/20240123153918/https://www.outsideonline.com/outdoor-adventure/climbing/smashing-guidings-glass-ceiling/.

Callaghan, Anna, and Jenny Vrentas. 'For female climbers, dangers go beyond avalanches and storms'. *New York Times*, (31 May 2024). https://web.archive.org/web/20240531100402/https://www.nytimes.com/2024/05/31/sports/mountaineering-sexual-harassment-abuse-nims-purja.html.

Cams, Mario. *Companions in Geography: East-West Collaboration in the Mapping of Qing China (c.1685–1735)*. Leiden: Brill, 2017. https://doi.org/10.1163/9789004345362.

———. 'Not just a Jesuit atlas of China: Qing imperial cartography and its European connections'. *Imago Mundi*, 69:2 (2017), 188–201. https://doi.org/10.1080/03085694.2017.1312114.

Capra, Frank (dir.). *Lost Horizon*. United States: Columbia Pictures, 1937.

Carr, Herbert R. C. *The Irvine Diaries: Andrew Irvine and the Enigma of Everest, 1924*. Reading: Gastons-West Col Publications, 1979.

Carter, Thomas F. 'Of spectacular phantasmal desire: tourism and the Cuban state's complicity in the commodification of its citizens'. *Leisure Studies*, 27:3 (2008), 241–57. https://doi.org/10.1080/02614360802018806.

Chakraborty, Ritodhi, Mabel D. Gergan, Pasang Y. Sherpa, and Costanza Rampini. 'A plural climate studies framework for the Himalayas'. *Current Opinion in Environmental Sustainability*, 51 (2021), 42–54. https://doi.org/10.1016/j.cosust.2021.02.005.

Chakraborty, Ritodhi, and Pasang Yangjee Sherpa. 'From climate adaptation to climate justice: Critical reflections on the IPCC and Himalayan climate knowledges'. *Climatic Change*, 167:3–4 (2021), 49. https://doi.org/10.1007/s10584-021-03158-1.

Chamberlain, Tim. 'Books of change: A Western family's writings on China, 1855–1949'. *Journal of the Royal Asiatic Society China*, 75:1 (2013), 55–76.

———. 'Mountains and mysticism: Escapism and authenticity in the cinematic exploration of the Himalaya'. Unpublished essay.

Chambers, Donna, and Tijana Rakić. 'Critical considerations on gender and tourism: An introduction'. *Tourism Culture & Communication*, 18:1 (2018), 1–8. https://doi.org/10.3727/109830418X15180180585112.

Cheung, Esther. 'Korean climber lost on Himalayas' Broad Peak'. *Korea JoongAng Daily*, (20 July 2021). https://web.archive.org/web/20210801213340/https://koreajoongangdaily.

joins.com/2021/07/20/national/socialAffairs/Kim-hongbin-hiker-missing/202107 20191800344.html.

Childs, Geoff. 'Trans-Himalayan migrations as processes, not events: Towards a theoretical framework.' In Toni Huber and Stuart Blackburn (eds), *Origins and Migrations in the Extended Eastern Himalayas*. Leiden: Brill, 2012, pp. 11–32. https://doi.org/10.1163/9789004228 368_003.

Cockrell, Will. *Everest, Inc.: The Renegades and Rogues Who Built an Industry at the Top of the World*. New York: Gallery Books, 2024.

Colebrook, Henry Thomas. 'On the height of the Himalaya mountains'. *Asiatick Researches*, 12 (1818), 253–93. https://archive.org/embed/dli.pahar.0053.

Coleman, Kevin P, Daniel James, and Jayeeta Sharma. 'Photography and work'. *Radical History Review*,132 (2018), 1–22. https://doi.org/10.1215/01636545-6942345.

Connell, R.W. 'Growing up masculine: Rethinking the significance of adolescence in the making of masculinities'. *Irish Journal of Sociology*, 14:2 (2005), 11–28. https://doi.org/10.1177/079160350501400202.

Cooper, Roland E. '"Native collectors" of primulas'. *Quarterly of the American Primrose Society*, 13:3 (1955), 98–102.

Corbett, Geoffrey. 'The word Himalaya'. *Himalayan Journal*, 1 (1929), 84–6. https://archive.org/details/dli.pahar.2410.

Craig, Sienna. 'A sacred geography: sonnets of the Himalaya and Tibet'. *Anthropology and Humanism*, 35:2 (2010), 240–7. https://doi.org/10.1111/j.1548-1409.2010.01071.x.

Czerwińska, Anna, and Wanda Rutkiewicz. *Zdobycie Gasherbrumów [Ascending Gasherbrums]*. Warszawa: Sport i turystyka, 1979.

Dahal, Shankar. 'Mt Everest in business class'. *Nepali Times*, (2022). https://web.archive.org/web/20240124191940/https://nepalitimes.com/banner/mt-everest-in-business-class.

Das, Sarat Chandra. *Narrative of a Journey to Lhasa in 1881–82*. Calcutta: Bengal Secretariat Press, 1885. http://hdl.loc.gov/loc.rbc/General.23029v2.1.

Davis, Wade. *Into the Silence: the Great War, Mallory, and the Conquest of Everest*. New York: Knopf, 2011.

Dawes, Heather, and Faye Rhiannon Latham. 'Introducing Faye Latham and her debut poetry collection, British Mountaineers'. *Little Peak Press*, (2022). https://web.archive.org/web/20220131124725/https://www.littlepeak.co.uk/news/news10/.

De la Cadena, Marisol, and Mario Blaser. *A World of Many Worlds*. Durham, NC: Duke University Press, 2018. https://doi.org/10.2307/j.ctv125jpzq.

Debarbieux, Bernard, and Gilles Rudaz. *The Mountain: A Political History from the Enlightenment to the Present*. Translated by Jane Marie Todd. Chicago, IL: University of Chicago Press, 2015.

Dec-Pustelnik, Sylwia. 'Kobieta na dachu świata, czyli kilka słów o historii oraz wizerunku medialnym Wandy Rutkiewicz [A woman on the world's roof, or a few words about the history and media image of Wanda Rutkiewicz]'. *Dziennikarstwo i Media*, 10 (2018), 25–36. https://doi.org/10.19195/2082-8322.10.2.

Dekleva, Janez, and Franci Savenc. 'Zahodni greben je najdaljša smer na najvišjo goro sveta [The West Ridge is the longest route on the world's highest mountain]'. *Delo – Sobotna priloga*, (12 May 1979), 26.

Della Dora, Veronica. *Mountain*. London: Reaktion, 2016.

Dent, C. T., W. M. Conway, and J. H. Wicks. 'Report of the Special Committee on Equipment for Mountaineers'. *Alpine Journal*, 15 supplement (1890–1891), 1–32. https://

Bibliography

www.alpinejournal.org.uk/Contents/Contents_1893_files/AJ%201893%20Vol%20 16%20Equipment%20Report.pdf

Derrick, Florence. 'How women-only treks are claiming space on Everest'. *Condé Nast Traveler*, (20 July 2021). https://web.archive.org/web/20230513211442/https://www. cntraveler.com/story/how-women-only-treks-are-claiming-space-on-everest.

Deslandes, Paul R. *The Culture of Male Beauty in Britain: From the First Photographs to David Beckham.* Chicago, IL: University of Chicago Press, 2021.

Diemberger, Hildegard. 'When lha lu spirits suffer and sometimes fight back: Tibetan cosmopolitics at a time of environmental threats and climate change.' In Riamsara Kuyakanon, Hildegard Diemberger and David Sneath (eds), *Cosmopolitical Ecologies Across Asia: Places and Practices of Power in Changing Environments.* London: Routledge, 2021, pp. 19–41. https://doi. org/10.4324/9781003036272-1.

Dodds, Klaus, and Sverker Sörlin. *Ice Humanities: Living, Working, and Thinking in a Melting World.* Manchester: Manchester University Press, 2022. https://doi.org/10.7765/978152 6157782.

Doney, Lewis. *The Zangs gling ma: The First Padmasambhava Biography: Two Exemplars of the Earliest Attested Recension.* Andiast: IITBS GmbH, International Institute for Tibetan and Buddhist Studies, 2014.

Donner, Jonathan. *After Access: Inclusion, Development, and a More Mobile Internet.* Cambridge, MA: MIT Press, 2015. https://doi.org/10.7551/mitpress/9740.001.0001.

Doran, Adele, Peter Schofield, and Tiffany Low. 'Women's mountaineering: accessing participation benefits through constraint negotiation strategies'. *Leisure Studies*, 39:5 (2020), 721–35. https://doi.org/10.1080/02614367.2020.1763439.

Douglas, Ed. *Himalaya: A Human History.* London: Vintage, 2021.

———. 'Remembering Audrey Salkeld'. *Climbing*, (4 Nov 2023). https://www.climbing. com/people/remembering-audrey-salkeld/.

———. *Tenzing: Hero of Everest, a Biography of Tenzing Norgay.* Washington, DC: National Geographic, 2003.

Drew, Georgina, and Mabel Denzin Gergan. 'Imagining Himalayan glacial futures: Knowledge rifts, disciplinary debates and icy vitalities at the Third Pole'. *Social Anthropology/ Anthropologie sociale*, 32:1 (2024), 80–95. https://doi.org/10.3167/saas.2024.320107.

Driver, Felix. 'Face to face with Nain Singh: the Schlagintweit collections and their uses.' In Arthur MacGregor (ed.), *Naturalists in the Field: Collecting, Recording and Preserving the Natural World from the Fifteenth to the Twenty-First Century.* Leiden: Brill, 2018, pp. 441–69. https:// doi.org/10.1163/9789004323841_016.

———. *Geography Militant: Cultures of Exploration and Empire.* Oxford: Blackwell, 2001.

———. 'Hidden histories made visible? Reflections on a geographical exhibition'. *Transactions of the Institute of British Geographers*, 38:3 (2013), 420–35. https://doi.org/10.1111/j.14 75-5661.2012.00529.x.

———. 'Intermediaries and the archive of exploration'. In Shino Konishi, Maria Nugent and Tiffany Shellam (eds), *Indigenous Intermediaries: New Perspectives on Exploration Archives.* Canberra: ANU Press, 2015. https://doi.org/10.22459/II.09.2015.02.

Driver, Felix, Lowri Jones, and Royal Geographical Society. *Hidden Histories of Exploration: Researching the RGS-IBG Collections.* London Royal Holloway, 2009. https://web.archive. org/web/20240125215741/https://issuu.com/rgs_ibg/docs/hidden_histories_of_ exploration.

Driver, Felix, Mark Nesbitt, and Caroline Cornish, eds. *Mobile Museums: Collections in Circulation.* London: UCL Press, 2021. https://doi.org/10.2307/j.ctv18kc0px.

Bibliography

Driver, Felix, Eugene Rae, and Sarah L. Evans. *A History of the Society's Collections Catalogues.* *Higher Education Resources*, Royal Geographical Society with IBG 2023, accessed 31 Jan 2024, https://web.archive.org/web/20240131212330/https://www.rgs.org/research/higher-education-resources/a-history-of-the-societys-collections-catalogues.

Du Halde, J.-B., and Emanuel Bowen. *A Description of the Empire of China and Chinese-Tartary: Together with the Kingdoms of Korea, and Tibet: Containing the Geography and History (Natural as well as Civil) of those Countries: In Two Volumes.* London: Edward Cave, 1738.

Dyson, Laurel Evelyn. 'Framing the indigenous mobile revolution.' In Laurel Evelyn Dyson, Stephen Grant and Max Hendriks (eds), *Indigenous People and Mobile Technologies*. New York: Routledge, 2016, pp. 1–21. https://doi.org/10.4324/9781315759364.

Eades, Gwilym Lucas. *The Geography of Names: Indigenous to Post-Foundational.* London: Routledge, 2017. https://doi.org/10.4324/9781315715636.

Edney, Matthew H. *Mapping an Empire: The Geographical Construction of British India, 1765–1843.* Chicago, IL: University of Chicago Press, 1997.

Ehrhard, Franz-Karl. 'The role of "Treasure Discoverers" and their writings in the search for Himalayan sacred lands'. *Tibet Journal*, 19:3 (1994), 3–20. http://www.jstor.org/stable/43300512.

Ekvall, Robert B. *Fields on the Hoof: Nexus of Tibetan Nomadic Pastoralism.* New York: Holt, Rinehart and Winston, 1968.

Elliott, Alan. 'Rhomoo Lepcha'. *Botanics Stories RBGE Personal & Project Stories*, Royal Botanic Garden Edinburgh 2013, accessed 9 Sept 2023, https://web.archive.org/web/2022072719 1559/https://stories.rbge.org.uk/archives/4256.

Ellis, Sam. '"No Name Intelligible to Civilised Men": Hidden Voices in Mount Everest's Nomenclature'. *Charleston Hub*, 2022, accessed 9 August 2023, https://web.archive.org/web/20240123174437/https://www.charleston-hub.com/2022/09/no-name-intelligible-to-civilised-men-hidden-voices-in-mount-everests-nomenclature/.

Ellis-Pedersen, Hannah. 'Climate change to blame for up to 17 deaths on Mount Everest, experts say'. *Guardian*, (30 May 2023). https://web.archive.org/web/20240110200157/https://www.theguardian.com/world/2023/may/30/climate-change-to-blame-for-up-to-17-deaths-on-mount-everest-experts-say.

Engelhardt, Isrun. *Tibet in 1938–1939: Photographs from the Ernst Schäfer Expedition to Tibet.* Chicago, IL: Serindia, 2007.

Escobar, Arturo. *Designs for the Pluriverse: Radical Interdependence, Autonomy, and the Making of Worlds.* Durham, NC: Duke University Press, 2018.

Expeditions, High Adventure. 'List of women who have climbed Mount Everest'. (4 February 2023). *Haexpeditions.com.* https://web.archive.org/web/20240122225520/https://haexpeditions.com/advice/list-of-women-who-have-climbed-mount-everest/.

Farrar, J. P. 'The Everest Expeditions. Conclusions'. *Alpine Journal*, 34 (1922), 452–6. https://alpinejournal.org.uk/Contents/Contents_1922_files/AJ%201922%20Vol%2034%20452-456%20Farrar%20Everest.pdf

Faull, Janette. *Climbing Mount Everest: Expeditionary Film, Geographical Science and Media Culture, 1922–1953.* PhD thesis, Royal Holloway, University of London, 2019. https://pure.royalholloway.ac.uk/en/publications/climbing-mount-everest-expeditionary-film-geographical-science-an (uk.bl.ethos.855254).

Fibicher, Arthur. 'Dufour, Pointe.' In *Dictionnaire historique de la Suisse (DHS)*. 2005. https://hls-dhs-dss.ch/fr/articles/008784/2005-11-07/.

Finch, George Ingle. *Climbing Mount Everest.* 3rd ed. London: G. Philip & Son, 1933. https://archive.org/details/climbingeverest1932inglefinch.

Bibliography

Finch, George I. 'The Second High Climb'. *Geographical Journal*, 60:6 (1922), 413–22. https://doi.org/10.2307/1781078.

Fitzgerald, William. 'A school for explorers'. *Pearson's*, 9:3 (1903), 243–51.

Fleetwood, Lachlan. *Science on the Roof of the World: Empire and the Remaking of the Himalaya*. Cambridge: Cambridge University Press, 2022. https://doi.org/10.1017/978100912 8117.

Fleming, Anna. 'Herstory 6: Lhakpa Sherpa's long dream of Everest'. *UK Climbing*, (31 May 2023). https://web.archive.org/web/20231002160212/https://www.ukclimbing.com/articles/features/herstory_6_lhakpa_sherpas_long_dream_of_everest-15196.

Fokkema, Douwe Wessel. *Perfect Worlds: Utopian Fiction in China and the West*. Amsterdam: Amsterdam University Press, 2011.

Forman, Harrison. *Through Forbidden Tibet. An Adventure into the Unknown*. New York; Toronto Longmans, 1935.

Freshfield, Douglas W. 'The conquest of Mount Everest'. *Geographical Journal*, 63:3 (1924), 229–37. https://doi.org/10.2307/1780935.

———. 'Further notes on "Mont Everest"'. *Proceedings of the Royal Geographical Society and Monthly Record of Geography*, 8:3 (1886), 176–88. https://doi.org/10.2307/1800965.

———. 'The highest Mountain in the world'. *Geographical Journal*, 21:3 (1903), 294–8. https://doi.org/10.2307/1775805.

———. 'Mount Everest v. Chomolungma'. *Alpine Journal* 34 (1922), 301–2. https://alpinejournal.org.uk/Contents/Contents_1922_files/AJ%201922%20Vol%2034%20 300-303%20Freshfield%20Everest.pdf

———. 'Mount Everest: the story of a controversy'. *Nature*, 71:1830 (1904/11/01 1904), 82. https://doi.org/10.1038/071082a0.

———. 'The Sikhim Himalaya'. *Scottish Geographical Magazine*, 21:4 (1905/04/01 1905), 173–82. https://doi.org/10.1080/14702540508554648.

Fricke, Thomas. 'Introduction: Human ecology in the Himalaya'. *Human Ecology*, 17:2 (1989), 131–45. https://doi.org/10.1007/BF00889710.

Frischmann, Brett M. *Infrastructure: The Social Value of Shared Resources*. New York: Oxford University Press, 2012.

Frohlick, Susan. 'The hyper-masculine landscape of high-altitude mountaineering'. *Michigan Feminist Studies*, 14 (1999–2000), 81–104. http://hdl.handle.net/2027/spo.ark5583.0014.004.

———. '"That playfulness of white masculinity": Mediating masculinities and adventure at mountain film festivals'. *Tourist studies*, 5:2 (2005), 175–93. https://doi.org/10.1177/1468797605066926.

———. '"Wanting the children and wanting K2": The incommensurability of motherhood and mountaineering in Britain and North America in the late twentieth century'. *Gender, Place & Culture*, 13:5 (2006), 477–90. https://doi.org/10.1080/0966369060085 8820.

———. '"Who is Lhakpa Sherpa?" circulating subjectivities within the global/local terrain of Himalayan mountaineering'. *Social & Cultural Geography*, 5:2 (2004), 195–212. https://doi.org/10.1080/14649360410001690213.

Frydenlund, Shae A. 'Situationally Sherpa: race, ethnicity, and the labour geography of the Everest industry'. *Journal of Cultural Geography*, 36:1 (2019), 1–22. https://doi.org/10.108 0/08873631.2018.1516601.

Gagné, Karine. *Caring for Glaciers: Land, Animals, and Humanity in the Himalayas*. Seattle, WA: University of Washington Press, 2019.

Bibliography

Gamble, Ruth. 'The mountain's many faces: How geologists mistook Chomolungma for Everest.' In Alison Bashford, Adam Bobbette and Emily M Kern (eds), *New Earth Histories: Geo-Cosmologies and the Making of the Modern World*. Chicago, IL: University of Chicago Press, 2023, pp. 53–69. https://doi.org/10.7208/chicago/9780226828596-007.

———. *Reincarnation in Tibetan Buddhism: The Third Karmapa and the Invention of a Tradition*. Oxford: Oxford University Press, 2018. https://doi.org/10.1093/oso/9780190690779.001.0001.

———. 'Surviving Pemakö's pluriverse: Kunga Tsomo, the goddess, and the LAC'. *Critical Asian Studies*, 54:3 (2022), 398–421. https://doi.org/10.1080/14672715.2022.2069140.

Garrett, Frances Mary, Elizabeth McDougal, and Geoffrey Samuel. *Hidden Lands in Himalayan Myth and History: Transformations of sbas yul through Time*. Leiden: Brill, 2021. https://doi.org/10.1163/9789004437685.

Garrington, Abbie. 'What does a modernist mountain mean? Auden and Isherwood's *The Ascent of F6*'. *Critical Quarterly*, 55:2 (2013), 26–49. https://doi.org/10.1111/criq.12043.

Gates, Barbara T. *In Nature's Name: An Anthology of Women's Writing and Illustration, 1780–1930*. Chicago, IL: University of Chicago Press, 2002.

Gauchon, Christophe. 'Nommer les biens du Patrimoine mondial: processus de patrimonialisation et réinvention toponymique'. *EchoGéo*, 53 (2020). https://doi.org/10.4000/echogeo.19973.

Gellner, David. 'Caste, ethnicity and inequality in Nepal'. *Economic and Political Weekly*, 42:20 (2007), 1823–8.

Gesing, Lars. 'Eric Larsen: The long way to Tweeting atop Mount Everest'. *CU Independent*, (14 February 2014). https://web.archive.org/web/20240126180636/https://www.cuindependent.com/2014/02/14/eric-larsen-talk/.

Ghosh, Kaushik. 'A market for aboriginality: Primitivism and race classification in the indentured labour market of Colonial India'. *Subaltern Studies*, 10 (1999), 8–48.

Gianotti, Carla. 'Female Buddhist adepts in the Tibetan tradition. The twenty-four jo mo, disciples of Pha dam pa sangs rgyas'. *Journal of Dharma Studies*, 2:1 (2019), 15–29. https://doi.org/10.1007/s42240-019-00038-x.

Gibbs, H. R. K. *The Gurkha Soldier*. Calcutta: Thacker, Spink & Co, 1944.

Gilchrist, Paul. 'Embodied causes: Climbing, charity, and 'celanthropy''. *International Journal of the History of Sport*, 37:9 (2020), 709–26. https://doi.org/10.1080/09523367.2020.1783250.

———. 'Heroic leadership, mountain adventure and Englishness: John Hunt and Christ Bonington compared.' In Chris Hart (ed.), *Heroines and Heroes: Symbolism, Embodiment, Narratives & Identity*. Kingswinford, West Midlands, UK: Midrash Publications, 2008, pp. 247–66.

———. '"Motherhood, ambition and risk": mediating the sporting hero/ine in Conservative Britain'. *Media, Culture & Society*, 29:3 (2007), 395–414. https://doi.org/10.1177/0163443707076182.

———. 'Mountains, Manliness and Post-war Recovery: C.E. Montague's "Action"'. *Sport in History*, 33:3 (2013), 282–302. https://doi.org/10.1080/17460263.2013.826436.

Gillman, Peter. 'Audrey Salkeld obituary'. *Guardian*, (1 Nov 2023). https://web.archive.org/web/20231103130722/https://www.theguardian.com/world/2023/nov/01/audrey-salkeld-obituary.

Gillman, Peter, and Leni Gillman. *The Wildest Dream: Mallory, His Life and Conflicting Passions*. London: Headline, 2001.

Giraut, Frédéric, and Myriam Houssay-Holzschuch. *The Politics of Place Naming: Naming the World*. London; Hoboken: ISTE; Wiley, 2022. https://doi.org/10.1002/9781394188307.

Bibliography

Graaff-Hunter, James de. 'Heights and names of Mount Everest and other peaks'. *Occasional Notes of the Royal Astronomical Society, London*, 15:3 (1953), 37–53.

Grebowicz, Margret. *Mountains and Desire: Climbing vs. the End of the World*. London: Repeater Books, 2021.

Green, Stewart M. 'Sherpa and American teams climb first ascents in Rolwaling Himal'. *Alpinist* (9 November 2015). https://web.archive.org/web/20151116182848/https://www.alpinist.com/doc/web15y/newswire-sherpa-americans-climb-first-ascents-rolwaling-himal.

Greene, Graham. '"Lost Horizon" at the Tivoli'. *Spectator*, 158:5679 (30 April 1937), 805.

Greene, Maggie. 'Performing socialism at altitude'. *Performance Research*, 24:2 (2019), 63–72. https://doi.org/10.1080/13528165.2019.1624030.

Griffin, Gabriele. *A Dictionary of Gender Studies*. Oxford: Oxford University Press, 2017.

Griffiths, Alison. 'Cinema in extremis: Mount Everest and the poetics of monumentality'. *Film History*, 32:1 (2020), 40–71. https://doi.org/10.2979/filmhistory.32.1.02.

Grošelj, Viki. *Velikani Himalaje [Giants of the Himalayas]*. Ljubljana: Planinska zveza Slovenije, 2013.

Gross, Rachel S. 'Logos on Everest: Commercial sponsorship of American expeditions, 1950–2000'. *Enterprise & Society*, 22:4 (2021), 1067–102. https://doi.org/10.1017/eso.2020.31.

Grzeszczuk-Gałązka, Anna (dir.). *100 pytań do ... Wanda Rutkiewicz [100 questions to ... Wanda Rutkiewicz]*. Poland: TVP2, 1989.

Guibaut, André. *Tibetan Venture: In the Country of the Ngolo-Setas: Second Guibaut-Liotard Expedition*. London: Readers Union, 1949.

Gulatee, B. L. 'Mount Everest – Its name and height'. *Himalayan Journal*, 17 (1952), 131–42. https://archive.org/details/dli.pahar.2971.

Gupta, Poorvi. 'Meet legendary mountaineer Bachendri Pal – Scaling new heights leading an expedition of senior women'. *Herstory* (17 March 2022). https://web.archive.org/web/20230320093403/https://yourstory.com/herstory/2022/03/legendary-mountaineer-bachendri-pal-mount-everest-new-expedition-fitat50.

Haberman, David L. *Understanding Climate Change through Religious Lifeworlds*. Bloomington, IN: Indiana University Press, 2021. https://doi.org/10.2307/j.ctv21hrh8r.

Hall, Jenny, Emma Boocock, and Zoë Avner, eds. *Gender, Politics and Change in Mountaineering: Moving Mountains*. Cham: Palgrave Macmillan, 2023. https://doi.org/10.1007/978-3-031-29945-2.

Hall, Jenny, and Katrina Myrvang Brown. 'Creating feelings of inclusion in adventure tourism: Lessons from the gendered sensory and affective politics of professional mountaineering'. *Annals of Tourism Research*, 97 (2022), 103505. https://doi.org/10.1016/j.annals.2022.103505.

Hall, Jenny, and Martin Hall. 'Politics of representation in mountaineering: Conclusion.' In Martin Hall and Jenny Hall (eds), *The Mountain and the Politics of Representation*. Liverpool: Liverpool University Press, 2023, pp. 289–96. https://doi.org/10.2307/jj.1866848.20.

Hall, Jenny, and Maggie Miller. 'Troubling the silences of adventure legacies: Junko Tabei and the intersectional politics of mountaineering.' In Jenny Hall, Emma Boocock and Zoë Avner (eds), *Gender, Politics and Change in Mountaineering*. Cham: Palgrave Macmillan, 2023, pp. 31–50. https://doi.org/10.1007/978-3-031-29945-2.

Hall, Martin, and Jenny Hall, eds. *The Mountain and the Politics of Representation*. Liverpool: Liverpool University Press, 2023. https://doi.org/10.2307/jj.1866848.

Hanbury-Tracy, John. *Black River of Tibet*. London: F. Muller, 1938.

Hansen, Peter H. 'Commercialisation and Mount Everest in the twentieth century.' In Marco Armiero, Roberta Biasillo and Stefano Morosini (eds), *Rethinking Geographical Explorations in Extreme Environments: From the Arctic to the Mountaintops*. London: Routledge, 2023, pp. 144–56. https://doi.org/10.4324/9781003095965-10.

———. 'Confetti of empire: The conquest of Everest in Nepal, India, Britain, and New Zealand'. *Comparative Studies in Society and History*, 42:2 (2000), 307–32. https://doi.org/10.1017/S0010417500002486.

———. 'Coronation Everest: Empire and Commonwealth in the "Second Elizabethan Age".' In Stuart Ward (ed.), *British Culture and the End of Empire*. Manchester: Manchester University Press 2001, pp. 57–72. https://doi.org/10.7765/9781526119629.00009.

———. 'The dancing lamas of Everest: Cinema, Orientalism, and Anglo-Tibetan relations in the 1920s'. *American Historical Review*, 101:3 (1996), 712–47. https://doi.org/10.2307/2169420.

———. 'Hargreaves, Alison Jane (1962–1995), revised, with Tom Ballard (1988–2019).' In David Cannadine (ed.), *Oxford Dictionary of National Biography*. Online ed. Oxford: Oxford University Press, 2023. https://doi.org/10.1093/ref:odnb/58208.

———. 'Partners: Guides and Sherpas in the Alps and Himalayas, 1850s–1950s.' In Jás Elsner and Joan-Pau Rubies (eds), *Voyages and Visions: Towards a Cultural History of Travel*. London: Reaktion,1999, pp. 210–31.

———. 'Scott, Douglas Keith (Doug) (1941–2020).' In David Cannadine (ed.), *Oxford Dictionary of National Biography*. Online ed. Oxford: Oxford University Press, 2004. https://doi.org/10.1093/odnb/9780198614128.013.90000381698.

———. *The Summits of Modern Man: Mountaineering After the Enlightenment*. Cambridge, MA: Harvard University Press, 2013.

———. 'Tibetan horizon – Tibet and the cinema in the early twentieth century.' In Thierry Dodin and Heinz Rather (eds), *Imagining Tibet: Perceptions, Projections, and Fantasies*. Boston, MA: Wisdom, 2001, pp. 91–110.

———. 'Unsworth, Walter (Walt) (1928–2017).' In David Cannadine (ed.), *Oxford Dictionary of National Biography*. Online ed. Oxford: Oxford University Press, 2021. https://doi.org/10.1093/odnb/9780198614128.013.90000380378.

———. 'Vertical Boundaries, National Identities: Victorian Mountaineering on the Frontiers of Europe and the Empire, 1868–1914'. *Journal of Imperial and Commonwealth History*, 24:1 (Jan 1996), 48–71. https://doi.org/10.1080/03086539608582968.

———. 'Wildest dreams of Everest and modern mountaineering.' *La montagne: territoire du moderne? Les sports modernes n°1*. Neuchâtel: Éditions Alphil-Presses universitaires suisses, 2023, pp. 61–9. https://doi.org/10.33055/SPORTSMODERNES.2023.001.01.61. https://libreo.ch/de/view/610115/3768214/Les_sports_modernes_61.pdf.

———. 'Y is for Yak.' In Antoinette Burton and Renisa Mawani (eds), *Animalia: An Anti-Imperial Bestiary for Our Times*. Durham, NC: Duke University Press, 2020, pp. 213–18. https://doi.org/10.2307/j.ctv17db46q.30.

Hargreaves, Jennifer. *Heroines of Sport: The Politics of Difference and Identity*. Hoboken: Taylor and Francis, 2013.

Harris, Clare. 'Creating a space for performing Tibetan identities: A curatorial commentary'. *Trans-Asia Photography Review*, 9:2 (2019). https://doi.org/10.1215/215820251_9-2-202.

Harris, Clare, and Shakya Tsering. *Seeing Lhasa: British Depictions of the Tibetan Capital, 1936–1947*. Chicago, IL: Serindia, 2003.

Bibliography

Harris, Tina. 'Yak tails, Santa Claus, and transnational trade in the Himalayas'. *Tibet Journal*, 39:1 (2014), 145–55. http://www.jstor.org/stable/43741560.

Havenith, George. 'Benchmarking functionality of historical cold weather clothing: Robert F Scott, Roald Amundsen, George Mallory'. *Journal of Fiber Bioengineering & Informatics*, 3:3 (2010), 121–9. https://doi.org/10.3993/jfbi12201001.

Hawley, Elizabeth. 'Everest first ascent by a Nepalese woman and tragedy'. *American Alpine Journal*, 36 (1994), 211–13. https://web.archive.org/web/20240415155756/http://publications.americanalpineclub.org/articles/12199421100/Asia-Nepal-Everest-First-Ascent-by-a-Nepalese-Woman-and-Tragedy.

———. 'Seasonal stories for the Nepalese Himalaya 1985–2014.' *Himalaya Database*. 2014. https://web.archive.org/web/20230306221059/https://www.himalayandatabase.com/downloads/EAHSeasonalStories.pdf.

Hedin, Sven Anders. *Mount Everest och andra Asiatiska problem*. Stockholm: A.Bonner, 1922.

———. *Southern Tibet; Discoveries in former times compared with my own researches in 1906–1908*. Vol. 3, Stockholm: Lithographic Institute of the General staff of the Swedish Army, 1917.

Heflich, Waldemar (dir.). *Ślady na śniegu [Footprints in the snow]*. Poland: Interpress Film, 1990.

Helander, Kaisa Rautio. 'Toponymic silence and Sámi place names during the growth of the Norwegian nation state.' In Lawrence D. Berg and Jani Vuolteenaho (eds), *Critical Toponymies: The Contested Politics of Place Naming*. London: Routledge, 2009, pp. 267–80. https://doi.org/10.4324/9781315258843-20.

Hemmleb, Jochen, Larry A. Johnson, Eric R. Simonson, and William E. Nothdurft. *Ghosts of Everest: The Authorized Story of the Search for Mallory & Irvine of the Expedition Team that Found Mallory on Everest*. London: Pan, 2000.

Herrligkoffer, Karl M. 'The German-French Mount Everest expedition, 1978'. *Himalayan Journal*, 36 (1980).

Herzog, Maurice. *Annapurna*. New York: Dutton, 1952.

Hilton, James. *Lost Horizon*. New York: Pocket Books, 1939.

Hodgson, B. H. *Essay the First; On the Kocch, Bódo and Dhimál Tribes, in Three Parts*. Calcutta: J. Thomas, 1847.

———. *Miscellaneous Essays Relating to Indian Subjects*. London: Trübner & Co., 1880.

Hodgson, Brian Houghton. 'Native name of Mount Everest'. *Journal of the Asiatic Society of Bengal*, 25:5 (1856), 467–70.

Hollis, Dawn, and Jason König. *Mountain Dialogues from Antiquity to Modernity*. Bloomsbury Academic, 2021. http://doi.org/10.5040/9781350162853

Hollis, Dawn L. *Mountains before Mountaineering: The Call of the Peaks before the Modern Age* Cheltenham, UK: The History Press, 2024.

Holzel, Tom, and Audrey Salkeld. *First on Everest: The Mystery of Mallory and Irvine*. New York: H. Holt, 1986.

———. *The Mystery of Mallory and Irvine*. Rev. ed. London: Pimlico, 1999. https://archive.org/details/mysteryofmallory0000holz.

Hooker, Joseph Dalton. *Himalayan Journals, or, Notes of a Naturalist in Bengal, the Sikkim and Nepal Himalayas, the Khasia Mountains, &c*. London: John Murray, 1854.

Horvat, Tina. 'Ni jih poklical Tito, ampak sam Everest [It wasn't Tito calling, but Everest itself]'. *Slovenske novice*, (26 February 2019), 8.

Hou, Arnold. 'China's first woman on top of the world passes away'. *Womenofchina.cn*, (2 April 2014). https://web.archive.org/web/20160711083845/http://www.womenofchina.cn/womenofchina/html1/people/others/17/1863-1.htm.

Bibliography

Howard-Bury, C. K. 'The Mount Everest Expedition'. *Geographical Journal*, 59:2 (1922), 81–99. https://doi.org/10.2307/1781386.

Huber, Toni. *Sacred Spaces and Powerful Places in Tibetan Culture: A Collection of Essays*. Dharamsala: Library of Tibetan Works and Archives, 1999.

Huber, Toni, and Stuart Blackburn. *Origins and Migrations in the Extended Eastern Himalayas*. Leiden: Brill, 2012. https://doi.org/10.1163/9789004228368.

Huey, Raymond B, Richard Salisbury, Jane-Ling Wang, and Meng Mao. 'Effects of age and gender on success and death of mountaineers on Mount Everest'. *Biology Letters*, 3:5 (2007), 498–500. https://doi.org/10.1098/rsbl.2007.0317.

Humboldt, Alexander von. *Asie centrale. Recherches sur les chaines des montagnes et la climatologie comparée*. Paris: Gide, 1843.

———. *Sur l'élévation des montagnes de l'Inde*. Paris: Feugueray, 1814.

Hume, Abraham. *Philosophy of Geographical Names*. Liverpool: Benjamin Smith, 1851.

Hunt, John. 'Book Review: *The Irvine Diaries. Andrew Irvine and the Enigma of Everest*'. *Geographical Journal*, 146:2 (1980), 301–3. https://doi.org/10.2307/632896.

Hunt, John Hunt. *The Ascent of Everest*. London: Hodder & Stoughton, 1953.

Hunt, Rachel. 'Historical geography, climbing and mountaineering: route setting for an inclusive future'. *Geography Compass*, 13:4 (2019), e12423. https://doi.org/10.1111/gec3.12423.

Information Centre of Poland in India. 'Polish woman atop Mt. Everest'. *Polish Facts on File issued by the Information Centre of Poland in India*, 390 (1978), 10–1. http://nyka.home.pl/bibl_his/pl_ascii/12.htm.

Inkpen, Dani. *Capturing Glaciers: A History of Repeat Photography and Global Warming*. Seattle, WA: University of Washington Press, 2024.

———. 'Ever higher: The mountain cryosphere.' In Klaus Dodds and Sverker Sörlin (eds), *Ice Humanities*. Manchester: Manchester University Press, 2022, pp. 72–88. https://doi.org/10.7765/9781526157782.00011.

Isserman, Maurice, and Stewart Weaver. *Fallen Giants: A History of Himalayan Mountaineering from the Age of Empire to the Age of Extremes*. New Haven, CT: Yale University Press, 2008.

Ives, Katie. 'An oral history of the first U.S. ascent of Annapurna (Oh yeah, and it happened to be the first female ascent, too)'. *Outside Magazine*, (May 2017). https://web.archive.org/web/20220524224820/https://www.outsideonline.com/outdoor-adventure/climbing/annapurna-women/.

———. 'Sharp end: between the lines'. *Alpinist*, 51 (Autumn 2015), 11–12. https://web.archive.org/web/20240217210337/https://alpinist.com/departments/sharp-end/.

Jansen, Berthe. 'Serendipity among books: The van Manen collection.' In Alexander Reeuwijk (ed.), *Voyage of Discovery: Exploring the Collections of the Asian Library of Leiden University*. Leiden: Leiden University Press, 2017, pp. 126–31.

Johnson, Ryan. 'European cloth and "tropical" skin: Clothing material and British ideas of health and hygiene in tropical climates'. *Bulletin of the History of Medicine*, 83:3 (2009), 530–60. https://doi.org/10.1353/bhm.0.0252.

Jones, Lowri M. *Local Knowledge and Indigenous Agency in the History of Exploration: Studies from the RGS-IBG Collections*. PhD thesis, Royal Holloway, University of London, 2010 (uk.bl.ethos.531297).

Jones, Torquil (dir.). *14 Peaks: Nothing is Impossible*. United States: Netflix, 2021.

Kaczmarek, Agnieszka. 'Wanda Rutkiewicz and Ewa Matuszewska: Deliberations on the auto/biographical Na jednej linie [On One Rope].' In Martin Hall and Jenny Hall (eds),

The Mountain and the Politics of Representation. Liverpool: Liverpool University Press, 2023, pp.169–88.

Kambic, Matt. 'The Sherpa and the Beekeeper – Summit on Everest'. 2022. Unpublished Play.

Kamińska, Anna. *Wanda: opowieść o sile życia i śmierci: historia Wandy Rutkiewicz [Wanda: A story about the power of life and death]*. Kraków: Wydawnictwo Literackie Kraków, 2017.

Karki, Darshan, and Miriam Wenner. 'What is not in a name? Toponymic ambivalence, identity, and symbolic resistance in the Nepali flatlands'. *EchoGéo*, 53 (2020). http://journals.openedition.org/echogeo/19987.

Kaulback, Ronald. *Salween*. London: Hodder and Stoughton, 1938.

———. *Tibetan trek*. London: Hodder and Stoughton, 1934.

Keay, John. *The Great Arc: The Dramatic Tale of How India was Mapped and Everest was Named*. New York: HarperCollins, 2000.

Kellas, A. M. 'The nomenclature of Himalaya peaks'. *Geographical Journal*, 52:4 (1918), 272–4. https://doi.org/10.2307/1779902.

Kempson, E. G. H. 'The local name of Mount Everest.' In Hugh Ruttledge, *Everest, The Unfinished Adventure* London: Hodder & Stoughton, 1937, pp. 285–8. https://archive.org/details/dli.pahar.2660/page/284/mode/2up.

Khadka, Bishnu Kumar. 'Development of ELT in Nepal: An overview'. *Journal of NELTA*, 27:1–2 (2022), 124–40.

Kimmel, Michael S., and Amy Aronson. *Men and Masculinities: A Social, Cultural, and Historical Encyclopedia*. Santa Barbara, CA: ABC-CLIO, 2004.

King, Louis Magrath. *By Tophet Flare. A Tale of Adventure on the Chinese Frontier of Tibet*. London: Methuen, 1937.

———. *China in Turmoil, Studies in Personality*. London: Heath, Cranton, 1927.

———. *The Warden of the Marches, a Tale of Adventure on the Chinese Frontier of Tibet*. Boston, MA: Houghton Mifflin, 1938.

King, Rin-chen Lha-mo. *We Tibetans*. London: Seeley Service, 1926.

Kingdon Ward, F. 'The sacred mountain: A picturesque Tibetan pilgrimage'. *The Wider World Magazine*, (1911), 251–8.

Kingdon-Ward, F. *The Riddle of the Tsangpo Gorges*. London: Edward Arnold, 1926.

Kipling, Rudyard. *Kim. The works of Rudyard Kipling*. London: Macmillan, 1901.

Klak, Thomas, and Garth Myers. 'How states sell their countries and their people.' In Thomas Klak (ed.), *Globalization and Neoliberalism: The Caribbean Context*. Lanham: Rowman & Littlefield, 1998, pp. 87–109.

Kłosowicz, Marek (dir.). *Karawana marzeń [Caravan to dreams]*. Poland: TVN, 2007.

Konishi, Shino, Maria Nugent, and Tiffany Shellam. *Indigenous Intermediaries: New Perspectives on Expedition Archives*. Canberra: ANU Press, 2015. https://doi.org/10.26530/OAPEN_588812.

Kopit, Arthur. *The Day the Whores Came Out to Play Tennis & other Plays*. London: French, 1993.

Kormákur, Baltasar (dir.). *Everest*. United States: Universal, 2015.

Krajewski, Markus, and Peter Krapp. *Paper Machines: About Cards & Catalogs, 1548–1929*. Cambridge, MA: MIT Press, 2011. https://doi.org/10.7551/mitpress/9780262015899.001.0001.

Krakauer, Jon. *Into Thin Air*. London: Macmillan, 1997.

Kunaver, Dušica. 'Naučimo jih loviti ribe! = Let's teach them how to fish!'. In Peter Mikša, Mojca Volkar Trobevšek and Anže Logar (eds), *Z znanjem do zvezd: slovenska šola za nepalske gorske vodnike* = *Knowledge to reach for the stars: the Slovenian school for Nepalese mountain guides.* Ljubljana: Planinska zveza Slovenije, 2022.

———. *Od Triglava do treh vrhov sveta [From Triglav to three world summits].* Ljubljana: Didakta, 1994.

Kurczab, Janusz. *Polskie Himalaje: Część 4. Panie w górach [The Polish Himalaya: Part 4. Ladies in the Mountains].* Warszawa: Agora Warszawa, 2008.

Kurz, Marcel. 'Mount Everest – a century of history.' In Marcel Kurz (ed.), *Mountain World* London: George Allen, 1953, pp. 17–34.

Kuyakanon, Riamsara, Hildegard Diemberger, and David Sneath, eds. *Cosmopolitical ecologies across Asia: places and practices of power in changing environments.* New York: Routledge, 2021.

Lahiri, Ashish. 'Radhanath Sikdar and the final phase of measuring Peak XV'. *Indian Journal of History of Science*, 51:2 (2016), 280–8. https://cahc.jainuniversity.ac.in/assets/ijhs/Vol51_2016_2_1_Art10.pdf.

Lambert, Raymond. *A l'assaut des «quatre mille»: dix récits de haute montagne, suivis de «Altitude 8600» ou l'homme le plus haut du monde.* 2ème ed. Genève: Jeheber, 1953.

Landor, Arnold Henry Savage. *In the Forbidden Land: An Account of a Journey in Tibet, Capture by the Tibetan Authorities, Imprisonment, Torture, and Ultimate Release.* London: W. Heinemann,1899.

Larkin, Brian. 'The Politics and Poetics of Infrastructure'. *Annual Review of Anthropology*, 42:1 (2013), 327–43. https://doi.org/10.1146/annurev-anthro-092412-155522.

Latham, Faye Rhiannon. *British Mountaineers.* Yorkshire, UK: Little Peak Press, 2022.

Lazcano, Santiago. 'Ethnohistoric notes on the ancient Tibetan kingdom of sPo bo and its influence on the eastern Himalayas'. *Revue d'études tibétaines*, 7 (April 2005), 41–62. http://www.digitalhimalaya.com/collections/journals/ret/index.html.

Le Calloc'h, Bernard. 'Alexander Csoma De Koros, the heroic philologist, founder of Tibetan studies in Europe'. *The Tibet Journal*, 10:3 (1985), 30–41. http://www.jstor.org/stable/43300177.

Levine, Nancy E. 'A multifaceted interdependence. Tibetan pastoralists and their animals'. *Études mongoles et sibériennes, centrasiatiques et tibétaines*, 50 (2019). https://doi.org/10.4000/emscat.3822

Liechty, Mark. *Far Out: Countercultural Seekers and the Tourist Encounter in Nepal.* Chicago, IL: University of Chicago Press, 2017.

Lin Chao. 'Zhumulangma de fa xian yu mingcheng (The discovery and name of Everest)'. *Beijing da xue xue bao (Journal of Peking University)*, 4 (1958), 145–65.

Livingstone, Stephen, and Abbie Garrington. *Scaling the Heights – Miniature Mountaineering.* Durham: Oriental Museum, 2018.

Loland, Leif Rune. 'Commons of identity: Sherpa identity management'. *Dhaulagiri Journal of Sociology and Anthropology*, 1 (2005), 176–92.

Lopez, Donald S. *Prisoners of Shangri-La: Tibetan Buddhism and the West.* Chicago, IL: University of Chicago Press, 1998.

Macdonald, Alexander W. 'The lama and the general'. *Kailash: A Journal of Himalayan Studies*, 1:3 (1973), 225–33. https://himalaya.socanth.cam.ac.uk/collections/journals/kailash/pdf/kailash_01_03_05.pdf.

MacGregor, Arthur. *Naturalists in the Field: Collecting, Recording and Preserving the Natural World from the Fifteenth to the Twenty-First Century.* Leiden: Brill, 2018. https://doi.org/10.1163/9789004323841.

Malla, Kamal P. 'Sagara-māthā: The linguistic conquest of Mount Everest'. *Nepalese Linguistics*, 15 (1998), 19–28. https://himalaya.socanth.cam.ac.uk/collections/journals/nepling/pdf/Nep_Ling_15.pdf.

Mallory, George Leigh. 'Climbing Mount Everest is work for supermen'. *New York Times*, (18 March 1923). https://web.archive.org/web/20231115175618/https://www.nytimes.com/1923/03/18/archives/climbing-mount-everest-is-work-for-supermen-a-member-of-former.html.

———. 'The first high climb'. *Geographical Journal*, 60:6 (1922), 400–12. https://doi.org/10.2307/1781077.

Markowitz, Robert (dir.). *Into Thin Air: Death on Everest*. United States: Columbia Tristar, 1997.

Martin, Emma. 'Translating Tibet in the borderlands: networks, dictionaries, and knowledge production in Himalayan hill stations'. *Transcultural Studies*, 7:2 (2016), 86–120. https://doi.org/10.17885/heiup.ts.23538.

Martins, Luciana. 'Plant artefacts then and now: reconnecting biocultural collections in Amazonia.' In   Felix Driver, Mark Nesbitt and Caroline Cornish (eds), *Mobile Museums*. London: UCL Press, 2021, pp. 21–43. https://doi.org/10.2307/j.ctv18kc0px.8.

Mason, Kenneth. 'Karakoram Nomenclature'. *Geographical Journal*, 91:2 (1938), 123–52. https://doi.org/10.2307/1788003.

Mason, Kenneth, and Peter H. Hansen. 'Bruce, Charles Granville (1866–1939).' In H.C.G. Matthew and Brian Harrison (eds), *Oxford Dictionary of National Biography*. Oxford: Oxford University Press, 2004, vol. 8, pp. 284–5. https://doi.org/10.1093/ref:odnb/32130.

Mathieu, Jon. *Mount Sacred: A Brief Global History of Holy Mountains Since 1500*. Winwick, UK: White Horse Press, 2023.

Maury, Léon. *Les Noms de lieux des montagnes françaises*. Paris: J. Castanet; Bergerac, 1929.

Mazuchelli, Nina Elizabeth. *The Indian Alps and How We Crossed Them: Being a Narrative of Two Years' Residence in the Eastern Himalaya and Two Months' Tour into the Interior*. London: Longmans, Green and Co., 1876.

Mazzolini, Elizabeth. *The Everest Effect: Nature, Culture, Ideology*. Tuscaloosa, AL: University of Alabama Press, 2016.

———. 'Food, waste, and judgment on Mount Everest'. *Cultural Critique*, 76 (Fall 2010), 1–27. https://doi.org/10.1353/cul.2010.a402867.

McDonald, Bernadette. *Alpine Rising: Sherpas, Baltis, and the Triumph of Local Climbers in the Great Ranges*. Seattle, WA: Mountaineers Books, 2024.

———. *Alpine warriors*. Victoria, BC: Rocky Mountain Books, 2015.

———. *Freedom Climbers*. Seattle, WA: Mountaineers Books, 2013.

McKay, Alex. *Tibet and the British Raj: The Frontier Cadre, 1904–1947*. Richmond, Surrey: Curzon, 1997.

McMillan, Kelly. 'Controversy over "all-female" summit of K2—men aided climb'. *Nationalgeographic.com*, (7 August 2014). https://web.archive.org/web/20240123155214/https://www.nationalgeographic.com/adventure/article/140807-k2-women-nepal-pakistan-mountain-summit-controversy.

Members of the expedition, and Francis Younghusband. 'The Mount Everest Expedition: Organization and Equipment'. *Geographical Journal*, 57:4 (1921), 271–82. https://doi.org/10.2307/1780559.

Messner, Reinhold. *All 14 Eight-Thousanders*. Translated by Audrey Salkeld. Marlborough, UK: Crowood, 1988.

———. *The Crystal Horizon: Everest – the First Solo Ascent*. Translated by Jill Neate and Audrey Salkeld. Seattle, WA: The Mountaineers, 1989.

Mikša, Peter. 'The mountains that wrote them: Slovenians climbing and writing about eight-thousand-metre peaks. Góry, które ich napisały: Słoweńcy wspinający się na i piszący o ośmiotysięcznikach'. *Slavica Tergestina: European Slavic Studies Journal*, 28:1 (2022), 152–74. https://doi.org/10.13137/2283-5482/33711.

———. 'Od gore do simbola: Triglav in njegova vloga pri Slovencih = From a Mountain to a Symbol: Mount Triglav and Its Role among Slovenes'. *Geografija v šoli*, 29:2 (2021), 6–14.

Mikša, Peter, and Kornelija Ajlec. *Slovensko planinstvo = Slovene mountaineering*. Ljubljana: Planinska sveza Slovenije, 2011.

Mikša, Peter, and Jure Čokl. 'Slovensko osvajanje osemtisočakov (1975–1995) [Slovenian ascents of eight-thousanders]'. *Zgodovinski časopis*, 76:3–4 (2022), 510–32.

Mikša, Peter, and Urban Golob. *Zgodovina slovenskega alpinizma [History of Slovenian Alpinism]*. Ljubljana: Friko, 2013.

Mikša, Peter, and Matija Zorn. 'Nacionalni boj za gore in slovenska identiteta'. *Časopis za zgodovino in narodopisje*, 92:1 (2021), 67–88.

Miller, Daniel, and Jolynna Sinanan. *Visualising Facebook: A Comparative Perspective*. London: UCL Press London, 2017. https://doi.org/10.14324/111.9781911307402.

Miller, Maggie C., and Heather Mair. 'Between space and place in mountaineering: Navigating risk, death, and power'. *Tourism Geographies*, 22:2 (2020), 354–69. https://doi.org/10.1080/14616688.2019.1654538.

Miln, Louise Jordan. *The Green Goddess*. New York: A.L. Burt, 1922.

Mitchell, Breon. 'W. H. Auden and Christopher Isherwood: The 'German Influence''. *Oxford German Studies*, 1:1 (1966), 163–72. https://doi.org/10.1179/ogs.1966.1.1.163.

Mitchell, Ian R., and George W. Rodway. *Prelude to Everest: Alexander Kellas, Himalayan mountaineer*. Edinburgh: Luath, 2011.

Mitchell, Richard G. *Mountain Experience: The Psychology and Sociology of Adventure*. Chicago, IL: University of Chicago Press, 1983.

Moraldo, Delphine. 'Gender relations in French and British mountaineering. The lens of autobiographies of female mountaineers, from d'Angeville (1794–1871) to Destivelle (1960–)'. *Journal of Alpine Research | Revue de géographie alpine*, 101–1 (2013). https://doi.org/10.1080/09523367.2020.1819250

———. '"There is no manlier sport in the world". How hegemonic masculinity became constitutive of excellence in mountaineering.' In Jenny Hall, Emma Boocock and Zoe Avner (eds), *Gender Politics and Change in Mountaineering*. Cham: Palgrave Macmillan, 2023, pp. 51–70. https://doi.org/10.1007/978-3-031-29945-2_4.

———. 'Women and excellence in mountaineering from the nineteenth century to the present'. *International Journal of the History of Sport*, 37:9 (2020), 727–47. https://doi.org/10.1080/09523367.2020.1819250.

Morris, Jan. *Conundrum*. London: Faber and Faber, 1974.

———. *Coronation Everest*. London: Faber and Faber, 2003.

Morris, John. *Gurkhas*. Delhi: Manager of Publications, 1933.

Morshead, H. T., and F. M. Bailey. *Report on the Exploration of the North East Frontier, 1913* Dehra Dun: The Survey of India Trigonometrical Office, 1914. https://archive.org/details/ExplorationOnTheNorthEastFrontier1913.

Mort, Helen. *No Map Could Show Them*. London: Chatto & Windus, 2016.

Mu, Yang, Sanjay K Nepal, and Po-Hsin Lai. 'Tourism and sacred landscape in Sagarmatha (Mt. Everest) National Park, Nepal.' In Michael A. Di Giovine and Jaeyeon Choe (eds), *Pilgrimage Beyond the Officially Sacred*. London: Routledge, 2020, pp. 82–99. https://doi.org/10.4324/9781003007821-5.

Mundy, Talbot. *Om, the Secret of Ahbor Valley*. New York: A.L. Burt, 1924.

Mutrie, Tim. 'The Everest climber whose traffic jam went viral'. *New York Times*, (18 Sep 2019). https://web.archive.org/web/20211203202921/https://www.nytimes.com/2019/09/18/sports/the-everest-climber-whose-traffic-jam-photo-went-viral.html.

Nasr, Carmen. *The Climbers (NHB Modern Plays)*. La Vergne: Nick Hern Books, 2022.

Natarajan, Swaminathan, and Patrick Jackson. 'Lhakpa Sherpa: woman climbs Everest for record tenth time'. *BBC.com*, (12 May 2022). https://web.archive.org/web/20240123143127/https://www.bbc.com/news/world-asia-61424866.

Naylor, Simon. 'Spacing the can: Empire, modernity, and the globalisation of food'. *Environment and Planning A: Economy and Space*, 32:9 (2000), 1625–39. https://doi.org/10.1068/a32166.

Neate, Jill. *Mountaineering Literature: A Bibliography of Material Published in English*. Milnthorpe; Seattle, WA: Cicerone; Mountainbooks, 1986.

Neate, W. R., and Jill Neate. *Mountaineering and its Literature: A Descriptive Bibliography of Selected Works Published in the English Language, 1744–1976*. Harmony Hill: Cicerone Press, 1978.

Nebesky-Wojkowitz, René de. *Oracles and Demons of Tibet: The Cult and Iconography of the Tibetan Protective Deities*. The Hague: Mouton & Co, 1956.

Nepal National Mountain Guide Association. *IFMGA Mountain Guides*. https://web.archive.org/web/20230505201936/https://www.nnmga.org/international-guides/.

Nepal, Sanjay. 'Tourism and remote mountain settlements: Spatial and temporal development of tourist infrastructure in the Mt Everest Region, Nepal'. *Tourism Geographies*, 7:2 (2005), 205–27. https://doi.org/10.1080/14616680500072471.

Nestler, Stefan. 'Messner: 'First ascent a magic moment of mountaineering''. *DW* (29 May 2013). https://web.archive.org/web/20220813030534/https://www.dw.com/en/messner-first-ascent-a-magic-moment-of-mountaineering/a-16844185.

Neville, Tim. 'Brawl on Everest: Ueli Steck's story'. *Outside Online*, (2 May 2013). https://web.archive.org/web/20210921084337/https://www.outsideonline.com/outdoor-adventure/climbing/brawl-everest-ueli-stecks-story/.

Ngawang Shedrub Tenpe, Gyaltsen, and Jamyang Wangmo. *Dharma Wheel of Great Bliss: A Guide to the Thangme Gompa Dechen Chökhor Ling*. Kathmandu: Vajra Publications, 2008.

Ngawang Tenzin Norbu, and Ngag dbang bstan 'dzin nor bu. 'Bdud rtsi'i rol mtsho.' *Rnam thar 'chi med bdud rtsi'i rol mtsho*. n.p., n.d.

———. 'Gangs chen brgyad kyi ya gyal rdza rong phu yi gnas yig dad pa'i mgongs ldan dga' skyes dbyar gyi rnga sgra (The Sound of Summer's Drum that Delights the Faithful Peacocks, a Guide to the Sacred Sites of Dza Rongpu, Solitary among the Eight Great Snow Mountains).' *Ngag dbang bstan 'dzin nor bu's gsung 'bum (The Collected Works of Ngagwang Tenzin)*. Kathmandu: Ngagyur Dongak Choling Monastery, 2004, pp. 401–26.

Nodari, Maria Luisa. 'Why do some Tibetan women climb the highest mountains? Gendering mountaineering practices on the roof of the world'. *Inner Asia*, 15:2 (2013), 293–311.

Noel, John (dir.). *Climbing Mount Everest*. United Kingdom: Royal Geographical Society, 1922.

——— (dir.). *The Epic of Everest*. United Kingdom: BFI, 2013 [orig. 1924].

———. 'Photographing the Epic of Everest: How the camera recorded man's battle against the highest mountain in the world'. *Asia*, 27:5 (1927), 366–73.

Noel, J. B. L. *Through Tibet to Everest*. London: E. Arnold, 1928.

Norgay, Jamling Tenzing. *Touching My Father's Soul: A Sherpa's Journey to the Top of Everest*. Waterville, ME: Thorndike Press, 2001.

Norgay, Tenzing, and James Ramsey Ullman. *Man of Everest: The Autobiography of Tenzing*. London: Harrap, 1956.

———. *Tiger of the Snows: The Autobiography of Tenzing of Everest*. New York: Putnam, 1955.

Normand, Lawrence. 'Modernity and Orientalism in W. H. Auden and Christopher Isherwood's *The Ascent of F6*. *Modern Philology*, 108:4 (2011), 538–59. https://doi.org/10.1086/660366.

Norton, Edward Felix. *The Fight for Everest: 1924*. New York; London: Longmans; Arnold, 1925.

O'Connor, Bill. 'Nepal 1993'. *Alpine Journal*, 98 (1993), 263–6. https://www.alpinejournal.org.uk/Contents/Contents_1994_files/AJ%201994%20263-266%20Nepal.pdf.

Odell, Noel E. 'In memoriam: Andrew Comyn Irvine, 1902–1924'. *Alpine Journal*, 36 (1924), 386–89. https://archive.org/details/the-alpine-journal-vol-36-1924/page/n539/.

Oh, Young Hoon. *Sherpa Intercultural Experiences in Himalayan Mountaineering: A Pragmatic Phenomenological Perspective*. PhD thesis, University of California, Riverside, 2016. https://escholarship.org/uc/item/46b987r2.

Ollone, Henri d. *In Forbidden China. The D'Ollone mission 1906–1909; China--Tibet--Mongolia*. Translated by Bernard Miall. Boston, MA: Small, Maynard, 1912.

Olson, Ray. 'Mountains to climb'. *Mountain Lodges of Nepal*. https://web.archive.org/web/20240123005614/https://mountainlodgesofnepal.com/stories/mountains-to-climb/.

Ortner, Sherry B. *High Religion: A Cultural and Political History of Sherpa Buddhism*. Princeton, NJ: Princeton University Press, 1989. https://doi.org/10.1515/9780691218076.

———. *Life and Death on Mt. Everest: Sherpas and Himalayan Mountaineering*. Princeton, NJ: Princeton University Press, 1999.

———. 'The making and self-making of "the Sherpas" in early Himalayan mountaineering'. *Studies in Nepali History and Society*, 3:1 (1998), 1–34.

Ounoughi, Samia. 'Mapping in process: discourse analysis of the Alpine Club's periodicals'. *Studies in Travel Writing*, 24:2 (2020), 119–30. https://doi.org/10.1080/13645145.2020.1862953.

Pallis, Marco. *Peaks and lamas*. London, Toronto: Cassell, 1939.

Palmer, Catherine. '"Shit happens": The selling of risk in extreme sport'. *The Australian Journal of Anthropology*, 13:3 (2002), 323–36. https://doi.org/10.1111/j.1835-9310.2002.tb00213.x.

Pandey, Gyanendra. 'Voices from the edge: The struggle to write subaltern histories.' In Vinayak Chaturvedi (ed.), *Mapping Subaltern Studies and the Postcolonial*. London: Verso, 2000, pp. 281–99.

Parihar, Pragati. 'Bachendri Pal: The first Indian woman to climb the Mount Everest'. *Feminism in India*, (27 October 2022). https://web.archive.org/web/20240123001044/https://feminisminindia.com/2022/05/25/bachendri-pal-the-first-indian-woman-to-climb-the-mount/.

Pariseau, Russ (dir.). *Unity in Diversity*. Nepal: World Food Programme, 2008.

Parsons, Mike C., and Mary B. Rose. *Invisible on Everest: Innovation and the gear makers*. Philadelphia, PA: Northern Liberties Press, 2003.

Paul, G. Firth, Zheng Hui, S. Windsor Jeremy, I. Sutherland Andrew, H. Imray Christopher, G. W. K. Moore, L. Semple John, C. Roach Robert, and A. Salisbury Richard. 'Mortality on Mount Everest, 1921–2006: descriptive study'. *BMJ*, 337 (2008), a2654. https://doi.org/10.1136/bmj.a2654.

Peedom, Jennifer (dir.). *Sherpa*. Australia: Felix Media, 2015.

Pereira, Cliff, and Vandana Patel. 'Terra Nova for the Royal Geographical Society (with IBG): 2007 and the Bombay Africans strand of the "Crossing Continents: Connecting Communities" project.' In Laurajane Smith, Geoff Cubitt, Kalliopi Fouseki and Ross

Wilson (eds), *Representing Enslavement and Abolition in Museums*. London: Routledge, 2011, pp. 164–74. https://doi.org/10.4324/9780203808252.

Pfaff-Czarnecka, Joanna, and Gérard Toffin (eds.), *The Politics of Belonging in the Himalayas: Local Attachments and Boundary Dynamics*. New Delhi: SAGE, 2011.

Phillimore, Reginald Henry, and Survey of India. *Historical records of the Survey of India*. Vol. V, 1844–1861, Andrew Waugh. Dehra Dun: Survey of India, 1968.

Pickman, Sarah. 'Tool Users: Sun Protection'. *Alpinist*, 78 (Summer 2022), 28.

Pilcher, Jeffrey M. 'Culinary infrastructure: How facilities and technologies create value and meaning around food'. *Global Food History*, 2:2 (2016), 105–31. https://doi.org/10.1080/20549547.2016.1214896.

Pitches, Jonathan. *New Writing and Interviews | Performing Landscapes: Mountains*. 2024, https://web.archive.org/web/20240123174831/https:/performing-mountains.leeds.ac.uk/newwritingandinterviews/.

———. *Performing Mountains*. London: Palgrave Macmillan, 2020.

Pomfret, Gill, and Adele Doran. 'Gender and mountaineering tourism.' In Ghazali Musa, James Higham and Anna Thompson-Carr (eds), *Mountaineering Tourism*. Abingdon: Routledge, 2015, pp. 138–55.

Potocki, Mariusz, Paul Andrew Mayewski, Tom Matthews, L Baker Perry, Margit Schwikowski, Alexander M Tait, Elena Korotkikh, *et al.* 'Mt. Everest's highest glacier is a sentinel for accelerating ice loss'. *NPJ Climate and Atmospheric Science*, 5:1 (2022), 7. https://doi.org/10.1038/s41612-022-00230-0.

Pott, P. H., and Rijksmuseum voor Volkenkunde. *Introduction to the Tibetan collection of the National Museum of Ethnology, Leiden*. Leiden: E.J. Brill, 1951.

Potts, Mary Anne. 'Meet the woman taking the climbing world by storm'. *Redbull.com*, (11 July 2017). https://web.archive.org/web/20240123154500/https://www.redbull.com/gb-en/dawa-yangzum-sherpa-mountain-climber.

Pradhan, Sojen, and Gyanendra Bajracharya. 'Socio-economic impacts on the adoption of mobile phones by the major indigenous nationalities of Nepal.' In Laurel Evelyn Grant Dyson, Stephen and Max Hendricks (eds), *Indigenous People and Mobile Technologies*. London: Routledge, 2015, pp. 237–50. https://doi.org/10.4324/9781315759364.

Prown, Jules David. 'Mind in matter: An introduction to material culture and method.' In *Art as Evidence: Writings on Art and Material Culture*. New Haven, CT: Yale University Press, 2001, pp. 69–95.

Pugh, L. G. C. E. 'Scientific aspects of the Expedition to Mount Everest, 1953'. *Geographical Journal*, 120:2 (1954), 183–92. https://doi.org/10.2307/1791534.

Purandare, Nandini, and Deepa Balsavar. *Headstrap: Legends and Lore from the Climbing Sherpas of Darjeeling*. Seattle, WA: Mountaineers, 2024.

Purja, Nimsdai. *Beyond Possible: One Soldier, Fourteen Peaks: My Life in the Death Zone*. London: Hodder, 2022.

Pye, David Randall. *George Leigh Mallory: A Memoir*. Oxford: Oxford University Press, 1927.

Quintman, Andrew. 'Toward a geographic biography: Mi la ras pa in the Tibetan landscape'. *Numen*, 55:4 (2008), 363–410. https://doi.org/10.1163/156852708X310509.

Rai, Vishal. 'Blazing a trail to the top'. *ECS Nepal*, 149 (April 2014). https://web.archive.org/web/20230608173300/https://ecs.com.np/features/blazing-a-trail-to-the-top.

Raj, Kapil. *Relocating Modern Science: Circulation and the Construction of Knowledge in South Asia and Europe, 1650–1900*. Basingstoke: Palgrave Macmillan, 2007. https://doi.org/10.1057/9780230625310.

Rak, Julie. *False Summit: Gender in Mountaineering Nonfiction*. Montreal & Kingston: McGill-Queen's University Press, 2021.

———. 'Mediation, then and now: Ang Tharkay's *Sherpa* and *Memoires d'un Sherpa*'. *Primerjalnaknjiževnost*, 45:3 (2022), 125–44. https://doi.org/10.3986/pkn.v45.i3.08.

Rand, Christopher. 'The story of the first Sherpa to climb to the top of Mt. Everest'. *New Yorker*, (29 May 1954). https://web.archive.org/web/20240118060343/https://www.newyorker.com/magazine/1954/06/05/tenzing-of-everest.

Raztresen, Marjan. 'Odprave v tuja gorstva – Himalaja [Expeditions to foreign mountains – the Himalayas].' In Božidar Lavrič (ed.), *Planinski zbornik: ob 110-letnici Slovenskega planinskega društva in Planinske zveze Slovenije* Ljubljana: Planinska zveza Slovenije, 2003, pp. 245–86.

Reeuwijk, Alexander. *Voyage of Discovery: Exploring the Collections of the Asian Library of Leiden University*. Leiden: Leiden University Press, 2017.

Reinisch, Gertrude. *Wanda Rutkiewicz: A Caravan of Dreams*. Translated by Dieter Pevsner. Hindersley, UK: Carreg Ltd., 2000.

Rheingans, Jim. 'De-imagining Tibet: Beyond Orientalism, reverse Orientalism and other traps in the study of Himalayan histories'. *Journal of the Society of Asian Humanities*, 52 (2020–2021), 126–34. https://doi.org/10.3316/informit.036105030734709.

Richards, Thomas. *The Imperial Archive: Knowledge and the Fantasy of Empire*. London: Verso, 1993.

Rioux, Brigitte. 'Ascending marginalized stories to new heights'. (11 May 2022). https://web.archive.org/web/20230425082535/https://www.ualberta.ca/the-quad/2022/05/ascending-marginalized-stories-to-new-heights.html.

Robertson, David. *George Mallory*. London: Faber, 1969.

Robinson, Victoria. *Everyday Masculinities and Extreme Sport: Male Identity and Rock Climbing*. Oxford: Berg, 2008.

Robles, Pablo. 'Unfreezing the Everest economy'. *Bloomberg* (2020). https://web.archive.org/web/20201201095703/https://www.bloomberg.com/graphics/2020-everest-reopening-sherpa-supply-chain/.

Robles, Whitney Barlow. 'On nonhuman agency'. *Journal of Interdisciplinary History*, 54:3 (2024), 305–21. https://doi.org/10.1162/jinh_a_02000.

Roche, Clare. 'Women climbers 1850–1900: A challenge to male hegemony?'. *Sport in History*, 33:3 (2013), 236–59. https://doi.org/10.1080/17460263.2013.826437.

Rock, Joseph F. 'The land of the Yellow Lama'. *National Geographic Magazine*, 47:4 (April 1925).

———. 'Seeking the mountains of mystery'. *National Geographic Magazine*, 57:2 (Feb 1930), 131–85.

Rose, David, and Ed Douglas. *Regions of the Heart: The Triumph and Tragedy of Alison Hargreaves*. London: Penguin, 2000.

Rose-Redwood, Reuben, Derek Alderman, and Maoz Azaryahu. 'Geographies of toponymic inscription: new directions in critical place-name studies'. *Progress in Human Geography*, 34:4 (2010), 453–70. https://doi.org/10.1177/0309132509351042.

Royal Geographical Society, Alpine Club, and Mount Everest Expedition. *Catalogue of the Exhibition of Photographs and Paintings from the Mount Everest Expedition 1922*. London: The Society, 1923.

Royal Geographical Society with IBG. *Everest 24: New Views on the 1924 Mount Everest Expedition*. Washington, DC: Smithsonian Books, 2024.

Bibliography

————. *Everest Through the Lens*. https://web.archive.org/web/20240126232215/https://www.rgs.org/our-collections/stories-from-our-collections/online-exhibitions/everest-through-the-lens.

Rutkiewicz, Wanda. 'Mój Everest [My Everest].' In Karl M. Herrligkoffer (ed.), *Mount Everest ohne Sauerstoff: mit authentischen Berichten von 9 Gipfelbezwingern [Mount Everest Without Oxygen. With Authentic Reports from 9 Summiteers]*. Bamberg: Bayerische Verlagsanstalt, 1979, pp. 70–82.

Rutkiewicz, Wanda, and Ewa Matuszewska. 'Kobiecość kontrolowana [Controlled femininity], Uroda, May, 1987.' In Ewa Matuszewska (ed.), *Uciec jak najwyżej: nie dokończone życie Wandy Rutkiewicz*. Warszawa: Iskry Warszawa, 2004, pp. 142–8.

————. *Na jednej linie*. Warszawa: Wydawnictwo ISKRY, 2010.

Rutkiewicz, Wanda, and Barbara Rusowicz. *Wszystko o Wandzie Rutkiewicz: wywiad rzeka Barbary Rusowicz [Everything about Wanda Rutkiewicz: an extended interview by Barbara Rusowicz]*.Toruń: Comer & Ekolog, 1992.

Ruttledge, Hugh. *Everest: The Unfinished Adventure*. London: Hodder & Stoughton, 1937.

————. 'The Mount Everest Expedition of 1936'. *Geographical Journal*, 88:6 (1936), 491–519. https://doi.org/10.2307/1787082.

Said, Edward W. *Orientalism* New York: Pantheon, 1978.

Salisbury, Richard. *The Himalayan Database: The Expedition Archives of Elizabeth Hawley*. 2024, http://www.himalayandatabase.com/.

Salkeld, Audrey. *Climbing Everest: Tales of Triumph and Tragedy on the World's Highest Mountain*.Washington, DC: National Geographic, 2003.

————. *Mystery on Everest: A Photobiography of George Mallory*. Washington, DC: National Geographic Society, 2000.

————. *People in High Places: Approaches to Tibet*. London: Jonathan Cape, 1991.

Salkeld, Audrey, and John Boyle. *Climbing Mount Everest: The Bibliography: The Literature and History of Climbing the World's Highest Mountain*. Clevedon, Avon: Sixways Pub., 1993.

Sardar-Afkhami, Abdol-Hamid. *The Buddha's Secret Gardens: End Times and Hidden-Lands in Tibetan Imagination*. PhD thesis, Harvard University, 2001.

Satre, Lowell J. *Chocolate on Trial: Slavery, Politics, and the Ethics of Business*. Athens, OH: Ohio University Press, 2005.

Schaffer, Grayson. 'The controversial king of hardcore climbing'. *GQ Sports*, (19 January 2023). https://web.archive.org/web/20230119133927/https://www.gq.com/story/nims-purja-profile.

————. 'The disposable man: A Western history of Sherpas on Everest'. *Outside Online*, (10 July 2013), Updated Jun 26, 2021. https://web.archive.org/web/20150406020709/https://www.outsideonline.com/1928326/disposable-man-western-history-sherpas-everest.

————. 'The disposable man: Sherpas on Everest'. *Outside Magazine*, (August 2013), 64–71, 98–100.

————. 'Everest's darkest year'. *Outside Online*, (8 July 2014), Updated 30 Jun 2021. https://web.archive.org/web/20161114084454/https://www.outsideonline.com/1924596/everests-darkest-year.

————. 'Lhakpa Sherpa is the most successful female Everest climber of all time'. *Outside Online*, (10 May 2016), Updated 12 May 2022. https://web.archive.org/web/20240123142633/https://www.outsideonline.com/outdoor-adventure/climbing/most-successful-female-everest-climber-all-time-housekeeper-hartford-connecticut/.

Schaumann, Caroline. *Peak Pursuits: The Emergence of Mountaineering in the Nineteenth Century.* New Haven, CT: Yale University Press, 2020. https://doi.org/10.2307/j.ctv13 8wr6d.

Schlagintweit, Emil. 'Der Name des höchsten Berges der Erde'. *Petermanns Mitteilungen*, 47 (mars 1901), 40–3.

———. 'Der Name des höchsten Berges der Erde'. *Dr A. Petermanns Mitteilungen aus Justus Perthes' Geographischer Anstalt*, 36 (1890), 251–2.

Schlagintweit, Hermann. 'Gaurisánkar, or Mount Everest, in the Himálaya of Nepál.' In Hermann von Schlagintweit, Adolphe von Schlagintweit and Robert von Schlagintweit, *Results of a scientific mission in India and High Asia ... Atlas of panoramas and views*. Leipzig: F.A. Brockhaus, 1861. https://doi.org/10.11588/diglit.20836#0005.

Schnapp, Jeffrey T. *Staging Fascism: 18 BL and the Theater of Masses for Masses.* Stanford, CA: Stanford University Press, 1996.

Schultz, Kai, Jeffrey Gettleman, Mujib Mashal, and Bhadra Sharma. '"It was like a zoo": Death on an unruly, overcrowded Everest'. *New York Times* (26 May 2019). https://web. archive.org/web/20240120093921/https://www.nytimes.com/2019/05/26/world/ asia/mount-everest-deaths.html.

Scott, Doug, Ian Wall, and Jonathan Westaway. 'The Everest mess'. *Alpine Journal*, 123 (2019), 129–37. https://www.alpinejournal.org.uk/Contents/Contents_2019_files/AJ%202019 %20Vol%20123%20129-137%20Scott%20Wall%20Westaway%20Everest.pdf.

Sehgal, Saransh. 'Reinhold Messner on the future of climbing Mount Everest'. *The Diplomat*, (19 April 2017). https://web.archive.org/web/20180313093012/https://thediplomat. com/2017/04/reinhold-messner-on-the-future-of-climbing-mount-everest/.

Seven Summits Women Team. *Sevensummitswomen.org.* 2024, https://web.archive.org/web/ 20240123162624/http://sevensummitswomen.org/.

Shahid, Jamal. 'First Pakistani woman scales Mount Everest'. *DAWN.COM*, (20 May 2013). https://web.archive.org/web/20240122233506/https://www.dawn.com/news/1012 447/first-pakistani-woman-scales-mount-everest.

Sharma, Bhadra, and Mujib Mashal. '"I see no future": Sherpas leave the job they made famous'. *New York Times*, (7 May 2023). https://web.archive.org/web/20230507070603/ https://www.nytimes.com/2023/05/07/world/asia/sherpas-everest.html.

Sharma, Jayeeta. 'Producing Himalayan Darjeeling: Mobile people and mountain encounters'. *Himalaya*, 35:2 (2016), 87–101. https://digitalcommons.macalester.edu/himalaya/ vol35/iss2/12.

———. 'A space that has been laboured on: Mobile lives and transcultural circulation around Darjeeling and the eastern Himalayas'. *Journal of Transcultural Studies*, 7:1 (2016), 54–85. https://doi.org/10.17885/heiup.ts.23539.

Sherap, Paul, and G. A. Combe. *A Tibetan on Tibet Being the Travels and Observations of Mr. Paul Sherap (Dorje Zödba) of Tachienlu.* London: T.F. Unwin, 1926.

Sherpa, Jemima Diki, 'Three Springs'. *Whathasgood.* (23 April 2014). https://web.archive. org/web/20140426101013/http://whathasgood.com/2014/04/23/three-springs/.

Sherpa, Lhakpa. *Cloudscape Climbing.* 2024, https://web.archive.org/web/20240424025826/ https://cloudscapeclimbing.com/.

Sherpa, Pasang Yangjee. 'Climate change, perceptions, and social heterogeneity in Pharak, Mount Everest Region of Nepal'. *Human Organization*, 73:2 (2014), 153–61. https://doi. org/10.17730/humo.73.2.94q43152111733t6.

———. 'Ethnographies of the Sherpas in the High Himalaya: Themes, trajectories, and beyond.' In Jelle J.P. Wouters and Michael T. Heneise (eds), *Routledge Handbook of Highland*

Asia. Abingdon: Routledge, 2022, pp. 182–94. https://doi.org/10.4324/97804293457 46-16.

———. 'Institutional climate change adaptation efforts among the Sherpas of the Mount Everest region, Nepal.' In Donald C. Wood (ed.), *Climate Change, Culture, and Economics: Anthropological Investigations.* Leeds: Emerald, 2015, pp. 1–23. https://doi.org/10.1108/S0190-128120150000035001.

———. 'Sustaining Sherpa language and culture in New York'. *Book 2.0,* 9:1 (2019), 19–29. https://doi.org/10.1386/btwo_00003_1.

Sherpa, Pasang Yangjee, and Ornella Puschiasis. 'A reflexive approach to climate change engagement with Sherpas from Khumbu and Pharak in Northeastern Nepal (Mount Everest Region).' In Susan A. Crate, Mark Nuttall (eds), *Anthropology and Climate Change: From Transformations to Worldmaking.* London: Routledge, 2023, pp. 224–41. https://doi.org/10.4324/9781003242499.

Shipton, Eric. *The Mount Everest Reconnaissance Expedition, 1951.* London: Hodder and Stoughton, 1952.

Shyamal L. *Some unsung Lepcha collectors.* 2016, accessed 2 March, https://web.archive.org/web/20240124221836/https://muscicapa.blogspot.com/2016/03/some-unsung-lepcha-collectors.html.

Simon, Gregory L., and Peter S. Alagona. 'Beyond leave no trace'. *Ethics, Place & Environment,* 12:1 (2009), 17–34. https://doi.org/10.1080/13668790902753021.

Simpson, Thomas. 'Imperial slippages: Encountering and knowing ice in and beyond colonial India.' In Klaus Dodds and Sverker Sörlin (eds), *Ice Humanities.* Manchester: Manchester University Press, 2022, pp. 205–27. https://doi.org/10.7765/9781526157 782.00020.

Sinanan, Jolynna. 'Everest, Everestland, #Everest: A case for a composite visual ethnographic approach'. *Visual Anthropology,* 35:3 (2022), 272–86. https://doi.org/10.1080/08 949468.2022.2094187.

———. '#Everest: Visual economies of leisure and labour in the tourist encounter.' In Elisabetta Costa, Patricia G. Lange, Nell Haynes and Jolynna Sinanan (eds), *The Routledge Companion to Media Anthropology.* London: Routledge, 2022, pp. 245–57. https://doi.org/10.4324/9781003175605-24.

Škarja, Tone. *Everest.* Ljubljana: Mladinska knjiga, 1981.

———. *Slovenci v Himalaji = Slovenians in Himalaya.* Ljubljana: Planinska zveza Slovenije, 2004.

Sørensen, Ninna Nyberg, and Karen Fog Olwig. *Work and Migration: Life and Livelihoods in a Globalizing World.* London: Routledge, 2002.

Spender, Michael. 'Photographic surveys in the Mount Everest Region'. *Geographical Journal,* 88:4 (1936), 289–300. https://doi.org/10.2307/1786332.

Spoon, Jeremy, and Lhakpa Norbu Sherpa. 'Beyul Khumbu: The Sherpa and Sagarmatha (Mount Everest) National Park and Buffer Zone, Nepal.' In Josep-Maria Mallarach (ed.), *Protected Landscapes and Cultural and Spiritual Values.* Heidelberg: Kasparek, 2008, pp. 68–79.

Steele, Peter. *Eric Shipton: Everest and Beyond.* London: Constable, 1999.

Steers, J. A. 'A. R. Hinks and the Royal Geographical Society'. *Geographical Journal,* 148:1 (1982), 1–7. https://doi.org/10.2307/634237.

Stewart, Gordon T. 'The British reaction to the conquest of Everest'. *Journal of Sport History,* 7:1 (Spring 1980), 21–39.

Storti, Craig. *The Hunt for Mount Everest.* Boston, MA: Nicholas Brealey Publishing, 2021.

Bibliography

Stout, John C. 'Metapoetic explorations of Tibet in Victor Segalen's *Thibet* and André Velter's *Le Haut-Pays*'. *Sites: The Journal of Twentieth-Century/Contemporary French Studies revue d'études français*, 5:1 (2001), 63–78. https://doi.org/10.1080/10260210108456056.

Štremfelj, Andrej. 'Ko na vrhu ne veš, kaj bi: Everest med prvim vzponom in slovensko smerjo po Zahodnem grebenu leta 1979 [When you don't know what to do at the top: Everest during the first ascent and the Slovenian route along the West Ridge in 1979]'. *I-gore*, 1:2 (2003).

———. *Kristali sreče: avtobiografija alpinista [Crystals of Happiness: Autobiography of an Alpinist]*. Kranj: Založništvo N. Štremfelj, 2022.

Styles, Showell. *Mallory of Everest*. London: Hamish, 1967.

Subedi, Madhusudan. 'Afno Manchhe: Unequal access to public resources and institutions in Nepal'. *Dhaulagiri Journal of Sociology and Anthropology*, 8 (2014), 55–86. https://doi.org/10.3126/dsaj.v8i0.10722.

Summers, Julie. *Fearless on Everest: The Quest for Sandy Irvine*. London: Weidenfeld & Nicolson, 2000.

Svendsen, Nancy (dir.). *Pasang: In the Shadow of Everest*. USA: Good Docs, 2022.

Tabei, Junko, and Helen Y. Rolfe. *Honouring High Places: The Mountain Life of Junko Tabei*. Translated by Yumiko Hiraki and Rieko Holtved. Victoria, BC: Rocky Mountain Books, 2017.

Talbot, Joby, and Gene Scheer. '*Everest: Opera in One Act*'. London: Chester Music, 2017.

Tenzing, Tashi, and Judy Tenzing. *Tenzing Norgay and the Sherpas of Everest*. Camden, ME: Ragged Mountain Press, 2001.

Thamserku Trekking. *Our History*. https://web.archive.org/web/20240123002333/https://www.thamserkutrekking.com/about/history.

Tharchin, Gegen Dorje. 'The proper name of the Mount Everest'. *Yul phyogs so so'i gsar 'gyur me long = Tibet mirror*, 7:4 (1933), 27. https://archive.org/details/ldpd_6981643_000/page/124/mode/2up.

———. 'The proper name of the Mount Everest is'. *Yul phyogs so so'i gsar 'gyur me long = Tibet mirror*, 7:3 (March 1933), 21. https://archive.org/details/ldpd_6981643_000/page/118/mode/2up.

Tharkay, Ang, and Basil P. Norton. *Mémoires d'un sherpa*. Paris: Amiot-Dumont, 1954.

———. *Sherpa: The Memoir of Ang Tharkay*. Seattle, WA: Mountaineers Books, 2016.

Thévoz, Samuel. 'On the threshold of the "land of marvels": Alexandra David-Neel in Sikkim and the making of global Buddhism'. *Transcultural Studies*, 1 (2016), 149–86. https://doi.org/10.17885/heiup.ts.23541.

———. 'Visions of Tibet (1840–1910): Sacred landscape in French and British travelogues'. *Tibet Journal*, 45:1 (2020), 101–33.

Thomas, Nicholas. *Entangled Objects: Exchange, Material Culture, and Colonialism in the Pacific*. Cambridge, MA: Harvard University Press, 1991.

Thorington, J. Monroe. 'The Freshfield group'. *Alpine Journal*, 34 (1922), 387–99. https://alpinejournal.org.uk/Contents/Contents_1922_files/AJ%201922%20Vol%2034%20387-399%20Thorington%20Freshfield%20Group.pdf.

Thorpe, Holly. *Transnational Mobilities in Action Sport Cultures*. Basingstoke: Palgrave Macmillan, 2014. https://doi.org/10.1057/9780230390744.

Tilman, H. W. *Mount Everest, 1938*. Cambridge: Cambridge University Press, 1948.

Tournadre, Nicolas, and Hiroyuki Suziki. *The Tibetic Languages: An Introduction to the Family of Languages Derived from Old Tibetan*. Villejuif, France: Lacito Publications, 2023. https://lacito.cnrs.fr/wp-content/uploads/2023/09/TibeticAll-12-9-2023-1.pdf.

Bibliography

Tsering, Bhuchung K. 'Mi ti gu ti cha pu long na'. *Tibet Bulletin*, 8:4 (Oct-Nov 1985), 20.

Tuan, Yi-Fu. 'Language and the making of place: A narrative-descriptive approach'. *Annals of the Association of American Geographers*, 81:4 (1991), 684–96. https://doi.org/10.1111/j.1467-8306.1991.tb01715.x.

Tucci, Giuseppe. *To Lhasa and Beyond; Diary of the Expedition to Tibet in the year MCMXLVIII*. Roma: Istituto poligrafico dello Stato, 1956. https://archive.org/details/dli.pahar.3084.

Tulle, Emmanuelle. 'Rising to the gender challenge in Scotland: Women's embodiment of the disposition to be mountaineers'. *International Review for the Sociology of Sport*, 57:8 (2022), 1301–20. https://doi.org/10.1177/10126902221078748.

Turner, Hannah. *Cataloguing Culture: Legacies of Colonialism in Museum Documentation*. Vancouver, BC: UBC Press, 2020.

Twain, Mark. *More Tramps Abroad*. London: Chatto & Windus, 1897.

Unsworth, Walt. *Everest*. 2nd ed. London: Grafton, 1991.

———. *Everest: The Mountaineering History*. 3rd ed. Seattle, WA; London: Mountaineers; Bâton Wicks, 2000.

Van Schaik, Sam. *Tibet: A History*. New Haven, CT: Yale University Press, 2011.

van Spenger, Wim. *Tibetan Border Worlds: A Geo-Historical Analysis of Trade and Traders*. New York: Kegan Paul, 2000.

Vansittart, Eden. *Notes on Goorkhás: Being a Short Account of their Country, History, Characteristic, Clans, &c*. Calcutta: Superintendent of Government Printing, 1890.

Vansittart, Eden, and Bernhard U. Nicolay. *Gurkhās*. Handbooks for the Indian Army. Calcutta: Supt. Govt. Printing, 1915.

Varzi, Achille C. 'Introduction'. *Topoi*, 20:2 (2001), 119–30. https://doi.org/10.1023/A:1017944405193.

Venables, Stephen. *Everest: The Summit of Achievement*. London: Bloomsbury, 2013.

Von Brescius, Moritz. 'Empires of opportunity: German naturalists in British India and the frictions of transnational science'. *Modern Asian Studies*, 55:6 (2021), 1926–71. https://doi.org/10.1017/S0026749X19000428.

———. *German Science in the Age of Empire: Enterprise, Opportunity and the Schlagintweit Brothers*. Cambridge: Cambridge University Press, 2019. https://doi.org/10.1017/9781108579568.

Waddell, L. A. *Among the Himalayas*. London: Constable, 1899.

———. 'The environs and native names of Mount Everest'. *Geographical Journal*, 12:6 (1898), 564–9. https://doi.org/10.2307/1774275.

Walker, J. T. 'A last note on Mont Everest'. *Proceedings of the Royal Geographical Society and Monthly Record of Geography*, 8:4 (1886), 257–63. https://doi.org/10.2307/1801364.

Walker, Lucy (dir.). *Mountain Queen: The Summits of Lhakpa Sherpa*. USA: Netflix, 2024.

Waller, Derek J. *The Pundits: British Exploration of Tibet and Central Asia*. Lexington, KY: University Press of Kentucky, 2004.

Wang, Xinyuan. *Social Media in Industrial China*. London: UCL Press, 2016. https://doi.org/10.14324/111.9781910634646.

Wangdu, Pasang, and Hildegard Diemberger. *DBa' bzhed: The Royal Narrative Concerning the Bringing of the Buddha's Doctrine to Tibet; Translation and Facsimile Edition of the Tibetan text*. Wien: Verlag der Österreichischen Akademie der Wissenschaften Wien, 2000.

Wangmo, Jamyang. *The Lawudo Lama: Stories of Reincarnation from the Mount Everest Region*. Boston, MA: Wisdom Publications, 2005.

Ward, Michael. 'Review of *Sagarmatha-Mount Everest-Qomolungma*, by The National Geographic Society'. *Geographical Journal*, 155:3 (1989), 433–5. https://doi.org/10.2307/635257.

Waterhouse, David M. *The Origins of Himalayan Studies: Brian Houghton Hodgson in Nepal and Darjeeling, 1820–1858*. London: RoutledgeCurzon, 2004.

Waterman, T. T. 'The geographical names used by the Indians of the Pacific Coast'. *Geographical Review*,12:2 (1922), 175–94. https://doi.org/10.2307/208735.

Waugh, Andrew Scott. 'On Mounts Everest and Deodanga'. *Proceedings of the Royal Geographical Society of London*, 2:2 (1857), 102–15. https://doi.org/10.2307/1799335.

Westaway, Jonathan. "'Une bannière à l'étrange devise" Le poème *Excelsior* de Longfellow, idéalisme alpin et transcendance en alpinisme'. In Patrick Clastres, Delphine Debons, Jean-François Pitteloud and Grégory Quin (eds), *Gravir les Alpes du XIXe siècle à nos jours. Pratiques, émotions, imaginaires*. Rennes: Presses Universitaires de Rennes, 2021, pp. 29–37.

———. '"Men who can last": Mountaineering endurance, the Lake District Fell Records and the campaign for Everest, 1919–1924'. *Sport in History*, 33:3 (2013), 303–32. https://doi.org/10.1080/17460263.2013.826438.

———. 'Thinking like a mountain: The life and career of E. O. Shebbeare'. *Alpine Journal*, 122 (2018), 205–18. https://www.alpinejournal.org.uk/Contents/Contents_2018_files/AJ%202018%20Vol%20122%20203-218%20Westaway%20Shebbeare.pdf.

Whelan, Gregg. 'Here we are, let's go: Dartington College of Arts, 14 June 1997, Studio 11, 6.30 pm. A revision of Lone Twin's On Everest'. *Theatre, Dance and Performance Training*, 9:3 (2018), 431–44. https://doi.org/10.1080/19443927.2018.1503615.

Whelpton, John. *A History of Nepal*. Cambridge: Cambridge University Press, 2005.

Wigglesworth, Jennifer. *A Feminist Ethnography of Indoor and Outdoor Sport Climbing and Bouldering*. PhD thesis, Queen's University, 2021. http://hdl.handle.net/1974/29452.

Wilkinson, Freddie. 'The Khumbu Climbing Center: In the footsteps of Hillary and Norgay'. *National Geographic*, (15 March 2012). https://web.archive.org/web/20210509100821/https://www.nationalgeographic.com/adventure/article/sherpas-khumbu-climbing-center.

Williams, Danielle. 'Eight amazing Asian & Pacific Islander women climbers on Instagram'. *Melanin Base Camp*. Updated 31 July 2018, https://web.archive.org/web/20240122233306/https://www.melaninbasecamp.com/trip-reports/2018/7/31/eight-amazing-asian-pacific-islander-women-climbers-to-follow-on-instagram.

Williams, David, and Carl Lavery. *Good Luck Everybody: Lone Twin: Journeys, Performances, Conversations*. Aberystwyth: Performance Research Books, 2011.

Wilson, Jase, and Katherine Dashper. 'In the shadow of the mountain: the crisis of precarious livelihoods in high altitude mountaineering tourism'. *Journal of Sustainable Tourism*, 31:10 (2023), 2270–90. https://doi.org/10.1080/09669582.2022.2108038.

Wood, Henry, and Survey of India. *Report on the Identification and Nomenclature of the Himalayan Peaks as seen from Katmandu, Nepal*. Calcutta: Superintendent of Govt. Print., 1904.

World Economic Forum. *Global Gender Gap Report 2022*. (13 July 2022). https://www.weforum.org/reports/global-gender-gap-report-2022/.

Younghusband, Francis Edward. *The Epic of Mount Everest*. New York; London: Longmans, Green & Co.; E. Arnold, 1926.

Yü, Dan Smyer, and Erik de Maaker, eds. *Environmental Humanities in the New Himalayas: Symbiotic Indigeneity, Commoning, Sustainability*. London: Routledge, 2021.

Zakaria, Rafia. 'Pasang Lhamu Sherpa defied societal norms to climb Mount Everest: Nepal "needed a hero"'. *Washington Post*, (22 April 2018). https://web.archive.org/

web/20240123004408/https://www.washingtonpost.com/gender-identity/pasang-lhamu-sherpa-defied-societal-norms-to-climb-mount-everest-nepal-needed-a-hero/.

Zhang, Jimin. *The Yarlung Tsangpo Great Canyon: The Last Secret World.* Beijing, China: Foreign Languages Press, 2006.

Index

Page numbers in italic refer to illustrations. Literary works can be found under authors' names.

Index

Index

Index

Index

Index